Early Modern Military Identities
1560–1639

Early Modern Military Identities
1560–1639

Reality and Representation

Edited by
Matthew Woodcock and Cian O'Mahony

D. S. BREWER

First published 2019
D. S. Brewer, Cambridge

ISBN 978 1 84384 532 4

D. S. Brewer is an imprint of Boydell & Brewer Ltd
PO Box 9, Woodbridge, Suffolk IP12 3DF, UK
and of Boydell & Brewer Inc.
668 Mt Hope Avenue, Rochester, NY 14620–2731, USA
website: www.boydellandbrewer.com

A catalogue record for this book is available
from the British Library

The publisher has no responsibility for the continued existence or accuracy of URLs for
external or third-party internet websites referred to in this book, and does not guarantee
that any content on such websites is, or will remain, accurate or appropriate

This publication is printed on acid-free paper

2019286457

Contents

List of Illustrations   vii

List of Contributors   viii

Acknowledgments   ix

List of Abbreviations   x

Introduction
MATTHEW WOODCOCK   1

PART I: MODELS OF MILITARY IDENTITY

1 'Warlike prowesse and manly courage': Martial Conduct and
Masculine Identity in Late Tudor and Early Stuart England
D.J.B. TRIM   25

2 'The Breviarie of Soldiers': Julius Caesar's *Commentaries* and
the Fashioning of Early Modern Military Identity
MATTHEW WOODCOCK   56

3 'Souldiers, or Clarkes, or both': Ralph Knevet and the
Fashioning of Military Identity through Print and Performance
in Caroline Norwich
CIAN O' MAHONY   79

4 Thomas, First Lord Fairfax and 'The Highway to Heidelberg'
PHILIP MAJOR   100

**PART II: MILITARY IDENTITIES IN EARLY
MODERN IRELAND**

5 The Clergy and the Military in Early Modern Ireland
ANGELA ANDREANI AND ANDREW HADFIELD   121

6 'Trust, Desert, Power and skill to serve': The Old English and
Military Identities in Late Elizabethan Ireland
RUTH A. CANNING   138

7 Artifice in *Ormonius*: Why a Renaissance Latin Epic Falsified the
   Military History of a Tudor Irish General
   DAVID EDWARDS   158

8 Irish Savage and English Butcher: Military Identities and Tyrone's
   Rebellion, 1593-1603
   JAMES O'NEILL   177

9 A print in my body of this day's service': Finding Meaning in
   Wounding During and After the Nine Years War
   CLODAGH TAIT   197

PART III: STAGING MILITARY IDENTITIES

10 *Othello* and the Braggart Soldier in the Context of Elizabethan
    War Veterans
    ADAM N. MCKEOWN   221

11 'Lay by thine Arms and take the Citie then': Soldiery and City in
    the Drama of Thomas Middleton
    ANDREW HISCOCK   235

12 'Sometimes a figure, sometimes a cipher': Dramatic Assertions of
    Martial Identity, 1580-1642
    VIMALA C. PASUPATHI AND BENJAMIN J. ARMINTOR   256

    Afterword: The Way Ahead
    MATTHEW WOODCOCK   280

Bibliography   283
Index   309

Illustrations

Figures

9.1 Circle of Marcus Gheeraerts, Portrait of Henry Danvers,
     c.1599–1603. From the Woburn Abbey Collection   215
12.1 Observed vs predicted works asserting soldier identity by
     decade of composition   263
12.2 Observed vs predicted identity assertions by decade of
     composition   263
12.3 Percentage with assertions by genre and decade   265
12.4 Top 10 ED1642 authors by identity assertion   267

Table

12.1 Corpora used and referred to in the chapter   261

Contributors

Angela Andreani (University of Milan)

Benjamin J. Armintor (Columbia University, New York)

Ruth A. Canning (Liverpool Hope University)

David Edwards (University College Cork)

Andrew Hadfield (University of Sussex)

Andrew Hiscock (Bangor University)

Adam N. McKeown (Tulane University, Louisiana)

Philip Major (Independent Scholar)

Cian O' Mahony (Independent Scholar)

James O' Neill (Independent Scholar)

Vimala C. Pasupathi (Hofstra University, New York)

Clodagh Tait (Mary Immaculate College, Limerick)

D.J.B. Trim (Archives, General Conference of Seventh-day Adventists, Maryland)

Matthew Woodcock (University of East Anglia)

Acknowledgments

The editors would like to thank those who participated in and contributed to the Early Modern Military Identities conference, held at University College Cork and the Elizabeth Fort, Cork in August 2015, out of which several of the chapters in this volume developed. We gratefully acknowledge the dedication of Jane Grogan in supporting this event, as well as the financial assistance provided by the Society for Renaissance Studies, the Schools of English and of History (UCC), and the Cork City Heritage Fund. We are thankful too to participants in the military identities panel at the Sixteenth Century Society Conference held in Albuquerque in November 2018, and we are indebted to Paul Hammer for agreeing to chair. We are grateful to the Woburn Abbey Collection for granting permission to use the portrait of Henry Danvers and our gratitude goes to all of the contributors to this volume for the diligence, patience and enthusiasm shown during the course of this publication project.

We would like to thank all those who read drafts of individual essays or the manuscript in its entirety, especially Emily Mayne, Ruth Canning, Gary P. Baker, Andrew King, Dannielle Shaw and the anonymous publishers' readers. We are grateful to Caroline Palmer of Boydell & Brewer for backing this project initially and for the great support shown throughout its course. We are also indebted to Nick Bingham at Boydell for his help during production. Our thanks go to our families, and particular thanks go to Dannielle Shaw, not only for her extended engagement with the ideas of these essays and her assistance during the preparation of this volume, but for the love and encouragement she has provided throughout the project.

Abbreviations

BL	British Library, London
Bodleian	Bodleian Library, Oxford
Cal. Carew MSS	*Calender of the Carew Manuscripts*, 6 vols. (London, 1867–73)
CSPD	*Calendar of State Papers: Domestic*
CSPF	*Calendar of State Papers: Foreign*
CSPI	*Calendar of State Papers: Ireland*
CUL	Cambridge University Library
ELR	*English Literary Renaissance*
HLQ	*Huntington Library Quarterly*
HMC	Historical Manuscripts Commission
IHS	*Irish Historical Studies*
JBS	*Journal of British Studies*
NAI	National Archives of Ireland
NLI	National Library of Ireland
ODNB	*Oxford Dictionary of National Biography*
OED	*Oxford English Dictionary*
P&P	*Past and Present*
PMLA	*Publications of the Modern Language Association of America*
RES	*Review of English Studies*
Riverside Shakespeare	G. Blakemore Evans, ed., *The Riverside Shakespeare*, 2nd edn (Boston, 1997)
RS	*Renaissance Studies*
Salisbury MSS	*Calendar of the Manuscripts of the Marquis of Salisbury*, 24 vols. (London, 1883–1976)
SCJ	*Sixteenth Century Journal*
TCD	Trinity College, Dublin
TNA	The National Archives, Kew, London
TRHS	*Transactions of the Royal Historical Society*

Introduction

MATTHEW WOODCOCK

TO THE RIGHT NOBLE YOUNG LORD, WILLIAM, LORD HARBERT OF CARDIFFE

Most Noble young Lord, and of honourable expectation, although your yong yeares have scarse arrived yet to the bearing of Armes, neverthelesse on the assured hope conceived of your honourable partes, as so nobly each way descended, (whose vertue hath alwayes shined to the glorie of your name and house) I have emboldened my selfe to offer unto your Lordships view and protection, these Militarie discourses, penned upon occasion of conference had with sundry Gentlemen, and by them wished to be published. Many good reasons have moved me to dedicate them unto your Lordship, as well in respect of your owne vertues (resembling altogether that Noble Earle of Pembroke, your Graundfather, and that worthie Sir Phillip Sidney, your Uncle) as also in respect of the great and waightie Commandes which your Right Honourable father doth worthily hold over us in these our Westerne parts and Wales, under our dread Soveraigne. Such as they are, I humbly beseech your Lordship to accept, as from a souldier, who humbly offereth himselfe and his service unto your self, next unto my good Queene and deare Countrie.

Your lordships humbly at command

ROBERT BARRET

It is with the dedication above – and another addressed to William Herbert's father Henry, second earl of Pembroke – that the Elizabethan soldier and author Robert Barret opened his 1598 treatise *The Theorike and Practike of Moderne Warres.*[1] Barret invites his dedicatee to contemplate a particular way of viewing himself and assures him on the appropriateness of doing so, given Herbert's noble family and status. Although the eighteen-year-old Herbert had 'scarse arrived yet to the bearing of Armes', Barret responds to the great potential his

---

[1] Robert Barret, *The Theorike and Practike of Moderne Warres, Discoursed in Dialogue Wise* (London, 1598), sig. ¶3r.

dedicatee had evidently shown through his interest in military affairs, and to what is described to Herbert's father as 'the Martial vertues already shining in him'.[2] The dedication speaks too to expectations predicated by Herbert's social rank, and assumes a natural, inexorable connection between nobility and military identity. The association between Barret's military subject-matter and his dedicatee is further suggested by an intuitively perceived resemblance between the promise shown in Herbert and the martial reputation of his family. His grandfather and namesake, the first earl of Pembroke, led Mary I's army into France in 1557 and had helped capture the town of St Quentin. His uncle, the soldier-poet Sir Philip Sidney, fought and died in combat in the Low Countries during Herbert's youth. Herbert's father was also present at St Quentin and now continued to demonstrate his own loyal service to the sovereign in the office of Lord President of the Council in the Marches of Wales. Barret constructs a version of Herbert – an identity for Herbert – fashioned from the combination of an essential, lineal inheritance and the promising suggestion of future martial 'sympathie'.[3] The author then signs off the dedication by highlighting his own military identity when he enjoins Herbert to accept his book 'as from a souldier' and alludes to his own service to queen and country. Herbert never went on to assume the identity Barret fashioned for him in the 1598 dedication nor emulated his martial forebears, and he inclined instead towards more courtly, scholarly and literary spheres of activity.[4] Herbert, as third earl of Pembroke, is now perhaps best known as a literary patron (he was co-dedicatee of Shakespeare's First Folio) and for his long-standing relationship with Oxford University. His benefactions and donations to the Bodleian Library are remembered by the bronze statue of him that stands there in Old Schools Quadrangle. As befits his status and martial heritage, he is shown dressed in armour.

Barret's dedication nevertheless represents a useful illustration of the concept at the heart of this essay collection, and of some of the different ways of conceiving and articulating military identity that will be returned to and explored below. This book examines how early modern fighting men and their peers viewed and/ or represented themselves in military roles, and how they were perceived and fashioned by others. It gathers together new essays by historians and literary scholars offering multiple investigations into the construction, representation, perpetuation, interpretation and definition of military identity in the sixteenth and earlier seventeenth centuries. Adopting a range of different disciplinary approaches, and concentrating predominantly on sources concerning English, Irish and Anglo-Irish fighting men active between the 1560s

---

[2]   Barret, *Theoricke*, sig. ¶2v.
[3]   Barret, *Theoricke*, sig. ¶2v.
[4]   Victor Stater, 'William Herbert, third earl of Pembroke', *ODNB*.

and 1630s, the essays consider what was at stake in fashioning or fabricating a military identity, and draw much-needed critical attention to the complex, shifting ontology of both early modern soldiery and soldiers.[5] What was it that distinguished a soldier from the rest of society or from practitioners of other occupations? What was it that made a good soldier, or that necessarily made a soldier good? How was early modern military identity shaped by classical or medieval models and ideals? How was the military life perceived in this period by those who had first-hand experience of soldiery and the wars, or by those who would represent soldiers on the page and stage? This book also considers how military identity was closely bound up with confessional sympathies, and with contemporary conceptions of masculinity, honour and nobility. It explores too the fluidity of military identity, and how fighting men conceived of relationships between the worlds of court and camp, and between the arts of pen and sword. Military identity can also be collective as much as individual, and a number of the contributors to this volume approach the topic from the perspective of national, civic, religious, occupational and familial identities and modes of identification. Although the figure of the medieval fighting man and the rituals and communities of knighthood and chivalry have been well served by historians and critics,[6] scholarship on early modern military history and textual culture focuses predominantly on soldiers *en masse*, favouring examination of collective activity in battles or sieges, and matters such as army recruitment, formation and logistics, or the relative merits of different troop types, armaments or tactics.[7] The concept of military identity, however, and the kinds of reflexive questions posed above, occupy something of a lacuna in

---

[5]   The temporal scope of this volume broadly spans a period from the first campaign of Elizabeth I's reign through to the outbreak of the first Bishops' War in 1639. As noted in the Afterword, this volume concentrates on the nature of military identities in the period prior to the advent of widespread citizen soldiery during the Civil Wars of the 1640s.

[6]   Arthur B. Ferguson, *The Indian Summer of English Chivalry* (Durham, NC, 1960); Malcolm Vale, *War and Chivalry* (London, 1981); Maurice Keen, *Chivalry* (London, 1984); Arthur B. Ferguson, *The Chivalric Tradition in Renaissance England* (Washington, DC, 1986); Richard C. McCoy, *The Rites of Knighthood: The Literature and Politics of Elizabethan Chivalry* (Berkeley, 1989); Matthew Strickland, *War and Chivalry: The Conduct and Perception of War in England and Normandy, 1066–1217* (Cambridge, 1996); Peter Coss and Christopher Tyerman, ed., *Soldiers, Nobles and Gentlemen: Essays in Honour of Maurice Keen* (Woodbridge, 2009); Adrian R. Bell et al., ed., *The Soldier Experience in the Fourteenth Century* (Woodbridge, 2011); Adrian R. Bell et al., *The Soldier in Later Medieval England* (Oxford, 2013).

[7]   See, for example, Charles Oman, *A History of the Art of War in the Sixteenth Century* (London, 1937); C.G. Cruickshank, *Elizabeth's Army* (Oxford, 1966); Lindsay Boynton, *The Elizabethan Militia, 1558–1638* (London, 1967); John Keegan and Richard Holmes, *Soldiers: A History of Men in Battle* (London, 1985); Mark Fissel, *English Warfare, 1511–1642* (London, 2001); Charles Carlton, *This Seat of Mars: War and the British Isles, 1485–1746* (New Haven, 2011).

the current historiography of early modern warfare, falling as they do at the intersection of several different fields or areas of interest.[8]

Perhaps the most hotly contested area of scholarship for military historians over the last sixty years concerns the tactical, technological, social and political implications of the early modern military 'revolution': on how armies were formed, trained, supplied and deployed; on how towns and cities were fortified, besieged and defended; on how developments in gunpowder weaponry irrevocably transformed the nature of warfare and soldiery during the sixteenth and seventeenth centuries.[9] There has been comparatively little examination, however, of the impact of such changes (and the military revolution thesis) on perceptions of the early modern fighting man himself, and on how the changing nature of the profession of arms was viewed and written about by contemporaries. In part, this arises from the central thrust of the military revolution debate itself, which is inherently invested in constructing large-scale narratives concerning institutions, state-building and geopolitical motives and changes. Some of the debate's founding sources do begin by considering the smallest building block of an army – the rank-and-file soldier – but these then quickly broaden their focus in order to better comprehend the place of the individual soldier within a body of troops drilled to move and function as a single unit. Michael Roberts's seminal argument for an early modern revolution focused on Gustavus Aldolphus's perfection of volley fire and the close interaction of well-drilled pike and shot troops. However, he then used his observations as the first step of an ever-widening thesis linking a change in unit tactics and formation to a shift in grand strategy and military objectives necessitating bigger armies and a re-conception of the relationship

---

[8]   One of the only studies to tackle the concept of identity specifically in relation to warfare, albeit from a cross-chronological perspective, is Bertrand Taithe and Tim Thornton's essay collection *War: Identities in Conflict 1300–2000* (Stroud, 1998).

[9]   See Michael Roberts, *Essays in Swedish History* (London, 1967); J.R. Hale, *War and Society in Renaissance Europe, 1450–1620* (London, 1985); Jeremy Black, *A Military Revolution? Military Change and European Society* (Basingstoke, 1991); Frank Tallett, *War and Society in Early Modern Europe, 1495–1715* (London, 1992); C.J. Rogers, ed., *The Military Revolution Debate* (Oxford, 1995); Geoffrey Parker, *The Military Revolution: Military Innovation and the Rise of the West, 1500–1800* (Cambridge, 1996); David Eltis, *The Military Revolution in Sixteenth-Century Europe* (New York, 1998); M. Knox and W. Murray, ed., *The Dynamics of Military Revolution, 1300–2050* (Cambridge, 2001); Pádraig Lenihan, 'Conclusion: Ireland's Military Revolution(s)', *Conquest and Resistance: War in Seventeenth-Century Ireland*, ed. Pádraig Lenihan (Leiden, 2001), pp. 245–69; Geoffrey Parker, *The Army of Flanders and the Spanish Road, 1567–1659*, 2nd edn (Cambridge, 2004); James Raymond, *Henry VIII's Military Revolution: The Armies of Sixteenth-Century Britain and Europe* (New York, 2007); Paul E.J. Hammer, ed., *Warfare in Early Modern Europe, 1450–1660* (London, 2007); Frank Jacob and Gilmar Visoni-Alonzo, *The Military Revolution in Early Modern Europe* (Houndmills, 2016).

between the state and military.[10] Geoffrey Parker's modification of Roberts's thesis again starts small. He attributes the military revolution to (among other factors) innovations in infantry tactics initiated by Prince Maurice of Nassau and his brother, which placed a premium on volley fire and the role of the soldier armed with hand-held gunpowder weapons, led by commanders well-read in classical methods of drilling and counter-marching.[11] This argument too (unavoidably) considers the individual infantryman as but part of a disciplined whole. Indeed, as Maurice's tutor Justus Lipsius emphasised when writing in 1595 of recent experiments with classical drilling methods, the success of the Roman legions lay in their working in formation, not as individuals.[12] The essays in this volume do not profess to engage with the military revolution argument(s) directly, but they do persist in making the point that it is all too easy to lose sight of the figure of the soldier (and his profession) within the wider revolution debate.

Conceived at a larger, national level, military identity has been touched upon, albeit obliquely, in critical discussions of individual nations' martial character and reputation: in considerations of whether there was a distinctly English art of war in the sixteenth and seventeenth centuries, and in more recent revisionary works challenging the long-held view that English military expertise lagged behind that of the rest of Europe until around the 1580s.[13] A glorious national military identity could also be constructed retrospectively, as it was, for example, during the 1620s when recent martial achievements lacked efficacy or inspiration.[14] By the early years of James I's reign, following the cessation of the war with Spain in 1604, English martialists and polemicists could look back to a short, though frequently recalled list of laudable achievements when constructing the national military character and reputation: Crécy, Agincourt, the capture of Boulogne, the repulse of the Spanish Armada, the 1596 Cadiz raid and (at a push) the heroic defences undertaken at the sieges of Haddington (1548) and Ostend (1601–4). National military identity, as embodied by particular events, figures or martial trappings, was thus at

---

[10] Roberts, *Essays*, pp. 195–225.
[11] Parker, *Military Revolution*, pp. 6–44, and 'The Limits to Revolution in Military Affairs: Maurice of Nassau, the Battle of Nieuwpoort (1600), and the Legacy', *Journal of Military History* 71.2 (2007), 331–72.
[12] Parker, 'Limits', pp. 342–3.
[13] Fissel, *English Warfare*, esp. pp. 282–94; Raymond, *Henry VIII's Military Revolution*. In a similar vein, on the distinctive character of Irish warfare, see Donal O'Carroll, 'Change and Continuity in Weapons and Tactics', *Conquest and Resistance*, ed. Lenihan, pp. 211–55; and James O' Neill's essay below (Chapter 8) on the respective reputations and realities of English and Irish forces during the Nine Years War.
[14] Thomas Cogswell, *The Blessed Revolution: English Politics and the Coming of War, 1621–1624* (Cambridge, 1989), pp. 281–301. See also Philip Major's essay below (Chapter 4).

the core of what Susan Harlan usefully terms 'militant nostalgia'.[15] Celebrated martial personalities such as Sir Francis Drake, Sir Walter Ralegh and Robert Devereux, second earl of Essex were evoked regularly in Jacobean and Caroline expressions of nostalgia for the militaristic character of Elizabeth's reign.[16]

The investigations into military identity in this volume also intersect with the small number of works that discuss early modern soldiery in terms of professional or occupational identity. Mark Hailwood recently highlighted that historians of identity for this period rarely take occupations as their starting point.[17] He noted too that identity formation can be both 'internal' and 'external'; individuals or groups can take on or identify with a particular identity themselves, or their identity can be defined and constructed by others (just as Barret attempted to do for Herbert).[18] As Ian Roy's study of the profession of arms proposed, for early modern fighting men to see themselves as members of a distinct occupational group there needed to be certain defining attributes that constituted such a group in the first place, including a recognisable career structure, internal regulation (the 'laws of war') and a collective sense of purpose.[19] D.J.B. Trim likewise posited the concept of a 'discrete occupational identity' for fighting men when examining the relationship between sixteenth- and seventeenth-century continuations of the chivalric ethos and the contemporary rise in military professionalism.[20] And there are certainly examples of early modern soldiers who viewed and represented themselves as practitioners of a profession.[21] But as both Roy and Trim discuss, the shifting, evolving nature of the military profession during this period – and until the second half of the seventeenth century – complicates a ready equation of military identity with occupational identity. Keith Thomas included military

[15]   Susan Harlan, *Memories of War in Early Modern England: Armor and Militant Nostalgia in Marlowe, Sidney, and Shakespeare* (New York, 2016), p. 1.
[16]   Cogswell, *Blessed*, pp. 182–3, 286–7; Anna Beer, *Sir Walter Ralegh and his Readers in the Seventeenth Century* (London, 1997), pp. 119–22; Andrew Hiscock, '"Achilles alter": The Heroic Lives and Afterlives of Robert Devereux, 2nd Earl of Essex', *Essex: The Cultural Impact of an Elizabethan Courtier*, ed. Annaliese Connolly and Lisa Hopkins (Manchester, 2013), pp. 101–32.
[17]   Mark Hailwood, 'Broadside Ballads and Occupational Identity in Early Modern England', *HLQ* 79.2 (2016), 187
[18]   Hailwood, 'Broadside', 188.
[19]   Ian Roy, 'The Profession of Arms', *The Professions in Early Modern England*, ed. Wilfrid Prest (London, 1987), p. 187.
[20]   D.J.B. Trim, 'Introduction', *The Chivalric Ethos and the Development of Military Professionalism*, ed. D.J.B. Trim (Leiden, 2003), pp. 3–7. See also James Scott Wheeler, *The Making of a World Power: War and the Military Revolution in Seventeenth-Century England* (Stroud, 1999), pp. 66–93, on links between the creation of an English standing army and the reification of a military profession in the seventeenth century.
[21]   Geoffrey Gates, *The Defence of Militarie Profession* (London, 1579); Robert Monro, *Monro, His Expedition with the Worthy Scots Regiment* (London, 1637), sig. χ4r.

activity in his study of the ways in which work and vocation offered a means of achieving fulfilment in early modern England. He was compelled, however, to use a very elastic definition of the martial role(s) in which such activity was undertaken, encompassing those who saw the military life as a privilege or duty of rank as well as those for whom it was a profession or means of employment.[22] John Hale similarly spent a great deal of time probing the seemingly porous line between the soldierly and civilian spheres, and examining the difficulties of occupational differentiation in an era before the formation of regular standing armies in the British Isles.[23] Phil Withington, responding in part to Thomas, further interrogated distinctions between the soldier and civilian citizen in early modern Britain and Ireland, outlining the extent to which militarism had been 'insinuated' into urban life and experience by the eve of the Civil Wars.[24] More recently, Paul Scannell has surveyed the different categories of early modern soldier and identified how fighting men of the period themselves recognised distinctions between the paid professional, the mercenary and the 'gentleman volunteer' committed to the vocation of arms, even if they too – like modern historians – found it hard to pinpoint defining characteristics exclusive to each.[25] As is discussed further below, nomenclature and definitions prove evasive for the military profession, not least due to the casualness with which one could go off to the wars in this period.[26] And would individuals engaged in military activity necessarily have had a fixed conception of what soldiery, or being a soldier, actually entailed? Does what a soldier *does* always provide the individual involved with the same impression of what a soldier must *be*? Pasupathi and Armintor's contribution to this volume provides a valuable re-assessment of how such questions were explored on the Tudor and Stuart stage.

As several of the chapters reveal, investigations into the nature of military identity also complement the growing number of studies that examine the experiential dimension of early modern warfare. Recent scholarship on autobiographical writings, service journals and memoirs, eye-witness accounts of combat, and war poetry in an assortment of genres produced both by fighting men and those otherwise involved in conflicts in Ireland, continental Europe and the New World has revealed a body of materials that preserves the voices of those engaged in military activities and their reflexive commentaries upon

---

[22] Keith Thomas, *The Ends of Life: Roads to Fulfilment in Early Modern England* (Oxford, 2009), pp. 44–62.

[23] Hale, *War*, pp. 127–39.

[24] Phil Withington, 'Introduction – Citizens and Soldiers: the Renaissance Context', *Journal of Early Modern History* 15 (2011), 3–30.

[25] Paul Scannell, *Conflict and Soldiers' Literature in Early Modern Europe* (London, 2015), pp. 49–67.

[26] Hale, *War*, pp. 137–9.

the soldier's life and lot.[27] By demonstrating the variety of different sources and genres through which military identity is articulated and perpetuated, this essay collection also builds on the work of a number of scholars currently engaged with exploring links between early modern literature and martial culture – what Miguel Martinez recently dubbed the 'soldierly republic of letters'.[28]

Military identity is, therefore, by no means an entirely new concept or theoretical construct with which to be working here. The chapters of this volume – individually and collectively – do, however, make an original contribution to the criticism and historiography of early modern warfare and martial culture by bringing to the foreground both 'internal' and 'external' constructions of military identity. The next part of this introduction considers some of the ways in which the sorts of questions set out above were already being posed and discussed during the early modern period.

It would be easy to approach the subject of this essay collection by suggesting simply that early modern military identity was one and the same as noble identity. The association of noble and military identity does indeed largely reflect the operational reality of early modern armies. The aristocracy remained crucial to the formation of military forces throughout the sixteenth and seventeenth centuries either through the quasi-feudal system of special musters whereby the sovereign called on the nobility to raise troops from their households and estates, or through the newer system that saw armies recruited regionally under each county's lord lieutenant.[29] As Barret's dedication exemplifies, the equation of noble and military identity was one of the bases of his identification of innate military virtues in William Herbert. This kind of association was reiterated repeatedly during the period, with numerous contemporary authorities asserting that martial activity was vital for sustaining

---

[27] See, for example, Robert J. Knecht, 'Military Autobiographies in Sixteenth-Century France', and Henry J. Cohn, 'Götz von Berlichingen and the Art of Military Biography', *War, Literature, and the Arts in Sixteenth-Century Europe*, ed. J.R. Mulryne and Margaret Shewring (London, 1989), pp. 3–40; Yuval Noah Harari, *Renaissance Military Memoirs: War, History and Identity, 1450–1600* (Woodbridge, 2004), and *The Ultimate Experience: Battlefield Revelations and the Making of Modern War Culture, 1450–2000* (Basingstoke, 2008); David Edwards, ed., *Campaign Journals of the Elizabethan Irish Wars* (Dublin, 2014); Scannell, *Conflict*; Matthew Woodcock, 'Tudor Soldier–Authors and the Art of Military Autobiography', *Representing War and Violence in Later Medieval Europe*, ed. Joanna Bellis and Laura Slater (Woodbridge, 2016), pp. 159–77; Miguel Martinez, *Front Lines: Soldiers' Writing in the Early Modern Hispanic World* (Philadelphia, 2016).

[28] Martinez, *Front Lines*, p. 1. D.J.B. Trim, 'The Art of War: Martial Poetics from Henry Howard to Philip Sidney', *The Oxford Handbook of Tudor Literature, 1485–1603*, ed. Mike Pincombe and Cathy Shrank (Oxford, 2009), pp. 587–605; Adam McKeown, *English Mercuries: Soldier Poets in the Age of Shakespeare* (Nashville, 2009); Rory Rapple, *Martial Power and Elizabethan Political Culture* (Cambridge, 2009); Matthew Woodcock, *Thomas Churchyard: Pen, Sword and Ego* (Oxford, 2016).

[29] Fissel, *English Warfare*, pp. 82–4.

and affirming noble identity, and that it was an essential expectation of social rank.[30] Sir Richard Barckley, for example, writing in the same year that Barret's treatise appeared, neatly sums up not only the expectations of noble rank but the implications for personal identity should these not be fulfilled: '[A noble man] must take upon him a thousand enterprises in the wars, offer himself to an infinite number of perils, hazard his life, shed his blood to die in the bed of honour; otherwise he shall be accounted a carpet-knight, and effeminate man, and had in contempt'.[31]

Military identity formed an integral part of the long-running discourse about the nature and function of honour and nobility in the early modern state, and about the continued relevance (or not) of chivalric trappings and practices in contemporary warfare.[32] Military activity was deemed an essential means by which honourable identity was maintained, as several of the chapters here explore. (See Chapter 7 by David Edwards on the earl of Ormond, and Chapters 1 and 9 by D.J.B. Trim and Clodagh Tait respectively on the role of wounds as markers of virtuous martial identity.) The recording of the names of both victorious and fallen fighting men, and the preservation of their deeds, was a powerful motive behind the production of many of the printed accounts of overseas military actions published by early modern soldier-authors, including Thomas Churchyard, William Blandy, Geoffrey Gates, Thomas Digges, Henry Hexham and Robert Monro. Martialist authors were also especially interested in the kinds of literary genres that offered opportunities either to generate and perpetuate honour and renown, or to defend those of the military profession. The elegy or poetic 'epitaph', for example, was a particularly favoured genre, as were dedicatory verses written for or about fellow soldiers and soldier-authors. It is important to stress too that neither those engaged in recording the names and deeds of military men, nor their subjects themselves, were drawn exclusively from the ranks of the nobility and gentry.

As Roger B. Manning discussed at length, the concept of military identity was already recognised and commented upon in the period itself.[33] Manning takes up the distinction made in Sir Robert Naunton's character study of

[30] Trim, 'Introduction', p. 1; Steven Gunn, David Grummitt and Hans Cools, *War, State, and Society in England and the Netherlands 1477–1559* (Oxford, 2007), ch. 14. Links between soldiery and nobility were commented upon frequently on the early modern stage – not without circumspection; see Chapter 12 below, by Pasupathi and Armintor.

[31] Quoted in Thomas, *Ends*, p. 49. The ignoble figure of the effeminate and/ or 'civilian' concept of the carpet knight is returned to later in this introduction, and in Chapter 1.

[32] Mervyn James, *Society, Politics and Culture: Studies in Early Modern England* (Cambridge, 1986), pp. 308–415; Rapple, *Martial*, pp. 20–3.

[33] Roger B. Manning, *Swordsmen: The Martial Ethos in the Three Kingdoms* (Oxford, 2003), esp. pp. 1–50. See also Manning, *An Apprenticeship in Arms: The Origins of the British Army, 1585–1702* (Oxford, 2006), pp. 1–40.

Elizabeth I's courtiers, *Fragmenta Regalia* (c.1633), between those classed as the *militia* – effectively, the 'swordsmen' who looked to military action to display their honour and virtue – and their antithesis the *togati*, the 'gownsmen' or 'pen gentlemen'.[34] These kinds of categorisations and labels were used extensively by early modern writers and commentators themselves, with variants of the latter term used to draw contemptuous distinctions between the 'culture and career patterns' of the active swordsmen and the more idle, facile gownsmen – the carpet knights scorned by Barckley in the quotation above.[35] As the work of Manning and Rory Rapple has shown, there was no shortage of individuals at the courts of Elizabeth and James keen to play the swordsman and to fashion and promulgate military identities for themselves. Robert Dudley, earl of Leicester spent many years cultivating a martial identity for himself at court through the performative rites of Elizabethan knighthood.[36] He had also long been a rallying-point for militant Protestant swordsmen pushing for greater military intervention in the Low Countries to support their co-religionists in the revolt against the Spanish, and would eventually lead the English expeditionary force there in 1585. Leicester's nephew Sir Philip Sidney lost his life on the expedition, and his reputation as both a soldier and poet formed a key part of his posthumous identity.[37] The dying Sidney bequeathed his sword to the earl of Essex. Proving himself the spiritual heir of Sidney and Leicester, Essex made extensive use of the symbolic language of chivalry in the tiltyard, on the battlefield and in his interactions with Elizabeth, and he devoted himself to fashioning an identity founded on martial ambition and glory. Essex's career represents one of the greatest examples of martial self-fashioning, and of an individual of this period taking every opportunity to present himself as a soldier, be it in deeds, words or representations, and through his campaign to secure the office of Earl Marshal (principal military and heraldic officer of state).[38] (Not surprisingly, Essex and his military clientage feature in several of the chapters below.) The figure of the swordsman remained a presence at the Jacobean court even though it was clear from the outset of James's reign that there would be few opportunities for state-sanctioned military activity following the signing of the Treaty of London in August 1604, which ended the war

---

[34]   Sir Robert Naunton, *Fragmenta Regalia, or Observations on Queen Elizabeth, Her Times and Favorites*, ed. J.S. Cerovski (Washington, DC, 1985), p. 48.

[35]   Manning, *Swordsmen*, pp. 28–32.

[36]   McCoy, *Rites*, pp. 28–54.

[37]   Richard Hillyer, *Sir Philip Sidney, Cultural Icon* (New York, 2010), pp. 23–40.

[38]   McCoy, *Rites*, pp. 79–102; Wallace T. MacCaffrey, *Elizabeth I: War and Politics, 1588–1603* (Princeton, 1992), pp. 453–513; Paul E.J. Hammer, *The Polarisation of Elizabethan Politics: The Political Career of Robert Devereux, 2nd Earl of Essex, 1585–1597* (Cambridge, 1999), pp. 199–268; Janet Dickinson, *Court Politics and the Earl of Essex, 1589–1601* (London, 2012), pp. 5–23.

with Spain.[39] During the pacific first decade of James's rule, the king's eldest son Prince Henry became the focal point for military clients, and he both took on and enthusiastically accepted constructions of identity casting him as the new hope for militant Protestant activism and the restorer of national martial glory.[40] After Henry died, his brother Charles was similarly celebrated as an object of martial expectation. Once crowned, Charles I continued to project the image of himself as a warrior king, as captured in Anthony van Dyck's paintings of him armoured and on horseback.[41] Several of the chapters below examine attempts by English and Anglo-Irish nobles and gentry who similarly construct, or have constructed for them, narratives that emphasise and celebrate their military identity to a public or coterie audience.[42]

The distinct culture and value system of the early modern swordsmen, and the military identities that they constructed or that were ascribed to them, was also defined in response to the changes taking place in later sixteenth- and seventeenth-century warfare that were being noted by contemporary fighting men themselves. As warfare became ever more impersonal, fewer opportunities presented themselves for displays of individual martial prowess, or for ever meeting one's opponent face to face. Long-term sieges were replacing full-scale pitched battles and stalemates between the besieger and besieged of fortified cities or castles were often resolved more effectively by bombardment or starvation. In larger armies involving more costly weaponry there were fewer obvious roles for the heroic autonomy of the individual armoured fighting man. Declining too was the concept of a martial community that saw combat as a rules-bound ritual and their enemies as worthy opponents, the result of what Manning characterises as a newer kind of 'instrumental war in which the enemy was an evil force or an obstacle to be destroyed'.[43] The Elizabethan chivalric revival (charted by Arthur B. Ferguson, Richard McCoy and others), and the quasi-medieval martial identity this afforded, was, it is argued, a reaction to the growing impersonalisation of war and the more 'instrumental' warfare encountered by Englishmen fighting in continental Europe during the 1570–80s.[44] As Trim maintains, however, cultivation of chivalric martial identity was certainly not dichotomous with military professionalism in this

---

[39] Carlton, *This Seat*, pp. 78–81.
[40] David Lawrence, *The Complete Soldier: Military Books and Military Culture in Early Stuart England, 1603–1645* (Leiden, 2009), pp. 105–26; Roy Strong, *Henry, Prince of Wales and England's Lost Renaissance* (London, 1986), pp. 220–5; J.W. Williamson, *The Myth of the Conqueror: Prince Henry Stuart – A Study of Seventeenth-Century Personation* (New York, 1978).
[41] Cogswell, *Blessed*, pp. 62–9; Roy Strong, *Van Dyck: Charles I on Horseback* (New York, 1972).
[42] See the chapters below by Canning, Edwards, Major and Woodcock.
[43] Manning, *Swordsmen*, pp. 5–6.
[44] Fissel, *English Warfare*, p. 165; Manning, *Apprenticeship*, pp. 27–8.

period.[45] Nevertheless, the figure of the soldier was transforming during the late sixteenth and early seventeenth centuries as war was viewed less as a theatre of honour and more as *realpolitik*.[46] As historians of the military revolution have shown at length, greater emphasis was being placed – in theory and in practice – upon drilled fighting men working and moving as a disciplined group or collective 'organism', as Roberts put it.[47] Ultimately, this served to precipitate both the decline of a model of military identity based solely on individual effort and display of personal honour, and the gradual shift towards a more clearly defined sense of an occupational martial identity.[48]

Although noble identity may have carried with it the expectation of military activity and identity, military identity itself was by no means inevitably constructed or determined by class and social rank alone. This begs questions regarding exactly who might adopt a military identity in this period, and to what kind of individuals or groups we might ascribe military identities? The answers to such questions are complicated by the fact that it requires us to consider a range of different ways in which individuals would have seen themselves, or found themselves as fighting men. For those of the aristocracy, military activity was viewed, as indicated above, as a social obligation. It was an intrinsic duty and perquisite of rank rather than a trade undertaken for direct financial enrichment or as an occupation or profession in the modern sense.[49] One consequence of this was that until well into the seventeenth century it was commonly the case that noble or gentry rank, as opposed to martial ability or experience, was the principal qualification for military command and intermediate leadership roles. This remained a continued source of tension in English armies fighting in Ireland and continental Europe throughout the period and served to emphasise a fault-line between those who assumed a military identity by virtue of rank and office, and those – such as Sir John Norreys, Sir Roger Williams, Sir Francis Vere and his brother Horace – whose military identity was constituted more by battlefield practice and expertise born of field experience. Linked more to the latter group than the former were

---

[45] Trim, 'Introduction', pp. 1–3.

[46] Thomas, *Ends*, p. 62.

[47] Roberts, *Essays*, p. 198. See Lawrence, *Complete*, pp. 135–94; Parker, 'Limits', pp. 331–47; O' Carroll, 'Change', pp. 211–18.

[48] Trim, 'Introduction', p. 29. Bert S. Hall, *Weapons and Warfare in Renaissance Europe: Gunpowder, Technology, and Tactics* (Baltimore, 1997), pp. 234–5. The transformation of individual soldierly identity charted by historiographers of the early modern military revolution debate is a pendant to Michel Foucault's argument concerning the 'disciplining' of the soldier's body between the seventeenth and eighteenth centuries that transformed the 'homme de guerre' into a component of the greater military institution (or 'militaire'): *Discipline and Punish: The Birth of the Prison*, trans. Alan Sheridan (Harmondsworth, 1977), pp. 135–69.

[49] Trim, 'Introduction', p. 4.

those soldiers – generally, but not always, of lower military rank – who fought as gentleman 'volunteers' motivated by confessional or political sympathies, or by the promise of opportunities for adventure or financial enrichment. The issue of military identity thus forces us to consider questions of soldiers' motivations as well as self-perceptions. National identity could also be a motive. Steve Murdoch has discussed, for example, how Scottish regiments campaigning on the continent saw themselves as defenders of the honour of the House of Stuart following the Imperial invasion of the German Palatinate territories in 1620, and the defeat and exile of their ruler the Elector Frederick V, husband of James I's daughter, Elizabeth.[50]

Experienced early modern fighting men of lower ranks, such as Churchyard, Gates, Barnabe Rich and Thomas Trussell, evince a distinct sense of collective occupational identity when they felt pressed to defend or praise its practitioners in print.[51] Churchyard, for example, concluded his poem 'The Prayes of our Souldiars' by identifying the category of fighting man that exemplifies the growing cadre of committed military professionals of the later Elizabethan era:

Now must you mark, I mean not hierlings heer
Nor sommer birds, and swallows for the time
That wagis taeks, and sarvs but oens a yeer
And sprowts a whiell, as flowrs do in the prime
But thoes whoes minds, and noble manners shoes
In peace and warr, loe thear a soldior goes
Of lief moest cleer, of deed and word full Just
In triall still, a man of speshall trust.[52]

Monro informed readers of his printed account of service on the continent during the 1620s–30s that he wrote to honour not only the exercise of his countrymen in the martial profession, but their professionalism.[53] As many of the chapters reveal, military identities were also formed or consolidated by the need to distinguish the 'good' soldier and his peers from those mere 'hierlings', braggarts and would-be warriors, and to define themselves in relation to other distinct (potentially antithetical) communities, be it those of the courtier, scholar or what we would now call 'civilian'.[54]

[50] Steve Murdoch, 'The House of Stuart and the Scottish Professional Soldier 1618–1640: A Conflict of Nationality and Identities', *War: Identities in Conflict 1300–2000*, ed. Taithe and Thornton, pp. 44–6.
[51] See Thomas Churchyard, *A Generall Rehearsall of Warres* (London, 1579), sigs. L4v–P4v; Gates, *Defence*; Barnabe Rich, *A Path-way to Military Practise* (London, 1587), sigs. B1r–D3r; Thomas Trussell, *The Souldier Pleading his own Cause* (London, 1619).
[52] Thomas Churchyard, *Churchyardes Chippes* (London, 1575), sig. N4v.
[53] Monro, *Monro, His Expedition*, sigs. χ1r–χ4v.
[54] The word 'civilian', which one might expect to be a useful term against which to define those of a military occupation, was usually only used in this period to denote an expert

At the other end of the social spectrum from aristocratic fighting men were members of the male civilian populace of military age – i.e. aged between 16 and 60 – who were required by law throughout Elizabeth's reign, and in the Stuart period from 1613, to participate in county-based musters. As Canning shows in Chapter 6, comparable military obligations were in place in the Old English lordships of Ireland during this period. Musters were an opportunity for both the regional review of men and matériel, and several days of training in elementary weapons handling and drilling. The fruits of such occasions were mixed. Barnabe Rich complained of the lamentable quality of the citizen militias, and Shakespeare had similar impressions in mind when portraying a provincial muster as comic farce in *2 Henry IV*.[55] Machiavelli had earlier written at length praising citizen soldiery in his *Art of War* (1521), and looked to the Roman republican period as a model for how early modern states should constitute their armies. Machiavelli noted too the transformation a civilian individual underwent on becoming a soldier:

> he immediately changes not only his dress, but his behavior, his company, his air, his manner of speaking, and that he affects to throw off all appearances of anything that may look like ordinary life and conversation. For a man wanting to be ready-equipped for any sort of violence despises the formal dress of a civilian [i.e. civil apparel] and thinks no dress fit for his purpose but a suit of armor. And as to civility and politeness, how can we expect to find them in one who imagines that such things would make him look effeminate and that they would be a hindrance to his work [...] This indeed gives countenance to such an opinion and makes people look upon a soldier as a creature different from all other men.[56]

But did the mustered militia-man really consider that he was adopting or developing any kind of military identity, albeit temporarily and possibly rather impressionistically? There is limited evidence offering insight into how men of English shire militias viewed themselves or their role. And as Fissel observes, they were more likely to have perceived their service at a parochial level: as preparations to defend their locality rather than as part of a national

---

in civil law; see, for example, Thomas Palmer, *An Essay of the Meanes How to Make Our Travailes, into Forraine Countries, the More Profitable and Honourable* (London, 1606), sigs. E1r–E2r. (My thanks to Dannielle Shaw for bringing this text to my attention.) *OED*, s.v. 'civilian', dates the first usage of the word to denote 'a non-military person' to 1794. Chapter 12 below, by Pasupathi and Armintor, examines different kinds of collocations and oppositions found in references to soldiers on the early modern stage.

55 Barnabe Rich, *A Right Excelent and Pleasaunt Dialogue, betwene Mercury and an English Souldier* (London, 1574), sigs. G6r–G7v; Paul Jorgensen, *Shakespeare's Military World* (Berkeley, 1956), pp. 130–5, 143–8.

56 Niccolò Machiavelli, *The Art of War*, trans. Ellis Farneworth (New York, 1965), p. 3.

war effort.[57] Nevertheless, many martialists' manuals published from the 1570s onwards, such as Thomas Styward's 1581 *The Pathwaie to Martiall Discipline* or Barret's *Theorike and Practike*, offered detailed guidance to county gentlemen and muster-masters on how to train their local companies and shape the civilian into some form of military mould.[58]

The wide range of such treatises and manuals published during the sixteenth and early seventeenth centuries frequently discussed military identity in prescriptive terms, and returned repeatedly to questions of what made a good or ideal soldier. Drawing on the model of one of the most influential classical authorities on martial practice, Vegetius' *De Re Militaria* (written in the fourth century AD), early modern military manuals regularly attended not only to practical information about what soldiers should *do*, but to more theoretical matters regarding how a soldier should *be*.[59] They offered often very detailed examinations of the motives, character and qualities desired in the ideal soldier, and recognised that there was something distinct and exceptional about those of the martial profession.[60] Loyalty, piety, clemency and the assurance of plain-speaking honesty are frequently identified as core characteristics of the ideal soldier, as are learning and a general receptiveness towards acquiring knowledge of the more technical aspects of the early modern art of war. Barret, for example, maintained that a soldier should be guided by four principles: defence of true religion; honour of his prince; safety of his country; and 'diligently to learne the Art he professeth, which is warre'.[61] Gates placed confessional motivations at the core of his ideal soldier, whilst George Whetstone argued that 'learning is the most pretious Ornament of a Souldier, and the necessariest vertue'.[62] Chapters 2, 3 and 4, by Woodcock, O'Mahony and Major, examine the figure of the learned and literate soldier in more detail.

Although military manuals repeatedly declared the virtues of the ideal, disciplined soldier, fighting men as a group were routinely characterised

[57] Fissel, *English Warfare*, pp. 62–3.

[58] Eltis, *Military*, pp. 111–12. It should be stressed that for a long time there was little in the way of a consistent, universally adopted 'mould' and little national uniformity when it came to the practices, equipment and standards of regional musters. It was only in 1623 that a new book of prescribed training orders appeared, based on continental models, and was circulated throughout England and Wales: Boynton, *Elizabethan Militia*, pp. 237–41.

[59] Vegetius, *Epitome of Military Science*, trans. N.P. Milner (Liverpool, 1993), pp. 1–27 (book 1). On the reception of Vegetius' formulation of the ideal soldier: Christopher Allmand, *The De Re Militari of Vegetius: The Reception, Transmission and Legacy of a Roman Text in The Middle Ages* (Cambridge, 2011) pp. 261–9.

[60] Webb, *Elizabethan*, pp. 51–77.

[61] Barret, *Theoricke*, sigs. A4v–B1v.

[62] Gates, *Defence, passim*; George Whetstone, *The Honourable Reputation of a Soldier* (London, 1585), sig. F1r. Palmer, *Essay*, sigs. E2r–E2v, adds a knowledge of geometry and mathematics to his breakdown of what makes the 'compleat souldier'.

in extremely negative terms throughout the early modern period. (Indeed, many martialist authors were moved to write to counter the frequent negative characterisations of soldierly identity.) Such negative stereotypes were not without foundation, and civilian audiences of pamphlets and newsbooks could read with horror of atrocities taking place at soldiers' hands during the revolt in the Low Countries or in Germany during the Thirty Years War.[63] Comparable savagery was recorded in Elizabethan accounts of the ongoing wars in Ireland, both in operational documentation and service journals, and in published sources such as Churchyard's *A Generall Rehearsall of Warres* (1579) or John Derricke's *The Image of Irelande* (1581).[64] Closer to home, those men pressed in England for overseas service were routinely of very poor quality, in part because the Privy Council preferred to retain the comparatively better-trained militia-men at home in local defence, and because their ranks were sometimes filled out with released prisoners.[65] In September 1598, for example, the commissioners for musters in Norfolk wrote to the county's high constables with a request for men to be sent to Ireland that emphasised the need for better discernment to be exercised at a local level when selecting men. As they explained:

> because there is greate fault founde by their honours with the insufficiencie of such persons as have heretofore ben chosen for the like service, choise being made of idle and loose persons and the refues of the people, we are to pray you care for the helpe thereof, advertisinge you that it is their honours direccion that your selves doe either repaire to the townes to se good choise made of men of hable bodies and convenient yeres, or cause the persons to be brought before you to be by you veiwed [*sic*] and allowed before theie be presented to the mustars.[66]

Even those men mustered for county militias were frequently found wanting militarily and did little to amend the persistently negative stereotypes about soldiers – at home and abroad – that still continued to circulate widely at the eve of the Civil Wars.[67] William Cecil, Lord Burghley advised his son to avoid the soldier's trade, claiming

---

[63]   Carlton, *This Seat*, p. 21; David Randall, ed., *English Military News Pamphlets, 1513–1637* (Tempe, AZ, 2011).
[64]   See Edwards, ed., *Campaign Journals*; Churchyard, *Generall Rehearsall*, sigs. Q3v–Q4r; John Derricke, *The Image of Irelande* (London, 1581). See also O'Neill's essay below (Chapter 8).
[65]   Hale, *War*, p. 86; Paul E.J. Hammer, *Elizabeth's Wars* (Basingstoke, 2003), pp. 100–1; Manning, *Apprenticeship*, p. 44; Carlton, *This Seat*, p. 25.
[66]   Victor Morgan et al., eds., *The Papers of Nathaniel Bacon of Stiffkey: Volume IV, 1596–1602* (Norwich, 2000), pp. 57–8.
[67]   Barbara Donagan, *War in England, 1642–1649* (Oxford, 2008), p. 18.

he that sets up his rest only to live by that profession can hardly be an honest man or a good Christian, for war is of itself unjust unless the good cause may make it just. Besides it is a science no longer in request than [its] use for soldiers in peace are like chimneys in summer.[68]

Burghley's closing simile reveals once again the ontological instability of the soldier's life, implicitly querying what a soldier should do or be when not employed in the field. There are suggestions here too both of soldiers' obsolescence in peacetime – a frequent cause of complaint from the martialists – and of an associated fear that lack of employment abroad could generate social disorder at home.[69] Even when soldiery was not being viewed as a trade full of criminals and degenerates, there were plenty more negative military identities in circulation, ranging from the boastful braggart soldier of the *miles gloriosus* tradition (discussed in Chapters 10 and 11 by McKeown and Hiscock), to the figure of the 'ruffler' – a beggar feigning to be a wounded war veteran – found in early modern rogue literature and on the contemporary stage.[70]

Now that some of the different ways in which military identity was evoked, constructed and contemplated during the period covered by the essays in this collection have been outlined, it remains here to map out the shape of this volume and the areas upon which the contributors have focused. The approach taken, guided in part by the contributors' expertise and interests, has been to concentrate on three principal strands of investigation that examine: (1) different ways in which early modern soldiery and martial communities conceived and constructed military identity using models of masculinity, the literate soldier and family identity; (2) relationships between English, Irish and Anglo-Irish (or 'Old English') military identities during the Nine Years War (1594–1603); and (3) the numerous appearances made by soldier figures on the early modern stage and what they reveal about military identity. The book recognises, as noted above, that the concept of military identity can be situated in relation to several distinct areas of current critical interest in studies of military history and textual culture. It acknowledges too that early modern soldiery, whether viewed in terms of individuals or as a profession, has long been an under-studied aspect of military history.[71]

---

[68] Quoted in Rapple, *Martial*, p. 19.
[69] Carlton, *This Seat*, pp. 252–3. Chapters 9, 10 and 11 in this volume examine different ways in which soldiers' complaints about their perceived obsolescence, and the state's ingratitude, are articulated in documentary and literary sources.
[70] Arthur Kinney, ed., *Rogues, Vagabonds, and Sturdy Beggars* (Amherst, MA, 1990), pp. 92, 115–16; Nick De Somogyi, *Shakespeare's Theatre of War* (Aldershot, 1998), pp. 43–4, 131–85.
[71] This point is reiterated by Trim, 'Introduction', p. 2; Donagan, *War*, p. 43; Withington, 'Introduction', 5, 22.

The volume opens with D.J.B. Trim's chapter on martial conduct and masculinity. Drawing on both literary texts and archival sources, Trim argues that a large part of martial identity can be understood as masculine identity and shows that, among both the gentry/ nobility and the lower orders, military service and the performance of overtly courageous deeds of martial prowess were widely perceived as important, even preeminent ways to demonstrate and vindicate a man's honour and masculinity alike. Taking up the points made earlier linking military identity and the performance of honourable deeds, and responding too to Machiavelli's opposition of soldiery and effeminacy in the quotation above, Trim demonstrates that an honourable martial identity depended on actions that showed one to be manly as well as soldierly. His chapter also paves the way for subsequent work on both male and female roles and identities in the study of early modern warfare, complementing the lead taken by Barton Hacker and John Lynn.[72]

Matthew Woodcock's chapter takes a different approach to the activities by which martial identity could be constituted, and concentrates on the figure of the literate, learned soldier and the paradigmatic model of the writing fighting man provided by Julius Caesar and his campaign reports, or *Commentaries*. The chapter focuses upon Caesar's twin roles as both protagonist and author of the *Commentaries*, and on how Caesar's mastery with pen and sword provided a significant, much-imitated model of military identity during the early modern period. It then examines how this model was taken up and responded to in Sir Clement Edmondes's *Observations upon Caesar's Commentaries* (1600, 1604, 1609). More than simply an annotated translation of the *Commentaries*, Edmondes's text provided a programme for fashioning military identity based on the Caesarian ideal of the literate, rhetorically adept fighting man. Edmondes not only imitated Caesar to a degree himself through his annotations and short essays upon the original text, but he attempts to fashion one of the leading English generals of the late Elizabethan era, Sir Francis Vere, as the epitome of this Caesarian ideal. As Woodcock demonstrates, the study of Caesar's *Commentaries* complements the growing level of critical interest in soldier-authors and military life-writing (noted above). The link between literary and soldierly spheres is returned to by Cian O' Mahony in Chapter 3, which focuses on the writings of the Norfolk-based clergyman and scholar Ralph Knevet and his continued interest in both local and international military activity and identity. Although lacking any kind of combat experience himself, Knevet composed a discourse on military discipline, *Stratiotikon* (1628), in which he responds to perceived failures of the local militia system

---

[72]   Barton C. Hacker, 'Women and Military Institutions in Early Modern Europe: A Reconnaissance', *Signs: Journal of Women in Culture and Society* 6.4 (1981), 643–71; John A. Lynn II, *Women, Armies, and Warfare in Early Modern Europe* (Cambridge, 2008).

and links dereliction of martial duties at a civic level to England's tarnished military reputation during the 1620s. A similar preoccupation with associating local, national and international military identities manifests in Knevet's occasional play *Rhodon and Iris* (1631) and in his unpublished three-book addition to Edmund Spenser's *Faerie Queene*. As O' Mahony demonstrates, *A Supplement of the Faery Queene* (c.1628–35) uses chivalric representations of military identity to criticise the failings of James I, celebrate the success of Gustavus Adolphus and serve as an instruction manual to Charles I. Knevet's writings argue for the necessity for all citizens to become both soldier *and* clerk to safeguard Protestant statehood at home and abroad.

Whereas O' Mahony explores personal military identity in relation to civic and national martial communities, in Chapter 4 Philip Major looks at the construction of familial military identity as revealed through the work of Thomas, first lord Fairfax, a diplomat and veteran soldier who had served with Francis Vere and the earl of Essex in the Low Countries and France during the 1590s. The chapter focuses on a little-discussed prose tract, 'The Highway to Heidelberg', that Fairfax produced in the 1620s in response to the loss of two of his sons during the ill-fated defence of the Palatinate. In the first sustained critical analysis of this text, Major considers how Fairfax combines some of the more conventional anti-Spanish rhetoric found in manuscript and printed sources of the 1620s with an idiosyncratic construction of military identity shaped by both Calvinist piety and a powerful endorsement of the current and past service given by the Fairfax family.

Links between confessional sympathies, military service and the concept of the Christian soldier are found, as noted above, in many of the martialist manuals produced in this era. In Chapter 5, Angela Andreani and Andrew Hadfield approach this subject from a different angle by exploring the relationship between the clergy and the military in the late Elizabethan period. Their approach here is to concentrate on clergymen serving the military in late sixteenth-century Ireland, service that took the form both of clerical duties performed for armies whilst on campaign, and of preaching conducted ahead of expeditions. Building on John Hale's earlier work on English divines and the subject of war, Andreani and Hadfield place the clergymen Meredith Hanmer and Lancelot Andrewes in a tradition that looks back to the likes of Thomas Becon and Hugh Latimer, and their exhortations to obey one's prince and fight his wars. In doing so they demonstrate that divines played an important role in framing how Elizabethan soldiers viewed their own roles and responsibilities when they went to war.[73] Andreani and Hadfield return us once more to the

---

[73] J.R. Hale, *Renaissance War Studies* (London, 1983), pp. 487–517; Gunn et al., *War*, p. 266. Looking at the other end of the confessional spectrum to both the Henrician and Elizabethan divines, recent scholarship on Jesuits and war offers a useful examination of

notion of soldierly communities, but also remind us that the discussion of military identities and occupations, need not necessarily restrict itself solely to those directly engaged in combat.

Andreani and Hadfield's chapter is the first in Part II of the volume, which examines different aspects of both personal and national identities in late sixteenth- and early seventeenth-century Ireland. In Chapter 6, Ruth Canning examines the powerful sense of military identity maintained and propagated by the lordships descended from Ireland's original Anglo-Norman conquerors (also known as the Old English), and their defences in treatises and petitions of their martial responsibilities in preserving English rule in Ireland. The constant state of military preparedness of the Old English, and their continued confrontations with the Gaelic Irish shaped the particular individual and collective mentalities of this community. And as Canning shows, an emerging Old English identity came to be defined by its military traditions and martial men. David Edwards also looks to Old English military identity, and focuses on Thomas Butler, tenth earl of Ormond and the Latin poem *Ormonius* (published 1615) that celebrated his military career and constructed at length – and not without embellishment – a model of the earl as a long-serving, loyal military subject. Like Fairfax's 'Highway to Heidelberg' discussed in Chapter 4 by Major, *Ormonius* represented a significant exercise in identity politics, and combined an ameliorated version of the Butlers' service and familial identity with extended characterisation of Ormond as military hero – the sort of figure, it was hoped, that would warrant reward and preferment in the early Stuart state.

In Chapter 8, James O'Neill turns attention to the military identities and reputations of the Gaelic Irish forces led by Hugh O'Neill, second earl of Tyrone, and to the nature of their warfare against crown forces during the Nine Years War. Countering previous reductive characterisations of the war as being a contest between the primitive or savage Irish warrior and the thoroughly modernised English soldier, and building on more recent scholarship concerning manifestations of the military revolution in Ireland, O'Neill reveals that the Irish military were quicker to adapt to the changing nature of warfare than the English.[74] At the same time, O'Neill reassesses modern critical narratives characterising English military actions in Ireland during this period as wholly bloodthirsty and cruel. In doing so, O'Neill presents a valuable modification of the military identities used as convenient commonplaces in historiography of the Nine Years War. Clodagh Tait approaches the Nine

---

comparable involvements of chaplains within Catholic military communities; see essays by Vincenzo Lavenia, Gianclaudio Civale and Ariane Boltanski in the *Journal of Jesuit Studies* 4.4 (2017).

[74]   O'Carroll, 'Change'; Lenihan, 'Conclusion'.

Years War and its aftermath from the perspective of wounds and wounding, and focuses on a particularly problematic sub-category of military identity: the casualty. Her chapter explores how the injured, broken and scarred bodies of soldiers in this conflict become surfaces on which service, duty and loyalty can be inscribed, and the means by which military identities can be displayed. Drawing on emerging fields of scholarship looking at representations of disability and the emotional impact of early modern combat, Tait examines how wounds were a prized currency within the larger economy of honour vital to contemporary military identity (as discussed above, and in Chapter 1). After talking more broadly about the signification of soldiers' disabilities in this period, she presents the careers and woundings of Sir Griffin Markham and Sir Henry Danvers as case-studies.

The final section of the collection, Part III, focuses on the presence of the soldier on the early modern stage – or more precisely, in the playhouse, in London-based civic entertainments and in printed plays. As in many of the investigations of military identity in earlier parts of this volume, attention repeatedly turns to how individuals, groups and communities imagine and display themselves or are in turn represented. Adam McKeown in Chapter 10, for example, revisits the figure of the braggart soldier mentioned earlier and the associations of Shakespeare's Othello with the well-known *miles gloriosus* tradition. We are returned again to those representations of wounded veteran soldiers seen in Chapter 9, and to the larger issue of the physical, visceral and mortal costs of military service that is raised repeatedly throughout this volume.[75] McKeown demonstrates that the self-promotional language of the braggart soldier comes perilously close to that of the valorous veteran and/ or wounded fighting man seeking due reward for his service. Verbal constructions of military identity are vital within the economy of honour but are also hugely problematic, not only because of the linguistic proximity of the braggart and valiant soldier, but because of the wider difficulties of establishing the precise boundaries of the military profession in this period. In Chapter 11, Andrew Hiscock looks to Thomas Middleton's playhouse drama and civic entertainments and the questions that they posed about militarism and the role of the military profession during the Jacobean period. As well as exploring the relationship between martial and civic communities (as O'Mahony does), it demonstrates the full extent of Middleton's preoccupation with incorporating a variety of soldier figures within his dramatic works, and his interest in representing the problematic, potentially controversial nature of this figure and how he would be perceived. Hiscock also examines how Middleton's texts regularly addressed the challenge of responding positively to the policies of the *rex pacificus*, and engaged in many of the same debates found in earlier

[75] De Somogyi, *Theatre*, pp. 11–33.

seventeenth-century print culture concerning the decline in the nation's military identity and reputation.

Complementing McKeown and Hiscock's contributions on dramatic representations of soldiery, and the observations made above about the methodological difficulties of establishing the boundaries or defining criteria of military identity, Vimala C. Pasupathi and Benjamin Armintor focus in Chapter 12 on stative declarations and utterances of soldierly identity in Tudor and Stuart drama. Using traditional archival evidence as well as digital methods, Pasupathi and Armintor analyse an electronic corpus of dramatic works produced between 1580–1642 for linguistic patterns relating to both reflexive and ascriptive recognitions of martial identity – that is, where individuals either self-identify, or are identified by others, as soldiers. (The authors thus complement Trim's chapter, which addresses military identity asserted more by *doing* rather than *saying*.) Having examined linguistic data drawn from over 300 assertions about soldiers' identities, Pasupathi and Armintor present a 'grammar' delineating just how soldiers' identities are constructed and articulated in early modern drama. They use their data to respond to some of the questions noted at the start of this introduction about defining military identity, examining constructions and collocations that present the soldier figure in relation to other spheres and occupations, including those of the courtier and scholar. Pasupathi and Armintor's innovative research casts new light on the nature and frequency of references to soldiery in early modern drama, and paves the way for subsequent scholars accessing their dataset to drill down and explore individual playwrights' investment in soldiers' identities in greater detail.

This book does not pretend to offer a comprehensive history of the early modern soldier, or soldiery more generally, nor to cover every facet of military identity. It was not designed to provide an exhaustive or seamless survey of how Tudor and Stuart fighting men viewed themselves in their martial roles or were represented in such roles by others. The Afterword identifies areas for further analysis in our field. The essays here do not set out a single argument or 'line' on military identity although, as indicated above, recurrent themes, concerns and objects of analysis can be discerned. Taken together, the essays add a greater level of nuance to critical understanding of the early modern soldier and his profession, and of his place within the historiography of sixteenth- and seventeenth-century warfare and the early modern military revolution. They also provide a series of new investigations into representations of early modern martial culture, and into how and why military identities were formed, assumed, propagated and debated. Drawing upon a wide range of different disciplines and methodologies, the contributors demonstrate how the study of military identity – and military identities – intersects with that of life-writing, digital humanities, gender, disability, the history of emotions, and the relationship between literature and martial culture.

PART I

Models of Military Identity

1

'Warlike prowesse and manly courage': Martial Conduct and Masculine Identity in Late Tudor and Early Stuart England

D.J.B. TRIM

I

Manhood and masculinity once barely registered on the horizon of historians of early modern England. History was tacitly understood as being, on the whole, the record of actions by men; thus, while (male) historians grudgingly conceded that women's history might be justified, there was, to judge by their lack of interest, no need for men's history or for consideration of gender roles. This was true even when dealing with the history of war and soldiering, an area of life that was distinctly gendered (in theory and largely, though not entirely, in practice). In the historiography of early modern England up to the early 1980s, explicit treatment of gender roles was uncommon and cursory, even in cultural histories, while the concept of a whole separate history of masculinity seems never to have crossed the minds even of historiographical giants.[1] As late as 1992, Sir Geoffrey Elton – himself a Second World War veteran, and thus well aware of the masculine nature of armies – published an essay on war and the English people that ignores the female half of the population entirely and says nothing about gender roles or masculinity, despite passages that seem to cry out for critical reflection on how manhood was defined in early modern England.[2] Nor was this untypical of Elton's *oeuvre*.[3]

By the early 1990s there was wider historiographical interest in the roles of men and women, yet the sub-disciplines of gender history and men's history were still developing. They arose out of women's history and women's studies, especially from a growing awareness that treating women 'in isolation from

---

[1] See, for example, A.L. Rowse, *The Elizabethan Renaissance: The Cultural Achievement* (London, 1972), p. 299.

[2] Geoffrey Elton, 'War and the English in the Reign of Henry VIII', *War, Strategy, and International Politics*, ed. Lawrence Freedman et al. (Oxford, 1991), pp. 9, 11, 16.

[3] Elton's occasional references to the topic of gender indicate only passing interest: 'Tudor Government: The Points of Contact. III. The Court', *TRHS*, 5th ser., 26 (1976), 219.

men' was a limitation, and that omitting the comparative perspective of men's history 'wrenched [women's history] from its historical context'. Consequently, pioneers of women's history began to encourage gender history, on the grounds 'that we should be interested in the history of both women and men', since 'concentrating on women' begged serious questions about the relative position of the sexes.[4] Interest in early modern masculinity and manhood was initially rather more typical of scholars of literary and cultural studies than historians, as Elton's example suggests. In 1985, when David Underdown published a reflection on gender roles and patriarchy in early modern England, he was ahead of the historiographical curve. Over the next twenty years, however, historians joined literary critics in addressing masculinity, at first focusing on issues relating particularly to patriarchy but increasingly on other aspects of male identities.[5] The first wave of studies had little to say about violence and the construction of manhood but in the last twenty years, studies of masculine honour have appeared, based largely on archival, documentary sources rather than literature, which draw in the arena of masculine violence.[6]

The weakness of the new men's history of early modern England, however, is that it generally focuses on the domestic sphere; it is violence within families and communities, rather than the large-scale state-sponsored violence of war, that has been examined. There is little historical scholarship on the

[4] Natalie Zemon Davis, '"Women's History" in Transition: The European Case', *Feminist Studies* 3:3/4 (1976), 83, 90–1. See also Amy E. Leonard, 'Introduction: Attending to Early Modern Women—and Men', *Masculinities, Childhood, Violence: Attending to Early Modern Women—and Men: Proceedings of the 2006 Symposium*, ed. Amy E. Leonard and Karen L. Nelson (Newark, 2011), pp. 3–10.

[5] Pathbreaking essays include D.E. Underdown, 'The Taming of the Scold: The Enforcement of Patriarchal Authority in Early Modern England', *Order and Disorder in Early Modern England*, ed. Anthony Fletcher and John Stevenson (Cambridge, 1985), pp. 116–36; Anthony Fletcher, 'Men's Dilemma: The Future of Patriarchy in England 1560–1660', *TRHS*, 6th ser., 4 (1994), 61–81, and 'Manhood, the Male Body, Courtship and the Household in Early Modern England', *History* 84 (1999), 419–36; David Cressy, 'Gender Trouble and Cross-Dressing in Early Modern England', *JBS* 35 (1996), 438–65; Susan Dwyer Asmussen, '"The part of a Christian man": The Cultural Politics of Manhood in Early Modern England', *Political Culture and Cultural Politics in Early Modern England*, ed. Asmussen and Mark A. Kishlansky (Manchester, 1995), pp. 213–33; Cynthia Herrup, '"To pluck bright honour from the pale-faced moon": Gender and Honour in the Castlehaven Story', *TRHS*, 6th ser., 6 (1996), 137–59.

[6] Elizabeth A. Foyster, *Manhood in Early Modern England* (London, 1999); Alexandra Shepard, *Meanings of Manhood in Early Modern England* (Oxford, 2003). See also Peter Sherlock, 'Militant Masculinity and the Monuments of Westminster Abbey', *Governing Masculinities in the Early Modern Period: Regulating Selves and Others*, ed. Susan Broomhill and Jacqueline van Gent (London, 2011), pp. 131–52; and Courtney Erin Thomas, *If I Lose Honour I Lose Myself: Honour Among the Early Modern English Elite* (Toronto, 2017), ch. 1.

expression of manliness in the military arena.[7] Yet this was one of the chief sites for the demonstration of masculinity and provided the occasion for powerful articulation of distinctively male virtues. The lack of analysis is a strange lacuna, given that studies of masculinity in other periods recognise the central importance of soldiering in individual and collective masculine self-imagining.[8] At the same time, the currently buoyant sub-discipline of early modern English military history has largely focused on questions of technological and administrative developments, with concern for motivation mostly restricted to financial and confessional factors.[9] Military historians have shown little interest in masculinity, and historians of gender and manhood little interest in war or military identity.

Literary scholarship, meanwhile, has not been much concerned with war and soldiering either. Whether because 'English Lit' in political terms is of the Left, whereas military history is perceived (rightly or wrongly) as being of the Right, or for other reasons, literary critics since the rise of 'literary theory' have not found war a fit subject for study. When critics have concerned themselves with war in early modern England, they have tended to do so on their own terms, sometimes simply dismissing its manifestations on the sixteenth-century page or stage with disdain.[10] And yet not only is war prominent in early modern English drama and poetry (notably, *inter alia*, in the plays of Marlowe and Shakespeare), but war had a wider impact on English Renaissance literature.[11] There was a very considerable contemporary published literature on the art of war and on soldiering, including many works by soldiers; some were technical, some historical, but many were experiential, exemplars of martial poetics, whether written in prose or verse.[12] Some fifty years ago, martial poetics and its authors attracted some, albeit limited, interest from critics, before being sidelined for half a century and ignored by

---

[7] Sherlock, 'Militant Masculinity', and Keith Thomas, *The Ends of Life: Roads to Fulfilment in Early Modern England* (Oxford, 2009), pp. 44–62, are only qualified exceptions due to their limited scope.

[8] See, for example, Graham Dawson, *Soldier Heroes: British Adventure, Empire and the Imagining of Masculinities* (London, 1994).

[9] See David Lawrence, 'Reappraising the Elizabethan and Early Stuart Soldier: Recent Historiography on Early Modern English Military Culture', *History Compass* 9 (2011), 16–33.

[10] Jonathan Baldo, 'Wars of Memory in *Henry V*', *Shakespeare Quarterly* 47 (1996), 132.

[11] See the essays by McKeown, Hiscock, and Pasupathi and Armintor in this volume (Chapters 10, 11 and 12).

[12] D.J.B. Trim, 'The Art of War: Martial Poetics from Henry Howard to Philip Sidney', *Oxford Handbook of Tudor Literature, 1485–1603*, ed. Mike Pincombe and Cathy Shrank (Oxford, 2009), pp. 587–605.

literary theory. Only recently has this early modern literature of war started to attract scholars, from any discipline.[13]

A handful of books and essays by literary critics in the last quarter century may suggest continued limited interest (though perhaps they are the first cuckoos of spring). Some bring modern preconceptions too much to bear, and display limited understanding of early modern military institutions and the conduct of war.[14] Other critics, including Nick de Somogyi, Nina Taunton and Patricia Cahill, have read widely in the literature of war and their insights have value beyond their discipline.[15] There are also recent well-researched literary-biographical studies of soldier-poets such as Thomas Churchyard, George Gascoigne, and Barnabe Rich (second-rank but significant figures in the English literary Renaissance), nuanced work that provide insights into their martial poesy, as well as their lives and wider literary production.[16] One hopes that such works will 'encourage further investigation into Tudor military writing and the significance of the soldier-author in sixteenth-century English literature'.[17] But in any event, given the extent to which literary scholars have engaged with gender and masculinity since the 1970s, an obvious issue to explore would be what concepts of manhood are present in the early modern English literature of war and how that literature, especially the experiential writing of soldier-authors, shaped those concepts.

In fact, few literary critics have engaged with the interrelationship of masculinity and soldiering in early modern England. Fewer still take distinctly military literature, as opposed to the plays of Shakespeare and Marlowe, into account.[18] And of those scholars who have engaged substantively with contemporary descriptions of the theory and practice of war, while some provide provocative and insightful 'readings' of particular texts, in each case they view

---

[13]   See Adam N. McKeown, *English Mercuries: Soldier Poets in the Age of Shakespeare* (Nashville, 2009), p. 6; Matthew Woodcock, *Thomas Churchyard: Pen, Sword, and Ego* (Oxford, 2016), pp. 2–3.

[14]   Michael Hattaway, 'Blood is Their Argument: Men of War and Soldiers in Shakespeare and Others', *Religion, Culture and Society in Early Modern Britain*, ed. Anthony Fletcher and Peter Roberts (Cambridge, 1994), pp. 84–101; Curtis Breight, *Militarism, Surveillance and Elizabethan Drama* (London, 1997).

[15]   Nick de Somogyi, *Shakespeare's Theatre of War* (Aldershot, 1998); Nina Taunton, *1590s Drama and Militarism: Portrayals of War in Marlowe, Chapman and Shakespeare's Henry V* (Aldershot, 2001); Patricia Cahill, *Unto the Breach: Martial Formations, Historical Trauma, and the Early Modern Stage* (Oxford, 2008).

[16]   Woodcock, *Thomas Churchyard*; McKeown, *English Mercuries*, chs. 3 and 4; Gillian Austen, *George Gascoigne* (Cambridge, 2008); Willy Maley, 'Barnaby Rich', *ODNB*.

[17]   Woodcock, *Thomas Churchyard*, p. 3.

[18]   For example, Timothy Francisco's very slender study, *The Impact of Militarism and Social Mobility on the Construction of Masculinity in Elizabethan and Jacobean Drama* (Lewiston, 2007), has ambitions that are let down by its limited survey of early modern texts and its tendency to reify social categories.

these texts through a heavily theoretical lens and are more interested in making arguments about psychological indications allegedly evident across a range of texts than in drawing conclusions about the place of war and manhood in the value system with which martial poetic texts collectively engage.[19]

This chapter considers the place of martial values in the construction of manhood in English society from the death of Henry VIII to the Thirty Years War (i.e. from the late 1540s to the 1630s). I argue that the ways in which men (especially young men, of military age) understand, articulate and demonstrate their sense of manhood are always of great consequence. But because they evolve, adapting to contemporary conditions and concerns, the terrain of masculinity is not fixed: it requires historical analysis to identify its contours. And in the sixteenth and seventeenth centuries, 'soldierly' and 'manly' were largely coextensive, as is argued below. A large part of martial identity (the identity of soldiers) can be understood as masculine identity – the values of the soldier were typically expressed in distinctly masculine terms. Furthermore, among the nobility, military service – in particular, the performance of overtly courageous deeds of martial prowess – was widely perceived as the principal, even preeminent, way of demonstrating and vindicating a man's honour and manhood alike. This is an important point and with wider application than might be assumed, for I use 'nobility' in a way used by contemporaries, who generally understood the gentry as being part of the wider nobility, the *nobilitas minor* as opposed to the *nobilitas major* of the peerage.[20] And so in this study the terms 'noble' and 'gentle' are used interchangeably except where contemporary quotations are clearly referencing the peerage.

This chapter emphasizes the performative nature of military honour. My analysis thus accords to some extent with the insights of literary and cultural critics, and particularly with the view that gender identity is socially constructed and performative. I seek to extend that conceptual approach, however, by incorporating not only 'speech acts', but also physical actions, which were more important in the conceptualisation and personification of masculine identity in early modern England. In my analysis, *performativity* is about doing more than saying.[21] Proving oneself a true man (or true gentleman)

[19] See Diane Purkiss, *Literature, Gender and Politics during the English Civil War* (Cambridge, 2005), esp. pp. 34–44; Taunton, *1590s Drama and Militarism*, pp. 137–45; Alan Shepard, *Marlowe's Soldiers: Rhetorics of Masculinity in the Age of the Armada* (Aldershot, 2002). All three draw on wide reading of contemporary texts by and about soldiers, with Purkiss adding letters to published works.

[20] D.J.B. Trim, 'Fighting "Jacob's Wars": The Employment of English and Welsh Mercenaries in the European Wars of Religion: France and the Netherlands, 1562–1610', unpublished Ph.D. thesis (University of London, 2002), pp. 49–51. Hereafter cited as 'Mercenaries'.

[21] I draw particularly on Judith Butler, *Gender Trouble: Feminism and the Subversion of Identity* (rpt New York, 2006).

required performance – not on the stage (a point that is perhaps important to make in light of how many studies of early modern masculinity are studies of the contemporary theatre), but in the theatre of war.[22]

My sources in this chapter are, in the main, texts and documents by men who themselves had experience of war, including soldier-poets and playwrights. What is described is not just theory, but praxis. Many of the texts set out precepts for behaviour, but they also narrate actual episodes from campaigns and reveal that men's actions were shaped by what was valorised in the texts. Martial poetics tends to be both prescriptive and descriptive: its texts prescribe an ideal course of action and ideal virtues, but also describe how the ideals were practised and implemented. What follows, then, is a study of more than rhetoric. These texts reveal a value system which pushed men, firstly, to show that they could serve creditably as a soldier, making the experience of at least one military campaign a key *rite de passage*. Having gone 'to the wars', moreover, men serving as soldiers were then, secondly, impelled to exhibit *élan*, skill at arms, courage, and *sang froid*. Wounds bore powerful witness to a warrior's honour and manhood, even when injuries suffered in combat would in other circumstances have been seen as unmanning.[23] Because acts of bravery and prowess were the chief sources of an honourable reputation, martialists were therefore led, thirdly, to engage in increasingly dangerous and ever more conspicuous actions of gallantry and proficiency in combat. An honourable martial identity, in sum, depended on actions that demonstrated one to be manly as well as soldierly.

II

Military identity can be understood as masculine identity to a great degree. The attributes of the soldier were usually articulated in distinctly masculine terms; meanwhile, manliness – especially what we might call gentlemanliness or aristocratic manhood – was often described in martial terms. Soldierliness and manliness were similar and overlapping in their mental geography and their terminology, while want of warrior virtues occupied the same terrain as effeminacy. Thomas Churchyard, the doyen of early modern English soldiers-cum-authors, whose parallel military and literary careers spanned from Henry VIII through to Elizabeth I, wrote acidly in 1579 of how 'a man that hath [...] abidden the hazard of the Cannon [...] is no companion for punies, nor Milksoppes, whose manhoode and maners differs, as farre from the grave

---

[22]   A term used by early modern soldier-poets (see below, Section IV) as well as in the title of De Somogyi's 1998 monograph *Shakespeare's Theatre of War*; cf. 'theatre of operations', a standard technical military term for at least the last eighty years.

[23]   See Tait's essay below (Chapter 9).

Soldiour, as a [...] kite in courage and ambition, differs from a Jerfaucon'.[24] Geoffrey Gates, a soldier who authored just one book, praised English soldiers who served in the Dutch Revolt, arguing that their actions in war prove 'the olde English valiancy is not so extinguished [through] corrupt idlenesse' and 'shew that they [English] are not so far degenerate from [...] their ancestors'.[25] The equation of unmanly behaviour with unwarlike behaviour is plain, as is its opposite, which Churchyard expresses succinctly in his epitaph on the Elizabethan model of knightly behaviour, Sir Philip Sidney: 'manhood runnes in Armor'.[26] In another epitaph, on Sir Hugh Paulet, similar ideas emerge, as Churchyard praises his subject's skill, since youth, 'in armes and marciall feates' and terms him 'a maister of that arte/ Whiche oft in feeld and countreis cause, did plaie a manly parte'.[27] The part of a man, then, was to be skilful in use of arms and armour and to deploy his adeptness 'in [the] feeld'.

In a late work – part translation, part adaptation of the Dutch chronicler Emanuel van Meteren – Churchyard describes the English troops of John Norreys in 1580 campaigning, with allied Dutch troops, in the province of Brabant and praises them for their 'good order with manly courage'.[28] In 1579 Gates had praised 'the high courage and manlines' of 'those valiant and worthy souldiers'.[29] Courage was not gender neutral. Neither were strength and energy. William Blandy, writing of a campaign in the Low Countries in 1580, praised an English lieutenant 'for his manlynes and activitye, for his strength [...] in every weapon that belonges to a tall and expert Souldiar'.[30] Not only were military qualities such as courage distinctly masculine, but also, in Blandy's telling, such manly traits as height and strength were soldierly. He goes on to commend 'many more' English soldiers for their 'prowes [...] theyr singuler manhood and rare vertue'.[31] Manliness, in this view, was distinctly a martial virtue – and vice versa.

---

[24] *A Generall Rehearsall of Warres, Wherein is Five Hundred Severall Services of Land and Sea. And joined to the same some tragedies and epitaphes* [running title *Churchyard's Choise*] (London, 1579), sig. M2r.

[25] Geoffrey Gates, *The Defence of Militarie Profession* (London, 1579), p. 58.

[26] *The Epitaph of Sir Philip Sidney Knight, Lately Lord Governor of Floshing* (London, 1586), sig. A4r.

[27] *A pleasaunte Laborinth called Churchyardes Chance* (London, 1580), sig. A2r.

[28] T[homas] C[hurchyard], with Ri[chard] Ro[binson], *A True Discourse Historicall of the Succeeding Governours in the Netherlands* (London, 1602), p. 39. This draws on, but (especially when writing about English soldiers) is rather more than a translation of Emanuel van Meteren's *Historia Belgica* (1598) – the first edition of a celebrated work with its own complex textual history: see E.O.G. Haitsma Mulier and G.A.C. van der Lem, *Repertorium van geschiedschrijvers in Nederland 1500–1800* (Den Haag, 1990), pp. 284–6.

[29] Churchyard et al., *True Discourse*, p. 39; Gates, *Defence*, p. 58.

[30] William Blandy, *The Castle, or Picture of Pollicy* (London, 1581), sig. H3r.

[31] Blandy, *Castle*, sig. G3v.

This is brought into sharp relief by the regular depiction of feminine characteristics as both unmilitary and ignoble. This was a favoured theme of the prolific author Barnabe Rich, who late in life affirmed: 'I am a Souldier, a professed souldier, better practised in my pike then in my penne'.[32] While perhaps only six of his twenty-five books and pamphlets were on military themes, he often writes of soldierly characteristics in other works; a recent biographer identifies 'carpet knights', men who postured as soldiers, as his 'chief bugbears'. However, 'womanlike mynded men' could be added to that list; in 1574 Rich contrasts them (in the first of many expostulations on effeminacy) with 'the noble Souldier', whose exertions are what permits womanly males to 'injoy their delightes'.[33] Blandy draws a similarly sharp contrast, writing of the 'paynefull' soldier as 'delighting rather in brave furniture and glittering armor, then in deynty dyet, womanlyke wantonnes, and vayne pleasures'.[34] Churchyard sneers at courtly qualities as decidedly inferior to those that fit one for the field: 'Where Cannon roard, and Dromme did sounde,/ I did not learne, to daunce a rounde'.[35] Similarly, Francis Markham, who served in continental wars during the reigns of both Elizabeth I and James I, carves out martial honour as alien to the domestic sphere: 'Honour […] is a lover of Action, and will sit in no Theater, but where the clamour of good deeds may ring shrilly about it'.[36]

The feminisation of those who had not braved the cannon and the valorisation of the manhood of those who bore arms lent itself to certain figurative applications. Literary critics have been very inclined to see texts as embodying ideas about manly potency, and no doubt often with some justification; but 'weapon', 'sword', 'pike' (almost any term for a weapon with a long blade) can be applied figuratively to a male phallus, and there is perhaps too great a readiness to read sexual meaning into descriptions of weaponry. For example, Taunton quotes Leonard and Thomas Digges's *Stratioticos* (1590) on the perceived danger that, as Englishmen grew 'more delicate' like (allegedly) 'the Italian and French', they would stop using the pike, 'and thereby greatly weaken the forces of our land'. Her conclusion is that 'this economical little sentence'

---

[32]   Barnabe Rich, *A Short Survey of Ireland* (London, 1609), sig. A3r.

[33]   Maley, 'Rich'; Barnabe Rich, *A Right Exelaunt and Plesaunt Dialogue between Mercury and an English Souldier* (London, 1574), sig. M3v; see Trim, 'Art of War', p. 599. Shepard and Purkiss misread Rich, to my mind, as being fixated on the dangers of effeminacy, rather than being a theorist of manliness and its connection with military service: Shepard, *Meanings*, pp. 283, 288; Purkiss, *Literature*, p. 37.

[34]   Blandy, *The Castle*, sig. F2v.

[35]   *A Light Bondell of Livly Discourses Called Churchyardes Charge* (London, 1580), p. 7. This is part of a series of negative discourses on the court and courtiers. Churchyard's relationship with, and views of, these were alike ambivalent (and often voiced in his works): Woodcock, *Thomas Churchyard*, e.g. pp. 111–12, 198–9. Churchyard's effective feminisation of courtly activities is part of a wider trope of courtiers as effeminate: Cynthia Herrup, 'The King's Two Genders', *JBS* 45 (2006), 503–4.

[36]   *The Booke of Honour. Or, Five Decads of Epistles of Honour* (London, 1625), p. 4.

summarises perfectly 'the association of masculinity with that most phallic of weapons, the pike [and] of effeminacy with the "perfumed" European'. But this is not the natural reading of the original statement, which occurs as part of a long section of 'Notes to be remembered in the Musters, and ordering of men', the intent of which is that troops are turned out effectively. It refers to actual English forces in the field rather than any figurative phallic 'force' of metaphorical manhood. There is a connection to masculinity since the author is concerned that men who are too delicate will be unable to use the pike, but it goes no further than that. Taunton even overstates the jibe at continentals: the insertion of quotation marks around perfumed is curious, as it is not in Digges.[37] Sometimes a pike is just a pike.

What is certain, though, is that bearing a pike was perceived as one of the primary ways of demonstrating that one was distinguished by the warlike virtues. But these were, in turn, more particularly the virtues, not of men in general, but of noble or gentle men. Gates took for granted that those who 'exceede in militarie prowess and worthines, soe do they excell in [...] all noblenesse of hart'. When Churchyard sought to 'shew how Gentilitie begane, and where and in what sorte honour was first gotten and maintained', he pointed to 'the lives of noble Soldiours'. Blandy laments the death of an English captain who had demonstrated his 'manlynesse' but who, by his good service, had 'approved in himselfe every way to come of a gentle and noble race'.[38] It was not only martialists who had these views. The celebrated chronicler William Camden – inclined if anything to scepticism about soldiers – writes of how in 1566 some 'English [gentlemen], who for their naturall valour, thought themselves borne to live in Armes, and not in idlenes, seeing the Nobility of all parts, did rise at the report of the warre against the Turke, and carried their Armes and Courages into Hungarie'.[39] This underscores both how the values espoused by soldier-poets were widely accepted in elite culture and how unmanly attributes (idleness) tended to be contrasted with physical courage, military experience and 'nobility'.

Estimable military service could vindicate nobility and masculinity, or confer it. Blandy stresses that good service by a 'common, as private Souldiar is honorable' and, after praising the common soldiers alongside whom he served in the Netherlands for their good conduct, he declares that they had '*become* peerlesse, noble, and magnificent'.[40] Implicit in his choice of that word is a recognition that commendable military service brings honour to those

---

[37] Taunton, *1590s Drama and Militarism*, p. 138; Leonard and Thomas Digges, *An Arithmeticall Warlike Treatise Named Stratioticos* (London, 1590), pp. 376–7.

[38] Gates, *Defence*, p. 17; *Churchyard's Choise*, sig. M1r; Blandy, *Castle*, sig. G3v.

[39] William Camden, *Annales, The True and Royal History of Elizabeth, Queene of England*, trans. Abraham Darcie (London, 1625), book 1, p. 127.

[40] Blandy, *The Castle*, sigs. F2v and H1v (emphasis supplied).

who serve, regardless of social status, and confirms the virtue of the gentry or nobility who soldiered well. Moreover, it suggests that sometimes a man of ignoble birth could have a noble spirit in his heart, in which case honourable military service allowed the presence of aristocratic virtue to be manifested; said service then validated both gentility and masculinity. This recognition is also evident in the invocation by George Whetstone of the 'highe incouragement to bee valiant, when valour, by government, is able to raise a man from the Carte, to be a Soveraigne Captaine'.[41] The elision of soldierly, manly and aristocratic identities was epitomised by Markham: 'the fittest man to make a Souldier is a perfit gentleman'.[42]

III

To be soldierly and manly were thus to a great extent synonymous/ conflated. But what were the values of this ethos of martial manhood? To prove oneself a true man (or gentleman) was a matter of deeds more than words. To authenticate one's manliness, one had to perform: partly, no doubt, in bed;[43] but reputation derived, to a great extent, from deeds done in the public eye. If actions mattered more than words, however, one must ask in turn: what particular actions were valorised and served to prove that one was a true man?

The answer, as indicated earlier, is threefold: first, being manly and soldierly was, at its most basic, about 'being there', in a military unit in a war zone. While Shepard, in her study of violence and manhood, devotes much time to evidence from Cambridge (the violence 'of young men performing rituals of bravado', and rarely deadly violence),[44] one English soldier expressed his view of those who thought university a prime site for demonstrating manliness, writing that, though 'first in Cambridge I had spent my prime,/ And next at Inns of courte bestow'd some time', it was after he 'imploy'd my riper yeares in warres', that 'I thought [...] my yeares well spent'.[45] Taking part in a campaign served as a rite of passage for many early modern Englishmen, a proof of their worth as men and as gentlemen, since manliness and aristocratic status were bound up together. It was not necessary, then, to emulate Shakespeare's Hotspur, 'he that kills me some six or seven dozen of Scots at a breakfast, washes his hands, and says to his wife, "Fie upon this quiet life! I want work."'[46] A

41 George Whetstone, *The Honorable Reputation of a Souldier* (London, 1585), sig. B1r.
42 Francis Markham, *Five Decades of Epistles of Warre* (London, 1622), p. 26.
43 Cf. Fletcher, 'Manhood'; Foyster, *Manhood*; Shepard, *Meanings*.
44 Shepard, *Meanings*, pp. 93–9 (quotation at p. 93), 107–10.
45 Anon., 'The Souldiers Counterbluffe to the Cambridge Interludians', Folger Shakespeare Library, MS V.b.303, p. 301.
46 Shakespeare, *I Henry IV*, 2.5.95–7. (All references to Shakespeare are from the *Riverside Shakespeare*.) Herrup uses Hotspur as an example of allegedly changing conceptions of honour in early modern England ('Gender and Honour', 137).

number of veterans discovered a taste for war and became career soldiers after their first campaign; yet, for many, it was their one and only campaign. Having demonstrated and vindicated their manhood (to themselves, perhaps, as well as to others), they could continue with the rest of their lives.[47]

Early modern warfare was highly seasonal. To go on campaign meant serving probably at most from late spring to autumn, but sometimes just the summer months; then a soldier, especially a gentleman, might return home to England. Indeed, gentlemen warriors who had made soldiering their career, and were serving on the continent or in Ireland, often went home for part of the winter season.[48] Yet service – as long as it was steady and resolute service, even for such a limited time span – could provide masculine self-validation. Successful combat was desirable (as shown below), but not essential in the fashioning of an honourable reputation as a martialist and a man. The reasons reflected the nature of warfare.

Soldiers might only rarely find themselves in actual combat. At the heart of the art of war in the sixteenth and early seventeenth centuries were sieges, in which men wielded the spade more than the sword. Early in the Dutch Revolt, atrocities were common and cities and strongholds reluctant to surrender, but as the Eighty Years War wore on, and throughout most other wars of the era, the final, successful end to a siege tended to be not the storming of the walls but the surrender of the garrison on honourable terms, with sometimes few lives lost in combat. But only by manning the trenches, extending them by spadework, and guarding them against sorties, could the ultimate success of a capitulation be secured, while it was for the defenders to resolutely maintain watch from their ramparts, counter-mining and digging new trenches and working to build ad hoc bastions as needed. All this was unpleasant work and perilous, too, for there was the persistent threat of mortal danger from the enemy (even if it was infrequently realised), whether in a bombardment or counter-bombardment, or in the quick combat of a sortie. There was also constant risk of death from disease, the chief killer of soldiers on campaign up to the twentieth century. As the earl of Leicester reported from the Netherlands, when he was commander-in-chief there, it was 'the poor garrison-men [who] suffer presently the greatest miserie in the world for all thinges'; and yet, he reported, he was in 'good comfort' because so many of these men affirmed that, for honour's sake, 'they will suffer more yet' (though before long he was forecasting 'the foulest mutiny that ever was made' by weary soldiers in winter quarters).[49]

---

[47] For examples of soldiers, even captains of companies, serving only one year or just one campaign: Trim, 'Mercenaries', app. 3, pp. 351–2; app. 5, pp. 377, 382; app. 6, pp. 403ff.

[48] Trim, 'Mercenaries', pp. 239–41.

[49] Leicester to Lord Burghley, 14 Jan. 1586, and to Sir Francis Walsingham, 8 July 1586, *Correspondence of Robert Dudley, Earl of Leycester, During his Government of the Low*

Thus, to soldier steadfastly through a campaign season – even if one never took part in a battle or an attempted assault – or to loyally endure a winter in garrison were achievements that were still significant and were valued, which is why serving in even one campaign could be a *rite de passage* into manhood. Among those who did so was William Blandy, who presents the honour of the soldier as lying partly 'in the maintenaunce to death, of a good and rightfull cause: the condition no lesse paynefull then full of perill'.[50] Other authors, too, valorised not just the braving of peril but the steadfast endurance of pain and discomfort. Barnabe Googe, a friend of soldiers and author of several works on military themes, declared that only the 'fearefull hart refuseth [to take the] painefull way'.[51] The Elizabethan military theorist, Thomas Styward represents this painful option of persisting, of staying the course, as explicitly a masculine one, stressing the need for soldiers 'valiauntlie, and *manfullie to persist*, in [...] all enterprises' ordered by 'the Generall and principall officers'. Markham, while praising warriors who seek 'every place where hazards are most liberally bestowed', specifically includes among the soldiers who 'shall be [...] borne triumphantly into heaven' those who were simply 'mooved by a sollid and stedfast dutie'.[52]

Doing one's duty on a campaign – as long as one did not blot one's copybook by overtly dishonourable actions – could be a rite of passage, a way of demonstrating one's honour and manhood. For those who served on more than one campaign, but found that providence did not put them in a position where they could perform deeds of reckless daring or skill at arms, to stick it out and serve steadfastly was martial and manly.

IV

It was noted above that there were three types of conduct that authenticated one's status as a real man, true gentleman and 'proper soldier' (a term often used in the period). Having seen that the first was steady service through a campaign season, it was of course even better if one got the chance to demonstrate one's qualities while campaigning. And they *had* to be demonstrated, for honourable reputation, as a man and a martialist, accrued by public performance. Honourable reputation, moreover, was supremely important. Its loss drives Cassio in *Othello* to despair:

Countries, in the Years 1585 and 1586, ed. John Bruce (London, 1844), pp. 60, 339.

[50] Blandy, *Castle*, sig. F2v.

[51] Barnabe Googe, *The Shippe of Safegarde (1569)*, ed. Simon McKeown and William E. Sheidley (Tempe, AZ, 2001), p. 5.

[52] Thomas Styward, *The Pathwaie to Martiall Discipline* (London, 1581), p. 2 (emphasis supplied); Markham, *Epistles*, p. 11.

Reputation, reputation, reputation!
Oh, I have lost my reputation!
I have lost the immortal part of myself, and what remains is bestial.
My reputation, Iago, my reputation![53]

In attributing this emotion to a soldier on stage, Shakespeare was accurately representing what real soldiers thought. Sir Edward Norreys, veteran of the Dutch wars, wrote to his fellow soldier, the earl of Essex, after being subject of a 'Villanous slawnder' from another soldier, Captain Smythe. In Cassio-like language, Norreys bemoans 'the Trowble of my Mynde' and exclaims 'how moche the reputation and honor of a Man doeth Master every other affection'.[54]

It was, however, largely public perception which shaped a soldier's career, often despite his innermost qualities, underscoring that Cassio's concern was justified. William Pelham, for instance, who had soldiered in Scotland, France and Ireland before serving in the Netherlands from 1586 as the earl of Leicester's marshal of the field, came close to being unable to accept the latter appointment because, as he wrote, of the 'extremetie [to which] my reputation had bine brought'.[55]

It was because reputation and honour were not acquired in private that men could be impelled to take the public step of going on a campaign; and once there, activity was better than passivity. The latter might, as we have seen, be acceptable if no opportunities presented themselves for heroic action. But if they did, then, if a gentleman (actual or aspirational) was to preserve and vindicate his status – both his social standing and his status as man – he had no option, but to *do* – to perform, in fact, and in front of as many eyes as possible.

The oxygen of publicity was requisite for a good reputation, because a reputation was in effect the cumulative acknowledgement by one's peers of one's achievements and/ or status. In consequence, noblemen and gentlemen (and those who wanted to be thought of as such) had constantly to court, or at least to be conscious of, each others' good opinion. As Kristin Neuschel puts it in her insightful study of sixteenth-century French aristocratic culture (which was essentially similar to that in contemporary England), honour was 'accorded through the recognition of the community', and so it was necessary, not only 'to do "objectively" honorable deeds but to have one's behavior judged honorable'.[56] The types of deeds that, above all others, established one's claim as an honourable man and soldier, were those that publicly exhibited personal courage and prowess in combat.

---

[53] *Othello*, 2.3.246–8.
[54] Norreys to Earl of Essex, 5 Jan. 1596, Hatfield House, Cecil Papers, MS 171, fol. 47r.
[55] Pelham to Burghley, 25 Feb. 1586, BL, MS Harley 6993, fol. 129r.
[56] Kristen B. Neuschel, *Word of Honour: Interpreting Noble Culture in Sixteenth-Century France* (Ithaca, 1989), pp. 76–7; and Richard Cust, 'Honour and Politics in Early Stuart England: The Case of Beaumont v. Hastings', *P&P* 149 (1995), 70–89.

The performance of courage is a complex issue and will be dealt with in the next section. First, in this section, we consider demonstrations of a man's skill and proficiency as a soldier: excellent performance in personal combat and/ or successful exercise of the art of command. These imperatives are evident when Churchyard describes his purpose in writing a history of the Dutch Revolt and especially of English involvement in it. He tells his reader, his own excitement almost palpable, that this history is full of 'martiall affaires, and exployts done by […] valiant souldiers: that not onlie attained honour in the field […] but also wanne everlasting fame by their prowesse and service'; and declares: 'I took in hand to revive dead men and their actions (for fames sake which all men shoote at).'[57] Honourable reputation accrued in action. The battle or siege was the ultimate theatre of war, a figure of speech used by soldier-authors: 'Armes and Souldierie are the Cronicles of Princes, the hazards of Battayles their Theaters, [and] their warlike cause their Honor, Perfection and Tryumph'.[58]

This understanding of war's significance for *performance* is evident not just in soldiers' later writing about war, but in their actions during wartime. Sir Philip Sidney, for example, before leading English and Dutch troops to besiege Steenbergen, affirmed: 'I will undertake uppon my lyfe either to win it or make the enemy rais his seeg […] And it shall be done in the sight of the world which is most honourable and profitable'.[59] Sieges provided particularly good performative opportunities, because of the presence of walls (on both sides – the lines of circumvallation built by besieging armies to isolate the defenders often included ramparts and forts as well as entrenchments). The greater ease of observation along with the set-piece nature of siege operations optimised the chances of heroic deeds being noticed (as examples in the next section will demonstrate). As a result, major sieges were understood to be rare chances to make one's mark: both as a man and as a martialist.

This point is twice made explicitly by Churchyard. First, writing in 1579 of the siege of the Huguenot stronghold of La Rochelle in 1572–3, which English ships and troops helped to raise, Churchyard refers to other recent sieges: of Malta by the Ottomans in 1565; Haarlem in Holland in 1572–3, a siege in which English troops served both in the garrison and in William of Orange's army that tried unsuccessfully to raise the siege; and the rather less celebrated siege of Haddington.[60] This was an episode in a prolonged campaign between the

---

57   *True Discourse*, sig. A2v.
58   Markham, *Epistles*, p. 8. A similar usage is in Barnabe Rich, *Roome for a Gentleman, or the Second Part of Faultes* (London, 1609), sig. B1r, while 'theatre of war' is explicitly used by Edward Grimeston, *A Generall History of the Netherlands* (London, 1608), p. 1325.
59   Sidney to Earl of Leicester, 2 Feb. 1586, *The Correspondence of Sir Philip Sidney*, ed. Roger Kuin, 2 vols. (Oxford, 2012), 2: 1158–9.
60   *Churchyard's Choise*, sig. L4v.

English and Scotland's French allies who came to the aid of the country after it was invaded in 1547. Edward VI's regent, the duke of Somerset (one of Churchyard's early patrons), won an overwhelming victory at Pinkie, but French intervention helped to lead to stalemate. Churchyard served in and wrote about this war and was captured while part of a force trying to aid Haddington's garrison. The episode loomed large in his own life story but otherwise did not bear comparison with Malta, Haarlem or La Rochelle.[61] Churchyard's point, however, which would have been widely accepted (and was surely one reason he wanted to include Haddington) was that such sieges 'are monuments and patrons to shew that *manhoode maie woorke marvailes*, and [...] is not easely conquered. As Rotchell, and these places [...] doeth witnesse, and shall *whiles we are men* be daiely remembered.'[62] Writing nearly twenty-five years later, Churchyard makes a similar point, instancing the defence by 'Sir Frauncis Vere and the true Captaines of Ostend', during the epic Spanish siege of the Flemish port-town, as 'an example' of 'manlie enterprises'.[63] In 1622, Spanish investment of another strategic coastal fortress, Bergen-op-Zoom, 'brought many volunteers thither from divers parts of the Christian world', one of those who served there related, because men of many nations, 'being greedie of military honour, resorted thither in great numbers'.[64]

Either in the theatre-like setting of a siege, or in manoeuvres in the field, there was the opportunity to demonstrate soldierly and manly qualities. In 1579, looking back to his first experience of war, over thirty years earlier, Churchyard writes that then: 'All Chevalrie was cherished, Soldiours made of, and manhoode so much esteemed, that he was thought happest [...] that sought credite by the exercises of Armes, and dissipline of warre.'[65] Here the inherent connection perceived between manhood, military discipline and performance of expertise in arms, is explicitly stated. Elsewhere, it is the intrinsic connection perceived between demonstrated adeptness in the art of war, honour and nobility. Walter Morgan, a Welsh soldier who served in the Netherlands for many years, categorically asserted, 'hit ys not mans byrthe entitulyd wythe seremonis of honor that ys too stande an armie in effecte in that case, but his industrius spiritte of knowledge and value in Iudgement'.[66] Even without deeds of reckless daring, military qualities demonstrated inner nobility. They also fashioned an honourable reputation: Edward Chester, who fought with

[61] Woodcock, *Thomas Churchyard*, pp. 57–63.
[62] *Churchyard's Choise*, sig. L4v. Emphasis supplied.
[63] *True Discourse*, sig. A2v. Vere led the defence of Ostend in 1601–2 but Ostend was besieged a further two-and-a-half years, falling only in autumn 1604.
[64] William Crosse, *A generall historie of the Netherlands* (London, 1627), p. 1436.
[65] *Churchyard's Choise*, sig. A1r.
[66] Codrington Library, All Souls College, Oxford, MS 129, fol. 21r; see Trim, 'Mercenaries', pp. 452–3.

the Dutch in the early and mid-1570s, was praised by William of Orange for the 'good conduct […] and his diligent and vigilant actions', which gave him, William wrote, his 'mightily good reputation' in the Low Countries.[67] Similar language was used, forty-five years later, about Edward Cecil, who had risen from gentleman volunteer in Dutch employ to captain to colonel and finally general in both Dutch and English service. In his old age, Jeremy Leech, a military chaplain praised 'the renowned fame of your military science and heroicall valour, reported and confirmed unto the world, by the mouthes of so many witnesses'.[68] Cecil, then, coupled mastery of the art of war with heroic conduct in action; crucially, as his laudator acknowledges, his performance was widely witnessed and this was the foundation for his 'renowned fame'.

Describing a campaign in the autumn of 1585, Churchyard praises John Norreys, the commander of both English and Dutch forces in the Netherlands, for 'his determination and purpose' to 'annoy the enemie, and profit his Prince and Countrie'. He reports Norreys's successful capture of Spanish sconces near Arnhem, freeing the city from the threat of capture – and that then, despite the lateness of the year, Norreys 'marched with his forces toward the citie of Nimeghem [Nijmegen]; where by honourable force and Knightly chivalrie subduing another of the Enemies Sconces, he opened the passage from Colen [Cologne] and all the high Countries, which was a very profitable and readie helpe to all the English Campe'.[69] Elsewhere, as we shall see, Churchyard would applaud the physical courage and prowess in personal combat of 'Black Jack' Norreys, but here he singles out his skill in the art of war and his proficiency as a general. Churchyard describes what in modern terms would be strategic thinking; yet he still puts it in the context of the value system of martial manhood, writing of Norreys as 'honourable' and of his 'knightly chivalry'.

Another of Churchyard's evident favourites was Peregrine, Lord Willoughby d'Eresby. Among the points for which Willoughby is praised is that he 'from his youth forwards to his manhood proved pregnant in wit, prompt in knowledge, and practised especially in Martiall or Militarie actions: whereby he became the most rare, and surpassing ornament of his noble progenie'.[70] Churchyard, as we will see, elsewhere lauds Willoughby for his courage, but here he praises his practical knowledge of the art of war, and makes explicit that this is a proof of his 'manhood'.

---

[67] Orange to Burghley, 4 Jan. 1574, n.s., *Relations politiques des Pays-Bas et de l'Angleterre sous le regne de Philippe II*, ed. Kervyn de Lettenhove, 11 vols. (Brussels, 1882–1900), 7:27 (translation mine). See D.J.B. Trim, 'Edward Chester', *ODNB*.

[68] Jeremy Leech, *The Trayne Souldier: A Sermon Preached Before the Societie of the Captaynes and Gentle men* (London, 1619), sig. A2r.

[69] Churchyard et al., *True Discourse*, pp. 71–2.

[70] Ibid., p. 103.

V

If skill in the martial arts was an excellent way to demonstrate one's claims to masculine and martial worth, the primary way to assert worth was the performance of overtly (even outrageously) valiant feats of arms. A gentleman was impelled to demonstrate – to perform – courage, for his courage 'breath[e]s resolution into the Followers, and makes even Cowards to be valiant'.[71] As Leech advised: 'To the brave-spirited Souldier, there is nothing more hateful then the name of a Coward'.[72] Daring deeds in combat receive the highest praise in contemporary documents and texts, including the plays of Shakespeare: Jacques famously characterises the soldier as 'seeking the bubble reputation/ Even in the cannon's mouth'.[73] The primacy, in fashioning an honourable reputation, of conspicuously courageous conduct is also evident in the martial poetics of fellow soldiers.

So important is the performance of courage that this section is broken down into three sub-sections: first, we examine examples of the importance of bravery in battle, especially those that explicitly link it to masculinity. Second, having gained a deeper understanding of the worldview of martial poetics, we will consider the significance of recklessness. Third, we explore the cultural significance of wounds, which are especially relevant when considering manhood since, on the face of it, wounds carried the potential of dismembering and unmanning.

(1) Bravery and Masculinity

Two particularly flamboyant passages by Churchyard afford rich insight into the deeds and qualities that contributed most to early modern reputations. They form part of Churchyard's encomium about Lord Willoughby, which begin by praising him for his good service to Queen Elizabeth on an embassy to the king of Denmark.[74] However, Churchyard continues, 'after that [...] his Heroicall spirit, yet further affecting Militarie affaires', moved him to ask to be sent to the Netherlands to serve as a soldier. Diplomatic service, though at royal direction, was not as desirable in terms of accruing reputation as experience of 'military affairs'.

Willoughby received Elizabeth's blessing and soon arrived in the Netherlands. There, Churchyard tells us,

---

[71]   Leech, *The Trayne Souldier*, p. 38.
[72]   Ibid., p. 30.
[73]   *As You Like It*, 2.7.151–2.
[74]   Churchyard et al., *True Discourse*, p. 103.

his noble courage so conjoyned with dexteritie, and his forwardnes with such fortune, that he himselfe was formost in all attempts and enterprises of his forces, fiercelie like a Lyon he assayled the enimies, fought with them, spoyled them, and foyled them, wheresoever he came. So verilie and in such sort, as the Duke of Parma then himselfe confessed of this worthie Lord Willoughbie and his service (for foure yeers space in those Countries) never anie English man enterprised more boldlie to meete his enimies in the face, more bravelie encountered them, nor more painefullie pursued and sought them out neere and farre off, to their disgrace, spoile, and foyle, wheresoever he found them.[75]

Churchyard's rhetorical choices reveal the value system that impelled a soldier like Willoughby to act as he did, and the attributes and actions, whether of commanders or of the rank-and-file, that most added to martial reputation. These are: leading from the front (forwardness, being foremost in all attempts and enterprises); relentlessness as a commander, regardless of cost (painfully pursuing and seeking out the enemy near and far); a readiness, even eagerness, to do battle (assailing enemies, fighting wheresoever they were); facility to force battle on an enemy (dexterity and enterprise); an ability to gain victory for his army (disgracing, spoiling and foiling the Spanish); valour when personally in combat (courage; boldly and bravely meeting and encountering his enemies); and the ability to best opponents in person (fiercely like a lion assailing them). These were the primary sources of honourable military reputation. All testified to physical courage as a man as well as the moral courage of a commander.[76] All are linked, moreover, to social status ('his noble courage') and to manliness – for Churchyard's language is notable in stating 'never anie English *man*' did this. Willoughby received the ultimate endorsement of his honourable reputation, for it was acknowledged by his enemy, the duke of Parma, a distinguished and usually victorious commander, who Willoughby had faced when successfully defending Bergen in 1588.

This is Churchyard's overview of Willoughby's qualities in general. In describing his particular conduct at the battle of Zutphen in October 1586, at which Sir Philip Sidney was mortally wounded, Churchyard (who was no fan of the earl of Leicester, but criticises by hint and omission) reveals that Leicester, the commander-in-chief of the army, 'came not into the fight'. Willoughby, in contrast, 'more forward then the rest',

[75]   Ibid., p. 104.
[76]   The distinction is one commonly drawn by military historians: see Lawrence R. Velvel, 'Physical Courage, Moral Courage and American Generals', *Counterpunch* Online, 21 Apr. 2006: https://www.counterpunch.org/2006/04/21/physical-courage-moral-courage-and-american-generals (accessed 7 May 2019); Peter Olsthoorn, 'Courage in the Military: Physical and Moral', *Journal of Military Ethics* 6 (2007), 270–9.

met the enimies couragiouslie, brake his Launce in the middest of them, made way with his sword everie where, and so forciblie adventured his noble person through the thickest of them: that all his men nearest him much feared, when his bases were bereved from his bodie, his plumes pluckt awaie from his head, and his Armes be battered with blowes, [that] he should utterlie haue beene foyled in the fight, and spoyled [...] of life [...] he was so desperately endaungered every way.[77]

Yet instead, Willoughby emerged unscarred, having taken an enemy commander as his prisoner after defeating him in personal combat. Elsewhere, Churchyard writes of Zutphen: 'Touching the honour of the field there fought, as all our English Lords and Knights by their valours much diminished the enemies force and daunted his courage' and English chroniclers, stress that in the battle an Italian count was killed in hand-to-hand combat by Sir Thomas Parrot, while another 'one of the enemies commanders, was by the worthie Lord Willoughby taken prisoner'.[78]

These passages and the emphases in them indicate that not only was honour gained by fighting in the field, but in addition honour potentially could be a zero-sum game. Defeat in hand-to-hand combat could diminish a man's honourable reputation, depending on how he fought; the reputation of the victor would, however, increase – very possibly at the expense of the vanquished. Victory of the army in battle redounded to the credit of the commander (as with Willoughby, in the earlier long quotation, and unlike Leicester); victory in personal combat with opponents who were themselves men of honour, was a source of personal honour and this could be true, even if personal victory came in a wider defeat. For example, the heroic conduct of Sir Roger Williams and Sir Francis Vere in the siege of Sluys (1587) redounded to their credit, even though the port-town eventually had to be honourably surrendered to the Spanish. Likewise, though the British defenders of Mannheim, Heidelberg and Frankenthal in 1621–3 could not prevent the Spanish capturing all three cities and thus conquering the Palatinate, these 'places were lost at length for want of succors in due time', the defenders having first inflicted great 'losse to the victors', so that 'great honor [accrued] to the vanquished for their brave defence of these Townes'.[79]

Churchyard's valuable insights and observations are hardly unique, as will be seen. Some of the passages that follow were written well after the events by soldier-authors; others are contemporary reports from soldiers in the field. All are evidence of what men thought conduced to being of good repute (or of ill fame), but they also show how men acted as a result of that world view,

---

[77] Churchyard et al., *True Discourse*, pp. 104–5.
[78] Ibid., p. 90. Camden, *Annales*, book 1, pp. 115–16.
[79] See below, p. 50. Crosse, *Generall Historie Continued*, p. 1407.

and in particular how certain actions they took led to perceptions of them as honourable, soldierly and manly – and in particular how performance of courage demonstrated manhood. Churchyard makes this explicit when he shares his hope that his readers will 'mervaile at the most manlie enterprises […] that couragious souldiers dare adventure, take in hand, and accomplish'.[80] Such sentiments could almost be the inspiration for Shakespeare's Henry V before Agincourt:

> And gentlemen in England now a-bed
> Shall think themselves accurs'd they were not here,
> And hold their manhoods cheap whiles any speaks
> That fought with us upon Saint Crispin's day.[81]

But it is not only Churchyard and Shakespeare who present this view of courage, manliness and performance in combat. It occurs repeatedly in early modern military literature, including passages that are descriptive as well as, by implication, prescriptive.

Near Groningen in 1580, for example, according to Blandy's narrative, after the Spanish attacked John Norreys's English force, one of his officers, Captain Corne, was concerned 'that the enemy might thinke their Larum to have any maner wayes touched us with a shiver of feare' – which would have been judged dishonourable and unmanly. Corne wanted to demonstrate that he and his men were 'touched […] rather with a flame of furye' and so led a counter-attack 'with other Gentlemen and Souldiars of profe […] so that [the Spanish] should know and feel the force of English bloud'. Blandy reports a short speech Corne gave (so short that it likely is one of the few genuine battle-field speeches in military literature), telling his troops, 'my naturall and deare Countrymen, let us now stand fast [against] yonder cursed company […] Let them understand by our stomaches, what minde and spirite remaineth'. The result was a 'skirmish on both sides […] whott and violent', in which Corne and his lieutenant were both killed.[82] Corne's speech was not bravado, for it was followed up by audacious, even desperate, action: the reality of his rhet-oric, the proof of his and his men's honourable and masculine qualities. This is evident not just from the actions taken, but the language used to describe them – the language both of the protagonist and the reporter of his deeds (who was, however, himself part of the combat). Blandy references English *blood* and repudiates the '*shiver of feare*', while Corne addresses his soldiers, unusually, as 'country*men*' and speaks of their *stomach* as well as their *mind and spirit*. Rhetorically, martial metaphor is mixed with strikingly corporeal

---

[80] *True discourse*, sig. A2v.
[81] *Henry V*, 4.3.64–7.
[82] Blandy, *Castle*, sigs. G2v–G3v.

language, including that typically used to invoke male physicality. In control of their mind and emotions, the bodies of the English soldiers will not shake with fear; instead, by virtue of their blood and stomach – physical properties and thus literally manly, albeit applied figuratively – they will demonstrate their soldierly and manly qualities. This becomes explicit in Blandy's conclusion that Corne, though physically short proved his nobility of character and 'his manlynesse'.[83]

In a work published a year before Blandy served in the Netherlands, Church-yard, too, had stressed English military masculinity. Writing of a campaign by English troops in aid of the Huguenots in 1573, he writes that marvels could be achieved by 'manhoode […] joyned with courage', then describes an assault in which Belle Île was 'very valiauntly wonne […] In whiche service was many a hotte skirmishe, and many more matters worthie memorie putte in practice, wherein manhoode, and diligence of manne was throughlie tried'.[84] Manhood was tested but emerged from the crucible, its strength unquestioned.

In their works of 1579–81, Churchyard and Blandy may have been at pains to emphasise the intrepid and masculine qualities of English soldiers because, between 1573 and 1577, English troops serving in the Netherlands had not, distinguished themselves by their courage. Cowardice resulted in contempt and dishonour. This is evident in an English soldier's contempt for his compatriots in Holland in 1573: 'God send […] that they may be stabler and not to shit in their breeches and runne awaie as often they have done, and that some honor may be acheved.'[85] The lack of control over their bodies signals a degree of unmanning that stands in contrast to Blandy's depiction of Norreys and Corne's well-disciplined and resolute men, or Churchyard's of the English troops in 1573 whose manhood had been 'thoroughly tried'. In 1574, however, things had got worse: almost an entire English regiment serving near Leiden routed, among them, commanding a company, the poet George Gascoigne. As I argue elsewhere, Gascoigne undoubtedly felt personally ashamed by this, as his verse narrative of events reflected. He was at pains to highlight factors that mitigated the shamefulness, lest it permanently affect his reputation.[86]

Thanks to the disasters of 1573 and '74, the Dutch refused to employ English regiments again for four years. When they returned, however, they helped the Dutch win a signal victory at Rijmenam on 1 August 1578, a victory celebrated at length by Churchyard, writing a year later.[87] He returned to it in 1602, praising 'The first of the English Captaines which set upon the enemies [was]

[83] Ibid., sig. G2v.
[84] *Churchyard's Choise*, sig. L4v.
[85] S. Jewks to [?], 11 July 1573, *Relations politiques*, ed. Kervyn de Lettenhove, 6:792.
[86] D.J.B. Trim, 'Gascoigne the Soldier: Rhetoric, Representation and Reality', *New Essays on George Gascoigne*, ed. Gillian Austen (London, forthcoming).
[87] *Churchyard's Choise*, sigs. S1r–T1r.

William Marckham, a Nottinghamshire man, sterne of countenance, strong of hands, and couragious of heart'. As with Blandy's account of the Frisian campaign, Churchyard stresses Markham's male physicality. He goes on to praise John Norreys, colonel of the largest English regiment at Rijmenam, who proved his personal physical courage and prowess in combat: 'with greatest valour [he] pursued and subdued his enemies, being only weaponed with single sword and his pistols which he used: even so surely, as who had seene how couragiously he laid about him on every side, might well have said he had seene a new Hector, another Alexander, or rather a second Caesar foyling his enemies every where'.[88] This time, however, Churchyard is not engaged in special pleading: the Dutch commander-in-chief at Rijmenam reported to the Prince of Orange that Norreys had 'borne himself in such manner that a Caesar could not have done better'.[89] Norreys, along with two other captains, Richard Bingham and Rowland Yorke, had, by 'acquitting th[emselves] with very great value and reputacion' in the battle, acquired greater honour.[90] One of Elizabeth's privy councillors, Sir Francis Knollys, whose sons served with Norreys, wrote to Secretary of State Walsingham in something like delighted astonishment about 'this new "accident" of [Norreys] fronting the Spaniards with his regiment so manfully and skilfully beyond expectation'.[91] It was not only soldier-poets for whom military skill and manhood went together: this was an orthodoxy of early modern aristocratic culture.

Seven years later, in the autumn of 1585, after England agreed to aid the Dutch Republic, Norreys commanded an Anglo-Dutch army in Gelderland. Earlier in this chapter, we saw that Churchyard, in his narrative of this campaign, praises Norreys's ability as a commander and his skill in the art of war. Churchyard also lauds Norreys both for 'his own great valour and [the] diligence of his souldiers', repeating praise of 'his own valour' as well as the collective courage of his troops, highlighting his 'minde unconquerable', 'Knightly chivalrie', and 'most valiant heart'. But Churchyard puts these attributes in context in his comment that 'Generall Norice [...] continued [a] skirmish [...] so manfully' that the Spanish retreated.[92] Courage, skill in the art of war and combat, and manliness coalesced in a value system, a conjoined set of perspectives on what constituted masculine and aristocratic honour.

[88]   Churchyard et al. *True Discourse*, p. 32.
[89]   Comte du Bossu to William of Orange, 3 Aug. 1578, *Correspondance de Guillaume le Taciturne, Prince d'Orange*, ed. L.P. Gachard, 6 vols. (Brussels, 1850–5), 4: 57.
[90]   William Davison to Burghley, 2 Aug. 1578, *Relations politiques*, ed. Kervyn de Lettenhove, 10: 686.
[91]   Knollys to Walsingham, 10 Aug. 1578, *CSPF 1578–79*, pp. 130–1.
[92]   Churchyard et al., *True discourse*, pp. 71–3.

(2) Recklessness

Understanding this attitudinal co-occurrence allows us to see the significance of acts of daring that were reckless, even foolish on the face of things, but that contemporaries admired greatly. They are best understood as the martialist's attempts to stand out from the mass, to distinguish himself as a warrior *and* as a man, using the only currency that had value in the moral economy of honour: his own blood.

Conspicuous performance of courage necessarily entailed being forward in the fight – for officers this meant literally leading from the front. Blandy writes admiringly of Roger Williams, a Welsh career soldier who was probably the model for Shakespeare's Fluellen, who led a cavalry charge at a key moment in a battle in Friesland, telling his men: 'It is farr more honorable for us to charge them in this maner', than to retreat. 'This sayd, he hemselfe first with the rest of his gentlemen charged, and recharged to the great losse of the enemy.'[93] Churchyard praises Norreys for his personal conduct in battle against the Spanish in November 1585:

> he with a most valiant heart and cheerefull voyce encouraged his souldiers to the encounter: wherein he himselfe, for better emboldening of all under his charge, and for their only evident example of valour and courage, gave the first charge [...] which the Englishmen well perceiving, most venturously followed their fleeting fainting foes, with such furie that the Spaniards were by heapes laid levell with the ground.[94]

As Leech enjoined the officers and gentlemen of his company: 'If you would not be a Coward when you come into the field [...] look your enemie couragiously in the face.'[95] Looking steadfastly on the enemy in battle was a foundation of martial and manly honour.

In addition to being in the front lines in the field, forwardness in the assault was the other, even better, way to demonstrate bravery. Sieges offered particularly potent performative opportunities. Assaulting defended fortifications was desperately dangerous, especially for the initial storming parties. Again and again, however, English soldiers volunteered for this duty. Evidently, they saw an assault as an occasion for exhibiting obvious valour – at times soldier-poets surely overstate the enthusiasm of the rank-and-file for daring deeds, but the evidence is suggestive of the extent to which they, like the elites, valorised conspicuous courage.

At the climax of the siege of Guingan in Brittany in 1591, there were too many volunteers from Henry Norreys's regiment for the assault party on the

[93] Blandy, *Castle*, sig. H1r.
[94] Churchyard et al., *True Discourse*, p. 73.
[95] Leech, *The Trayne Souldier*, p. 30.

breach (something close to a suicide mission), which was to be of 200 men. We know this because the rest of his men diced for the honour of being included, while four captains led a force that was only about the size of two companies. The post of danger was desirable because of the honour that came with it.[96] In his memoirs, Sir Francis Vere describes the storming of Cadiz in 1596, and how his veteran soldiers from the Low Countries 'boldly attempted to climbe the wall [...] wanting no encouragements that good examples of the chiefs could give them [...] being as forward as any'.[97] Even more striking is an English military chaplain-cum-chronicler's report of the storming of Oldenzeel in the Netherlands, in 1626. When Ernest Casimir of Nassau, the commander of the besieging army, assigned to 'the Low Dutch Companies' the task of storming the fortress, the English 'being jealous of this supposed affront, (intrenching, as they thought, upon the honour of their Nation) told Count Ernest discontentedly, that they were no sit-stil souldiers, and surveryors of action, but meant, by his leave, to share danger and honour indifferently'.[98]

In particular, sieges were unparalleled opportunities for individuals to stand out from the crowd. At the siege of Doesburg, in the autumn of 1586, Williams's conduct in the trenches was reported by Leicester with a degree of wonder: he 'would need run upp and downe so oft out of the trench', despite having seen that other soldiers who left the 'trench to gaze and were strait hit'. It was not only that Williams braved enemy fire: he did so, as Leicester remarks in what seems like amazed admiration, 'with a great plume of feathers in his gylt morion, as so many shott coming at him he could hardlie escape with soe little hurt'; indeed there 'were never such marks [i.e., such targets] as he was, and within point-blanke [range] of a caliver'. He was duly wounded, having 'gott a blow throw the arme'.[99] But he survived, an already formidable reputation enhanced yet further.

A month after Williams's exploit at Doesburg, Leicester was again astonished by the courageous conduct of a gaudily garbed individual, this time at a Spanish fort that was the outer defence of Zutphen. According to Leicester, it 'little looked to be won so soone, and in all troth it is one of the strongest places for sure fights within, that ever I saw in all my life'.[100] Yet won it was, which Camden attributed to 'the valour of Edward Stanley who laying hold of a Spaniards Pike' – the intended instrument of Stanley's death – and then 'kept such fast hold that hee was by the Pike drawne into the Fort, whereat the Spaniards were in such sort amazed, that they fearefully fled'.[101] Churchyard,

---

[96]   Newsletter, May 1591, HMC, *Rutland MSS*, 4 vols. (London, 1888–1905), 1: 291–2.
[97]   *The Commentaries of Sir Francis Vere* (Cambridge, 1657), sig. F3v.
[98]   Crosse, *Generall Historie Continued*, p. 1584.
[99]   Leicester to Walsingham, 4 Sept. 1586, *Correspondence of [...] Leycester*, p. 406.
[100] Leicester to Walsingham, 6 Oct. 1586, *Correspondence of [...] Leycester*, p. 428.
[101] Camden, *Annales*, book 3, p. 116

who was probably Camden's source, had recounted the story thirteen years earlier but stresses Stanley conducted himself 'verie couragiouslie', and that he had already 'climed up the rampere of the Fort,' before the said Edward tooke [a pike] perforce out of [a Spanish defender's] hands, and held it stoutlie, and the more the enimie stroue to wrest it from him againe, the higher hee raised [him] so much more out of his reach'.[102] Importantly, Leicester witnessed every moment, as he wrote to Walsingham soon after, writing in clear astonishment:

> Since I was borne I did never se any man to behave himself as he did. First clime the brech, a pike-length before and above anie person that followed him, soe did he alone maintaine the fight, first with his pike, then with the stumpes of his pike, and afterward his sword, against at the lest ix or x [...] yet would he not back a foote, but kept himself in this sort without anie one man to gett upp to him, the ground was soe false being all sandie, insomuch as we all gave him [up for] lost if he had a c lives.[103]

Eventually, after 'he had longe thus dealt most valientlie and worthilie', his men were able to ascend the wall to his aid, and then 'thei speedilie dispatched the enemye'.[104]

In Churchyard and Camden's telling, Stanley might have been lucky. In Leicester's account, which stresses his skill at arms, athleticism and, above all, valour (literally not taking a backward step), Stanley makes his own luck. Leicester continues, as if awestruck, 'this gentleman shall I never forgett if I live a c yere' and declares 'I would God her majestie had sene this enterprise, [...] the willingnes of her subjects [and] their *valour in performing*'.[105] Stanley had hit the performative jackpot.[106]

Just as Williams wore a distinctive plume of feathers and a golden helmet, ensuring his courageous actions would be seen, Stanley had been dressed 'all in yellow saving his curatts', and this, according to Leicester, was why Stanley was widely observed – by 5,000 men, or so the earl estimated. Leicester concludes of Stanley, 'even so worthilie he did by Godes goodnes, as he was the cheife cause, of mans worke, of all the honour of this day'.[107] Successful performance of prowess, dexterity and daring brings 'honour' in Leicester's value system. But while reference to 'man's work' is obviously partly in contrast to 'God's goodness', surely it also had another purpose, at least in Leicester's

---

[102] Churchyard et al., *True Discourse*, p. 53.
[103] *Correspondence of [...] Leycester*, pp. 427–8.
[104] Ibid., p. 428.
[105] Ibid., pp. 428–9 (emphasis supplied).
[106] His rewards were financial as well as reputational: Churchyard et al., *True Discourse*, p. 53; Camden, *Annales*, book 3, p. 116.
[107] *Correspondence of [...] Leycester*, p. 428.

subconscious. It is striking that, in summing up the exceptional exploit he had witnessed, the term that came to his mind was 'man's work'.

A year later, Williams was commanding the defence of Sluys against Parma's army. One of his officers, Francis Vere, became well known to the besiegers of Sluys, and – upon the garrison's capitulation (on honourable terms) – had the signal honour of being singled out for praise by the Spanish. They were easily able to identify him, Williams recorded, because he was 'marked for his red mandilion, who stood alwaies in the head of the armed men at the assaults of the fort and Towne: being twise hurt' and, when asked by Williams 'and other his friends […] to retire, he answered, he had rather be kild ten times at a breach, than once in a house'.[108] It was his forwardness in combat and refusal to give ground that won Vere the approval of his comrades and enemies alike, but his crimson jacket made him conspicuous.

Similarly, Thomas Arundell recalled of his time fighting the Turks in Hungary during the 1590s, that, 'by reason of my Plumes of feathers, of my Armour [and] Furniture all full of Gould and silver [...] I was presently marked of all mens eyes'. He then showed his mettle in action. An imperialist general told the Emperor Rudolf II (so Arundell reports) 'that a certaine Englishe man of good accounte […] was the first man of marke, that was seen to charge and enter upon the enemies Ordnance'. He implies that his attention-grabbing dress helped to make his deeds of prowess visible.[109]

Vere continued to be conspicuous in costume as well as in conduct, though later it was surely in part so that his men could easily see him and be inspired by his leading from the front. The Dutch victory over the Spanish at Turnhout in 1597, where he led a decisive cavalry charge, was dramatised in the London theatre, with 'Sir Francis Vere upon the stage, killing, slaying and overthrowing the Spaniard' – and the actor 'that plaid [his] part got a beard resembling his and a watchet satten doublet, with hose trimd with silver lace' – Vere's blue doublet and silver lace was part of his public persona.[110] One of Vere's colonels, Edward Harwood, followed his mentor's example. An anonymous narrative of the siege of Maastricht in 1632 tells how Harwood 'was first hurt by a Granado'. The author stresses that this was 'a sufficient warrant to have exempted him from the Service', but that 'he would not leave the prosecution of the designe' – that is, to extend siege works towards the city. Harwood continued, moreover, his habitual practice of 'going often into the Trenches [...] in a Scarlet Coate'.[111] Such dress again was probably partly to help him inspire his soldiers, but as

---

[108] Roger Williams, *Works*, ed. John X. Evans (Oxford, 1972), p. 49.
[109] CUL, MS Mm.i.43, pp. 145–6.
[110] Rowland Whyte to Robert Sidney, 26 and 27 Oct. 1599, HMC, *Report on the Manuscripts of Lord De L'Isle and Dudley*, 3 vols. (London, 1925–36), 1: 406, 408.
[111] *The Advice of that Worthy Commander, Sir Ed. Harwood, Collonel* [...] *Also a Relation of his Life and Death* (London, 1642), sig. B3v, and cf. sig. B2v.

with Vere, Arundell, Stanley and Williams, bold dress also bore witness to the bravery of its wearer.

Flamboyant attire presented a more prominent target and so references to ostentatious costume in contemporary reports are part and parcel of the testimonies of intrepidity, and they would have been understood as such, rather than as simply attention-seeking devices. But the reason for dressing thus and so risking one's life even more than by one's audacious actions, was partly to ensure that the deeds of daring were observed and recounted. 'To pluck bright honour from the pale-faced moon' was of little value if it were not noticed.[112]

Conspicuous courage could also be marked by what one did not wear, which could also become a marker. The earl of Sussex, writing home from the English expedition to Spain and Portugal in 1589 of a battle near La Coruña, stresses that the gentlemen of the force 'took their pikes in their hands'. He writes admiringly of how Norreys led the English troops wielding a pike 'in his doublet and hose'. His brother Edward Norreys was 'hurt in the head' but Sussex reports that 'it is said that [Thomas] Sidney did kill him that wounded Sir Edward'.[113] John Norreys was clearly impelled by the exigency of the situation rather than a calculation of how to promote his reputation, but the passage tells us something about the values of aristocratic martial manhood, given what the author chooses to highlight – especially since this was not a text intended primarily for public consumption. Arguably, too, the passage illustrates how these values impelled the men (and 'especially the gentlemen') in the combat. Edward Norreys was so forward in the fight that he was wounded and thus his courage is implied. Thomas Sidney's skill at arms is not stated but is clear, since he is said to have killed an enemy in personal combat. Sussex makes plain John Norreys's personal prowess at arms, and also foregrounds his valour by adverting that Norreys forewent armour yet was in the forefront of combat. Moreover, because he did not deign to protect his body, there is a clear implication about his manhood. What Sussex stresses tells us what he saw as important. But it also shows that veteran martialists had internalised the symbiotic values of soldierliness and manliness. Edward Norreys, like Sidney, went into the front ranks, even though, as colonels of regiments, both would normally have stayed at the back of the pike formation.[114] This was even truer of Norreys, the commanding general, yet when the occasion demanded, he did not take time to put on armour, nor remain in the rear, directing his troops, but instead sprang immediately into action. That courage had to be performed was not simply a theoretical virtue, promoted by authors of published texts; it was the default understanding of many soldiers.

[112] Shakespeare, *1 Henry IV*, 1.3.200.
[113] Sussex to Walsingham, 16 May 1589, *The Expedition of Sir John Norris and Sir Francis Drake to Spain and Portugal, 1589*, ed. R.B. Wernham (Aldershot, 1988), p. 159.
[114] Ibid., pp. 343–8.

(3) *Wounds and* Sang Froid

In the honour economy, wounds were valuable currency. As Leech put it, a soldier had to be prepared to 'die in the maintenance of his quarrell', his life bearing witness to his honour, sealing it with his blood.[115] Wounds demonstrated willingness to give one's life rather than conduct oneself dishonourably; the blood that flowed from them was an indisputable proof of personal bravery. A pamphlet on the English victory over the Armada praises 'the prowesse of such woorthy men as still with their bloud do paint out, the woorthiness of their resolutions'.[116] Wounds were the external signifiers of honourable and manly performance in the theatre of war.

When a narrative of Leicester's first campaigns in the Netherlands reports, for example, that in a battle near Grave, Captain John Burgh 'had a finger stroken off with a musket shot', it is clearly intended as implicit commendation.[117] The father of Thomas Poyntz, who served in the Netherlands in the late 1590s and the 1600s, kept a piece of a bullet removed from his son's arm 'as a testemonie of [his] forwardnes upon all services'.[118] Edward Herbert, himself a soldier, wrote with satisfaction of his younger brother Richard who 'went to the Low Countreys, where he continued many years with much reputation, both in the wars and for fighting single Duels, which were many, in so much that between both, he carried [...] the scars of four and twenty wounds upon him to his grave'.[119] The divine who preached the funeral sermon for William Proud in 1633, in going through the soldier's distinguished career, declared that it was when Proud was wounded in the thigh by a musket ball that he 'got the first badge of his honour'.[120]

The widespread perception of a wound as a badge of honour is evident in the words Shakespeare gives to Henry V in his St Crispin's Day speech:

He that shall see this day, and live t'old age,
Will yearly on the vigil feast his neighbours,
And [...] will he strip his sleeve and show his scars,
And say 'These wounds I had on Crispin's day'.[121]

[115] Leech, *The Trayne Souldier*, p. 37.
[116] D.F.R. de M., *An Answer to the Untruthes Published in Spaine, in Glorie of Their Supposed Victorie Against our English Navie*, trans. J[ames] L[ea] (London, 1589), sig. A2v.
[117] T.D., *A Briefe Report of the Militarie Services Done in the Low Countries, by the Erle of Leicester: Written by One that Served in a Good Place There* (London, 1587), sig. B1v.
[118] Daniel Poyntz to Thomas Poyntz, 18 Apr. 1606, Koninklijke Bibliotheek, The Hague, MS 132.G.27; see Trim, 'Mercenaries', p. 389.
[119] *The Life of Edward, First Lord Herbert of Cherbury*, ed. J.M. Shuttleworth (London, 1976), p. 8.
[120] Francis Rogers, *A Sermon Preached on September the 20 1632. At the Funerall of William Proud* (London, 1633), sig. D1r.
[121] *Henry V*, 4.3.44–8.

In addition, demonstrations of sangfroid after being wounded were highly valued. While suffering wounds alone could help accrue honourable reputation, the way one publicly reacted to being wounded could further serve to prove one soldierly and manly. Leicester uses no such adjectives or adverbs in reporting Sir William Pelham's response to being shot in the stomach at Doesburg but his admiration is plain: 'Thinking himself slayne, [he] turned about, speaking verie cheerfully to me, and thanked God it was his happ to be betwene me and that blow, with very comfortable and resolute speeches to me.' The fact that Pelham survived his wound did not lessen Leicester's approbation. In 1602 Ernst Casimir of Nassau writes to an older brother in similar terms about the wounding of Horace Vere, who had been shot in the hip.[122]

Modern studies of early modern manhood have argued that 'the process of fighting' could undermine the 'hard masculinity which soldiers struggled to build'.[123] This indubitably was true at times. In the attack on Zutphen's outworks in which Edward Stanley distinguished himself, one of Leicester's dispatches notes that 'an honest proper yong gentleman [...] called Cooke [was] even at the first attempt [...] shott [by] a canon [ball in] his belly', which struck him, Leicester recounts, 'so strangely as I never saw; armour broken with a hole as bigg as a bullet himself with a piece of the armour cut alonge his bellye, ij inches deep, and yet his bowells whole, and I am in hope of his life'.[124] Here the wound is chiefly a curiosity: it objectifies the 'young man' as a victim of modern military technology rather than epitomising his courage, much less his manhood.

The unmanning effect of wounds has perhaps been overstated by scholars, however, because they discount how wounds functioned. Because they were evidence of valour, proofs of virility, even terrible physical injuries did not necessarily unman a soldier, for he might have manifested his masculinity in the course of being maimed. Sir John Norreys petitioned the Privy Council to award a pension to his client Oliver Lambert, who had been badly wounded and lost his leg in Ireland in early 1585, declaring that, as 'a[n] eye Wittnes of his doinges, I am to Com[m]end him also to your L[ordshi]ps for his value and manly behaveour'.[125] The stress that Norreys had witnessed the action in which Lambert was wounded highlights the need for courageous actions to be publicly corroborated, but his wording makes it plain that Lambert had not been unmanned – either literally or figuratively – since his wounding testified to his military abilities and manhood. Similar *sangfroid* is shown by a young

---

[122] Leicester to Walsingham, 31 Aug. 1586, *Correspondence of [...] Leycester*, pp. 401–2. Ernst Casimir to Willem-Lodewijk, 7 Jan. 1602, *Archives ou correspondance inédite de la maison d'Orange-Nassau*, ed. G. Groen van Prinsterer, 2nd ser. (Utrecht, 1856–61), 2: 115.
[123] Purkiss, *Literature*, p. 45; cf. Shepard, *Meanings*, p. 214.
[124] Leicester to Walsingham, 6 Oct. 1586, *Correspondence of [...] Leycester*, p. 429.
[125] Norreys to Privy Council, 7 Mar. 1585, TNA, SP 63/115/14.

English gentleman volunteer 'of about 23 years of age' who, having had one arm shot off by a cannon during a sally from besieged Ostend, brought the limb back with him into the town and, arriving at the surgeon's quarters, cast it down before him, declaring, 'Behold the arm, which but at dinner helped its fellow!'[126] He had been dismembered but his response asserts that he was not unmanned.

VI

In the end, martial conduct that served to shape an honourable reputation was a performance. To perform successfully could be literally deadly and was certainly dangerous. But even given that the meanings of 'perform' and 'performance' have evolved, there is ample evidence that contemporaries understood the performative nature of honourable martial masculinity, and of military identity as a whole. It was because of Sir Philip Sidney's sense of being on a public stage and needing to live up to his classical and poetic models that he did without his cuisses in the cavalry action at Zutphen, in which Willoughby performed the deeds of prowess celebrated by Churchyard, and in which Sidney was fatally wounded in his unarmored thigh.[127] Sidney's friend and panegyrist, Fulke Greville, appropriately acknowledged the performative nature of military service, in concluding that 'honourable act[s]' prove that 'greatness of heart is not dead [and] that war is both a fitter mould to fashion it, and stage to act it on, than peace can be'.[128] Performance – personal conduct in the theatre of war – was a key moment in the fashioning of masculine and military identity. One final proof of contemporary awareness of this comes from Willoughby, who (remarkably) seems never to have suffered a serious wound. He suffered, nevertheless, in his last dozen years from persistent fever; the queen commiserated with his 'vexation' at being 'restrained by any indisposition of body, from following those courses, which, to your own reputation, and our great satisfaction, you have formerly performed'.[129]

As this chapter has shown, warlike prowess and courage were fountainheads of masculine honour in early modern England. More important than domestic violence (whether within the household or within a community)

---

[126] Vere, *Commentaries*, sig. T3r.
[127] John Gouws, 'Fact and Anecdote in Fulke Greville's Account of Sidney's Last Days', *Sir Philip Sidney: 1586 and the Creation of a Legend*, ed. Jan van Dorsten et al. (Leiden, 1986), pp. 69–70.
[128] Quoted in ibid., p. 74.
[129] Elizabeth to Willoughby, 7 Oct. 1594, *Somers Collection of Tracts*, 2nd edn, ed. Walter Scott, 13 vols. (London, 1809–15), 1: 265 fn.4. Willoughby may have suffered from malaria contracted during his 1589 campaign in France, when his army was severely afflicted by illness. In the sixteenth century it was possible to treat malarial symptoms but not the disease, which in that case remains in the body.

was the violence men were called to perform as part of demonstrating their manhood. There are, moreover, wider implications for the conclusions drawn here: just as the study of early modern military identity necessarily entails the exploration of male identity and its articulation during the sixteenth and seventeenth centuries, so adding the military dimension to modern studies of masculinity will likewise bring a fuller understanding of how manhood was conceived and demonstrated in this period. How men conducted themselves on campaigns and in combat was crucial to how men fashioned their identity in early modern England.

2

'The Breviarie of Soldiers': Julius Caesar's *Commentaries* and the Fashioning of Early Modern Military Identity

MATTHEW WOODCOCK

Julius Caesar's reports of campaigning in northern Europe and during the Roman civil war were widely read and imitated by soldiers, politicians, colonial administrators, historians, writers and soldier-authors throughout the early modern period. But the utility of Caesar's *Commentaries* in this period extended way beyond the spheres of historical record or, indeed, battlefield tactics. This chapter sets out to demonstrate that the *Commentaries* had a much wider field of application, and that they represented an influential, authoritative model of military identity in sixteenth- and early seventeenth-century England. My focus here is upon Caesar's twin roles as the text's protagonist and author, and upon the legacy of these paired roles in the *Commentaries*' applied reception history. The chapter begins by considering prominent aspects and models of military identity provided both within the text and by Caesar's composition of the *Commentaries* themselves. It then argues that Caesar's apparent mastery with both pen and sword formed a particularly resonant model of military identity during the early modern period. In particular, I examine how this distinct conception of military identity was translated into English (and England) through successive editions of Sir Clement Edmondes's *Observations upon Caesar's Commentaries* (1600, 1604, 1609), and how it is epitomised for Edmondes by his friend Sir Francis Vere. This chapter argues that Caesar's *Commentaries* provided early modern writers, fighters and writing fighters with a vital paradigmatic template for how the arts of the pen and the sword might be productively aligned or synthesised. As will be shown, Caesar's *Commentaries* constituted a significant resource for both battle-hardened and study-bound polemologists in this period as they returned to perennial questions about how one goes about making a good soldier, and concerning the relative value of martial book-learning and practical personal experience.

Caesar's *Commentaries* and military identity

Julius Caesar produced seven books of *commentarii* concerning expeditions made into Gaul, Germany and Britain between 58–52 BC – a text usually known as *De Bello Gallico* – and a further three books on the civil war (*De Bello Civili*) waged against Pompey between 49–48 BC.[1] Caesar's officers added four more books to these detailing operations in Gaul, Egypt, Africa and Spain up to 45 BC – the year before Caesar's assassination.[2] *BG* follows Caesar's campaigning from the initial confrontation with the Helvetii from modern Switzerland, and onwards into successive conflicts with Gallic and German peoples, two short-lived expeditions to Britain, and the revolt led by Vercingetorix that ended with the Roman victory at Alesia in 52 BC. *BC* is more politically focused and begins with Caesar's reconstruction of machinations at Rome that precipitated his opposition to Pompey. It then takes a more martial turn, tracing Caesar's successes against Pompey's forces in Spain, and his defeats against the same in Africa and at Dyrrachium, before culminating in Caesar's decisive victory at Pharsalus in 48BC. Caesar was not the first Roman general to record his military achievements but his are the only extant examples of any appreciable length.[3] The *Commentaries* were composed more as a working military memoir than as a history or annal.[4] For the most part they are focalised through Caesar, drawing upon the author's perspective, knowledge, experience and achievements. There are, however, sections where he repeats things he could not have seen, such as the battles in book 5 and Gallic war council in book 7 of *BG*, or scenes in Rome at the start of *BC*. One of the most distinctive and arresting features of the *Commentaries* is that they are almost wholly written in the third person, maintaining a pose of objectivity and detachment, as if the narrator joins the reader in observing, scrutinising and admiring the figure at their centre.[5] At the start of *BG*, when the Romans learn that the Helvetii are on the march, factual reports about Caesar's expeditious response appears alongside insights into the protagonist's informed decision-making process; we are made privy to objective and subjective, 'external' and 'internal' information (*BG*, 1.7). Caesar's text thus often sees him adopting

---

[1]   Quotations and citations from *De Bello Gallico* (hereafter *BG*) and *De Bello Civili* (hereafter *BC*) are from the Loeb editions of Caesar: *The Gallic War*, trans. H.J. Edwards (London, 1917); *The Civil War*, trans. Cynthia Damon (London, 2016).

[2]   Edmondes does not include the non-Caesarian books in his editions, and they feature little in the following discussion.

[3]   Adrian Goldsworthy, *Caesar: The Life of a Colossus* (London, 2006), pp. 224–5.

[4]   On the *Commentaries'* distinct form: F.E. Adcock, *Caesar as Man of Letters* (Cambridge, 1956), pp. 6–18; Christina S. Kraus, 'Bellum Gallicum', *A Companion to Julius Caesar*, ed. Miriam Griffin (Oxford, 2009), pp. 160–61.

[5]   On the particular qualities of the *Commentaries'* narration: Andrew M. Riggsby, *Caesar in Gaul and Rome* (Austin, 2006), pp. 150–5. Shakespeare appears to imitate the

multiple complementary roles as he witnesses, evaluates and memorialises events, in addition to initiating and participating in the same.[6]

As well as seeing Caesar the conquering general at work, the author's contemporaries greatly admired the *Commentaries'* composition, particularly their narrative and linguistic simplicity. Cicero wrote that they were composed 'like nude figures, straight and beautiful; stripped of all ornament of style as if they had laid aside a garment', and he highlighted their sense of immediacy and provisional, preparatory nature, averring that Caesar's aim 'was to furnish others with material for writing history'.[7] Caesar's proficiency as an orator and his authorship of several now-lost works – including a book on grammar, *De Analogia*, written while traversing the Alps – have been much praised by classical and modern commentators.[8] Critical attention has also been paid to the quality of Caesar's writing in the *Commentaries* themselves, including his use of earlier Greek sources in descriptions of warfare and his attempts to construct a vocabulary for representing – and in some ways simplifying – the confusion of battlefield realities.[9] Though their general accuracy has been confirmed by historical and archaeological evidence, the *Commentaries* were also written as instrumental, self-promotional and, at times, nakedly propagandistic documents.[10] Critics are divided over many aspects of the *Commentaries'* composition and formation but it appears Caesar likely wrote in the field during the campaigning year, or as he wintered in Cisalpine Gaul. Each year he sent what amounted to a book of the *Commentaries* back to Rome in order to support his bid for consulship or otherwise win him popular approval.[11] Together with regular correspondence to and from camp, the *Commentaries* enabled Caesar to

Commentaries' narration when he has his Caesar speak in the third person: *Julius Caesar*, act II, scene 2, lines 41–8 (cited from *The Riverside Shakespeare*).

[6]   Kraus, '*Bellum Gallicum*', p. 427.

[7]   Cicero, *Brutus*, trans. G.L. Hendrickson (Cambridge, MA, 1971), p. 227.

[8]   See Lindsay G.H. Hall, '*Ratio* and *Romanitas* in the *Bellum Gallicum*', *Julius Caesar as Artful Reporter*, ed. Kathryn Welch and Anton Powell (Swansea, 1998), pp. 22–4; Goldsworthy, *Caesar*, pp. 224–30; Christopher Pelling, 'Judging Julius Caesar', *Julius Caesar in Western Culture*, ed. Maria Wyke (Oxford, 2006), pp. 15–20; Richard Billows, *Julius Caesar: The Colossus of Rome* (London, 2009), pp. 192–204. Caesar was not the only soldier engaged in literary activity during the Gallic campaign. Quintus Cicero (younger brother of orator Marcus) penned four tragedies while in Britain during 54BC: Josiah Osgood, 'The Pen and the Sword: Writing and Conquest in Caesar's Gaul', *Classical Antiquity* 28 (2009), 345.

[9]   J.E. Lendon, 'The Rhetoric of Combat: Greek Military Theory and Roman Culture in Julius Caesar's Battle Descriptions', *Classical Antiquity* 18 (1999), 273–329; Anton Powell, 'Julius Caesar and the Presentation of Massacre', *Julius Caesar as Artful Reporter*, ed. Welch and Powell, pp. 111–37.

[10] Kraus, '*Bellum Gallicum*', p. 165; Riggsby, *Caesar*, pp. 207–14.

[11] T.P. Wiseman, 'The Publication of *De Bello Gallico*', *Julius Caesar as Artful Reporter*, ed. Welch and Powell, pp. 1–9; Goldsworthy, *Caesar*, pp. 226–7; Riggsby, *Caesar*, pp. 9–11. Some critics posit another (not wholly incompatible) compositional model and identify

remain away from Rome for nearly nine years and thus to stay alive politically (as Josiah Osgood puts it) while campaigning.[12] They functioned as his textual surrogates back in Rome, and would have had particular urgency as the civil war progressed, serving to justify his cause and undermine his opponents.[13]

So what makes the *Commentaries* an important source for examining military identity? Caesar does not address or name the concept of military identity overtly, not least because he never attempts to establish his text as an analytical or theoretical exposition on the art of war comparable to the authoritative later Roman treatises by Vegetius, Onosander and Frontinus. Caesar clearly intended his works to be read by others but there is little sense of textual or expositional self-consciousness in the *Commentaries*, or moments where he talks about himself as being author as well as protagonist of what is written.[14] The *Commentaries*' form and genre is such that their instructive potential derives from the countless examples of practice they present, accompanied by Caesar's reflections upon the decisions behind them or implications of what occurred. Unlike those later Roman military manuals (and those of their early modern imitators), or indeed historical accounts by Polybius and Josephus containing significant discursive excurses on Roman warfare, the *Commentaries* teach by example rather than by setting out precepts or providing exposition on tactics or training. Caesar assumes his audience knows all about the structure, formations and equipment of the late Republican army, and thus does not pause for further explanation when describing, say, how he drew his legions into the favoured triple battle-line (*triplex acies*) to fight the Helvetii, or when noting how the enemy formed a phalanx in response (*BG*, 1.24).[15] It tends only to be exceptional or foreign military practices that warrant further comment: German battle tactics (*BG*, 1.48), Gallic siege methods and musters (*BG*, 2.6; 5.56), British use of chariots (*BG*, 4.33), the guerilla tactics of the Morini and Menapii tribes (*BG*, 3.28), or the 'new and untried' type of trench warfare experienced at Dyrrachium (*BC*, 3.47). Of greatest interest here is the way in which the *Commentaries* are full of exemplary episodes and passing authorial comments addressing questions of what it means to be a soldier, what it means to be a *good* soldier, and what it means to be an effective leader of fighting men. For Caesar, military identity is closely bound up with the cultivation and

---

a degree of patterning to the *Commentaries* suggesting that they were revised prior to circulation: Adcock, *Caesar*, pp. 77–96; Kraus, 'Bellum Gallicum', p. 421.

[12]   Osgood, 'Pen and Sword', 345.

[13]   Adcock, *Caesar*, pp. 89–96.

[14]   There is a rare moment where we do glimpse Caesar in the act of making his text, and distinguishing his roles as protagonist and author: 'As for these points [a request from Pompey's commanders regarding their opponent's demands] Caesar did not think that they needed a response even then, nor do I now feel that there is sufficient reason for putting one on record' (*BC*, 3.17).

[15]   Adcock, *Caesar*, p. 53.

preservation of honour, rigid maintenance of discipline (personal and collective), and the continued accrual of martial experience. Time and again Caesar underlines the importance of adhering to orders and the grave implications of the failure of discipline; witness his treatment of the legates Sabinus and Cotta when the former disobeys orders leading to severe Roman losses at Atuatuca (*BG*, 5.29–37). Experience is frequently held up as the means by which individual soldiers become habituated to martial regimen (e.g. *BG*, 2.20, 6.39; *BC*, 3.28, 3.50). The inherently masculinist nature of such discipline is highlighted from the opening of *BG*, albeit characterised by its opposite, in passages where Caesar writes of those who have slipped from martial readiness into effeminate habits of living (*BG*, 1.1, 4.2).[16] Indeed, for Caesar *virtus* – literally 'manliness' – is perhaps the pre-eminent characteristic that forms military identity: the ability to meet the enemy courageously, maintain one's martial reputation, and eagerly fight again to recover a reputation lost through defeat.[17]

Caesar himself, as author–protagonist, is obviously the principal exemplar of what constitutes military identity in the *Commentaries* as we are made privy to his strategic decision-making, and see the vital transformative effect of his very presence on the battlefield, including during battles against the Veneti and at Alesia (*BG*, 3.14, 7.87–8). At times it looks as if Caesar alone is the sole point of movement and initiative in an engagement, as in the clash with the Nervii on the river Sambre:

> Caesar had everything to do at one moment – the flag to raise, as signal of a general call to arms; the trumpet-call to sound; the troops to recall from entrenching; the men to bring in who had gone somewhat farther afield in search of stuff for the ramp; the line to form; the troops to harangue; the signal to give. A great part of these duties was prevented by the shortness of the time and the advance of the enemy. The stress of the moment was relieved by two things: the knowledge and experience of the troops […] and the fact that Caesar had forbidden the several lieutenant-generals to leave the entrenching and their proper legions until the camp was fortified. [...] Caesar gave the necessary commands, and then ran down in a chance direction to harangue the troops [which] was no more than a charge to bear in mind their ancient valour, to be free from alarm, and bravely to withstand the onslaught of the enemy. [...] In whichever direction each man chanced to come in from the entrenching, whatever standard each

---

[16] Machiavelli commented on this particular aspect of Caesar's military identity: *The Art of War*, trans. Ellis Farneworth (New York, 1965), p. 211. Trim's essay above (Chapter 1) discusses military masculinities in greater detail.

[17] On the importance of *virtus* in the *Commentaries*: Lendon, 'Rhetoric', 306–16; Riggsby, *Caesar*, pp. 83–96; J.E. Lendon, 'Julius Caesar, Thinking About Battle and Foreign Relations', *Histos* 9 (2015), 9–22.

first caught sight of, by that he stood, to lose no fighting time in seeking out his proper company. (*BG*, 2.20–1)

Individual soldiers are but armoured parts of the greater whole here, their disciplined responses making them appear as compliant, efficient automata.[18] As Caesar's description shows, however, collective military identity is also important, and the men of his favoured Tenth Legion are encouraged not only to fight courageously but to draw upon their shared memory of past battle experience. Caesar conceives of military identity at an individual level too when praising the virtues of particularly heroic soldiers such Sextius Baculus, the friendly rivalry of centurions Titus Pullo and Lucius Vorenus, or the name-less eagle-bearer of the Tenth who urges men forward when landing in Britain (*BG*, 2.25, 4.25, 5.44, 6.38). Identifying with the troops – who they are and what they want – is shown to be a powerful rhetorical move for Caesar's subordinate commander Gaius Curio when addressing soldiers before the battle of Utica (*BC*, 2.32–3).[19] There are also occasions where Caesar clearly adopts a soldier's-eye-view, or at least imagines how his men will respond to particular events or conditions, when he works hard to control the damaging effects of fear on his troops (e.g. *BG*, 1.40–41).

It is important to note too that the preoccupation throughout much of the *Commentaries* is with Roman military identity specifically, and of Caesar as an exceptional but not unique exemplar.[20] As one might expect, the friends (*amici*) of Rome come in for high praise (e.g. *BG*, 4.12) whilst the military identity of Gallic foes is denigrated and found wanting by comparison. Vercingetorix, for example, is said to have levied a group of 'beggars and outcasts' ('*egentium ac perditorum*') who were 'unaccustomed to toil', and his countryman Crito-gnatus's otherwise rousing speech is undermined by its suggestion that Gauls besieged at Alesia might resort to cannibalism to survive (*BG*, 7.4, 7.30, 7.77). Caesar faces a greater challenge when writing of a Roman opponent in *BC* but even here he contrasts his own military strategy and identity with the far more 'foreign' policies of Pompey and the un-Roman taste for luxury exhibited at the latter's camp (*BC*, 3.96).[21]

So far attention has focused on the significance of military identity within the *Commentaries* themselves. Although, as noted above, Caesar rarely men-tions his role as author, there are many places in the text where he foregrounds the efficacy and value of the literate, rhetorically adept soldier. We see this

[18] See too the descriptions of soldiers at the siege of Quintus Cicero's camp (*BG*, 5.40).
[19] Montaigne later commended Caesar for addressing his soldiers as 'companions': *The Complete Essays*, trans. M.A. Screech (London, 2003), p. 834.
[20] Adrian Goldsworthy, '"Instinctive Genius": The Depiction of Caesar the General', *Julius Caesar as Artful Reporter*, ed. Welch and Powell, pp. 193–219.
[21] Goldsworthy, '"Instinctive Genius"', pp. 211–12.

in those moments where Caesar and others convince soldiers to master their fear of the enemy and in an episode during the siege of Quintus Cicero's camp where a critical message is conveyed using a letter written in Greek attached to a javelin (*BG*, 5.48). But it is the very act of Caesar writing his text while on campaign – and his role as author-protagonist – that establishes the most striking, most significant and certainly the most enduring model of military identity presented by the *Commentaries* as a whole. It is a model of military identity founded on a circularity of words and deeds, and the implicit valorisation of individuals skilled and experienced in both. Plutarch offers a vignette of Caesar the soldier-author at war, describing how when the Roman general travelled he had a slave writing down everything he dictated, while another stood behind him bearing his sword.[22] As will be shown, it is this image – of Caesar armed and active with pen and sword – that became for early modern martialists and soldier-authors the definitive example of writing produced from the field by a fighting man, and that made the *Commentaries* a popular template for authors of military memoirs and manuals throughout the period. It is this model of military identity that I want to examine further below.

Early modern reception and transmission of the *Commentaries*

The *Commentaries* were widely admired and imitated throughout the early modern period, and remained one of the most frequently printed and translated classical histories between the fifteenth and seventeenth centuries.[23] The *editio princeps* of the *Commentaries* was first printed in Rome in 1469. Printed translations appeared in German in 1507, in Italian in 1512 and in French in 1531. The first English translation was published in 1530, comprising of sections from *BG* books 4 and 5, describing Caesar's British campaigns. This is usually ascribed to John Tiptoft, first earl of Worcester, who was active in the mid-fifteenth century, though in the 1530s it would read as a timely illustration of native military prowess opposing a Roman foe. Arthur Golding published a complete translation of *BG* in 1565 accompanied by limited apparatus to help the reader (contextual topographic notes and a glossary) and prefatory praise of Caesar's stylistic purity.[24] As discussed below, Clement Edmondes's

---

[22] Plutarch, *Roman Lives*, trans. Robin Waterfield (Oxford, 1999), pp. 315–16.
[23] Peter Burke, 'A Survey of the Popularity of Ancient Historians, 1450–1700', *History and Theory* 5 (1966), 136–40. On the *Commentaries'* reception history: Jorit Wintjes, 'From "Capitano" to "Great Commander": The Military Reception of Caesar from the Sixteenth to the Twentieth Centuries', *Julius Caesar in Western Culture*, ed. Wyke, pp. 269–84; *Companion to Julius Caesar*, ed. Griffin, chs. 22–4.
[24] Arthur Golding, *The Eyght Bookes of Caius Julius Caesar* (London, 1565), sigs. *3v–*4r.

annotated translation of the first five books of *BG* appeared in 1600 followed by the seven-book edition in 1604 and addition of *BC* in 1609.[25] John Cruso appended an annotated abridgment of the *Commentaries* to his translation of Henri, duc de Rohan's treatise on ancient and modern military practice, published as *The Complete Captain* (1640).

The *Commentaries* remained a popular fixture on school curricula in the early modern period, their linguistic simplicity making them a favoured text for elementary Latin learners.[26] Caesar himself was the object of continued fascination, scrutiny and critique by humanist scholars across Europe for his political and military achievements, and for his dual roles as both historical protagonist and author. He was evoked at the foundation of what would eventually become the Bodleian library, Oxford when the formative donor Humphrey, duke of Gloucester was compared to the Roman general for his shared commitment to books and arms.[27] Petrarch read and studied Caesar, as did Leonardo Bruni, and the Caesarian genre of *commentarii* became a popular autobiographical model with the Italian humanists.[28] Castiglione used the *Commentaries* to illustrate the virtue of combining arms and learning.[29] Peter Ramus published detailed commentaries on Caesar's text and in the preface to *Liber de Caesaris militia* (1559) defended the seeming incongruity of a professor of letters writing of martial matters.[30] Michel de Montaigne's *Essais* reveal a sustained, if ambiguous engagement with the *Commentaries* including an essay specifically offering 'Observations on Julius Caesar's methods of waging war' that claimed the Roman general 'ought to be the breviary of every fighting-man'.[31] Montaigne evinces particular interest in literate soldiers and fascination in Caesar's role as both historical agent and author, rehearsing (without citation) Plutarch's vignette of the general attended by secretary and

---

[25] Citations from Edmondes, unless otherwise stated, are from *Observations upon Caesars Commentaries* (London, 1609). Pagination can be confusing because the 1604 and 1609 editions begin the numbering again as new material is added (*BG* books 6–7 in 1604; *BC* in 1609). In-text references here use the abbreviations *GW* (for *BG*) and *CW* (for *BC*) to indicate which parts of the *Observations* are cited. Edmondes's *Observations* were reprinted in 1655, 1677, 1695.

[26] T.W. Baldwin, *William Shakspere's Small Latine and Lesse Greeke*, 2 vols. (Urbana, IL, 1944), 1: 125, 312, 334, 387, 446. See Freyja Cox Jensen, *Reading the Roman Republic in Early Modern England* (Leiden, 2012), pp. 25–44. John Brinsley, *A Consolation for our Grammar Schooles* (London, 1622), sigs. I4v–K1r, praised the educational benefits of the Commentaries and Edmondes's translation.

[27] Henry Anstey, ed., *Epistolae academicae Oxon.*, 2 vols. (Oxford, 1898), 1: 177–8.

[28] Martin McLaughlin, 'Empire, Eloquence and Military Genius: Renaissance Italy', *Companion to Julius Caesar*, ed. Griffin, pp. 336–42.

[29] Baldesar Castiglione, *The Book of the Courtier*, trans. G. Bull (Harmondsworth, 1967), p. 93.

[30] Carol Clark, 'Some Renaissance Caesars', *Companion to Julius Caesar*, ed. Griffin, p. 361.

[31] Montaigne, *Essays*, p. 833.

sword-bearer.[32] For Montaigne, Caesar warrants study for his text and knowledge, as well as for the man himself and his actions – even if sometimes the admirable nature of Caesar the author does not align with Caesar the protagonist's cruelty and ambition.[33] One of the most striking contemporary illustrations of Caesar's conjunction of arms and letters is Nicolas de Cholières' *Des lettrez et guerriers* (1585), a dialogue between a character named 'Jules', who personifies and advocates study and letters, and another called 'Caesar' who defends the profession of arms.[34] As often in humanist debates on this theme, opposition is contrived only to conclude with reconciliation.

During the sixteenth century, Caesar's text was being read as part of a culture in which classical military theory and practice were playing a vital role in shaping advancements in the tactics of contemporary warfare. The *Commentaries* were used to draw contrasts between Roman military discipline and the shortcomings seen in contemporary armies. As McLaughlin writes, they 'afforded Italians deprived by their lack of success against foreign powers in the Italian wars, a consolatory backward glance at a happier military past', when (amongst others) France had been bested by the Romans.[35] Machiavelli cited Caesar frequently in his *Art of War* (1521); Francesco Patrizi produced a study drawing instructive parallels between ancient and contemporary military practice; Justus Lipsius's *De militia Romana* (1595–6) used Caesar alongside Polybius to advocate military reform.[36] Andrea Palladio had made a similar case in a handsomely illustrated Italian translation of the *Commentaries* (published 1575), which exemplified how Caesar's text was increasingly being accompanied by a range of visual and verbal paratexts (glosses, essays, maps, reconstructions of formations or battles) that elucidated and transposed Roman practice into forms readily applicable to sixteenth-century audiences.[37]

Caesar's dual role in the *Commentaries*, and his military identity as a soldier-author, spoke to scholars and soldiers alike. Although not as instrumental within the 'Maurician' military reforms as more analytical classical manuals

[32] Montaigne, *Essays*, p. 835. See also James J. Supple, *Arms Versus Letters: The Military and Literary Ideals in the 'Essais' of Montaigne* (Oxford, 1984); Jennifer Waldron, 'Beyond Words and Deeds: Montaigne's Soldierly Style', *Philological Quarterly* 82 (2003), 38–59; Louisa Mackenzie, 'Imitation Gone Wrong: The "Pestilentially Ambitious" Figure of Julius Caesar in Michel de Montaigne's *Essais*', *Julius Caesar in Western Culture*, ed. Wyke, pp. 129–47.
[33] Montaigne, *Essays*, p. 469.
[34] Supple, *Arms*, pp. 76–7.
[35] McLaughlin, 'Empire', p. 333.
[36] Jeanine de Landtsheer, 'Justus Lipsius's *De Militia Romana*: Polybius Revived, or How an Ancient Historian Was Turned Into a Manual of Early Modern Warfare', *Recreating Ancient History*, ed. Karl A.E. Enenkel et al. (Leiden, 2002), pp. 103–4.
[37] J.R. Hale, *Renaissance War Studies* (London, 1983), pp. 471–86; McLaughlin, 'Empire', pp. 350–4.

such as Aelian's *Tactica* or Vegetius' *De re militaria* – and thus associated less with the early modern military revolution – the *Commentaries* were still immensely influential on how military history was written from the early modern period onwards.[38] Military historian John Keegan made such a claim with the formal model of the set-piece battle narrative in mind.[39] One might make just as bold a claim for Caesar's influence upon constructions of military identity and indeed on the figure of the soldier-author himself, whose writings are informed by battlefield experience or drafted in the field.[40] Blaise de Monluc, for example, was one of many sixteenth-century military memoirists attracted to the image of Caesar 'being careful to record by night the actions he performed by day'.[41] For those employed in comparable projects of conquest to those Caesar described in *BG*, the *Commentaries* offered both literary and military models: Lord Deputy of Ireland Sir Henry Sidney was familiar with Caesar's *Commentaries*, as was one of his successors Charles Blount, Lord Mountjoy.[42] One of the best-known professional soldiers of the late Elizabethan era, Sir Roger Williams, cited the *Commentaries* approvingly in his own martial writings and is then himself mentioned in Edmondes's *Observations* (*CW*, sig. T3v).[43] As discussed below, Sir Francis Vere's memoir of military service undertaken between 1589 and 1604 was posthumously cast in a Caesarian mould when published in 1657 as the (by then) long-departed author's *Commentaries*.[44]

Caesar's *Commentaries* can also be situated within early modern debates concerning whether one could ever write authoritatively on war without actually having been a soldier, and on the comparative value of book-learning and

[38] On Maurice of Nassau and the early modern military revolution, see the discussion and directions to further reading in the Introduction to this volume (pp. 4–5).

[39] John Keegan, *The Face of Battle* (Harmondsworth, 1978), pp. 63–8.

[40] Yuval Harari, *Renaissance Military Memoirs: War, History and Identity, 1450–1600* (Woodbridge, 2004), pp. 190–5, discusses how widely Caesar was read by early modern military memoirists though contends – albeit working with a restrictive definition of what constitutes imitation – that the *Commentaries* had little influence on the actual 'style, values and messages' of martial autobiography in this period.

[41] Blaise de Monluc, *The Habsburg-Valois Wars and the French Wars of Religion*, ed. Ian Roy (London, 1971), p. 32.

[42] Henry Sidney, *A Viceroy's Vindication? Sir Henry Sidney's Memoir of Service in Ireland, 1556–78*, ed. Ciaran Brady (Cork, 2002), pp. 8–10; Brandie R. Siegfried, 'Rivalling Caesar: The Roman Model in Sir Henry Sidney's Memoir of Ireland', *Sidney Journal* 29 (2011), 187–208; John McGurk, 'Terrain and Conquest, 1600–1603', *Conquest and Resistance: War in Seventeenth-Century Ireland*, ed. Pádraig Lenihan (Leiden, 2001), p. 96.

[43] Sir Roger Williams, *Works*, ed. John X. Evans (Oxford, 1972), pp. 4, 33, 55.

[44] *The Commentaries of Sir Francis Vere* (Cambridge, 1657). Manuscript copies of Vere's memoir were in circulation from 1606: D.J.B. Trim, 'Sir Francis Vere', *ODNB*.

field experience.[45] As veteran soldier Robert Barret concluded in 1598, some military books

> have beene penned by learned men, as Politicians, Geometricians, and Mathe-
> maticians, which never saw any warres; Some by men of small learning, but by
> their practise and long continuance in warres; Some againe have beene penned
> by men both of good learning and long experience in warres: the last of these
> are to bee best approved.[46]

The *Commentaries* fall into this third 'approved' group. We might further extend the conceptual implications of Caesar's dual role as author-protagonist, and the exemplary nature of this kind of hybrid identity, by placing the *Commentaries* within early modern humanist discourse about how best to cultivate, exhibit and utilise *virtus* in the interests of the social and public good. (We saw above how *virtus* was also fundamental to military identity in Caesar's text.) As Quentin Skinner and others have shown, underlying 'virtually the whole framework for civic humanist discussions of the active life' was Cicero's *De officiis*, which propounded the primacy of the active, public life of *negotium* over the solitary life of scholarly, contemplative withdrawal (*otium*).[47] One area into which debates about the active life extended pertained to how military service constituted a way of demonstrating virtuous character and advancing the common good.[48] *De officiis* placed a premium on civic aspects of the active life (i.e. service as a governor, law-maker or counsellor) over the military, and the greater rewards that the former carried over the latter. As Cicero put it 'let arms unto the toga yield the laurel to men's praise' ('*cedant arma togae concedat laurea laudi*').[49] *Eloquentia*, in this view, was deemed of greater use to the state than the arts of war.[50] This kind of Ciceronian model of active public virtue still tends to dominate critical perceptions of the orthodox humanist ideal. But as Richard Tuck and others have identified, by the 1590s learning becomes increasingly associated with the arts of war – partly in response to the martialist culture fostered by the war with Spain and by the martial entourage

---

[45] Henry J. Webb, *Elizabethan Military Science: The Books and the Practice* (Madison, 1965), pp. 21–2, 35–6.
[46] Robert Barret, *The Theorike and Practike of Moderne Warres* (London, 1598), sig. A3r.
[47] Quentin Skinner, *Visions of Politics – Volume 2: Renaissance Virtues* (Cambridge, 2002), p. 218.
[48] Markku Peltonen, *Classical Humanism and Republicanism in English Political Thought, 1570–1640* (Cambridge, 1995), pp. 40–4.
[49] Cicero, *On Obligations*, trans. P.G. Walsh (Oxford, 2000), p. 27.
[50] Rory Rapple, *Martial Power and Elizabethan Political Culture* (Cambridge, 2009), p. 27. Edmondes himself offers qualified endorsement of Cicero's dictum at one point (*CW*, sig. K6r), though adds that the art of discourse is more effective when accompanied by cunning and deceit.

of Robert Devereux, earl of Essex.[51] This 'militarised conception of scholarship' has largely been discussed in relation to the reception of Tacitus and yet the *Commentaries* too – and Caesar the soldier-author – represent an alternative 'un-Ciceronian' model for reconciling the intuitively opposed poles of the contemplative and active lives.[52] Lisa Jardine and Anthony Grafton discussed at length how classical military texts were 'studied for action' in this period, and show indeed how Caesar was read as preparatory for action by Gabriel Harvey and Sir Philip Sidney.[53] From Harvey we learn that Sidney was a devoted, attentive reader of the *Commentaries*:

> Sir Philip Sidney esteemes [no] particular historie, Roman, or other, like the singular life, and actions of Cesar: Whome he values above all other, and reputes the greatest a[u]ctour, that ever the World did afforde [and] of none makes so high reckoning as of Cesars owne Commentaries.[54]

Edmondes's *Observations upon [...] Caesars Commentaries* are also the fruit of this late Elizabethan martialist culture and constitute different kinds of reading Caesar for action. As shown below, they represent significant interventions in contemporary controversies about the importance of books and reading for the art of war, and about military identity characterised by a combination of the arts of pen and sword.

Edmondes's *Observations* on the *Commentaries*

Sir Clement Edmondes combined careers as a scholar, civic official and statesman with practical and literary interests in military affairs. Never a combatant himself, Edmondes was nevertheless present at the battle of

---

[51] Richard Tuck, *Philosophy and Government, 1572–1651* (Cambridge, 1993), pp. 31–64, 104–8. See also R. Malcolm Smuts, 'Court-Centred Politics and the Uses of Roman Historians, c.1590–1630', *Culture and Politics in Early Stuart England*, ed. Kevin Sharpe and Peter Lake (Stanford, 1993), pp. 21–43; Paulina Kewes, 'Henry Savile's Tacitus and the Politics of Roman History in Late Elizabethan England', *HLQ* 74 (2011), 515–51.

[52] Edward Paleit, *War, Liberty, and Caesar: Responses to Lucan's 'Bellum Civile', c.1580–1650* (Oxford, 2013), p. 112.

[53] Lisa Jardine and Anthony Grafton, '"Studied for Action": How Gabriel Harvey Read his Livy', *P&P* 129 (1990), 30–78. See also Paleit, *War*, p. 96; Fred Schurink, 'War, What is it Good For? Sixteenth-Century English Translations of Ancient Texts on Warfare', *Renaissance Cultural Crossroads*, ed. S.K. Barker and B.M. Hosington (Leiden, 2013), pp. 121–38.

[54] Quoted in Jardine and Grafton, 'Studied', 55. Hubert Languet used Caesar's example to confront excuses made by his friend Sidney about why the latter had been too busy to maintain regular correspondence, declaring 'As the excuse for your delay you give the [1575] Progress, and the need to accompany His Excellency your father. But Caesar, who was busier than you, wrote his Commentaries from camp'; see Roger Kuin, ed., *The Correspondence of Sir Philip Sidney*, 2 vols. (Oxford, 2012), 1: 588–90.

Nieuwpoort in Flanders in July 1600, at what would prove to be a significant
and decisive engagement against the Spanish in the long-running war in
the Habsburg-controlled Netherlands.[55] No doubt through the graces of his
'honourable friend' Vere, he was privy to the English and Dutch war council
at Nieuwpoort and subsequently carried dispatches back to England following the battle. Edmondes dedicated *Observations upon the Five First Bookes
of Caesars Commentaries* (1600) to Vere, acknowledging not only his patron's
'continued incouragement' in the translation project but also the text's continued utility among Vere's military circle: 'this worke of Caesar hath alwaies
beene held in your particular recommendation, as the Breviarie of soldiers'.[56]
It was another of Vere's clients, Sir John Scott, 'whose desire to understand
the true sense of this history, and the mysterie of that discipline' moved
Edmondes to undertake his translation and annotation.[57] Later editions of the
Observations included dedications to Henry, Prince of Wales, who became a
significant military patron during the early Jacobean period.[58] King James VI
and I had earlier recommended Caesar's *Commentaries* to Henry in *Basilikon
Doron* (1599), and the 1604 and 1609 editions of Edmondes's text aligned
perfectly with deepening iconographic associations being made between the
Stuarts and the Caesars within early Jacobean political culture.[59]

Edmondes's *Observations* present a loose, abridged translation of the *Commentaries* that render Caesar's text into a functional English prioritizing utility
over style or accuracy. As Edmondes tells his readers: 'I have not tied my selfe

[55] Stephen Porter, 'Sir Clement Edmondes', *ODNB*; 'Clement Edmondes', *The History of
Parliament: The House of Commons 1604–1629*, ed. Andrew Thrush and John P. Ferris. 6
vols. (Cambridge, 2010), 4: 166–7.
[56] Clement Edmondes, *Observations upon the Five First Bookes of Caesars Commentar-
ies* (London, 1600), sig. *2r. On Vere's biography: Clements R. Markham, *The Fighting
Veres: Lives of Sir Francis Vere and Sir Horace Vere* (Boston, 1888); Tracy Borman, 'Sir
Francis Vere in the Netherlands, 1589–1603: A Re-evaluation of his Career as Sergeant
Major General of Elizabeth I's Troops', unpublished Ph.D. thesis (University of Hull,
2007); Trim, 'Vere'. On Vere's military circle: David R. Lawrence, *The Complete Soldier:
Military Books and Military Culture in Early Stuart England, 1603–1645* (Leiden, 2009),
pp. 93–100.
[57] Edmondes, *Observations upon the Five First Bookes*, sig. *2r. Edmondes further signals
his connection to Vere's circle in an epistle to Scott's stepson Sir Robert Drury inset
between his treatment of *BG* 5.23 and 5.24 in the 1600 *Observations*, sig. Y4r. He credits
Drury with encouraging him to complete his translation of book 5, professing that his
original intention was to publish an edition that concluded with Caesar's British expedition.
[58] On Prince Henry's military circle: Lawrence, *Complete*, pp. 105–26.
[59] [James VI and I], *Basilikon Doron, Or His Majesties Instructions to his Dearest Sonne,
Henrie the Prince* (London, 1603), sigs. H7r–H7v; Paulina Kewes 'Julius Caesar in Jacobean England', *The Seventeenth Century* 17 (2002), 155–86; Jensen, *Reading*, pp. 148–51;
Thomas James Dandelet, *The Renaissance of Empire in Early Modern Europe* (Cambridge, 2014), p. 259.

to a litterall translation of the history, but followed the sense; not daring to make any resemblance of the sweetnesse of that stile, but desirous to gratifie our better sort of souldiers, with the pourtraiture of that discipline.'[60] Each book of Edmondes's translation is broken down into sections, although these do not always correspond to the *Commentaries*' original chapter divisions. Each translated section is furnished with contextual, expository, discursive and polemical observations – usually between two and five per section – drawn both from Edmondes's personal experience and his extensive reading in classical and contemporary history and military theory.[61] The *Observations* on *BC* are particularly well-glossed, their copious marginal cross-references to other sources displaying just how well-read the author had become in military matters and how keen he was to stress the scholarly nature of the 1609 edition. As Paulina Kewes notes, whereas the 1600 *Observations* looked to an imagined audience among the soldiery, the Jacobean editions were directed towards a royal readership.[62] The Jacobean editions also included a number of detailed illustrations depicting engagements mentioned in the *Commentaries*, something that had featured in continental editions of Caesar's text for many decades. As noted above, there was already a well-established tradition of publishing editions of Caesar with supporting apparatus and commentary. Edmondes may have had in mind earlier annotated translations, such as Palladio's 1575 edition or Brancaccio's *Il Brancatio, della vera disciplina, et arte militare sopra i Commentari di Giulio Cesare*, as working models for his *Observations*. The latter book – which Edmondes cites (*GW*, sig. Q3v) – presented a translation of *BG* divided into sections, with each section accompanied by explanatory 'avertimenti'.[63] Edmondes was no doubt also influenced by annotated English translations of other classical authors that proliferated in the 1590s, including those of Tacitus produced by Henry Savile.[64] And in his concerted attempts to highlight the desired applicability of ancient warfare to modern practice, Edmondes was indebted too to the works of Patrizi and Lipsius mentioned above.

One important source for the *Observations* that Edmondes never acknowledges is Montaigne. We saw above how he evokes Montaigne's description of the *Commentaries* as being the 'breviary of every fighting-man', though attributes

[60] Edmondes, *Observations upon the Five First Bookes*, sig. *2v.
[61] Edmondes's identified referents include Homer, Herodotus, Xenophon, Polybius, Sallust, Strabo, Thucydides, Lucan, Livy, Seneca, Plutarch, Virgil, Ovid, Tacitus, Appian, Suetonius, Josephus, Onosander, Frontinus, Cassius Dio, Vegetius, Eusebius, Philippe de Commines, Francisco Guicciardini, Ramus, Patrizi, Giulio Cesare Brancaccio, Giovanni Botero, Lipsius, Raphael Holinshed and William Camden.
[62] Kewes, 'Julius Caesar', 166–7.
[63] Giulio Cesare Brancaccio, *Il Brancatio, della vera disciplina, et arte militare sopra i Commentari di Giulio Cesare* (Venice, 1582).
[64] Kewes, 'Henry Savile's Tacitus', 515–25.

this, flatteringly, to Vere. Edmondes also re-appropriates the opening lines of Montaigne's essay of 'Observations' on Caesar, about 'leaders in war' holding particular books in 'special esteem', so as to link Vere's use of Caesar to Marcus Brutus' high regard for Polybius and that of Charles V for Commines.[65] Elsewhere, he repeats (in translation) a paragraph from Montaigne commending swimming 'as a thing of much consequence in the use of Armes' (*CW*, sig. G4r).[66] He also incorporates Montaigne's essay on the battle of Dreux (1562) into an observation on the dangers of pursuing a routed enemy (*GW*, sigs. P4r–P4v).[67] Illustrating a point about the role of reason and passion at a war council (using the example of Cotta and Sabinus), he concludes 'so powerful is passion in the government of the soule, and so interested in the other faculties. And this is one cause of the uncertainty of man's judgement' (*GW*, sig. Z3v). He then uses exactly the same lines from Marcus Manlius quoted in Montaigne's essay 'Of the Uncertainty of our Judgment'.[68] The lack of attribution is hard to explain, though such unidentified appropriations are themselves another way in which Edmondes imitates Montaigne. Edmondes's evident debt to Montaigne helps us to understand how the *Observations* were produced. Taking his cue from Montaigne, and feasibly the first edition of Francis Bacon's *Essays* (1597), Edmondes frequently uses the process of annotation, not simply to add explanatory historical or topographical information but to reflect on a range of matters and problems prompted by his reading of Caesar. One can imagine that individual sections of observations developed out of annotations made at an intermediate stage between Edmondes's reading of Caesar's text and composition of the *Observations* themselves. As such, the *Observations* offer a valuable early contribution to the history of the English essay form. They represent a remarkable illustration of an author using an informed close reading of the *Commentaries* as the basis for his own original meditations on a wide range of matters both military and civil. Edmondes's initial readership certainly recognised and lauded the fact that the *Observations* were far more than just a translation. In his prefatory poems to the 1609 edition, Ben Jonson celebrated how his friend Edmondes was restoring Caesar to life and, through the annotations, producing something truly original:

> For where his person lived scarse one just age,
> And that midst envy and Parts; then, fell by rage;
> His deedes too dying, save in bookes: (whose good
> How few have read! How fewer understood!)
> Thy learned hand, and true Promethean Art,

---

[65]   Montaigne, *Essays*, p. 833.
[66]   Montaigne, *Essays*, p. 840.
[67]   Montaigne, *Essays*, pp. 306–7.
[68]   Montaigne, *Essays*, pp. 319–20.

As by a new creation, part by part,
In everie councell, stratageme, designe,
Action, or Engine, worth of thine,
T'all future time, not only doth restore
His Life; but makes, that hee can dye no more. (*GW*, sig. A3v)

Samuel Daniel too appended a poem to the same edition praising Edmondes for distilling the essence of the *Commentaries* and their author 'Whose Work, improv'd here to our greater gaine,/ Makes CAESAR more then CAESAR to containe' (*GW*, sig. A3r).

Throughout the *Observations*, Caesar's idiosyncratic voice and perspective are framed and put into dialogue with the translator–annotator and his sources. Edmondes proceeds, through an inductive method, to draw precepts from Caesar's practice, aligning the *Commentaries* with more theoretical classical and contemporary military treatises. Caesar's text frequently becomes a jumping-off point for Edmondes to pen a short essay on military practice, personnel or equipment.[69] On other occasions he adopts a more homiletic register and draws moral lessons from military conduct, as when the Helvetii grow over-confident after defeating some Roman cavalry:

> This example [...] maie lesson a commander, not to waxe insolent upon every overthrow which the enemie taketh, but duely to waie the true causes of a victorie gotten or an overthrowe taken; that apprehending the right currant of the action, he maie neither vaunt of a blinde victorie, nor be dismaied at a casuall mishappe. (*GW*, sig. C1r)

Elsewhere, individual observations are of a reflective or enquiring nature, more akin to Montaigne's essays, and take up broadly discursive themes: on 'whether men have greater courage in their owne or in a strangers country' (*GW*, sigs. F2v–F3v); on how civil life weakens a warlike people (*GW*, sigs. c4r–c4v); on the perils of the attraction of political novelties (*GW*, sig. n2r); on how 'the neglect of Ceremonies and formes in matter of State, is the ruine and abolishment of a Common-weale' (*CW*, sigs. C2r–C2v). Caesar's text often becomes the pretext for Edmondes's excurses on matters never directly contemplated in the *Commentaries*, including a spirited, if outmoded advocacy of archery (*GW*, sigs. m1r; *CW*, sigs. G5–5v); a rather equivocal statement concerning the role of women in war (*CW*, sig. O2r); and a curious suggestion that the British Druids 'proveth an auncient singularitie in the inhabitants of this Iland, touching the studie of Arts and matter of learning [...] In witnesse whereof I appeale to the two Universities of this land, as a

---

[69] See, for example, Edmondes's essays on legions, musters, siege-engines and the virtues of soldiers exercising (*GW*, sigs. H4r–I2r, b1v–b2v; *CW*, sigs. E4r–E4v, G2r).

demonstration of the love which our nation hath ever borne to learning'
(*GW*, sigs. d4r–d4v).

Edmondes's treatment of his subject is overwhelmingly positive, and there
is little negative critique of Caesar found in the *Observations*, nor accusations
regarding the *Commentaries*' accuracy or the conduct of war represented.[70]
There is little evidence of Edmondes engaging with contemporary condemnation of Caesar as an opponent of liberty or criticism of his ruthlessness as a
conqueror, such as we find, for example, in the scornful response of the scholar
Thomas Fenne:

> I much mervaile how [Caesar] could register and set downe with his owne pen
> the whole discourse of his warres and victories [...] without blushing cheeks,
> wonderful shedding of teares, and deepe sighes from the heart to thinke that
> for his owne vaine glorie and pride of heart, so manie Nations were subdued,
> so manie stately Townes beaten downe and sacked, so manie people slain and
> murdred most lamentably, that all Europa stood floating with the blood of his
> slaughters.[71]

Instead, Edmondes pointedly avoids condemnation of the more unapologet-
ically cruel or genocidal acts in *BG*. He dismisses the episode where Roman
cavalry hunt down German women and children at the Rhine as affording
'little matter of warre' (*GW*, sig. S3r), and he simply omits any form of
observation upon the section describing Caesar's use of terror tactics against
the Suebi and Sicambri tribes (*GW*, sigs. S4v–T1r).

Edmondes's concern throughout was to make the *Commentaries* relevant to
contemporary warfare. He queries, for example, the strategic benefits of higher
ground and, reversing the traditional military consensus, believes that for a
modern gunner advantage may lie with lower ground since there is less risk
of shot falling from the barrel if one fires uphill (*GW*, sig. C2r). Elsewhere,
comparisons are drawn between Caesar's practice and strategies employed
in the French Wars of Religion, during the 1588 Armada campaign, and at
the siege of Ostend (1601–4) (*GW*, sigs. C2v, P4r–P4v, T3v–V1v, L3v; *CW*, sig.
K3v). Edmondes makes a particularly topical comparison when commenting
on the guerrilla warfare conducted by the Morini (and Menapii) peoples: 'The
Irish rebels, having the like commoditie of woods and bogs, doe entertaine the
like course of warre, as the Morini did with Caesar: the meanes which he used
to disappoint them of that practise, was to cutte downe the woods' (*GW*, sigs.

---

[70] On contentious early modern interpretations of Caesar: David Norbrook, *Writing the
English Republic: Poetry, Rhetoric and Politics* (Cambridge, 1999), pp. 23–62; Jensen,
Reading, pp. 125–62; Paleit, *War*, pp. 111–23; Domenico Lovascio, 'Rewriting Julius Cae-
sar as a National Villain in Early Modern English Drama', *ELR* 47 (2017), 218–50.

[71] Thomas Fenne, *Fennes frutes* (London, 1590), sig. D1v.

Q4v–R1r). This passage, relating to *BG*, 3.28, was very likely written in the late 1590s prior to or around the same time as Essex's abortive Irish campaign.

The stand-out moment of contemporary application, which served simultaneously to illustrate the *Commentaries*' continued utility and the ability of Edmondes's patron to reference the very text the reader has before them, comes in an observation on *BG*, 6.7–8 concerning good generalship and the value of retaining superior ground. It sees Caesar's example put into practice at the battle of Nieuwpoort. On 2 July 1600 an army of the Dutch States-General under Maurice of Nassau fought along the beach and dunes near Nieuwpoort against a Spanish force led by Archduke Albert of Austria. The Dutch army, including English regiments led by Francis Vere and his brother Horace, gained superiority over the Spanish (it is argued) through sustained volley fire from musketeers drilled in infantry manoeuvres based on those that Maurice read of in Aelian and Vegetius.[72] The episode appears in part of the *Observations* first published in 1604, and actually relates to *BG*, 7.19, in which Caesar restrains his army from ceding higher ground to attack Vercingetorix's camp en route to Avaricum, 'which passage', writes Edmondes, 'was urged to good purpose by Sir Francis Vere in the yeare 1600 at a consultation before the battell of Newport'. Since this episode functions as an exemplary illustration of study being put into action, and of Vere's Caesarian inheritance, I quote it at length:

> For the armie of the Netherlanders being possest of the Downes [...] and the enemie making a stand upon the sands at the foote of those hils, and so cutting off the passage to Oastend, it was disputed by the Commaunders, whether they should leave the Downes, and go charge the enemie where he stood imbattelled upon the sands, or attend him in the fastnesse of the Downes whereof they were possest. The whole Councell of warre were earnestly bent to forsake the Downes, and to hazzard the fight on equall terms, as impatient that their passage and retreit to Oastend should be cut off. But Sir Francis Vere well knowing how much it imported the businesse of that day to hold a place of such gaine and advantage, perswaded Count Maurice by many reasons, and specially by this of Cesar which I last alledged [i.e. *BG*, 7.19], not to forgo the help of the Downes, but to expect the enemie in that place, and so make use of that benefite upon the first encounter, rather then to adventure the successe of the battell in worse tearmes, in hope of clearing the passage: and shewing also many probable conjectures, that the enemie would not continue long in that gaze. Wherein as his opinion then prevailed, so all that were present were eye-witnesses both of the truth of his conjecture, and the soundnesse of his judgement. For the

---

[72] Geoffrey Parker, 'The Limits to Revolutions in Military Affairs: Maurice of Nassau, the Battle of Nieuwpoort (1600), and the Legacy', *Journal of Military History* 71 (2000), esp. 347–54. See also C.E.H.J. Verhoef, *Nieuwpoort 1600: De bekendste slag uit de Tachtig-jarige Oorlog* (Soesterberg, 2000), esp. pp. 112–39.

enemie within a while after comming on to charge the troupes of the States, was received with such a counterbuffe from the hils, and were violently beaten backe in such rude manner, as our men had the execution of them for the space of a quarter of a mile or more, which was no small advantage to the fortune of that day. (*GW*, sig. c3v)

Edmondes's attention here to the advice Vere gives Maurice accords with the emphasis placed throughout the *Commentaries* and *Observations* on the place of verbal arts upon the battlefield. Witness the many episodes in Caesar's text depicting councils, orations and advice, and those where the general and his officers work to control their soldiers' fear of the enemy. Battlefield rhetoric is shown to be just as significant and effective a component of the art of war as the organisation of formations or selection of specific troop types and weapons. The Nieuwpoort episode also illustrates the strategic value of both Caesar and his interpreter Vere, and serves as an endorsement not just of the *Commentaries* – and thus Edmondes's edition – but of the decisive role that applied reading of the ancients could have in modern warfare.[73] Nieuwpoort was undoubtedly a significant victory in the ongoing struggles of the States-General against Spanish rule, but what Edmondes does is to trace the germ of this success to a critical decision made at the commanders' council, a decision apparently informed by Vere's reading of Caesar. For a moment it seems like Dutch independence was won on the battlefields of Gaul, the Nieuwpoort episode offering an alternative example of classical theory applied in combat. Edmondes thus endeavours to establish Caesar as a martial authority for contemporary fighting men and to consciously fashion a military identity for Vere in a Caesarian mould, as both reader and imitator of Caesar.

The literate soldier

Vere's use of Caesar at Nieuwpoort endorses the argument Edmondes sets out at the start of every edition of the *Observations* in an essay bearing a title leaving no doubt as to its principal lesson: 'Reading and Discourse are requisite to make a souldier perfect in the Arte militarie, how great soever his knowledge may be, which long experience and much practise of Armes hath gayned.' Edmondes's prose lacks the clarity or simplicity of Caesar's but his essay questions the value of battlefield experience alone and asks what constitutes

---

[73]   The chronology proposed by Lawrence, *Complete*, p. 100, that sees Vere's application of Caesar at Nieuwpoort as inspiration for Edmondes's *Observations* is questionable; the not insubstantial work of translating and annotating at least the first five books must already surely have been underway by early July 1600, when the episode occurs, since they appear in print the same year. The alternative scenario imagines that Edmondes dashes this off in no more than nine months (i.e. July–March 1600, using 'old style' dating).

'useful' experience, citing an example where the Roman general's own 'infinit' experience failed to prepare him for Pharnaces' attack at Zela in 47 BC (*GW*, sig. A2r). Taking a traditionalist stance in the ongoing 'ancients vs. moderns' debate about which era produced the best soldiers, Edmondes maintains that the conduct of warfare in more recent 'subtler ages' is a pale imitation of the valour and honour seen in the actions of 'ancient Heroes' (*GW*, sig. A3r).[74] What value, therefore, is experience based wholly on contemporary warfare? In answer to his key theme – 'whether reading or practice have the first place in this Art [of war]' – Edmondes concludes by proposing a circular relationship between the two:

> reading ought to go before practise (although it follow it in course of time, for there is no reading, but of something practised before) [...] both these partes were by our soldiers so regarded, that neither practice might march in obstinate blindnesse without learned knowledge; nor this againe be entertained with an idle apprehension without practise: but that both of them may be respected, as necessarie partes to make a compleat nature. (*GW*, sigs. A3v–A4r)

The essay effects a synthesis between reading and practice positing an imitative chain of well-read soldiers practising combat and applying theories they have read; said soldiers then write up such experiences and insights for subsequent bookish fighting men.

The 1604 and 1609 *Observations* are themselves working examples of how this circular relationship functions since they include a drill manual composed by Edmondes – entitled *The Maner of Our Moderne Training, or Tactike Practise* – that draws upon his reading in classical theory and experience of the Maurician innovations witnessed alongside Vere in the Netherlands. Edmondes's was the first manual printed in English to describe the organisation and 'warlike motions' of a company of soldiers and to include commands and directions for manoeuvres such as opening and closing ranks, wheeling and countermarching.[75] Edmondes does not include the diagrams of individual postures and group formations commonly seen in continental drill manuals but he impresses upon the reader that 'tactike practise' can be learnt from instructions such as his; reading and practice are indeed inseparable. Taken as a whole, the *Observations* offer multiple layers of readers, writers, fighters and

---

74   To illustrate his point, Edmondes contrasts ancient and modern political history as represented by Livy and Guicciardini (*GW*, sig. A3r). On the ancients vs. moderns debate: Webb, *Elizabethan Military Science*, pp. 17–50; Mark R. Geldof, 'The Pike and the Printing Press: Military Handbooks and the Gentrification of the Early Modern Military Revolution', *International Exchange in the Early Modern Book World*, ed. Matthew McLean and Sara Barker (Leiden, 2016), pp. 147–68. I'm grateful to Chris Warner for the latter reference.

75   Lawrence, *Complete*, pp. 144–7.

expositors: Caesar's text is translated and annotated by Edmondes, prefaced with a cogent argument pertaining to how reading and practice interact, and the editor then provides proof of this in the form of his own praxis-oriented drill manual. As Robert C. Evans points out, the multiple levels of reading in the 1609 *Observations* were apparent to Jonson in his first prefatory epigram to Edmondes, which deals, rather dizzyingly, with 'Caesar as a reader (and writer) of himself, with Edmondes as a reader of Caesar, with Jonson as a reader of Edmondes (but also of Caesar), with us as readers of Jonson reading Edmondes and Caesar, and thus with our own readings of these two as coloured by our reading of Jonson'.[76] The poem signals that Jonson too – who briefly served as a soldier in the early 1590s, very likely under Francis or Horace Vere – had read the *Observations* and implicitly endorsed the argument of its prefatory essay. Ultimately, the *Observations* construct a model of military identity based upon Caesar the soldier-author, offering a meditation and exposition on the contemporary value of such a hybrid figure by including within them an influential illustration of a highly successful reader and inheritor of that Caesarian tradition.

One key question remains, however, concerning the true extent of Caesar's influence upon Vere. That may seem an odd thing to claim, given everything set out above. But it is only through Edmondes's testimony that we learn of Vere's practical application of the *Commentaries* at Nieuwpoort. In Vere's own account of the war council included in his posthumously published military memoir, it is his reasoning and vehemence – rather than strategic deployment of Caesar – that win over Maurice. As he writes:

> I was moved to say, that all the world could not make me change my counsel. The Count Maurice was pleased to like of it, resolving not to passe any further towards the enemy, and for the ordering of things, reposed so much trust in me, as that he believed they were well, without viewing the places or examining the reasons of my doings.[77]

Only from Edmondes do we hear about Vere's recommendation of Caesar as being 'the Breviarie of soldiers'; and, as we saw, the phrase was taken from Montaigne. Edmondes's bias must also be considered, and contemporaries at Elizabeth's court noted that the account of Nieuwpoort he presented there was 'so partial, as yf no man had strooke stroke but the English, and among the English no man almost but Sir Francis Vere'.[78] Edmondes *was* present at the Nieuwpoort war council, but the reality of whether or not events actually

[76]   Robert C. Evans, *Habits of Mind: Evidence and Effects of Ben Jonson's Reading* (Lewisburg, 1995), p. 224.
[77]   Vere, *Commentaries*, sig. N2v.
[78]   Quoted in Borman, 'Vere', p. 142.

occurred as he described – with the *Commentaries* playing a pivotal role – is, one proposes, obscured by his desire to celebrate Vere as a reader and Caesar as his authority, and by using this example to advance his case for the literate and articulate fighting man. Vere's memoir is not bookish in any way and makes no reference to any classical or contemporary military authorities, Caesar included; the onus is all on practice rather than reading, as in the original Roman *Commentaries*. One should stress, nevertheless, that Vere was a committed reader and collector of military books, and his collection was later donated to the Bodleian.[79] The playwright Cyril Tourneur, who had read Vere's memoir, certainly highlighted their author's dual facility in arms and letters in an elegy for the deceased general that praised him as a 'Martialist' – an image of the 'compleate' man lauded within that anti-Ciceronian tradition discussed earlier, perfected 'aswell in actives, as contemplatives'.[80]

In 1657, when the Cambridge academic and 'entrepreneur of letters' William Dillingham published Vere's memoir as *The Commentaries of Sir Francis Vere*, he too consciously fashioned and celebrated his subject as being a reader and imitator of Caesar.[81] Dillingham made this connection explicitly in his prefatory poem:

> Look (Reader) how from Neuport hills he throws
> Himself a thunder-bolt amongst his foes;
> And what his Sword indited, that his Pen
> With like success doth here fight o're agen:
> What Mars performed Mercurie doth tell;
> None e're but Cesar fought and wrote so well.
> Why may not then his Book this title carry,
> The second part of Cesar's Commentary?

Vere's printed *Commentaries* were just as much a multi-vocal, portmanteau work as Edmondes's *Observations*. Both books presented a military autobiography framed by extensive editorial contextualisation and exposition. Dillingham added, for example, several synoptic narratives of actions described in the memoir that were written by the Dutch historian Isaac Dorislaus, and by Vere's friends and fellow soldier-authors Henry Hexham and Sir John Ogle.[82] To these were added Edmondes's reminiscences of Vere's employment of Caesar

---

[79]   Lawrence, *Complete*, pp. 97–8.
[80]   Cyril Tourneur, *A Funerall Poeme Upon the Death of the Most Worthie and True Souldier, Sir Francis Vere, Knight* (London, 1609), sig. C3r.
[81]   On Dillingham's literary activities: W.H. Kelliher, 'William Dillingham', *ODNB*.
[82]   Hexham published several military works in England and the Netherlands during the 1630s–40s, see Paul Hoftijzer, 'Henry Hexham (c.1585–1650), English Soldier, Author, Translator, Lexicographer, and Cultural Mediator in the Low Countries', *Renaissance Cultural Crossroads*, ed. Barker and Hosington, pp. 209–25. Ogle too was another

at Nieuwpoort, which Dillingham reads in a way that appears to present the veteran English soldier as a better model for 'the exact effigies of a good General' than the Caesarean original.[83] The only direct reference made in the 1657 *Commentaries* to Vere's application of Caesar returns us back to Edmondes. All of the other links made therein between Vere and Caesar – from the allusive title onwards – are formulated by Dillingham and the editorial paratexts.

The idealised figure of Vere as Caesar *redivivus* was the most important, and as it transpired, most enduring creation set out in the *Observations*. Vere represents the net result of adding together all of those different components of Edmondes's edition; he embodies – or is *made to embody* – theory in practice. Indeed, Vere is fashioned as a working exemplar of the value of the text Edmondes translates and annotates. What is clear from Edmondes's *Observations* and Dillingham's edition is that they both endeavour to shape Vere as an active reader and imitator of Caesar, with the 1657 text taking its lead from the earlier Jacobean work. They are both indebted to a particular model of military identity established in Caesar's *Commentaries*, that hybrid figure of the literate fighting man whose service with a sword complements and enhances that with a pen, and whose expertise with the latter is drawn upon subsequently by those that recognise the value of combining martial practice with acquisition of knowledge of the art of war.

---

bookish military man. As Henry Peacham noted, Ogle's house in Utrecht 'seemed many times a little Academie [...] whither resorted many great Schollers and Captaines, English, Scottish, French, and Dutch, it had beene enough to have made a Scholler or Souldier, to have observed the severall disputations and discourses among many strangers' (*The Compleat Gentleman* (London, 1622), sig. Cc2r).

[83]   Vere, *Commentaries*, sig. P4v.

3

'Souldiers, or Clarkes, or both': Ralph Knevet and the Fashioning of Military Identity through Print and Performance in Caroline Norwich

CIAN O'MAHONY

It may seem unusual that the concept of military identity would be a persistent and constant driving force for literary endeavour for a rural clergyman, with no direct experience of war, living in Norfolk in the pre-Civil War period. This chapter argues, however, that Ralph Knevet (1600–71) – in both his published work and private holograph writing – was consistently preoccupied with the formation, modelling and representation of contemporary military identity across a range of genres, including dedicatory poems and verse treatises, public entertainments drawing on contemporary pastoral drama and masque, and romance–epic.[1] This chapter will examine Knevet's writings in order to demonstrate that a keener understanding of military identity can deepen our awareness of the significance of regional, national and international influences on poetic interpretations of statehood and cultural identity. The majority of this chapter establishes Knevet's representation of military identity in his first work, *Stratiotikon* (1628), before going on to consider how his approach changes and becomes more varied in his later works, *Rhodon and Iris* (1631) and the unpublished manuscript continuation of Edmund Spenser's great poem, *A Supplement of the Faery Queene* (c.1628–35).[2] By examining Knevet's approach to military identity as a unifying theme for these works, I aim to jux-tapose the insular and localised focus of his writings with the under-explored national and international scope of his political outlook and interests, and his wider ambitions for his writing. In doing so, the chapter positions Knevet as a

---

[1]   On Knevet's biography: W. Moelwyn Merchant, 'Ralph Knevet of Norfolk, Poet of Civill Warre', *Essays and Studies* 13 (1960), 21–35; Alastair Fowler, 'Ralph Knevet', *ODNB*.

[2]   For editions of the first two texts: Amy Charles, ed., *The Shorter Poems of Ralph Knevet: A Critical Edition* (Columbus, OH, 1966), hereafter cited as *Poems*; for the latter, see Christopher Burlinson and Andrew Zurcher, eds., *A Supplement of the Faery Queene* (Manchester, 2015), hereafter cited as *Supplement*.

significant regional voice in response to burgeoning concerns for the Protestant faith during the early stages of Charles I's Personal Rule and following the
abortive attempts at re-establishing English and Protestant martial glory such
as the ill-fated Île de Ré campaign of 1627.

Knevet employs a combination of classical, chivalric and contemporary
examples to inform his work with the express intent of inspiring and instilling native military identity. Although, as is explored below, his purpose is
underpinned by his Protestant world view, he maintains conciliatory attitudes
towards representations of Catholicism in much of his work. As a tutor to William Paston (1610–63), first baronet of Oxnead, Norfolk, it is perhaps unsurprising – given the accusations of recusancy attached to the Paston family
– that Knevet tempers the specifically confessional thrust of his rhetoric.[3] He
does appear, however, to associate himself with other significant figures possessing actual continental fighting experience, such as John Cruso, who also
detested the more vitriolic expressions of Protestant faith. This chapter seeks
to demonstrate, then, that the type of military identity that Knevet attempts
to propagate throughout his writings is at once regional, national and international in its outlook. Knevet's particular formation of military identity is
founded on faith, but temperate in its zeal, and it is informed both by the
combat experience of others and by native literary traditions.

A poetic muster

Knevet's *Stratiotikon, Or A Discourse of Military Discipline Shewing the Neces-
site thereof According to these Perilous Times*, represents his first known foray
into print and it appeared ten years after his education at Cambridge (1616–18),
during which time he had served as tutor to the young William Paston. The
subtitle of the work may lead one to expect a manual of military instruction
of the practical type that had become increasingly popular in England since
the 1570s.[4] The practice of producing or importing translated material on a
martial theme represented a lucrative exercise for booksellers and printers,

---

[3]   On Knevet's connections with Paston: *Poems*, pp. 8–11. See also R.W. Ketton-Cremer,
       Norfolk Assembly (London, 1957), pp. 17–40.
[4]   Henry J. Webb, *Elizabethan Military Science: The Books and the Practice* (Madison,
       1965); Barbara Donagan, 'Halcyon Days and the Literature of War: England's Military
       Education before 1642', *P&P* 147 (1995), 65–100; David R. Lawrence, *The Complete Sol-
       dier: Military Books and Military Culture in Early Stuart England, 1603–1645* (Leiden,
       2009). Lawrence notes over ninety such texts in circulation in the early Stuart period (p.
       261). He also indicates the contentious use of 'military discipline' as a term which by this
       point was increasingly being identified specifically with the godly nature of Gustavus
       Adolphus's campaigning (pp. 225–6). The Irish captain, Garret Barry, produced a practi-
       cal work in 1634 called exactly that – *A Discourse of Military Discipline* – aimed at Irish
       and English soldiers joining the forces of Catholic powers.

and the popularity of such works demonstrates a widespread interest in military education in the pre-Civil War period. Knevet, however, offers something different: a poetic text laden with classical references and allegorical representations of Protestant internationalism, prefaced by a significant number of poems addressed to members of the Norwich militia and Norfolk county hierarchy. The text itself extends to 1,025 lines of iambic pentameter couplets and incorporates elements of dream vision, classical allusion and beast fable. After praising the martial exercises of the Norwich Military Yard, Knevet contrasts English martial prowess with that of France and Spain, as demonstrated by victories at Agincourt and in 1588 (*Poems*, pp. 120–5). The poem then takes a decidedly fantastical turn as the poem's speaker travels to the kingdom of Circe, shapeshifts to a Lion and then undergoes a period of instruction by 'ape-men'. He overhears a dragon and griffon – intended as allegories of the Catholic powers – proclaim their plots against the 'Lyons of the North' (*Poems*, pp. 137–8). The latter was a recognisable term applied most commonly to the Swedish king, Gustavus Adolphus, whose forces' activities in defence of the Protestant faith on the international stage were popularised in circulated corantos of the period.[5] The poem is noteworthy in that it demonstrates Knevet's refusal to rely on contemporary nostalgic approaches to English military identity, in lieu of any discernible military successes. The contemporaneous popularity of works such as Michael Drayton's *The Battaile of Agincourt*, and the enduring public interest in publications such as Samuel Daniel's *Civil Wars* (1595) indicate a readership yearning for a return to the days when English martial supremacy was unquestioned.[6] Knevet, however, is eager to dismiss anachronistic references to such successes in favour of realistic assessments of the early modern battlefield and contemporary weaponry. He sets aside nostalgic laments over the loss of technological supremacy and instead positions his work as an appeal to the innate English military character and identity, as he describes it, which has been diminished by its lack of discipline:

> These [soldiers] with their Bowes, of stiffe, and trustie Eugh
>   The Cavalrie of France oft overthrew [...]

---

[5]   On the English reception of Gustavus Adolphus's militant Protestantism and his initial successes against Catholic forces on the continent before his untimely death in 1632: Simon McKeown, 'The Reception of Gustavus Adolphus in English Literary Culture: The Case of George Tooke', *RS* 23.2 (2009), 200–20.

[6]   Drayton's publication of *The Battaile of Agincourt* in 1627 is particularly noteworthy in relation to tensions in contemporary expressions of military identity in England. Drayton's much shorter and more accessible *Ballad of Agincourt* (1604) demonstrates that the cultural memory of the battle is a long-held literary interest for him, but in the *Battaile* he combines significant emphasis on the medieval supremacy of English archery and the symbolism of the English fighting man with extensive depictions of contemporary siege weaponry and the effect of cannon during the siege of Harfleur.

> But now the fierie weapons have cashierd
> Those ancient Armes, that made our name so fear'd
> Through all the World, nor hath ease so decay'd
> Our courage, or our nerves, but by the aid
> Of Discipline, we may retrieve that Fame
> Which we so lately lost, and rayse a name. (*Poems*, p. 140)

Expressing a complaint frequently voiced during the 1620s, Knevet laments of English military identity as a neglected but recoverable virtue, and offers a local, regional perspective on the problems with the national martial reputation.

The paratextual elements of *Stratiotikon* return repeatedly to the difficulties with contemporary English military identity. In addition to the threnody appended to the end of the text, describing the deaths of John Burroughs and William Heydon during the disastrous Île de Ré campaign, Knevet's poem is prefaced by thirty-seven poems addressed to local figures with some involvement in the Norwich militia. The prefatory verse also provides further evidence of Knevet's perception of his own role in relation to propagating military identity and his place as a non-combatant among fighting men. They range in tone from the laudatory appraisals of unheralded heroes, such as Captain Henry Shelton, to the polite assessment of social superiors, such as Sir William de Gray, for whom Knevet writes: 'I take thy name on Fames bare word (Sir Knight)/ I know thee not: yet sweare I think th'art right' (*Poems*, pp. 94–5, 104).[7] Other notable figures within the militia structure singled out for praise include: his kinsman Thomas Knevet of Ashwellthorpe, who 'art the Glasse in which the World may see/ What once our Gentrie was, and still should bee';[8] the young Sir Roger Townsend 'on whose honourd name/ More noble Vertues are scor'd up by fame/ Then time hath lent you yeares'; and Sir Charles Le Grosse, who is ''mongst the chiefest of the Arts few friends' (*Poems*, pp. 96–8). Significant local personalities are also addressed, including Sir Miles and Sir John Hobart, John Hevingham and Framlingham Gaudy. One might assume that such a broad range of dedicatory poems would represent a wide-ranging bid for patronage among the local powers that be. But the author appears to be preoccupied far more with military identity and the instilling of good discipline. This becomes even more apparent when the pattern of the prefatory poem series is assessed against the wider sociopolitical context of the text's

---

[7]   Henry Shelton (1576–1634) was the third son of Ralph Shelton, who served as Sheriff of Norfolk in 1571.

[8]   More commonly spelled 'Knyvett' in records of this branch of the family, it may be an effort on Knevet's part to inculcate himself with this distant relative by aligning his name orthographically with the author's own. He addresses Thomas' brother, Edmund in a similar fashion (*Poems*, p. 112). See R.W. Ketton-Cremer, *Norfolk Portraits* (London, 1944), esp. pp. 22–5, and Bertram Schofield, ed., *The Knyvett Letters, 1620–44* (Norwich, 1949), for more on the Knyvetts of Ashwellthorpe and the Paston families.

production. Put simply, Knevet's writing of *Stratiotikon* appears to be compelled as much, if not more, by public and national political motives as it is by personal and private hopes for local preferment.

The Captain of the Norwich militia, Henry Shelton, is the initial dedicatee in the procession: the head of the column, as it were. There is a high degree of personal appreciation on Knevet's part in this initial poem and Shelton's place is likely warranted by his service in the Low Countries (*Poems*, p. 154). Surprisingly, sixteen of the dedicatees that follow Shelton in the procession could easily be regarded as having greater social importance within local and national society due to their position as knights, parliamentary representatives or local authorities.[9] As such, any of them would present greater prospects, were patronage the chief aim of Knevet's first publication. Despite the number of dedicatees included, the author excuses himself from censure by those who fail to make the cut and, in doing so, declares his authorial intent:

> To any to whom I write
>> Blame not my Muse, thou that dost find thy Name
>> Not Marshal'd here, as thou would have the same:
>> No blemish tis to thy repute: for (know it)
>> I act no Herald here (Sir) but a Poet. (*Poems*, p. 93)

In spite of Knevet's protestations of poetic licence, his attitude towards his dedicatees is highly nuanced and the arrangement of the prefatory poems is clearly purposeful in its intent. The dedicatory poems aim to achieve several interlinked objectives: to demonstrate the worth of the ordinary soldier; to promote and give preference to experience; to attack complacency and apportion blame for militia failures; and, finally, to position Knevet as the primary voice in representing local military identity, by publishing what could be considered a poetic muster.

The primary positioning of Shelton, elevated above his social betters in the martial procession of the prefatory poems, may well represent the fundamental argument of *Stratiotikon*: that the potential of the ordinary soldier can only be achieved with the tacit support of the city and county hierarchy, which in turn underpins an efficient national training programme through the reform and maintenance of a successful militia. Amy Charles, in her assessment of Knevet's purpose in including so many dedicatees of elevated rank, states that he

> could hardly have been trying to urge the benefits of military preparedness upon men deeply involved in the military organisation of the county and responsible for its safety; but in this first publication [...] even the names of men already

[9]   In addition to serving as commissioners for the Forced Loan in 1626, five of those listed served at various times as deputy lieutenants, with twelve holding the position of sheriff of the county, and nine serving as MPs.

established in the public regard might serve to recommend Knevet's proposi-
tions to his readers. (*Poems*, p. 23)

There is undoubtedly some degree of truth to Charles's observation. But
Knevet does explicitly challenge the organisational structure and dedication
of the militia itself as it stands, and towards the end of *Stratiotikon* calls for
much more frequent exercise:

> Yee, that have charge of Bands, your dutie tis
>> To train them up, with frequent exercise.
>> Not by your Mustr'ing once, or twice a yeare,
>> Doe yee discharge your duties, but I feare
>> If forraine foes should drive us to our fence,
>> We all should suffer for your negligence.
>> Tis rather fitting, that each Month should yield
>> A day, to draw your Souldiers to the field. (*Poems*, p. 140)

Such admonishments could only be aimed at those with the power to gather
those soldiers for exercise, rather than those charged with the practical elements of training, such as Shelton.

An alternative objective for the arrangement of the prefatory poems highlights Knevet's preoccupation with the formation and instilling of military
identity. Shelton, the experienced captain with direct knowledge of war, is
placed in the van, but equally important is the strength of the rear. This position is occupied in Knevet's column of dedicatees by the sergeant, John Cruso,
who may have drawn on real fighting experience on the continent in his role
as a practical instructor at the Norwich muster in August 1628. Inasmuch as
Knevet claims to 'act no Herald here (Sir) but a poet', it seems he is performing
exactly that role: positioning himself as a literary herald announcing a poetic
muster. There is a processional pageantry and inherent visual nature to the role
of order of the dedicatees. With experienced men as exemplars to the front and
rear, youthful, inexperienced members, such as Knevet's own student William
Paston (that 'Yong hopefull sprigge'), can be ensconced in the middle, to be
schooled in military learning from the best available examples (*Poems*, p. 107).

But what of the social superiors, whose positions may be usurped by Shelton in this parade? Despite Charles's claim that these men were integrally
involved in military preparedness, the historical account of Norwich's militia tells a different story, since it had effectively collapsed during this period.
Anthony Fletcher outlines how the militia in the region was in a deplorable
state in the period 1625–8, following King Charles's accession, and links this
to the concurrent local failures in securing a portion of royal finances and the
subsequent ill-feelings that the Forced Loan and subsidies engendered in the

region.[10] While local authorities in other counties sought to gain advantage through their zeal to collect for the king, Norfolk's commissioners were more recalcitrant. Examples from studies of the successful collection of subsidies for Herefordshire in the period 1626–8 show, by comparison, a sharp decline of over thirty per cent in Norfolk during the same period, which is indicative of the obstructionist attitude adopted by some of the very same illustrious figures included in Knevet's poetic parade.[11] One dedicatee, Sir Hamon Le Strange, for example, stepped down as deputy lieutenant over the controversy; another, Sir John Heveningham, had been imprisoned for refusing to pay the Forced Loan and was one of five gentlemen who mounted a legal case against the king's summary imprisonment of those who resisted his prerogatives.[12] Even more pertinent to the publication of *Stratiotikon* and its assessment of the militia's activities in 1628 is the involvement of Sir John Hobart, who Knevet describes as '[s]ole master of your selfe, and pelfe [...]/ Which is a freedome among great men rare' (*Poems*, p. 103). Hobart had levelled accusations against some of his colleagues, alleging widespread bribe-taking from men seeking to avoid impressment overseas. One consequence of this corruption was a notable rise in criminality and disorder in the region, as those who paid such bribes had to source the money for them.[13] Conflict existed between city authorities and county deputies: the mayor of the city stood trial in 1626 for refusing to supply 2 ships of war; in July 1627, the city refused a demand by the deputy lieutenants for 25 men towards a county-wide levy of 250, sending instead only their required quota of 17. Furthermore, the issue of billeting 400 Irish soldiers in the county in 1628 led to further accusations of corruption against the deputy lieutenants – that they had levied more money than was required to meet their cost – at the July courts session, just one month before the militia exercise in Norwich.[14]

The office-holders addressed by Knevet in his prefatory poems may not have been directly involved in such cases, but it seems clear that – despite Charles's assessment of their integrity with regard to military preparedness in the region – some of them had overseen a period of sharp decline in militia activity and so were perhaps more worthy, albeit oblique, targets for the admonitory tone Knevet adopts. He is careful to direct more obvious criticism

---

[10] Anthony Fletcher, *Reform in the Provinces: The Government of Stuart England* (New Haven, 1986), pp. 282–316.

[11] Ian Atherton, *Ambition and Failure in Stuart England: The Career of John, first Viscount Scudamore* (Manchester, 1999), pp. 97–8, for tabulated comparisons of subsidy yields for Herefordshire, Norfolk and Cheshire in this period.

[12] Fletcher, *Reform*, pp. 297–300; Mark Kishlanksy, 'Tyranny Denied: Charles I, Attorney General Heath, and the Five Knights' Case', *Historical Journal* 42.1 (1999), 53–83.

[13] Fletcher, *Reform*, p. 304.

[14] Francis Blomefield, *An Essay towards a Topographical Study of Norfolk: History of Norwich*, ed. Charles Parkin (London, 1860), p. 373; Fletcher, *Reform*, p. 303.

in his address to subordinate members of the company, such as the newly promoted cavalry captain, William Bladwell:

> Joy be to thee, of thy new place (say I)
> That seem'st to affect noble cavalrie,
> A glory which Fraunce vaunts of, to our shame
> We are become so careless of our fame
> Some tripping Hackney, we had rather backe
> Or dastard race-horse, or some snafled Jacke,
> Then mount the praunsing Courser, by whose pride
> The Riders courage might be multipli'de.
> And yee our Knights have yee forgot your name
> Or do you willfully neglect your fame;
> Yee by your Spurres seeme to be Chevaliers
> But by your Steedes y'are Northern Borderers,
> Or some Heath-scourers, fitter farre to flie
> Then mannage combate 'gainst an enemie.
> O sleepe not still; least yee contend too late,
> Your honours from the dust to vindicate. (*Poems*, pp. 110–11)

The poem is worth considering in full, both for its subtle criticism of those
figures already mentioned as bearing responsibility for the militia's diminished
state, given that the new captain could hardly be responsible for the state of the
cavalry, and for what it tells us about Knevet's use of chivalric topoi – specifically, his use of the mounted fighting man as an emblem of military identity.[15]
(I will return to this latter component when considering *A Supplement of the
Faery Queene*.) Bladwell may not be the ultimate target of Knevet's ire here
and he serves as a proxy. Indeed, the problem of the poor provisioning of the
cavalry was a long-running and frustrating one in this period, and not just for
Norfolk.[16] By questioning the integrity of those who would assume the status
of knight, Knevet creates a deliberate blurring or indistinction between the use
of the term as a contemporary social rank, its symbolism as a referent of the
chivalric medieval image of the properly equipped mounted warrior, and its
place within the cultural memory as an emblem of superior English military
identity. In doing so, Knevet seeks to use Bladwell's appointment as an opportunity to attack the complacency behind particular aspects of the militia's
under-performance. Ultimately, neither such veiled attacks nor his appeal for

---

[15]   Bladwell's promotion helps to locate the printing of *Stratiotikon* as an event contemporaneous to its composition in 1628 as Bladwell was 'Captain of a troop of horse reviewed
by Sir Thomas Woodhouse on August 20, 1628' (*Poems*, p. 158).

[16]   Lindsay Boynton's account of the militia during Knevet's lifetime indicates that cavalry
strength had been a notable deficiency affecting the area muster since at least 1608: *The
Elizabethan Militia* (London, 1967), pp. 211, 251–5.

monthly exercises within the poem had any discernible effect on his intended audience. The situation deteriorated even further, as Anthony Fletcher notes:

> From August 1628 until the following autumn the militia in Norfolk barely existed. Cumulative pressures from the centre had turned the deputy lieuten-ants into the scapegoats of the county community. Since they felt there was no way they could break the deadlock between them and their fellow gentry and countrymen, they merely went through the motions of their office.[17]

For Knevet, the final objective of publishing such a carefully structured work focusing on militia preparation in the region is to establish himself as an authoritative voice that can speak for and represent local military identity in order to negotiate his way around his personal lack of military experience. He seeks to do so in several ways: (i) by positioning himself as a poet capable of epic subject-matter; (ii) by blurring the lines between social roles and soldierly personas; (iii) by associating himself with another distinctive and highly sig-nificant writer in the city possessing extensive military knowledge, John Cruso. It is unsurprising that Knevet would be so ambitious in relation to his potential epic reach, given that he undoubtedly had designs for – or may have already embarked upon – his 18,000-line, three-book continuation of Spenser's *Faerie Queene*. He notes the difficult social tensions that surround the soldier and his role in society when away from the battlefield, declaring to Shelton: 'Nor art thou lesse expert to live belov'd/ In Peace, then Warre'. Knevet's own sense of potential epic success is evident when addressing Shelton and his legacy:

> Had *Homer* (whom seven cities strove to owne)
>   Not beene: then who had great *Achilles* knowne
>   Or *Hector* in these times. Then let none blame
>   My Muse, although she beares a part with fame
>   In thy due praise. (*Poems*, p. 95)

Such bold ambitions aside, Knevet also employs more subtle strategies towards assuming a poetic voice capable of representing military identity in the region. A key element of this is how he works to reduce the distance between himself, other non-combatants, and the actual participants in the militia exercise, who are both his literary focus and part of his intended readership for *Stratiotikon*. We have already seen his disdainful treatment of knights who 'wilfuly neglect your fame'. Knevet further seeks to subvert social hierarchies when he addresses his supposed audience (the thirty-seven dedicatees of the prefatory poems) in his opening lines to the same: '(Kind Gentlemen) Souldiers, or Clarkes, *or both*/ My Muse as gentle greetes you well (in troth)' (*Poems*, p. 94, empha-sis mine). Though at first glance, while it may appear an inclusive address,

---

[17]   Fletcher, *Reform*, p. 304.

welcoming all readers of whatever social strata by constructing homogeneity amongst his audience, and thereby broadening the potential readership of the text, it is highly likely to serve a more particular purpose. While gentlemen of rank would undoubtedly take pride in the appellation of the term 'souldier', they would hardly be satisfied with the term 'clarke'. I would therefore argue that it is the 'or both' where Knevet's interest primarily lies, given the implicit and explicit criticisms of the upper ranks that follow in the prefatory poems and text of *Stratiotikon* itself. This initial line is an act of social levelling that is particularly important with regard to Knevet's conception of military identity, and the veracity of the construct of the citizen-soldier. With the criticisms contained in the text, as outlined above, this address takes on greater significance as it becomes a conscious ploy by Knevet to define and control his audience and thus position himself as an authoritative public voice on the literary presentation of military identity in the region.

John Cruso, the final figure in the column of dedicatees, is especially significant in Knevet's estimation, but it is somewhat surprising to note that it is not for any actual military experience in the Low Countries that Knevet lauds him, but rather his poetic judgement and capacity:

> Thou that art farre more worthy of the bayes,
> Daigne to assist my home-spunne untun'd layes
> With gracious censure, for upon thy tong,
> Depend the grace, and fortune of my song.
> So sharpe a wit, and judgement dwell in thee,
> *Apollo's* trees may grow else-where, then on
> Our greene *Parnassus*, or our *Helicon*. (*Poems*, p. 114)[18]

Four years after *Stratiotikon* appeared, Cruso published the first of five works on military tactics and instruction: *Militarie Instructions for the Cavallrie: or Rules and Directions for the Service of Horse Collected Out of Divers Forrain Authors Ancient and Modern, and Rectified and Supplied, According to the Present Practice of the Low-Country Warres* (1632).[19] Cruso capitalised on the evident marketplace for pragmatic native and translated military handbooks and instructional works, which had grown steadily from the late Elizabethan

---

[18] Charles describes Cruso's inclusion in the final position of Knevet's parade as being 'almost an afterthought' (*Poems*, p. 23), most probably due to the biographical error regarding authorship of the later military handbooks by Cruso. Ole Peter Grell, *Calvinist Exiles in Tudor and Stuart England* (Aldershot, 1996), p.72, corrects the previous misattribution of authorship of *Militarie Instructions* and subsequent works to Cruso's son of the same name.

[19] This manual was published by Roger Daniel, the Cambridge University printer, and reprinted by the same in 1644 due to increased interest in cavalry tactics during the Civil War.

period onwards. Lawrence notes that Cruso's first published work, focusing on contemporary and reformed cavalry tactics, is one of only two such texts to appear in English during this period out of approximately ninety texts in circulation.[20] We have already noted Knevet's interest in equestrian descriptions and the use of horses as mimetic figurings of their riders in his Bladwell poem. As we shall see, the use of the mounted fighting man is an important emblem of military identity informing the allegorical descriptions of horses in *A Supplement*.

Knevet's praise of Cruso as a poet, prior to his success in print, gives some indication of a discourse community that is intrinsically invested not only in the performance of the local militia, but also in the production of literature offered in support of the region's military identity. Cruso is lauded as a poet and an authority for Knevet, and serves as a ready example of Knevet's ideal for pan-European militant Protestantism that combined martial prowess with literary engagement. Such an ideal drew inextricably on the exemplar of the soldier-poet Sir Philip Sidney and was one that dominates Knevet's later works, particularly in his allegorical rendering of Gustavus Adolphus as the knight Callimachus in Book Eight of *A Supplement*. The crucial inspirational role of practical literature in support of military identity would be endorsed by Cruso himself, and is even elevated above the importance of authorship in his *Militarie Instructions*:

> If my annotations be displeasing to any, they may use them like country stiles, and step over them. To others they may serve to shew the truth of that assertion. That a meer practicall knowledge cannot make a perfect souldier: for had we not been beholding to books, the militarie art (in all likelihood) had been utterly obscured from our knowledge.[21]

This statement would reflect Knevet's own educational aim in *A Supplement* when he borrows from Horace to state that '[t]he end of writeing Bookes, should be rather to inform the understanding, then please the fancy [...] *Omne tulit punctum, qui miscuit utile dulci*' (*Supplement*, p. 43). It seems from the dedicatory poem that Knevet enjoyed some access to Cruso's own poetic compositions. Cruso's satirical treatment of radical religious figures in his commonplace book would certainly indicate a like-minded figure to the author of *Stratiotikon*,[22] whose next public presentation of military identity, *Rhodon and Iris*, would direct its strongest criticism against members of local authorities:

20 Lawrence, *Complete*, pp. 16–17. For analysis of *Militarie Instructions* and its significance: Lawrence, *Complete*, ch. 5; and Donagan, 'Halcyon Days', 81–3.
21 John Cruso, *Militarie Instructions* (London, 1632), sig. A3.
22 Cambridge, St John's College, MS 548 (U.26). On Cruso's non-military poetics: Christopher Joby, 'Classical and Early Modern Sources of the Poetry of Jan Cruso of Norwich (1592–fl.1655)', *International Journal of the Classical Tradition* 21.2 (2014), 89–120.

'that are so pure and sage/ That they doe utterly abhorre a Stage/ Because they would be still accounted holy/ And know, the Stage doth oft bewray their folly' (*Poems*, p. 173).

Though seemingly relatively innocuous, the threnody appended to the end of *Stratiotikon* is another useful paratextual signpost as to the intent of the work, and to Knevet's recurrent interest in military identity. He depicts Sir William Heydon as a ship 'new set afloate' and his demeanour in death is heroic: 'Disdaine was fix'd upon his brow/ As if he yeelding up his breath,/ Had scornd that fate which made him bow' (*Poems*, p. 147). That this is somewhat at odds with the ignominious nature of Heydon's actual death, where he was trampled by his own fleeing men and drowned while attempting to land at Île de Ré in 1627, is understandable given the prominence of the Heydon family in the county of Norfolk. His death as a 'yong sonne, untimely shent' is made representative of the loss of English Protestant militant youth in the expedition (*Poems*, p. 149). However, with the inclusion of the death of Sir John Burroughs, who was not a Norfolk man, Knevet politicises the text in a subtle but very significant way. Burroughs, the experienced man, whose advice to the expedition's leader, the duke of Buckingham, not to lay siege to the citadel was ignored, subsequently suffered a wound from the citadel artillery and died shortly afterwards.[23] As James Doelman examines, Burroughs's death became a subversive topic for coterie dissemination, with elegies circulating widely in manuscript.[24] By including him here in print, Knevet boldly positions his work as both a critique of local militia failures, as examined above, and as an indictment of the incompetence of leadership on a national level, which results in the wasteful deaths of paragons of military identity like Heydon and Burroughs.

Rhodon and Iris and the case for military intervention

The Privy Council edict of 1623 regarding the performance environment in Norwich was explicit in its requirement for the city corporation to maintain control over its manufacturing industries, and broad in its remit to curtail the activities of 'severall Companyes of Players Tumblers and the like', which were alleged to be 'more prejudicial to that Cytty more th[a]n other places'. The corporation, seeking to avoid disruption in the city 'wherein multitudes of people and familyes are set one work whoe [are] apt to bee drawne away from their

---

[23]   Mark Charles Fissel, *English Warfare, 1511–1642* (London, 2001), p. 265.
[24]   James Doelman, "'Not as the mourning of some private fate": John Earle's Funeral Elegy on Sir John Burroughs', *ELR* 41 (2011), 485–502. Doelman notes over twenty-five extant witness manuscript versions of the text to attest to its widely circulated, yet clandestine nature; the text was not printed until 1656.

labour and business by [the players] occassions', seemed particularly zealous in their application of the power granted in the edict, which 'authorise and require you not to suffer any Companyes of players Tumblers or the like sorte of persons to acte any playes or shew or exercise any other feates and devices within that Cyttye'.[25] David Galloway notes the dearth of recorded public performances in Norwich for this period, and the performance of *Rhodon and Iris* for the Florists' Festival on 3 May 1631 is the only event for which we have an extant witness.[26] Records certainly suggest that some performances were permitted, but many visiting players were more likely to appear in the Mayors' Court records for punishment and expulsion than in the Chamberlains' accounts for payment, as letters and licences from the Master of Revels' office were ignored and players were even paid not to perform.[27]

It seems unusual, then, that an occasional play in a city that actively regulated dramatic performance should have received so little critical interest. Early studies focused primarily on failures of generic expectation and structural deficiencies that this self-declared 'Pastorall' displayed.[28] Amy Charles declared it 'primarily a masque with a few external characteristics of the pastoral' in her edition (*Poems*, p. 31). She echoed previous critics' complaints when noting that Knevet's characters in the text 'though they were devotees of Flora, he called them not gardeners but shepherds and shepherdesses', and that Knevet further confounds definition of the play by locating it in Thessaly. Many of the interpretative cruces of the play regarding its plot and Knevet's motives can be solved by once again considering his political viewpoint and consistent focus on the promotion of native military identity. Knevet had already begun *A Supplement* at this point, though *Rhodon and Iris* represents a crucial development in his public poetic persona and a necessary demonstration of his capacity in the initial phase of the Virgilian (and Spenserian) *cursus*: allegorical pastoral.[29] Knevet draws heavily upon contemporary masque forms, but also displays an evident familiarity with how the pastoral genre had become a poetic mode of dissent and withdrawal in the 1610s and 20s but had been subsequently

---

[25] David Galloway, ed., *Records of Early English Drama: Norwich: 1540–1642* (Toronto, 1984), p. 187.

[26] Galloway, *Records*, p. xxxi, notes that evidence for *Rhodon and Iris* is entirely self-contained with the printed text.

[27] Galloway, *Records*, p. xxxiv. Richard Dutton, *Mastering the Revels: The Regulation and Censorship of English Renaissance Drama* (Basingstoke, 1991), pp. 235–6.

[28] See Homer Smith's 'Pastoral Influence in the English Drama', *PMLA* 12.3 (1897), 355–460; W.W. Greg, *Pastoral Poetry and Pastoral Drama* (Oxford, 1906), pp. 327–9. For a more comprehensive guide to the evolution of Renaissance pastoral in the context of *Rhodon and Iris*: Sukhanta Chaudhuri, *Renaissance Pastoral and its English Developments* (New York, 1989), pp. 369–75.

[29] C. Bowie Millican, 'Ralph Knevet, Author of the *Supplement* to Spenser's *Faerie Queene*', *RES* 14.53 (1938), 44–52.

reabsorbed into popular and court culture.[30] Given Knevet's propensity for appropriation, the 1629 re-publication of John Fletcher's *The Faithfull Shepherdess* is particularly noteworthy as it might address Charles's concerns over Knevet's choices of location and style. Also set around shepherds in Thessaly, it was first performed in 1608, published in 1610 and subsequently performed for Henrietta Maria in 1634. The 1629 volume, however, was prefaced by poems from Ben Jonson and George Chapman, which insisted that the re-mediation of the text in print would dispel the poor initial reception of Fletcher's performed work and reveal the genius in the text. There was evidently a case to be made for the continued relevance of pastoral drama in this period.

There are two core issues in *Rhodon and Iris* that make it especially significant for the discussion of how the author continues to connect his local community with international military affairs: (i) Knevet's satirical treatment of local figures, whom he depicts as falsely obtaining military rank; and (ii) his allegorical rendering of the political and religious conflict of the Thirty Years War. Charles points to the first, localised reason as the motivation for the rapid appearance of the work in print, citing its irregular rhyming scheme and structure as indicative of a rushed response to apparent criticism levelled against the performance in Norwich (*Poems*, pp. 36–7).[31] While this reason is undoubtedly significant, it does not take into account the rather unusual printing conditions of *Rhodon and Iris*, which was produced in two distinct editions for sale in Norwich and London.[32] Its author (or printer) evidently thought that the text would sell beyond the local marketplace.[33] I would argue,

---

[30]   On changes in pastoral production and meaning in this period: Michelle O'Callaghan, 'The Shepheards Nation': Jacobean Spenserians and Early Stuart Political Culture, 1612– 1625 (Oxford, 2000), pp. 188–230; David Norbrook, *Poetry and Politics in the English Renaissance* (Oxford, 2002), pp. 172–98. See also Leah Marcus, 'Politics and Pastoral: Writing the Court on the Countryside', *Culture and Politics in Early Stuart England*, ed. Kevin Sharpe and Peter Lake (Basingstoke, 1994), pp. 139–59. Eliza Fisher Laskowski, 'Performance, Politics, and Religion: Reconstructing Seventeenth-Century Masque, unpublished Ph.D. thesis (University of North Carolina, 2006), examines the variety to be found in masque production at this time, and further contextualises Norfolk performance spaces by considering the later masque performed at the Paston home in Oxnead, John Cayworth's *Enchiridion Christiados* (1637).

[31]   Performed on 3 May 1631, the text appears in the Stationers' Register for 12 November 1631 as 'a Booke called a fflora show at Norwich': Edward Arber, ed., *A Transcript of the Registers of the Company of Stationers of London, 1554–1640*, 5 vols. (London, 1875–94), 4: 230.

[32]   The play is one of only two such dual imprints in Norwich in this period; the other, Alexander Neville's *Norfolk Furies*, trans. Richard Woods (1615), is a text with regional and national significance in its depiction of Kett's rebellion (printed for Edmund Casson and reprinted in 1623).

[33]   Identical other than the frontispieces, the Norwich text is marked for sale by 'E. Causson' or Edmund Casson, a local bookseller and head of the city's short-lived Guild of Stationers in 1622–3. The texts are printed by M. Sparke, most likely the son of the

however, that the play is noteworthy both within the context of contemporary responses to the crisis facing the Protestant faith on the continent, and in its relation to Knevet's continued preoccupation with military identity and his own role as a commentator on martial affairs.

As befits the occasion of its performance, the play features a number of characters named after flowers: the shepherds, Rhodon and Acanthus, who begin by discoursing on the nature of love; Iris, Rhodon's object of affection, for whom he has set aside his previous pursuit of Eglantine; and Violetta, Rhodon's sister who has been mistreated and dispossessed by Martagon and Cynosbatus. A subplot includes the malicious figures of Poneria and Agnostus, who are allegorical representations of wilful malice and ignorance. The text, which begins with theories of love, quickly descends into romance of near farcical levels as disguises are assumed and dropped, providential cures for poisoning are presented, and Rhodon and Acanthus become entangled in a conflict with Martagon and Cynosbatus in order to rescue Violetta. The play relies on the omnipotent figure of Flora, who abruptly ends the impending battle in the final scene in a unilateral fashion, enforcing the amicable resolution of the tension through presenting uncontested decrees to the characters.

The parodic portrayal of a young lawyer in the subplot character of Agnostus as a 'villain under a Scarlet Gowne' may well indicate the local application of the play and the cause of the antipathy that the work itself suggests. Knevet highlights that his reason for printing *Rhodon and Iris* was local misunderstanding of the text, and this extends far beyond personal insult, intended or otherwise:

> These [detractors], out of their malicious discretion [...] by mere misprisions, and under pretense that I should abuse a Corporation, would faine engage me in your Cities hatred [...] But whereas they accuse me for taxing of some private persons, I am contente to referre this controversye to the arbitrement of any that is ingenious. (*Poems*, p. 173)

Agnostus, who acts as a malicious but stupid and easily manipulated anti-masque character, is rewarded with the rank of Colonel for his efforts to undermine Rhodon as he prepares for conflict with Martagon. Similarly, the character of Gladiolus, the servant of Rhodon's previous love, Eglantine, whose only dramatic function is to berate female characters for the controversial act of wearing make-up, is instantly conferred the rank of Captain for simply acting as a messenger (*Poems*, p. 236). In this way, we begin to see how Knevet has continued his focus on military identity and its relationship to local authority. These unearned promotions are indicative of Knevet's disdain

---

Michael Sparke who would shortly attract the attention of the authorities for perceived veiled insults of Henrietta Maria in the publication of *Histriomastix* (1633).

for those who hold rank without experience or demonstrable intelligence, and his vitriolic portrayal of those who might fit that description in local authority is evident in his theatrical enrobing of Agnostus in the gown of office 'like the main stud of a Corporation', where Agnostus questions his colleague Poneria on the nature of leadership:

> *Agnostus*: How heavy is the burden of authority
> *Poneria*: 'Tis true, authority is heavy, I confesse
> But not so heavy that an Asse may bear't. (*Poems*, p. 197)

Of perhaps greater significance, and potentially the cause for Knevet rushing the work to print, may be the structure of political and contextual allusions underpinning the work concerning the Protestant faith and the need for military intervention on the continent – an aspect of the play that has been overlooked to date. The political urgency and topicality of this kind of interpretation of *Rhodon and Iris* would have been intensified all the more by current events in continental Europe, in particular the brutal siege and sacking of Magdeburg that took place during the very same week in which the play was first performed.[34] In the play, Rhodon, the central character, must delay his union with Iris until he rescues Violetta, his sister, from the oppression of Martagon. His cautious attitude towards this action and his reluctance to adopt a military approach to resolving the issue can be read as an allegorical depiction of King Charles and his reluctance to be more actively involved in European affairs, especially in the case of the Palatinate and the cause of his sister, Elizabeth of Bohemia, wife of the exiled Elector Frederick V. Furthermore, the oppositional pairing of Martagon and Cynobastus as the Catholic faith and Philip IV of Spain respectively is supported by Rhodon's setting aside of Eglantine, his former lover and Cynosbatus' relative, in careful reversal of his initial expressions in praise of passionate chivalric love. Eglantine represents the Spanish Infanta and Knevet, like many authors of the period, attempts to retrospectively excuse and negotiate the chaotic episode surrounding the Spanish Match of 1623 in Rhodon's depiction of Eglantine and his love for her:

> Whose rare endowments both of art and nature
>   Well corresponding with high birth and fortune,
>   Did moderately attract my sincere love,
>   Which love conspiring with a strong desire,
>   To see the Customes of some forraine Nations,
>   And know the manners of people farre remote,

---

[34] Peter H. Wilson, *Europe's Tragedy: A New History of the Thirty Years War* (London, 2009), pp. 467–70.

> Made me to greet the Princely Dame
> With a personal visitation. (*Poems*, pp. 182–3)[35]

The martial tone of Knevet's pastoral is also reflected in its use of music, which is almost exclusively employed in military situations in the play. Acanthus's description of Rhodon's massed forces and the 'splendour of their glistering armes' emphasises the 'bellowing drums and trumpets shrill'; the false military man Agnostus is captured and exposed, followed immediately by the stage direction 'Drum beats a march within'; and, finally, 'Musicke sound', following Rhodon's eventual declaration of martial righteousness and identity when confronting Martagon: 'For *Violettas* sake I took up armes,/ Whom thou unjustly has opprest' (*Poems*, pp. 217, 239–40).

Resolution in the play is only possible through the direct intervention of Flora, whose unilateral pronouncements obviate the need for any further dramatic action. In this way, Knevet adapts the contemporary masque form in order to propose that the adoption of a military role and commitment to act in the name of the Protestant cause will result almost instantaneously in success. The justice of Rhodon's cause would appear to win the day before the floral armies clash. In terms of our interest in military identities, it is significant to note that the only figures to suffer the true punishment of exile are Poneria and Agnostus, the anti-masque or subplot figures, who employed disguises and assumed false military identities to mislead both sides and foment unrest. Taken as a whole, the play demonstrates again the depth of Knevet's concerns with English involvement in international military affairs, and his commitment to articulating such concerns to both a local and national book-buying audience.

Chivalric romance and Stuart military identities

Described as a 'pastiche of Spenser' and as a text that 'inevitably disappoints any reader expecting Spenser's larger reach', Knevet's unpublished three-book *A Supplement of the Faery Queene* uses the concept of military identity to provide an overarching explanatory framework that has yet to be fully recognised by critics.[36] Designed to follow Spenser's original six books, the *Supplement's*

---

[35]   On the political implications and reception of the proposed marriage: Glyn Redworth, *The Prince and the Infanta: The Cultural Politics of the Spanish Match* (New Haven and London, 2003). On the efforts of royal panegyrists to negotiate the failed marriage after Charles's actual marriage in 1625: Karen Britland, 'A Fairy-tale Marriage: Charles I and Henrietta Maria's Romance', *The Spanish Match: Prince Charles's Journey to Madrid, 1623*, ed. Alexander Samson (Aldershot, 2006), pp. 123–38.

[36]   R.M. Cummings, *Edmund Spenser: The Critical Heritage* (London, 1995), pp. 170–1; Fowler, 'Ralph Knevet'. For a recent introduction to Knevet's poem: *Supplement*, pp. 10–27.

first book, Book Seven, depicts the virtue of Prudence in the character Albanio; the knight, Callimachus, represents Fortitude in Book Eight; while the characters of Gratian and Belcouer exemplify the concept of Liberality in Book Nine. The action of each book is connected, as it is in *The Faerie Queene*, by the interventions of Arthur. Knevet further connects his work to revived contemporary interest in chivalric literary tropes and figures at the Caroline court by dedicating his work in the proems to each book to King Charles, to whom he states: 'Thou sittest in Arthur's seate, and dost maintaine/ The antique glory of the Britons strong' (*Supplement*, p. 47).[37] The overall allegorical framework of Knevet's *Supplement* requires careful interpretation, but once again the author's preoccupation with military identity and contemporary conflicts in Europe provide a key. Knevet directs his work as an instructional manual on military identity and kingship to Charles by first exposing and degrading James I's failings as a chivalric figure represented through Albanio in Book Seven, who literally un-mans himself in terms of military prowess. In Book Eight, Knevet focuses on Callimachus, a knight who represents the virtue of Fortitude and operates as an allegorical rendering of Gustavus Adolphus. In Book Nine, Knevet considers the state of knighthood and poetic arts through Belcouer and Gratian, who come to represent different positive aspects of Charles's own martial capacities.

Albanio's chivalric reduction is self-inflicted. He clearly talks himself into an enfeebled and effeminate state (*Supplement*, pp. 85–6). And unlike the redemption that Spenser's Artegall receives, after undergoing similar challenges with enforced effeminisation at Radigund's hands,[38] Albanio's eventual re-education at the intervention of Arthur at the end of the Book is in no way indicative of his assumption of his assigned virtue of Prudence or wisdom. As mentioned earlier, the trope of the mounted warrior – present in Knevet's work as an allegorical figure for worth and character – is most readily appreciated here. As Albanio's chivalric identity and martial appearance implodes, his named steed, Dracontes, changes dramatically from a mighty 'courser' to a humble 'palfrey' as the text continues to demonstrate his unsuitability and lack of integrity in terms of military identity (*Supplement*, p. 86).[39] In the

---

[37] On the significance of chivalric symbolism at court: Richard Cust, 'Charles I and the Order of the Garter', *JBS* 52.2 (2013), 343–69. Charles, for example, commissions Peter Heylyn to write a re-edifying history of that most chivalric figure of romance military identity, St George: *The Historie of that Most Famous Saint and Souldier of Christ Jesus, St George of Cappadochia* (London, 1633).
[38] See John Henry Adams, 'Assembling Radigund and Artegall: Gender Identities in *The Faerie Queene*', *Early Modern Literary Studies* 18.1 (2015).
[39] 'Hee full of disdaine/ Mounts his proud *Palfrey*, leaving her behind' (*Supplement*, p. 88). On the signification of horses in this period: Peter Edwards, *Horse and Man in Early Modern England* (London, 2007); Kevin De Ornellas, *The Horse in Early Modern English Culture: Bridled, Curbed and Tamed* (Madison, 2013).

Supplement, as in *Stratiotikon*, the horse is a symbol of military preparedness and a reflection of the character's military identity. However, it can also be employed to characterise the state's failure to provision and support those that are capable of taking righteous action and displaying true military identity. As a clear example of the latter, Knevet's criticism of the lack of support for Sir Horace Vere and his under-resourced expeditionary force of 1620–1, which suffered defeat at Mannheim, is reflected in his depiction of Corleon in Book Eight, defeated in chivalric combat 'through the fault of his Vallets perchance/ Who had his horse not well accoutered' (*Supplement*, p. 120).

Knevet's allegorical representation of Gustavus Adolphus in the character of Callimachus as the exemplar both for the tripartite framework of the text and for Charles himself is as likely a cause for the lack of a contemporary printing of *A Supplement* as England's vacillating policies regarding Spain in this period.[40] The suppression of news regarding the Swedish king's successes in defence of the Protestant faith is a significant contextual element that exposes the potential dangers of authoring a long, politically laden epic in the fast-moving evolving news culture that had developed significantly since Spenser's day.[41] In Book Eight, Knevet consciously sets aside the singular combat characteristic of the genre with which he works to move toward representations of modern warfare involving massed forces. Of particular significance is Book Eight's initial conflict, in which Callimachus intervenes on behalf of the young untested character of Sir Tendron, who comes (briefly) to represent the state of the English Protestant youth. Callimachus castigates Tendron for his lack of preparation and failure to adopt a proper military identity:

> How happens it that in thy youthful age,
> When now thy limbes with vigour are supplide,
> That thou rid'st not not in warlike equipage,
> But looks't like one fitt for a scenicke stage? (*Supplement*, p. 106)

Callimachus knights and attempts to re-educate the wayward youth in martial discipline but Tendron is almost immediately killed in an ambush (*Supplement*, p. 112). Subsequently, Callimachus can be seen to be under a similar threat of the implosion of his military identity as that experienced by Albanio in Book Seven, although he casts aside his chivalric trappings through righteous anger rather than weakness: 'His [Tendron] fall did so Callimachus incense/ That desp'rately he threw away his shield/ Reckles of deadly danger, or defence' (*Supplement*, p. 112).

---

[40] Norbrook, *Poetry*, p. 206.
[41] The suppression order issued by Charles on 17 October 1632, shortly before Gustavus Adolphus's death at Lützen that November, focused particularly on the circulation of *The Swedish Intelligencer*. On literary uses of Adolphus as a 'political gesture of disapprobation and defiance': McKeown, 'Reception', pp. 200–20.

Though far less complete a degradation than that suffered by Albanio, Calli-machus also requires the intervention of Arthur as well as a period of recovery in the House of Panarete. Callimachus demonstrates the supplementarity of Knevet's text in his recovery, when he recounts, when called upon, the tales of *The Faerie Queene*: the deeds 'of Arthegall, Sir Guyon, and faire Britomart/ Eke of Sir Calidore he mention made/ Who whilome did the Blatant Beast enthrall' (*Supplement*, p. 115). He becomes inspired by his own telling of the Redcrosse Knight's story and sees the opportunity to seize his mantle as a paragon of the Protestant faith. In effect, *The Faerie Queene*, which Knevet seeks to extend with his books, is offered as an historical and prophetic source for the allegor-ical actions on which Callimachus/ Gustavus Adolphus is about to embark.

The palimpsestic relationship, revolving around native military identity, between Knevet and Spenser, between Callimachus and Redcrosse, and between the lamentable state of English military identity and the actions of Gustavus Adolphus, is the central element of Knevet's *Supplement*. Through extensive allegorical positioning, he aligns with contemporary war-reporting from the continent to treat Gustavus Adolphus as 'an honorary Englishman'.[42] In doing so, he completes a chiliastic depiction of the Swedish king, who is soon to die for the cause, by offering the death of English youth as a primary motive for his actions. Crucially for Knevet, who must negotiate his own lack of practical military identity, it is literature, specifically native English romance-epic, that 'informs the understanding' and inspires such actions in defence of the Protestant faith. Akin to Arthur and Guyon's transformative experience of reading the British and Elfin histories at the House of Alma,[43] it is Callimachus's knowledge of, and act of reading aloud the 'histories' of *The Faerie Queene* that leads him to glory:

> So did Callimachus in heart retaine
> Those trophyes, which the Redcrosse Knight did weare,
> An equall meede resolving to obtaine,
> Or by his hideous foe to bee subdue'd, and slaine. (*Supplement*, p. 116)

This chapter has demonstrated how Knevet's sustained interest in military affairs and military identity specifically provides a means of explaining and understanding his most significant literary works. It has shown too how mil-itary identity can be articulated in relation to local civic and regional com-munities, and how the local and regional forms a part of the wider political discourse concerning the martial ideals and shortcomings of the Stuart state during the 1620s and 30s. The chapter also returns us to that much-discussed contemporary controversy regarding whether someone without experience

---

[42] McKeown, 'Reception', p. 206.
[43] Edmund Spenser, *The Faerie Queene*, ed. A.C. Hamilton (London, 2001), II.ix.

of combat possessed the requisite knowledge to write authoritatively of military matters.[44] Knevet's works consistently and convincingly show that they could. While avoiding a teleological narrative in relation to the Civil War, it is also important to note that Knevet's writing largely ceases after the 1630s. He accompanied Paston to Europe in 1638, avoided any form of military employment and then returned to Lyng in rural Norfolk to serve the church there until his death in 1671. His only writing that may have come from this later period is his accomplished holograph emulation of George Herbert's *The Temple* (1633). In that work Knevet sets aside advocacy for early modern military identities in the public sphere in favour of a private focus on militancy of the soul.

[44] See Webb, *Elizabethan*, pp. 17–50; Lawrence, *Complete*, pp. 216–29.

4

Thomas, First Lord Fairfax and 'The Highway to Heidelberg'

PHILIP MAJOR

I

The writings of the celebrated parliamentarian general, Thomas, third Lord Fairfax (1612–71), which include Psalm translations, poems, epigrams, a translation of Vegetius, and a treatise on horse-breeding, have come under belated scrutiny in recent years.[1] Nearly all of these works are attributed to the period after Fairfax's retirement as commander-in-chief of parliamentarian forces in June 1650, and further contextualize the earlier literary accomplishments of the Fairfax family, such as the lavishly praised translation of Tasso's *Gerusalemme Liberata* by Thomas's great uncle, Edward Fairfax (1580?–1635). Yet hitherto, scant scholarly discussion has taken place on a substantial unpublished work by the *first* Baron Fairfax, Thomas (1560–1640), grandfather to the general. This Fairfax served in Queen Elizabeth's reign as a soldier in the Low Countries and on diplomatic missions to the future James I. He reputedly ruled his Yorkshire estate, and oversaw his grandson's upbringing, with military precision. Two of his sons were killed defending the Palatinate in 1621. 'The Highway to Heidelberg', a 15,000-word manuscript treatise written in the mid-1620s, was the literary undertaking into which his resulting grief was channelled.[2] Principally, it argues the ways and means for the European Protestant powers to attack a recrudescent expansionist Spain in America, but it is also vitally concerned with family military identity: with cementing the Fairfaxes' reputation as one of the most notable godly military families in England. In this chapter I explore the religious, political and literary-historical context of 'The Highway', its relationship to the military conflict from which

---

[1]   See Andrew Hopper, *'Black Tom': Sir Thomas Fairfax and the English Revolution* (Manchester, 2007); Andrew Hopper and Philip Major, eds., *'England's Fortress': New Perspectives on Thomas, Third Lord Fairfax* (Farnham, 2014); Philip Major, *The Writings of Thomas, Third Lord Fairfax* (Manchester, forthcoming).

[2]   BL, Add. MS 28326. All quotations from the treatise are taken from this manuscript, with page numbers included parenthetically in the text.

its title derives, and the martial tropes of honour with which it is infused. I show that although the treatise is influenced by the local and the familial, its scope is self-consciously ambitious. In places it resembles the early modern military memoir in eschewing autobiography. It does so, however, not simply for stylistic reasons, but to more convincingly inform contemporary debate on geopolitical decision-making.

II

The version of 'The Highway to Heidelberg' held by the British Library is a forty-eight-page folio autograph manuscript complete with a title page, and bearing Fairfax's signature. Given its minimal number of insertions and revisions, it is almost certainly the original copy. There are two fair copies containing numerous amendments, both of which are in the possession of the current Lord Fairfax. One of these, running to 136 quarto pages, is, like the original, in Fairfax's autograph; the other, at 65 folio pages, is in a Secretary hand.[3] The manuscript has never been published. 'The Highway' belongs to the genre of English literary responses to the Thirty Years War (1618–48), a subject which has received much critical attention in recent decades, though almost entirely with regard to print rather than manuscript sources.[4] The Palatinate was the capital of the German dominion ruled by the Elector Frederick V, son-in-law (through his marriage to Princess Elizabeth) to James VI and I. When it was overrun by Spanish Habsburg forces under Don Ambrogio Spinola in the early 1620s, it became both a strategic and symbolic focus of the newly energised Protestant cause. Undated, the particular moment of Fairfax's treatise is likely to be the collapse of negotiations on the Spanish Match, when in the summer of 1624 Parliament was at last given licence by the king to debate foreign affairs.[5] Charles and the duke of Buckingham were now adopting a militaristic stance towards the Spanish, at last aligning the court's position with that of the majority of the godly in the House of Commons. With the German commander Ernst, Count Mansfeld feted in London as he sought money and

---

[3] I am grateful to the present peer for granting me access to these manuscripts.

[4] See, for example, David Coast, *News and Rumour in Jacobean England: Information, Court Politics and Diplomacy, 1618–25* (Manchester, 2014); Jayne E.E. Boys, *London's News Press and the Thirty Years War* (Woodbridge, 2011); David R. Lawrence, *The Complete Soldier: Military Books and Military Culture in Early Stuart England, 1603–1645* (Leiden, 2009).

[5] This was the proposed marriage between the Infanta and Prince Charles through which James hoped to extend his irenic policy towards Spain; see Glyn Redworth, *The Prince and the Infanta: The Cultural Politics of the Spanish Match* (New Haven and London, 2003), pp. 120–33; Alexander Samson, ed., *The Spanish Match: Prince Charles' Journey to Madrid, 1623* (Aldershot, 2006).

men for an armed campaign against Spain, the 'blessed revolution' in English foreign policy was underway.[6]

Pre-existing military identity played an important role in literary responses advocating recovery of the Palatinate. Fairfax had already fought for the Protestant cause in the Dutch wars, captaining a troop of lancers under the earl of Leicester in 1585–86. As with countless veterans, it was a family commitment: his younger brother Charles had served under Sir Horace Vere and Sir John Ogle at Nieuwpoort in 1600, before being killed at Ostend.[7] Thomas's funerary monument, in the south transept of Otley Parish Church in Yorkshire, commemorates in Latin the Elizabethan martial achievements of a man 'who, after he had discharged the various duties of war among the French, Germans and the Dutch, obtained his dismission from this warfare of troubles'.[8] Other veterans of earlier campaigns, such as Secretary of State Edward Conway, were also to the fore in espousing military solutions to the current crisis.[9] Thus the emergence of a public sphere of debate and discussion in England, catalysed by events in Germany, was influenced by the perspective of men who had already seen active service against Spanish Habsburg forces on mainland Europe.

Fairfax's sons, John and William, had recently served with distinction among the English volunteers in Germany. His friend, Edmund, Lord Sheffield, President of the Council of the North, informed him that the service of one of them had come to the attention of the court: '[T]he worthy carriage of your son hath been much observed, and is here reported to his great applause and commendation'.[10] In 1620, Fairfax briefly visited his sons' camp on their way to the Palatinate, before returning home due to his wife's death. According to William, he was 'received here with very great respect; the memory of his former actions, as well in these parts as in France, being the chiefest cause thereof'. The 'white-headed' old soldier evidently relished his cameo: he had 'grown forty years younger than he was before' and 'was never in better disposition'. Nor, it seems, was his visit purely one of moral support: he had 'provided himself of horse and arms, and all other necessaries'.[11]

---

[6]   Simon Healy has speculated that the treatise may have been drafted at the request of Viscount Doncaster, earl of Carlisle, a strong supporter of Mansfeld: 'Thomas Fairfax (1560–1640)', *The History of Parliament: The House of Commons 1604–1629*, ed. Andrew Thrush and John P. Ferris. 5 vols. (Cambridge, 2010), 4: 218–22.

[7]   Clements R. Markham, *A Life of the Great Lord Fairfax* (London, 1870), p. 5.

[8]   Harry Speight, *Upper Wharfedale [...] from Otley to Langstrothdale* (London, 1900), p. 65.

[9]   Thomas Cogswell, *The Blessed Revolution: English Politics and the Coming of War, 1621–1624* (Cambridge, 1989), pp. 69–76.

[10] George W. Johnson, ed., *The Fairfax Correspondence: Memoirs of the Reign of Charles I*, 2 vols. (London, 1848), 1: xlv.

[11] Ibid., 1: xxxvi–xxxvii.

News of his sons' being killed in action at Frankenthal in 1621 was broken to Fairfax by the sergeant-major general of the English regiment in the Palatinate, Sir John Burroughs: '[D]uring the siege of this place, it pleased God to dispose your two sons, I doubt not, to a far better dwelling.' They 'had died with a general fame of honest men and valiant gentlemen'. And West Riding neighbour, Henry, Lord Clifford 'never took pen in [his] hand with more grief' than in 'declaring the death of your valiant and brave sons', whose 'never-dying virtues of valour and Christianity came to them by descent from your Christian and valiant self'.[12] The 'Analecta Fairfaxiana', a compendium of family history compiled by Fairfax's antiquarian youngest son Charles (1597–1673), records the Latin inscription commemorating their lives in the Dutch church at Frankenthal, beginning

IN GRATISSIMAM MEMORIAM
DNI GENEROSI GVLIELMI FAIRFAX,
ANGLO BRITTANI, HONORATISSIMI DNI
DE THO: FAIRFAX DE DENTON[13]

When Fairfax pens 'The Highway', then, he does so with personal and poignant familial experience of combatting the Spanish Habsburgs. Accordingly, it cannot be viewed as an abstract literary exercise, but rather as a deeply personal contribution to a debate in which an increasingly literate public was immersed.

At the same time there is also an important cultural motivation for writing the treatise. The 'Analecta Fairfaxiana' records in detail the status and attainments of generations of Fairfaxes, witnessed in the illustrious genealogy of its various branches, its coats of arms and, not least, its literary achievements. 'The Highway' is deemed eminently worthy of inclusion, appearing, with a synopsis, first on a list of Fairfax's compositions (all of them unpublished), which also includes works on local militias, household matters and horse-breeding.[14] The literary acumen of its soldiers was an important component in building and enhancing the early modern military family's reputation. But the reason for the pre-eminence of 'The Highway' in the 'Analecta' is not only formal and thematic – based on its impressive length and the breadth of subject matter – but its intended readership. In a preface found elsewhere in the Fairfax papers there is evidence that it was addressed to 'the sacred majestie of kings Princes of States to whom the greatness of Spain is or may be dangerous', with the

---

12   Ibid., 1: xlviii–xlix.
13   Leeds, Brotherton Library, MS Yorks 1, 'Analecta Fairfaxiana', fol. 128v.
14   Leeds, Brotherton Library, MS Yorks 2, 'Analecta Fairfaxiana', fol. 187r. Doubtless with Fairfax family prestige in mind, the synopsis accentuates the wide purview and relevance of the work: its 'Argument beinge the present state of Christendome' and 'How the estate of Spaine has growne in few yeares from a Molehill to a Mountain'.

immediate recipient James, Fairfax's 'Dread Souvraigne' and 'most mighty prince of Great Brittain'.[15]

There is no proof that the king received the treatise. However, that he was even the proposed reader signals a striking confidence and ambition in the author. The national and international military crisis of the Palatinate gave rise to deeply held feelings of pan-European Protestantism; yet it also provided opportunities for self-advancement, not only through military service but via literary intervention. In the preface, there is of course the conventional disclaimer: Fairfax beseeches the king to 'vouchsafe this pore present, and though I am not ignorant that it discords my presumption and weakness in handling soe great a subject yet it manifesteth my dutie and humble affection to your service. And love covereth a multitude of sins.'[16] Nevertheless, Fairfax was a man pushing the boundaries of kingly favour and familial kudos, emboldened by previous assistance rendered to the king, to whom he had been sent by Elizabeth on successful diplomatic missions in 1589, 1590 and 1593. In this context of assiduous self-promotion, it is instructive that within a few years of composing 'The Highway' Fairfax had acquired (for £1,500) a Scottish barony, becoming in 1627 the first Lord Fairfax of Cameron.

The position of the gentry in Yorkshire in the 1620s shows how local factors combined with national and international to form the backdrop to the treatise. By the 1620s, the nobility of England's largest county had, following the Wars of the Roses and the suppression of the Northern Rebellion, long since relinquished its old feudal power. The apparent military demise of the aristocracy (and by extension the gentry) meant that its status increasingly derived from social standing, wealth, court connections and office-holding.[17] An increased emphasis on the value of education, which saw a large number of grammar schools founded and endowed in Yorkshire, was one of the important results. There was a military angle to this too, and younger sons sent abroad to gain martial experience studied a variety of topics. Thomas Fairfax, the parliamentarian general, obeyed his grandfather's instructions by going into the Low Countries, like generations of British soldiers before him.[18] At Dordrecht, he

[15] Bodleian, MS Clarendon 34, fols. 7r–v. 'The Highway' was the first but not the last occasion on which Fairfax proffered written advice to a Stuart. In 1633, he dedicated an eighty-five-page folio manuscript to James Stuart, duke of Lennox, on the 'Discourse of Court and Courtiers'; see Hopper, *'Black Tom'*, p. 15.

[16] MS Clarendon 34, fol. 7v.

[17] J.T. Cliffe, *The Yorkshire Gentry: From the Reformation to the Civil War* (London, 1969), p. 3.

[18] Hugh Dunthorne, *Britain and the Dutch Revolt 1560–1700* (Cambridge, 2013), p. xv; Roger B. Manning, *An Apprenticeship in Arms: The Origins of the British Army 1585–1702* (Oxford, 2006), pp. 24–40.

learned skills in arms, fencing, dancing and mathematics.[19] With renewed alacrity many members of the Yorkshire gentry took up their pens. Family histories, diaries, prose pamphlets and poetry sprang forth.[20] Inevitably a sense of literary competition resulted, both within and between Yorkshire families competing for prestige. The Saviles of Bradley and Methley produced three brothers of erudition. The best-known, Sir Henry, translated Tacitus. Another, Sir John Savile, was a founder member of the Society of Antiquaries and a companion of William Camden. This was the Savile to whom Fairfax was bitterly opposed in the elections to Parliament of 1620 and 1624, and one can reasonably infer that political rivalry spilled over into academic. With a large group of Yorkshire gentry jostling for social status, and knighthoods in Yorkshire scarcely a rare commodity, an even greater premium than usual was placed on elevation to the peerage.[21]

As already indicated, however, a stronger accent on cultural achievement within the Yorkshire gentry in the 1620s did not mean that the pen now eclipsed the sword; rather, there was complementarity. The remilitarization of the English peerage in the decades before the English Civil Wars featured men, like Fairfax, who had seen active service on the continent, an experience which brought them into close contact with European, particularly French, martial values.[22] This in turn heralded a rediscovery of military heritage in the early seventeenth century: rechivalrization went hand in hand with remilitarization. Evidenced by the growing number of heraldic visitations in Yorkshire, there was a heightened interest in lineage, blood, pedigree, coats of arms and gene-alogy, abundantly demonstrated by the 'Analecta Fairfaxiana'. As one com-mentator has recently observed, 'Generations of peers and gentlemen became enthusiastic students of their ancestral heritage, poring over muniments to establish the distinguished achievements of their forebears and, if possible, trace their line back to the Norman Conquest.'[23]

Montaigne had asserted that the proper occupation of the *noblesse d'épée* remained functional: the display of valour in battle.[24] It was a model to which the aristocracies of the Three Kingdoms readily turned. Volunteering to fight for the Protestant cause in Europe, be it in the Dutch wars or the Thirty Years

---

[19]   Roger B. Manning, *Swordsmen: The Martial Ethos in the Three Kingdoms* (Oxford, 2003), p. 130.

[20]   Dunthorne, *Britain and the Dutch Revolt*, p. 82.

[21]   As part of James's mass dubbing of a thousand new knights in 1603–4, sixty new knights were created at York in 1603.

[22]   Fifty-four per cent of English peers in 1620 were military veterans, fifty-seven per cent in 1625 and sixty-three per cent in 1630: Manning, *Swordsmen*, p. 15. See also John Ad-amson, 'Chivalry and Political Culture in Caroline England', *Culture and Politics in Early Stuart England*, ed. Kevin Sharpe and Peter Lake (London, 1994), pp. 161–98.

[23]   Richard Cust, *Charles I and the Aristocracy, 1625–1642* (Cambridge, 2013), p. 14.

[24]   Manning, *Swordsmen*, p. 31.

War, was a public validation of honour. But the rechivalrization of elite culture also entailed fluid movement between court and camp, soldier and scholar. To swordsmen, with Sir Philip Sidney the exemplar, it was important that government was not left at the mercy of the *noblesse de robe*.[25] Hence the increased focus on scholarly pursuits also yielded an outpouring of military treatises and manuals, as well as translations of classical works by military authors, especially Vegetius.[26] This had a distinctly pragmatic, not merely cultural, dimension: early modern warfare had become a problem to be solved through intellectual means.[27] A translation of Vegetius' *De Re Militari* did not simply adorn a gentleman's library; it gave field commanders key insights into the training and disciplining of large numbers of infantry. Thus, with regard to later, domestic conflict in the 1640s, 'intellectually, the country was prepared by a literature that had little to do with chivalric romance and much to do with the professional practice of modern soldiers'.[28] It is essentially, though not wholly, within the newly flourishing field of *practical* military literature that 'The Highway' operates.

III

Absence rather than presence makes the most immediate impression in Fairfax's treatise. For nowhere is the fate of Fairfax's sons at the siege of Frankenthal, three years earlier, even hinted at, much less mentioned. The author had doubtless met Clifford's expectation that he would 'overcome the great grief in losing two such inestimable jewels, the honour of our time and kingdom', by 'bearing this blow with a Christian valour'.[29] Moreover, it risked redundancy, even indecorousness, to refer to a private matter of this kind in a work dealing with affairs of state. But Fairfax's relatively impersonal prose style, illustrated in the almost exclusive use of 'we' rather than 'I', is another influencing factor. It is a style which chimes in harmony with early modern military writing more generally, and which is indebted too to classical sources: exemplars such as Xenophon's *Anabasis* and Julius Caesar's *Commentaries* rarely used

[25] Ibid., pp. 31, 33.

[26] The third Lord Fairfax's translation of Vegetius is BL, Harleian MS 6390. See Mark Geldof, 'The Pike and the Printing Press: Military Handbooks and the Gentrification of the Early Modern Military Revolution', *International Exchange in the Early Modern Book World*, ed. Matthew McLean and Sara Barker (Leiden, 2016), pp. 153–8; and Michael King Macdona, 'Thomas, 3rd Lord Fairfax and Vegetius', *Modern Language Review* 113.2 (2018), 307–20.

[27] Lawrence, *Complete Soldier*, p. 21.

[28] Barbara Donagan, 'Halcyon Days and the Literature of War: England's Military Education before 1642', *P&P* 147 (1995), 68.

[29] Johnson, *Fairfax Correspondence*, 1: xlix.

'I'.[30] Though martial identity was reinforced in the writing and preserving of treatises such as 'The Highway', explicitly stated authorial involvement in the events described invariably remained (with notable exceptions) suppressed. To the extent that it describes events in which Fairfax has had personal or – through his sons – vicarious experience, 'The Highway' in some respects resembles a military memoir. And Renaissance military memoirs, though written by men with 'unique desires, emotions and interests', are (as Yuval Harari writes) conspicuously anti-individualistic texts; where they do so at all they almost always describe emotions, including grief, collectively.[31] Honour underscored the writer's authority and honesty far more than the witnessing of or personal participation in events described.

The reverse side of the same military memoir coin was a clear focus on naming historical protagonists rather than on abstract entities such as the state. In many ways 'The Highway' aligns with the medieval and early modern tradition of military history writing that broadly consisted of the retelling of acts of valour performed by one nobleman or another, for their own sake. In presenting the backstory to the present state of affairs, Fairfax conjures a pageant of the famous and infamous, including Alexander the Great, Julius Caesar, Holy Roman Emperors, popes, bishops, kings and princes. Inordinate detail is presented on how this ruler or that came to power, instanced in an excerpt dealing with the unification of the Spanish kingdoms:

> Naples and Sicily were given by the pope to this Duke of Anjou, and soe it came into the line of France, but they were supplanted by the pope's excommunication, who gave it to the familie of Durazzo. Alphonsus of Arragon was adopted by Joan queen of Naples for her successor, but after shee disliking her choice made a new election, and by the consent of Martin the pope did adopt Reni brother to the French kinge, who havinge to encounter king Alfonsus (who was alredy settled in the kingdom) did resign [...] to lewis the eleventh of France, against whom Alfonsus still held his possession, and left the same to John his sonne, from whom it came to this Ferdinand by adophin, who married Isabelle. (8–9)

[30] Matthew Woodcock, 'Tudor Soldier-Authors and the Art of Military Autobiography', *Representing War and Violence, 1250–1600*, ed. J. Bellis and L. Slater (Cambridge, 2016), p. 163.
[31] Yuval Noah Harari, *Renaissance Military Memoirs; War, History, and Identity, 1450–1600* (Woodbridge, 2004), p. 45. The writings of George Gascoigne and Thomas Churchyard, to name but two, provide an important counter-argument to Harari; see J. Bellis, '"I Was Enforced to Become an Eyed Witnes": Documenting War in Medieval and Early Modern Literature', *Emotions and War*, ed. S. Downes, A. Lynch and K. O' Loughlin (Palgrave, 2015), pp. 133–51; Woodcock, 'Tudor Soldier-Authors', pp. 173–6.

Such information is superfluous to the current situation in the Palatinate. But it is highly pertinent to advertising access to historical sources, and thereby to self-fashioning the image of a scholar. The specific books Fairfax consulted in writing 'The Highway' are not known; the diffusion of the Fairfax family archives is a subject unto itself. However, his library at the family seat in Denton, in the West Riding, was considered one of the finest in Yorkshire.[32] It certainly contained a splendid first edition of Froissart's *History* (1559–61), edited by Denis Sauvage and inscribed by Fairfax. This could well have provided useful background material for his generous treatment of the rise of continental dynasties germane to the early modern geopolitical balance of power.[33]

If its stress on individual actors characterises the text as late Renaissance, the rise of the nation state in Europe, all too evident in the present conflagration in Germany, sees geopolitics also take centre stage. The military veteran who writes on the Yorkshire militia and on horse-breeding widens his literary purview to national and international events. The writer–fighter equation is being recalibrated. Like his contemporaries, Fairfax is not solely interested in chivalric acts undertaken by noblemen, but in their implications for the present-day continental crisis.[34] Thus the machinations of Spain and its Catholic League allies, and the responses from Britain, France, the Low Countries, Germany, Denmark and Transylvania are diligently dissected. In this manner, the kudos-carrying display of learning continues, knowledge acquired not only from historical works but from a plethora of unnamed contemporary sources. For having contextualised the formation of the nation state protagonists and the rise of their leaders, Fairfax proceeds to examine the sanguinary events which since 1618 marred mainland Europe, culminating in the loss of the Palatinate and the resulting 'miserable condition that his Majesty's only daughter [Elizabeth of Bohemia] and her plentifull princely issue are reduced unto' (30).

Available contemporary accounts of developments in the Palatinate were legion.[35] Fairfax may partly have drawn on the weekly corantos – the first English newspapers – which from the outset of the Thirty Years War began to educate, inform and titillate an English reading public whose appetite for news and comment on the subject seemed insatiable. His son, Ferdinando, was an

---

[32]   W.J. Connor, 'The Fairfax Archives: A Study in Dispersal', *Archives* 11 (1973–4), 76–85.
[33]   *The Fairfax Library and Archive*, Sales Catalogue, Sotheby's, London, 14 December 1993 (London, 1993), lot 20.
[34]   Fairfax's work formed part of a wider textual response to the Palatinate crisis and complements other anti-Spanish tracts produced during the mid-1620s; see Cogswell, *Blessed*, pp. 69–76. Chapter 3 above also discusses contemporary literary responses to the Thirty Years War.
[35]   See Paul Salzman, *Literature and Politics in the 1620s: 'Whisper'd Counsells'* (Basingstoke, 2014), pp. 159–84.

MP throughout the period 1618–24 and could quite easily have brought corantos home to Denton from the capital, the news hub of the country. Recent
research has largely debunked the notion of county insularity with regards
to national and international news.[36] The weekly corantos were disseminated
via carriers to large towns and cities throughout the country, including those
in the Northern Home Counties, the South and West of England, the East
Midlands and Yorkshire.[37] Indeed, formal and informal mechanisms for news
circulation prompted a wide spectrum of unsolicited foreign policy advice to
the king, often to James's irritation.[38]

While the sensationalist corantos tended to cater for the lower end of the
reading market, the elite did not shun them altogether.[39] But in any case, if
one had the right connections there were many other authorities from which
to choose, including merchants, diplomats, volunteers, traders, migrants and
embassies.[40] Until their deaths, Fairfax had received regular news from his
sons on the front line, both directly and through their correspondence with his
other sons, to inform his own strategic views.[41] His finger was also kept on the
news pulse by Sir John Ogle, with whom he exchanged a series of pessimistic
letters on the growing military threat from the Habsburgs and the dangers of
the Spanish Match.[42]

The Fairfax–Ogle correspondence raises the important question of military
connections, the network of veteran officers and their various patron-client
relationships to which the author belonged and owed allegiance. Of relevance
here is that Fairfax had been knighted by Robert Devereux, second earl of
Essex, at the siege of Rouen in 1591.[43] More than most Elizabethan martial
luminaries, Essex hovered spectrally over debates on foreign policy in the
1620s, urging the godly towards conflict with Spain.[44] In creating twenty-two

[36] Coast, *News and Rumour*; Jason Peacey, 'Print and Public Politics in Seventeenth-Century England', *History Compass* 5.1 (2007), 85–111.
[37] Michael Frearson, 'The Distribution and Readership of London Corantos in the 1620s',
Serials and Their Readers 1620-1914, ed. Robin Myers and Michael Harris (London,
1993), p. 13.
[38] David Randall, *Credibility in Elizabethan and Early Stuart Military News* (London,
2008), pp. 43–5.
[39] Frearson, 'Distribution', p. 17.
[40] Boys, *London's News Press*, p. 7.
[41] Johnson, *Fairfax Correspondence*, 1: xl–xliii.
[42] Bodleian, MS Fairfax 30, fols. 152, 158, 163.
[43] Sir Thomas Coningsby, *Journal of the Siege of Rouen, 1591*, ed. John Gough Nicholls
(London, 1847), p. 71.
[44] Instanced in Thomas Scott's treatise, *Robert Earle Essex his Ghost, Sent from Elizian*
(London, 1624). See John Adamson, 'Chivalry and Political Culture in Caroline England',
Culture and Politics in Early Stuart England, ed. Kevin Sharpe and Peter Lake (London,
1994), p. 167; Richard C. McCoy, 'Old English Honour in an Evil Time: Aristocratic

knights in Normandy he had dubbed men further down the military peck-
ing order than usual, including captains like Fairfax, and non-commissioned
volunteers. His main purpose in doing so was to form a group of loyalists
around him dependent on his patronage. Fairfax's former commanding officer
in the Low Counties, Robert Dudley, earl of Leicester, was another symbol
of Elizabethan military honour resurrected in the newly belligerent literary
atmosphere.[45] There were also close ties to Sir Horace Vere, with whom Fairfax had served in the Dutch wars, who led the English expeditionary force
to the Palatinate in 1620.[46] In 1624, Vere and Ogle, to whose regiment Fairfax's seventeen-year-old grandson Thomas was attached in 1629, were both
on the Council of War, comprised exclusively of veterans from Elizabethan
campaigns. Under the watchful eye of Buckingham and Charles, the Council
was laying the groundwork for a military response to Spain at around the time
'The Highway' was composed.[47] And Gervase Markham's celebrated treatise
on Elizabethan military glory, *Honour in his Perfection* (1624), sought to establish a chain of army patrons stretching back to the days of Caesar, featuring
Essex, the Veres and another officer to whom Fairfax was connected, Peregrine
Bertie Willoughby.[48]

It is important to remember that a military patronage circle was, as David
Lawrence writes, 'more than just a haven for soldiers, it also served as a forum
for discussion of military and political affairs, and it is in these circles that we
find evidence of the use of military books in knowledge transactions taking
place between members of these groups'.[49] Indeed, while he was serving as
the Lord Governor of Utrecht, and still a full colonel, Ogle's home became
something of a military salon to eminent soldiers and scholars.[50] Thus the
intellectual milieu of such groups, not just the general strategic views they
held, had to some extent prepared and even conditioned Fairfax to enter into

---

Principle in the 1620s', *The Stuart Court and Europe: Essays in Politics and Religious Culture*, ed. R. Malcolm Smuts (Cambridge, 1996), pp. 134–5.

[45] Cogswell, *Blessed*, p. 94.

[46] Clements R. Markham, *The Fighting Veres: Lives of Sir Francis Vere and Sir Horace Vere*
(Boston, 1888), pp. 394–420.

[47] Cogswell, *Blessed*, p. 97. Links between the Veres and the Fairfaxes were strengthened
further in 1637 with the marriage between the future parliamentarian commander,
Thomas Fairfax, and Sir Horace's daughter Ann; see Jacqueline Eales, 'Anne and Thomas
Fairfax, and the Vere Connection', *England's Fortress*, ed. Hopper and Major, pp. 145–68.
Buckingham's son, George Villiers, the second duke, married the general's daughter,
Mary, in 1657.

[48] Gervase Markham, *Honour in his Perfection* (London, 1624). See also Woodcock's essay
in this volume (Chapter 2) that discusses Sir Francis Vere and those of his military circle.

[49] Lawrence, *Complete Soldier*, p. 51. The possibility exists of the circulation of Fairfax's
manuscript among his military friends; this may account for its two variants displaying
copious additions and amendments, as noted above.

[50] Ibid., p. 117.

the national debate on the Palatinate. Military identity was still governed chiefly by deeds of valour on the battleground, but again, the fully rounded soldier should also, like Sidney and Essex, possess the ability to discuss and communicate the *arte militaire*. Hence soldier-authors who had been on active duty in the Low Countries or the Anglo-Irish wars, like Gervase and Francis Markham, John Bingham, Edward Davies, Henry Hexham, Robert Ward and Garret Barry – many of whom Fairfax knew – produced a host of instructional military works in the 1620s.[51]

IV

If war with Spain was a unifying principle among veterans like Fairfax, the precise military strategy to be adopted had been contentious. By the time the last Protestant forces had been overrun in the Palatinate in late 1623, however, a consensus had started to form that a land assault would be treacherous, if not suicidal.[52] Accordingly, Fairfax recognises that the 'Spanyard wilbe master of the river [Rhine] and make bridges at his pleasure to transport his people' (31). Instead, he turns his attention to the Indies:

> The Kinge of Spain is att this day reputed the greatest prince in the world, for his dominions be not only extended into the three ancient known parts therof, as into Europe, Affrick and Asia, but also hath latly acquired the souvraignty of a new found world [...]. It abounds in Treasure of all sorts, as in [...] Diamonds, all variety of pretious stones, gould and silver, hearbs, drougs, fruits [...] soe as it may be said of him who hath America, owneth nothinge that the world can afforde. (6)

There was far greater potential for military success 'by a way of diversion'; that is, by attacking these burgeoning New World colonies:

> Every man knows that a tree is more easily lopped than cut down, though it have many branches and but one body, and that by taking away the top with the boughs the stock will wither and dy – even so this mighty empire of Spain, if you cut off the remote members from it, though they be but fingers or toes, yet may they gangrene to the heart. Then may we do well to seek the Palatinate in America. (36)

In some ways, it is counterintuitive that Fairfax, so at home in the military camp, should have favoured a tactical naval war with Spain rather than a head-on confrontation involving cavalry and infantry. On the other hand, the loss of his sons at Frankenthal, though adding a glorious new chapter to the

---

[51]   Ibid., p. 197.
[52]   Cogswell, *Blessed*, pp. 74–5.

family's military history, had convinced him of Spain's military superiority on the European mainland. A letter from his son John reveals how numerically disadvantaged were the Protestant forces:

> It is said that from the Maine are landed 3 or 4,000 Italians, near Coblentz, and there make a stand, not knowing whether the Netherlands or these parts shall have greater need of them. Yet Spinola hath already 52,000 foot and 9,000 horse for the field, besides men in every garrison. Our regiment, of late, is very weakened, because for want of means many are run away.[53]

Fairfax wrote an epitaph on the death of Sir Edward Yorke in 1622, which according to Charles Fairfax 'hath equal Refference to himselfe'. Though ortho-dox in its privileging of sword over gown, it is hardly a ringing endorsement of war on the continent:

> Wee that have seene the Belgick bloudy wares
> There slaught'red People and there batter'erd townes.
> France her Intestine, And some other Jarres
> First offr'ed upp our Armour for our Gownes
> And now our Soules wee render, With the Breath
> To him that gave us life soe oft in Death.[54]

In addition to which, one of the keynotes of 'The Highway' is Spanish military power, manifested in the wondrous imperial reach of Philip: 'to this exces-sive greatness is the might of Spain growne, as no girdle can goe about him less than almost the circle of the sun, for he embraceth the yet known world on every side' (12). A renewed appetite for armed conflict with Spain, there-fore, did not necessarily lead veterans of earlier conflicts to posit a gung-ho approach. Personal experience, and the intellectualisation of modern warfare, played important roles in late Jacobean military identity. Old soldiers like Fairfax certainly expressed hawkish intentions:

> [F]or my own part (if necessarily I must fight) I had rather give then take the first blow, and therefore as Christendome knows that his master [James] has a godly sceptre, and Solomon's wisdom to wield it in peace, so I wish that he would let them see he has a sharp sword, and David's valoor to handle it in war. (48)

And the sacrifice of generations of English officers in previous conflicts with Spain was a legitimate rallying cry: '[L]et the like occasions be that was, and I know there will be found English blood in English veins still, the same that we received from our fathers and the same that we will leave to our sonnes'

---

[53]   Johnson, *Fairfax Correspondence*, 1: xliii.
[54]   Brotherton Library, MS Yorks 2, 'Analecta Fairfaxiana', fol. 182v.

(41). But for the most part, veterans respected and were even in awe of the strength of the enemy; they were not going to allow Protestant, anti-Spanish sentiment, however keenly felt, to cloud their strategic judgement. For Fairfax, the highway to Heidelberg was perforce a circuitous one. The House of Commons agreed; by 1624, virtually all MPs favoured a diversionary war.[55]

Nonetheless, caution and rationality did not prohibit sentimentality. On the contrary, calls for a naval war gave Fairfax the opportunity to invoke a fabled name:

> I have heard Sir Francis Drake say that he would undertake with 60 or 70 good saile of ships to lie upon the coast of Spain, he would distress both Spain and the Indies so, as the king should within one year beg his peace [and] give any conditions for the same. [...] We remember that the famous Sir Francis Drake with a very few sails did sack Carthagena, San Domingo and divers other towns upon the coast of America. (42, 44–5)

Dropping the name of an Elizabethan military legend did no harm to family prestige; doubtless for these references alone 'The Highway' qualified as a treasured Fairfax literary artefact. The author hereby taps into a widespread revival of the Drake cult in the 1620s, exemplified in the publication of his authorized biography and in Buckingham's installing at Newhall a mural depicting the vice admiral at sea.[56] Naturally, the defeat of the Spanish Armada fitted neatly into the paradigm, with the hand of providence to the fore. Philip II, Fairfax recalls, 'did [...] dreame of conquests of England and Ireland; the one he sent his great Armado, and into the other his man of war, those were by the mercies of god dissipated and the loss and shame fell upon his own hand' (19). Newsbooks, periodicals and other publications echoed 'The Highway' in reprising a golden age of Gloriana, piquantly recalling the plundering by English ships of Spanish wealth in the Americas. Fairfax's memory was apparently undimmed:

> I did see in the glorious and happy days of Qu Elizabeth the frequent navigations of my worthy country men, and that in tyme of war with the spanyard we were inriched by ther spoyles. Never did England shine in more honor or abound in more wealth [...] Every brave spirit was taken up with some action that made him worthy of esteem our court and camps did glitter in Spanish gold, our ships

---

[55] See S.R. Gardiner, *A History of England under the Duke of Buckingham and Charles I*, 2 vols. (London, 1975), 1: 21–5. In the event, a 'blue water' policy was only partially implemented, and not in the Americas. A disastrous joint naval and land expedition to Cadiz in 1625, planned by Buckingham, lent Fairfax's proposals an unwanted aspect of prescience.

[56] Cogswell, *Blessed Revolution*, pp. 97, 182.

had sails of gold and silver cloths, so as then it seemed that the mines of Peru
were ours and the spanyard did but dig them for our uses. (40–1)

To reminisce thus over the Elizabethan naval past was an act of unashamed
nostalgia. But it was generated by, and harnessed to, a present-day emergency.
Fear of Philip's 'terrible' and 'dreadfull' power 'by reason of his countries,
armies, navies, ports, forts, mynes of treasure [and] the sinews of war to
support them' was palpable, the danger imminent. In pursuing a naval war
with 'the Hollanders [...] and other Adventurers', Fairfax claims, 'we are
assured that that we shall either make ourselves greater fortunes abroad' – in
the manner of Drake, Ralegh and their fellow privateers – 'or at the worst
reduce the Christian world here in Europe to their former happiness and so
stay the bells that ring our funeral peales before our deaths' (46). In these and
in other areas, such as the call to attack Spain in the West Indies, Fairfax's text
covers similar ground, with comparable political and confessional commitment, to Fulke Greville's *Dedication to Sir Philip Sidney* (written c.1612–14,
published 1652).[57]

   As this last quotation highlights, for military men in the 1620s a heightened sense of English patriotism mingles with a Protestant *sensus fidelium*,
an imperative to serve – and to save – the European-wide Protestant cause.
The international context of the Thirty Years War enabled men like Fairfax to
construct and express a self-identity indissolubly linked to issues well beyond
county boundaries. As an elect nation, England's duty and destiny was not
simply self-preservation but to safeguard the future of the Protestant Christian
world. Unsurprisingly, therefore, 'The Highway' is vehemently anti-papal. The
pope abuses his prerogative as 'the sole monarch of the church' to oppress
Protestant dissenters. His temporal power is as absolute as his spiritual: 'He
doth fly from Peter's faith to Peter's sword, and doth uphold his pretended
succession and power over the church by Armes'. The pope's dual role reeks
of hypocrisy: 'He doth buy Armes and wage war as he is a temporal Prince,
and may invade his enemies contries with sword and fyre, though as Pope he
be meeke humble and servant of servants', while '[t]he sword may inlarge his
temporall dominions which are measured my Myles, but not Christs which is
numbered by soules' (4–5). Naturally, in the present situation it is the pope's
support for the King of Spain, 'this overgrown fish' in Christendom's 'fair pond'
(7), which is the most troubling. The pontiff works hand in glove with Philip
in an unholy alliance

   telling the king that it is meritorious to fight gods battles (though in truth they
   be only his) making love to the spanyard in calling him the most catholic king,
   and his eldest son, sending him [...] hats and swords with ther cheap presents:

⁵⁷   I am grateful to Matthew Woodcock for this point.

the king entertains this, draws his sword for his holiness, brings the professant people (whom he can conquer) to the obedience of the pope in spiritual things but resynes to himself ther temporal estates; And this also the king hath further of this pope, that he cannot want titles to any part of the world, but he must get his possession as he can: yet will he further the king with his excommunications and interdictions, and will absolve any sated from his natural allegiance by his bulls. (24)

Such hostility presses many of the usual buttons. The Fairfaxes were already known, and were to continue to be known, as a godly Yorkshire family, in a county where puritanism among the gentry, not least in the West Riding, had grown rapidly since the 1570s.[58] The third Lord Fairfax wrote virulently anti-papal poems, and print and manuscript works by numerous other authors in the 1620s expressed similar sentiments, routinely yoking the Black Legend of Spanish cruelty to the Holy See.[59] Concerns over the Spanish Match melded with the usual iconic events – the Armada, Gunpowder Plot and Irish revolt – in a climate where 'every generation of English people between the 1580s and the 1640s had personal experience of a popish assault on English independence'.[60]

However, to the extent that Fairfax's military identity was Protestant in kind (which it certainly was), in 'The Highway' it is comparatively restrained, and in places positively conciliatory. Granted, as well as his assault on the pope, there are some traditional Calvinist tenets on the primacy of the Word: 'The government of the Church [...] hath reformed to man, but the worde is his and must not be changed', for 'if we alter one little of his words or wrest the same from his meaning [...] that which is our meat wilbe our poyson' (4). But his overriding concern with 'the estate of Christendome att this day' does not entirely comport with the flood of anti-Catholic sermons and pamphlets published in 1624.[61] Instead, emphasis is placed on the common enemy of Catholic and Protestant alike, the Ottoman Empire: 'The Turke is he that hath confined the bounds of Christendome within soe narrow limits, as the hearts of all Christians doe well to remember, whose daunger is yet more to be feared' (2). Instead of uniting to fight the shared foe, the present condition of Christendom

is such as was Jerusalem's by the seditious, rather seekinge to ruin one another rather then to oppose the enemies att the gate who threatened destruction to

---

[58]   Cliffe, *Yorkshire Gentry*, pp. 256–81.
[59]   Bodleian, MS Fairfax 40, p. 607.
[60]   Peter Lake, 'Anti-Popery: the Structure of a Prejudice', *Conflict in Early Stuart England: Studies in Religion and Politics 1603–1642*, ed. Richard Cust and Ann Hughes (London and New York, 1989), p. 80.
[61]   Cogswell, *Blessed*, pp. 281–301.

all. O envie above malice! O foolishness above folly! We slaughter one another whilst the Turk like vulturs croke over us to prey upon our dead bodies. (2)

Several English authors were counselling a Christian holy war against the Turks, among them a man with the ear of the king: Francis Bacon.[62] And there were germane familial considerations underpinning Fairfax's position: he lost another son, Thomas, fighting in Turkey in 1621, while the martial influence on his own funerary monument extends to the placing of a Saracen's head at the foot of Lady Fairfax, betokening an ancestor's participation in the Crusades.[63]

Such differences as exist between the two Christian traditions should in any case, Fairfax argues, be placed in their proper context:

> But how comes this to pass shall wee servinge one maister which is Jesus Christ and professinge one Gospell, should thus massacre one another as if we had twoe Maisters, and shall they but command contrary things? Surlie this fault must be in our selves, and (confessinge that) we must acknowledge ther is a mighty punishment due for our transgressions. Christ did give this for a new Comaundment Love one another, how dwells the love of god in us? (3)

He even suggests an international forum in which doctrinal and ceremonial disputes could be settled:

> Seinge that the present estate of Christendome is such as every man's dagger is att his Neighbour's throate […] might not the Christian princes agree to have the controversies disputed in some free assembly, and reform ether churches in those things which shall be holy scripture. (3)

The imperial ambition of Spain – realised on the continent by Philip II and Philip III, and now by Philip IV – was seen as the true source of danger to Christendom, not confessional allegiance or religion itself: 'Thus I conceive this war in Christendom not occasioned by the differences in religion but the swelling pride of this mighty monarch still thirsting after new conquests and swallowing poor states and kingdoms to make his stomach capable of greater gorging' (5).

Taken at face value, Fairfax's inclusive outlook on Christianity stands as a corrective to the notion that English military identity in the Thirty Years War was shaped wholly by confessional allegiance. In this respect, it is of note that he had close ties to Yorkshire Catholics such as the Bellasis family, and stood for Parliament in 1624 and 1625 with his good friend Sir Thomas Wentworth, later earl of Strafford, 'who was no Puritan and if anything a supporter of the

---

[62] Francis Bacon, 'An Advertisement Touching an Holy War', *The Works of Francis Bacon*, 10 vols. (London, 1861), 3: 467–92.
[63] I am indebted to Allan Boddy, member of Otley Parish Church, for this information.

[Spanish] Match'.[64] However, it is also likely that the stridency of Fairfax's Protestantism is deliberately tempered in order to secure a more receptive royal
audience for his treatise. A moderate Calvinist, 'European by education and
almost totally European by outlook', James's *rex pacificus* stance towards Spain
was predicated on his regarding a confessional war as 'a disaster to be avoided
at all costs'.[65]

If a relatively pacific attitude towards Catholicism was partially a politic
aspect of 'The Highway', there is good reason to suppose that the work's funda-
mentally pro-monarchist tenor was wholly authentic: 'Can ther be any bonds
in the world to oblige loyalty soe much as to be the born subject of a rightful
prince, and to receive life and education in that aire wherin all his predeces-
sors have been bred?' (20). Indeed, given his views on the crown, Fairfax's
death in 1640 may have made it easier for both Ferdinando and his grandson,
the third Lord, to take arms against royalist forces in the Civil Wars. Even so,
Fairfax's royalism does not exclude opprobrium for 'tyrannous kings, whose
wills be ther laws, and policies ther Religions', nor from reminding the 'Mighti
Monarchs' addressed in his preface that 'god hath not placed you in thrones
of Majesty for your owne glorie but his whom you serve who is incomparably
more transcendent over you than you are over subjects'.[66] It is not Fairfax's
place as 'the unworthiest of subjects to compare souvraignes, and to lay the
attribute of tyrant upon any whom god hath called gods', for 'we know ther
powers be from god and by him princes rule'; however, 'a kinge may be evell in
rigarde of himselfe, yet all is good in god' (1–2). Plausibly, some of these more
contingent expressions of loyalty percolate down into the third Lord's writing
when the latter, in retirement at Nun Appleton, imputes hubris to 'inconstant'
kings and princes whose 'crownes hath nothing sweete but ther names nor
riches than ther appearance'.[67]

Drawing on a variety of unnamed news sources, which almost certainly
included family members and close military friends like Vere and Ogle, 'The
Highway' contributes to the plethora of English literary responses to the loss
of the Palatinate, within a wider climate of the remilitarization – and to some

[64]   Richard Cust, 'Politics and the Electorate in the 1620s', *Conflict*, ed. Cust and Hughes, p.
       147.
[65]   Bruce Lenman, *England's Colonial Wars: Conflicts, Empire and National Identity* (Lon-
       don, 2001), p. 285. See also Simon Adams, 'Spain or the Netherlands? The Dilemmas of
       Early Stuart Foreign Policy', *Before the English Civil War: Essays on Early Stuart Politics
       and Government*, ed. Howard Tomlinson (London, 1983), p. 87. For a study of James's
       ecumenical approach and desire to achieve religious reconciliation among Christians of
       different stripes: W.B. Patterson, *King James VI and I and the Reunion of Christendom*
       (Cambridge, 1997), passim.
[66]   Bodleian, MS Clarendon 34, fol. 7r.
[67]   Thomas, third Lord Fairfax, 'The Thoughts of Eternity': Cambridge, Fitzwilliam Muse-
       um, MS CFM 13, p. 5.

extent rechivalrization – of Britain in the early Stuart period. Its specific political moment is the 'Blessed Revolution' of 1623–4, following the collapse of the Spanish Match, its main purpose to offer urgent, remedial military advice to the monarch. Yet in common with other contemporary treatises it is influenced by Elizabethan legend and the soldier–scholar networks formed in earlier conflicts. Fairfax's text epitomizes the anti-Spanish and anti-papal sentiment prevalent in much of this literature, but his acknowledgement of Habsburg military hegemony in Europe, and his call for Christian unity in the face of the common Ottoman threat, led to more carefully crafted proposals than might have been predicted. Though he is silent on the recent death of two of his sons at Frankenthal, his emotional investment in the early years of the Thirty Years War ensures that this is no dry academic exercise. Produced by an ambitious member of a dynasty for whom martial valour, family history and religious devotion were intertwined preoccupations, 'The Highway to Heidelberg' proves an instructive case-study in how, on a literary–strategic level, early modern military elites sought to influence contemporary affairs and, simultaneously, to fashion their own identity and status.

PART II

Military Identities in Early Modern Ireland

5

The Clergy and the Military in Early Modern Ireland

ANGELA ANDREANI AND ANDREW HADFIELD

This chapter will explore the relationship between the clergy and the military in late sixteenth-century Ireland. Connections to religious teaching and ritual were vital for early modern armies, yet these links remain underexplored in works on military culture of the period. The Erasmian *Militis Christiani* tradition has often been invoked to explain Christian attitudes, particularly in studies of an assertive proselytising culture prevalent from the late Middle Ages onwards, but it is relatively infrequently applied in terms of actual military service and identity.[1] As this chapter demonstrates, the clergy played two principal roles in martial culture: justifying military action in sermons; and accompanying armies in order to carry out the normal duties of clergymen, which included preaching to the officers and men. In return, the army provided those clergy who were prepared to serve it with ample reward.

In the first part of this chapter we will look at the careers of clergymen who served the military in Ireland and, in the second part, examine sermons delivered prior to military action. We will concentrate principally on the career of Meredith Hanmer (1544/5–1604), a chaplain to military governors in Ireland who also had a distinguished career as a translator and polemicist. Hanmer is an especially interesting case because of the wealth of information about his life that remains and, extrapolating from his example, we are able to reconstruct how clergymen behaved in times of conflict and participated in martial culture. Hanmer's career suggests that clergymen were pragmatic, prepared to adapt their service and knowledge according to the situation in which they found themselves. The second half of this chapter will concentrate on sermons, the principal extant material that enables us to reconstruct the intimate and vital relationship between clergymen and military men. We will analyse a number of military sermons, in particular, Lancelot Andrewes' sermon preached before Robert Devereux, second earl of Essex's expedition to

---

[1] David L. Jeffrey, *A Dictionary of Biblical Tradition in English Literature* (Grand Rapids, 1992), pp. 506–9. For a specific application: James A. Parente, *Religious Drama and the Humanist Tradition: Christian Theater in Germany and in the Netherlands, 1500–1680* (Leiden, 1987), pp. 69–70.

Ireland in 1599. We will look at the rhetoric Andrewes employed, including his adoption of the tradition of the *Militis Christiani*, as well as his warning to his congregation that there had to be a clear distinction between true Christians and those in thrall to Satan.

The clergy and the military in Ireland in the 1590s

At the beginning of the 1590s, the south of Ireland was a particular concern for the English authorities. The government was actively involved in the development of the Munster plantation, which had been established in the mid-1580s through the allotment of seignories to the English undertakers who agreed to populate the area, to run and maintain the estates and so, it was hoped, to make the area loyal to the crown.[2] This circle of 'English colonists, settlers, officials, and soldiers'[3] was soon to be followed by a small cadre of Protestant clergymen brought over from England to fill vacant benefices and to preach in those parishes that had been deprived by the Court of Faculties because they were occupied by Irish clergymen with no obvious Protestant affiliations.[4] Among this group of preachers was Meredith Hanmer. A distinguished, Oxford-educated Church of England divine, Hanmer was a vociferous polemicist against the Jesuits in London in the early 1580s, and produced the first printed translation into English of Eusebius' *Auncient Ecclesiastical Histories*, the standard history of the first 600 years of Christianity.[5] Hanmer, who seems to have been something of a dedicated collector of ecclesiastical offices, in Ireland as well as in England, soon became attached to a variety of royal officials and powerful military figures. As a preacher to the army he accompanied the military through the campaigns of the Nine Years War and witnessed the upsurge in violence from the beginnings of the Ulster rebellion in 1594 to the final overthrow of the Munster plantation in 1598.

Hanmer is exceptional because of the amount of information that has survived about him, but his experience was certainly not unique. The names of a number of fellow clergymen who arrived in Ireland in the 1590s and served alongside Hanmer have been identified by Alan Ford: John Albright, Thomas Tedder, John Chardon, Robert Graves, Christopher Hewetson, Anthony Sharpe and William Withrede.[6] All were ordained clergy and all were

---

2   Robert Dunlop, 'The Plantation of Munster, 1584–89', *English Historical Review* 3 (1888), 250–69; Michael McCarthy-Morrogh, *The Munster Plantation: English Migration to Southern Ireland, 1583–1641* (Oxford, 1986).
3   Andrew Hadfield, *Edmund Spenser: A Life* (Oxford, 2012), pp. 11, 198–200.
4   Alan Ford, *The Protestant Reformation in Ireland 1590–1640* (Dublin, 1997), pp. 31–2.
5   Eusebius, *The Auncient Ecclesiasticall Histories of the First Six Hundred Yeares after Christ* […] *Translated out of the Greeke Tongue by Meredith Hanmer* (London, 1577).
6   Ford, *Protestant Reformation*, pp. 30–5.

university graduates;[7] the majority were between their late twenties and early thirties.[8] Only two of these preachers were distinguished enough to become bishops, and the careers of most of the rest saw them gravitate to Dublin and Munster.[9] Thanks to extant archival evidence, we can reconstruct the details of the livings earned by these men and their day-to-day life as preachers.

The context in which they arrived was tough. Contemporary reconstructions of the conditions of the Irish parishes by English officials paint a picture of isolation and pluralism, in which the benefices were overwhelmingly poor and remote, and preachers far too few. From the mid-1560s, Alexander Craik, the first Protestant bishop of Kildare, and Sir Henry Sidney pleaded repeatedly that preachers be sent over from England.[10] Edmund Spenser noted that the benefices in Ireland were so mean that they could not provide 'competent maintenance for any honest minister to live upon'.[11] Henry A. Jefferies has provided important data of the 'incredible absence' of preachers in Irish parishes throughout Elizabeth's reign that closely matches the accounts handed down to us by contemporary observers.[12] The poor conditions of the Irish parishes and the sense of the Protestant clergy as a scattered community of isolated ministers were exacerbated by the state of violence which overwhelmed the country after the outbreak of the Ulster rebellion.

A vivid sketch of the troubled state of affairs in March 1594 is preserved in a report-letter sent to Lord Burghley from Dublin in which Hanmer conveyed his 'knowledge and vew of these thinges and the state of this land'.[13] In the north the situation was 'toe bad': Hugh Maguire, Brian McHugh Oge and Collo McBrian were 'out in open action' to the point that the English officials sent to negotiate with the Irish chieftains of the rebellion in Ulster 'might

[7]   Hanmer was at Corpus Christi College, Oxford; Graves, Albright and Hewetson were at Cambridge; Chardon was at Exeter College, Oxford; Tedder is styled as a university scholar but no details are given.

[8]   The exception are Chardon and Hanmer, both in their forties. Albright was born c.1559; Graves in 1560; Hewetson in 1562; see *A Cambridge Alumni Database* at http://venn. lib.cam.ac.uk; 'John Chardon', *ODNB*; Henry Cotton, *Fasti Ecclesiae Hibernicae*, 5 vols. (Dublin, 1848–78), 1: 238; 5: 61, 65, 83.

[9]   Chardon was bishop of Down and Connor. Graves was consecrated bishop of Ferns and Leighlin, succeeding Richard Meredith as bishop of Leighlin, but died a sudden death (with all of his family) by drowning in the bay of Dublin on 1 October 1600 (Cotton, *Fasti*, 1: 238). It is possible that Hanmer's career may have been hindered because he made too many enemies, as the surviving evidence of his life suggests.

[10] Henry A. Jefferies, 'Elizabeth's Reformation in the Irish Pale', *Journal of Ecclesiastical History* 66.3 (2015), 531.

[11] Andrew Hadfield and Willy Maley, eds., *Edmund Spenser: A View of the State of Ireland. From the First Printed Edition* (1633) (Oxford, 1997), pp. 87–8.

[12] Jefferies, 'Elizabeth's Reformation', 531.

[13] TNA, SP 63/173/273.

see afore their departure the [contrey] smokinge with the fire of the rebells'.[14] Hugh O'Neill, earl of Tyrone – Hanmer continued in his report – was greatly feared and able to command 700 horses and 3,000 footmen, which was 'farre beyond the powre of the late Earle of Desmond'. Within a few hours, moreover, he could count on the additional support of the Scots. As an illustration of the power and viciousness of the 'rebels', Hanmer described the destruction in the west, where Donel McCarta had burned, robbed and murdered, and it was feared that he could still perpetrate greater destruction. In the south, Fiach McHugh O'Byrne and his followers were 'greatlie feared', and 'yet not meaninge as it seemeth to reforme them selfe', even after the burning down of the castle of the sheriff of Kildare, in which the custodian had perished horribly together with his wife and children.[15]

This report captures the critical worsening of the conflict, as well as the role of a clergyman as an eye-witness to the evil deeds of the Irish chieftains, who were out of control and could count on Catholic backing. Since the outbreak of the war, in fact, the available Protestant English clergy became part of the war effort as chaplains and preachers, and the network of their connections naturally centred upon the military. Service in the army could provide protection and an institutional network in which to operate, given the disrupted state of several 'wasted' benefices, like the bishoprics of Cork, Cloyne and Ross.[16] Furthermore, since the income from the benefices was minimal, service in the army surely represented the main source of revenue for these men.

A survey directed from the secretariat in Westminster to account for the expenses of war states that preachers had been most commonly maintained by stipends given to them by the Lord Deputy and the councillors, and by the chief officers, captains and commanders of the army. These sums were taken 'out of their private purses' according to rates agreed upon voluntarily, making the document a particularly interesting testimony of the significance of the military for the clergy, and vice versa.[17] While service in the army was

---

[14] Sir Robert Gardiner and Sir Anthony St Leger were in Dundalk to meet the Irish chieftains O'Neill and O'Donnell and conduct negotiations towards a resolution of the recent Ulster rebellion in Ulster. For a recent discussion of the meeting: Hiram Morgan "'Tempt not God too long, O Queen": Elizabeth and the Irish Crisis of the 1590s', *Elizabeth I and Ireland*, ed. Valerie McGowan-Doyle and Brendan Kane (Cambridge, 2014), p. 213.

[15] TNA, SP 63/173/273. The burning of the castle of the sheriff of Kildare clearly affected Hanmer badly, and another version of the same event exists in his manuscript notes (TNA, SP 63/214).

[16] TNA, SP 63/206/308.

[17] The documents seem to be related to a survey initiated by the Westminster secretariat to account for the expenses of war, and to check that nobody received money without serving. The aim appears to have been to restore to the crown money paid out to preachers and surgeons not actually serving in Ireland. One such survey endorsed by Robert Cecil is TNA, SP 63/207/2, fol. 183.

evidently a source of income and a viable career alternative for these preachers, the arrangement for their maintenance – they were supported from within the army by military officials – reveals the importance of their role for the garrison in question.

For example, as chaplain to Thomas Butler, tenth earl of Ormond (c.1531–1614), Hanmer was receiving 'the moiety of a man's lendings of all the bands serving in Leinster, Connaught, and on the northern borders of the Pale'.[18] In December 1599 this sum was 33s and 4d per week, as recorded in a list of the preachers to the army and their revenue. Among the other preachers in the list are Robert Graves, dean of Cork and future bishop of Leighlin and Ferns; the dean of Christchurch Jonas Wheeler; and William Lyon, bishop of Cork, Cloyne and Ross. Out of the fourteen listed, five were actually involved in military campaigns: Hanmer, who attends Ormond 'in all journeys'; Mr Palmer at Athlone, preacher 'bothe to the Town and Garrison'; Mr Webbe (most likely William Webbe), then prebendary of St Patrick, preacher to the garrison at Newry but in Dublin at the time of the census; Denis Campbell, dean of Limerick; and 'one Cornewall' (probably Gabriel Cornwall), appointed in the place of Mr Lynacker, and preacher to the garrison at Drogheda.[19] Army preachers in Ireland were thus directly in contact with soldiers beyond the urban environment and the space of the church; their lives intersected on the field too, in the day-to-day reality of martial experience.

Beyond their role in the army, the duties expected of the clergy included taking services in their several parish churches; preaching a sermon every Sabbath day at St Patrick's Cathedral; and a public sermon before the state in Christ Church Cathedral, 'which they duelie performe with greate studie and care', being for the most part resident 'either in theire Rectories in the Countrie or within the lymittes of the Cathedrall Churche'.[20] These duties are outlined in a certificate of the ecclesiastical livings, dignities and prebends in the diocese of Dublin. Several well-known English ministers were included in the document, which listed the names of those earning over £30 per year, including Adam Loftus, the archbishop of Dublin, Jonas Wheeler and Thomas Ram, the chaplain of Lord Mountjoy, prebendary of St John's in Christ Church and future bishop of Fern and Leighlin. Also featuring in the list were the army preachers already found in Ireland in 1599, including Webbe and Cornwall, in addition to Hanmer and his colleagues brought over in the early 1590s: Christopher Hewetson, John Albright and Luke Challoner.[21] These men had

18   TNA SP 63/208/1, fol. 256.
19   TNA, SP 63/206/308. Cornwall acted as precentor of Cork, and was appointed to the bishopric of Derry, Raphoe and Clogher in 1603, but he died before the consecration (Cotton, *Fasti*, 2: 395; 3: 315).
20   TNA, SP 63/216/59.
21   TNA, SP 63/216/59.

remained in Ireland and at the end of the war they were earning well above the average revenue of the majority of Irish, and even English, benefices. Just as serving in Ireland could be rewarding for soldiers, for this select group of preachers, service in the Church of Ireland during the war had indeed represented an opportunity.

With just a few exceptions, the livings in the diocese of Dublin were under the church patronage of the archbishop of Dublin and of the dean and chapter of Christ Church. Only the deanery of Christ Church and of St Patrick were under crown patronage, and Yagoe and Maynooth overseen by the Kildare family. These had escaped lay impropriation and impoverishment, and provided the clergy with stipends above the average annual income, calculated by Steven Ellis at just over IR£22 (approximately £15).[22] Even so, £30 was considered the minimum annual income to adequately maintain a preaching minister, and pluralism was rife.[23] During his protracted residence in Ireland, Hanmer was appointed vicar, archdeacon, treasurer, rector, warden, prebendary and chancellor of over ten benefices and it is not clear which of these he actually occupied, what duties he performed, or whether he appointed deputies in his place and pocketed the difference between what he paid them and the income from the benefice.

Hanmer's ecclesiastical career fared much better and he accumulated far more money in Ireland than he was likely to have done in England. As the prebendary of St Michan's he was the only one of the three attached to Christ Church Cathedral to equal or exceed the yearly income of £30. From his first arrival in Munster – after 1590 and before 1593 – Hanmer rapidly developed connections to the key figures in English colonial government.[24] He was certainly in demand with the military and campaigned as an army preacher with Sir John Norreys, one of the most celebrated soldiers of his day, before serving (as noted) as chaplain to Ormond, the Lord Treasurer and Lord Lieutenant General of Ireland, distant cousin to Elizabeth I and one of her favourite courtiers.[25] From one of the letters of recommendations praising Hanmer's service as an army preacher we learn that he had been brought over to Ireland by the bishop of Cork William Lyon, and that he had started his service in the

---

[22]   Steven G. Ellis, 'Economic Problems of the Church: Why the Reformation Failed in Ireland', *Journal of Ecclesiastical History* 41.2 (1990), 251.

[23]   Ellis, 'Economic Problems', 254.

[24]   The earliest evidence of Hanmer's connection to Munster is the appearance of his name as archdeacon of Ross and vicar of Timoleague in the reports of visitations to the southern Irish dioceses undertaken by the Court of Faculties in 1590 while he was still in England (TCD, MS 566 fol. 168). A summons from the English Privy Council notes him as already resident in Ireland in 1593.

[25]   The most comprehensive study of Ormond's influence in this period is David Edwards, *The Ormond Lordship in County Kilkenny, 1515–1642: The Rise and Fall of Butler Feudal Power* (Dublin, 2003).

army in the north with Norris.[26] Norris had campaigned in Ulster from the late summer to the autumn of 1595, when a truce was reached with the leader of the Irish rebellion, Tyrone.[27] As was usual, the army was disbanded, and at times of truce both soldiers and army preachers gravitated to the city. Details of their lives at such times can be filled in by documents like the campaign journal of the Lord Deputy William Russell. In Russell's journal we can read of both his attendance at Sunday service in Dublin cathedral, and the names of the preachers delivering sermons, which included Hanmer, who was clearly now living in the city. It appears from the journals that there were several occasions in which two preachers each delivered a sermon, or delivered it jointly, with Humphrey Fenn and Jonas Wheeler two of the most regular presences in the mid-1590s alongside Loftus and Graves.[28]

After Norris's death the royal army was re-organised through new appointments, but the military preachers remained in service, and, in the case of Hanmer, former associations granted subsequent preferment. Hanmer was in service under the earl of Ormond from 1597, and followed him in all his journeys throughout Ireland.[29] Therefore, from the itineraries of Ormond's campaigns, we can follow the progress of his chaplain across the country: between 1597 and 1599 Hanmer probably accompanied the general on his campaigns in the mid-south and south-west, covering an area that stretched beyond Kilkenny, the earl's territories, to Kilmallock, in south Limerick near the Cork border. From May 1599 Ormond's garrison was mostly employed to the north and north-east of Kilkenny, at Ballyragget, Athy and Naas in County Kildare. Hanmer must have spent the months between August and November 1599 predominantly in Dublin.[30] Probably through the patronage of Ormond, at the end of 1599 Hanmer received an appointment by royal letters patent to the wardenship of the new Collegiate Church of St Mary in Youghal, County Cork, where he moved in the spring of 1600 to be inducted.[31]

Ormond interceded to obtain more for his chaplain, and in 1600 wrote to the government in London asking that 'Mr Meredith Hanmer, doctor of

---

[26]   TNA, SP 63/201/59.
[27]   John S. Nolan, *Sir John Norreys and the Elizabethan Military World* (Exeter, 1997), p. 224.
[28]   Humphrey Fenn was associated with Thomas Cartwright and the Presbyterian movement; see Alan Ford, *James Ussher: Theology, History, and Politics in Early Modern Ireland and England* (Oxford, 2007), p. 42. Jonas Wheeler features in the list of puritans in Dublin compiled by Hanmer (TNA, SP 63/214/36; see also Ford, *James Ussher*, pp. 54–5). The names of the preachers of Sunday sermons in Dublin are given by Russell: David Edwards, ed., *Campaign Journals of the Elizabethan Irish Wars* (Dublin, 2014), pp. 208 and ff.
[29]   TNA, SP 63/206/308.
[30]   *CSPI, 1599–1600*, pp. 11–13, 20, 36–8; Edwards, *Ormond Lordship*, pp. 251–62.
[31]   *The Irish Fiants of the Tudor Sovereigns*, ed. K.W. Nicholls, 4 vols. (Dublin, 1994), no. 6345; NLI MS 43,144/4/92, and MS 43,283/3, item 7.

divinity, attendant [...] on myself ever since my Lieutenancy', could be granted a very small bishopric 'long void and wasted by traitors' in regard of the services performed and of the 'sufficiency of the man'.[32] As late as 1601 Hanmer was still closely connected to the household of his erstwhile military patron and delivered a sermon at the funeral of his wife, Lady Elizabeth Sheffield, held at the Cathedral Church of Kilkenny on 21 April 1601, demonstrating how important – and, undoubtedly, remunerative – was his role in military culture.[33] Hanmer probably spent most of his last years in Dublin. He was briefly imprisoned in Dublin Castle, sometime before April 1604, allegedly due to drunkenness. A compelling account of this episode survives written by the Jesuit Henry Fitzsimon. In his correspondence with the Superior General of the Jesuits, Claudio Acquaviva, Fitzsimon tells us that Hanmer had been pressed to engage in controversy with him while they were both in jail, but that he ended up lending him books from his library, together with a barrel of beer and one of flour.[34] Sometime after April 1604 Hanmer died in Dublin and was buried in St Michan's church.

Hanmer stands as a figure who was both exemplary and eccentric.[35] He undoubtedly had a serious commitment to the Christian faith, but may have seen his ecclesiastical career as a means of supporting his scholarship rather than as the result of a specific devotion to preaching (although we cannot be sure as little evidence remains of his sermons). Furthermore, we do not know the exact nature of his faith, beyond his commitment to the institution of the church which employed him. It is hard, also, to believe that many Church of England priests were quite as combative as he was, a feature that predates his time as an army chaplain. What we can state is that he was clearly valued as a chaplain and preacher, perhaps because he was prepared to go to Ireland which was notoriously short of committed Anglophone reformed priests. Hanmer was prepared to do his duty, and he was valued as an effective preacher by his commanders. Military culture undoubtedly suited Hanmer and he gained a great deal from his service. He had accumulated benefices and other monetary

---

32   TNA SP 63/207/6/277 (31 December 1600).
33   NLI, GO MS 64, fol. 32. We are indebted to Dr Stuart Kinsella for directing us to the funeral entries.
34   Hanmer had in fact been one of the most vociferous anti-Jesuit pamphleteers in the early 1580s in London, author of *The Great Bragge and Challenge of Mr Champion* [i.e. Edmund Campion] and of *The Jesuits' Banner*. The letter, and a later (1614) account of the encounter between Fitzsimon and Hanmer, are printed in Edmund Hogan, *Words of Comfort to Persecuted Catholics* (Dublin, 1881). For a discussion of Hanmer's anti-Jesuit polemic: Angela Andreani, 'Between Theological Debate and Political Subversion: Meredith Hanmer's Confutation of Edmund Campion's Letter to the Privy Council', *Aevum* 3 (2016), 557–73.
35   For further discussion: Angela Andreani, 'Meredith Hanmer's Career in the Church of England, c.1570–1590', *Explorations in Renaissance Culture* 44.1 (2018), 47–72.

rewards, which he probably used to further his scholarship – an indication that common bonds and mutual interest cemented links between the church and the army.

As John Hale has argued, preachers dealt with war not only in their sermons, but also through their involvement in the facilitation of military activity, for instance by storing armour in their churches.[36] As our study of Hanmer's example shows, military identity could encompass a wider variety of roles than simple soldiery. It demonstrates too that the lives of preachers and the military were physically close, since providing spiritual comfort and blessings to soldiers on the battlefield meant that preachers had to travel and camp with them, sharing the actual experience of martial life.

Preaching to the Army in Ireland

The testimony of the military officials during the Nine Years War reveals a number of important though generally neglected aspects of the Protestant clergy in Ireland. Reading these documents, we learn of the clergy's commitment to the service of the church and their congregations, as well as to preaching. It is clear that they were thought to play an important role for the garrison, as is demonstrated by the stipends that were voluntarily paid by royal officials from their own purses to maintain the clergy attached to the army. Further evidence of the significance of their spiritual role is provided by the several references to their preaching and accounts of their attendance to their pastoral duties. Robert Graves, Jonas Wheeler and Humphrey Fenn were all regular preachers in Dublin during Russell's deputyship.[37] Thomas Norris had a special regard for Bishop Chardon, and he praised his learned preaching to the army at a time of difficulty during the Nine Years War and interceded to grant him protection and benefices.[38] Even amongst the clergy least persuaded of the adequacy of preaching there were regular preachers like Archbishop Loftus.[39] Hanmer appears to have been valued as a good and learned preacher by Loftus and Ussher, who signed their recommendation on his behalf, noting the 'great pains' taken by Hanmer in his service in Munster.[40] Ormond commended his

---

[36] J.R. Hale, *Renaissance War Studies* (London, 1983), pp. 490–1.
[37] Edwards, ed., *Campaign Journals*, pp. 208 and ff.
[38] Chatsworth House, Cork MS 1/31–2.
[39] George Browne preached only twice a year; Jones not more than four times and not in his diocese but in Dublin; Loftus referred to preaching as a futile exercise: Brendan Bradshaw, 'Sword, Word and Strategy in the Reformation in Ireland', *Historical Journal* 21.3 (1978), 485, esp. nn. 36–8.
[40] TNA, SP 63/201/59.

dutiful and respectful offices and services worthy of consideration, in addition to his learning and good sermons.[41]

The journal of the Lord Deputy supplies occasional, scattered comments on the preachers of Sunday sermons. For instance, we gather that Hanmer's preaching could be very bitter, though it is indeed possible that underlying this laconic comment were political and religious rivalries. Russell was a forward Protestant while Hanmer was a convinced 'anti-puritan' who was zealous enough to compile lists of non-conformists in Ireland; one such list features Russell himself and survives in Hanmer's manuscript notes now in the State Papers for Ireland.[42] Russell was also an old enemy of Sir John Norris, and a member of the circle of the earl of Essex, another rival to Hanmer's patron.[43] In fact, a great deal of the information that we have about these two figures reminds us that we need to pay close attention to personal feuds, political differences and local conflicts, as well as emphasising the mutual dependency of the military and the clergy, even in the context of war.

The importance of the sermon, the form of dramatic, rhetorically crafted oral delivery most frequently experienced in early modern England, has been much more commonly acknowledged in recent years.[44] Sermons, as the previous comments indicate, were probably the most significant aspect of a Protestant preacher's role, as the established church sought to become reformed and so repudiate the ceremonial nature of the late medieval and post-Reformation Catholic churches, concentrating on the word rather than the image. Inspiring soldiers as they were due to enter battle was the duty of a Protestant preacher and it is no coincidence that the rising star of the Elizabethan Church, Lancelot Andrewes (1555–1626), was chosen to preach the Ash Wednesday sermon before the Queen on 21 February 1599, 'At what time the Earle of Essex was going forth, upon the Expedition for Ireland.'[45] Essex was not appointed until 12

---

[41]   TNA, SP 63/207/6 fol. 277. Hanmer's portrait is somewhat in contrast with what emerges of his conduct from the Act book of Christ Church Cathedral, where he was a prebendary from 1594; see Raymond Gillespie, ed., *The Chapter Act Book of Christ Church Dublin 1574–1634* (Dublin, 1997).

[42]   TNA, SP 63/214. Hanmer's antagonism was also recorded by the Jesuit father Henry Fitzsimon in his correspondence with the Father General Aquaviva, printed in Hogan, *Words of Comfort*, p. 60.

[43]   Edwards, ed., *Campaign Journals*, p. 191; D.J.B. Trim, 'Sir John Norris', *ODNB*; Nolan, *Sir John Norreys*, pp. 141, 226–32.

[44]   See Peter McCullough, Hugh Adlington and Emma Rhatigan, eds., *The Oxford Handbook of the Early Modern Sermon* (Oxford, 2011); Peter McCullough, *Sermons at Court: Politics and Religion in Elizabethan and Jacobean Preaching* (Cambridge, 1998); Arnold Hunt, *The Art of Hearing: English Preachers and their Audiences, 1590–1640* (Oxford, 2010); Mary Morrissey, *Politics and the Paul's Cross Sermons, 1558–1642* (Oxford, 2011).

[45]   Lancelot Andrewes, *Sermons* (London, 1629), sig. R2r.

March, so Andrewes' sermon serves as a prelude to his campaign.[46] Andrewes' approach is to emphasise the justness of the Protestant cause in Ireland, in line with the familiar image repeated throughout the sixteenth century of the battle between the English Christian and the Irish Papist, a struggle of good against evil, God against Satan.[47] Andrewes' central theme is that of the just war of the Christian against the heathen, most famously explored in Erasmus's *Enchiridion Militis Christiani* (1501), regularly translated and reprinted in English as *The Manuell of the Christian Knight*. He opens the sermon with wordplay on 'host', which could mean an army, sacramental bread and an entertainer and lodger of guests:

> This our Host so going forth, our hearts desire and prayer unto GOD is, that they may happily goe, and thrise happily come againe; with joy and triumph, to Her Sacred Majestie; honour to themselves; and generall contentment to the whole Land. So shall they goe, and so come, if we can procure the Lord of Hosts, to goe forth with, and to take charge of our Hosts.[48]

The host which is received by the soldiers gathered as an army (a host) comes from God, the Lord of Hosts, and it will enable them to impose themselves on their hosts, the Irish, who, if they wish to be reconciled to God, need to understand that the invasion is just and for their own good. Host and guest will then be united and can take the host together.

Andrewes' sermon is replete with images of sinfulness and sinlessness, as he deftly draws on a wealth of Biblical images to make his simple central point that the godly are justified in imposing God's will on the godless. Moses is recast as a Christian soldier, a general who understands the 'skill what belonged to war, as one that forty yeares together was never out of campe'.[49] Andrewes employs the familiar image of the sinfulness of the times, and God's just anger at the backsliding of his flock, to argue that only if the English army behaves in an appropriately Christian manner will God favour them with the victory they desire and deserve: 'That now, this time of our going forth, we would goe forth against sinne too; and keepe us, from it, as we would keepe us from our enimie. If we could be but perswaded to reforme our former custome of

---

[46] Steven G. Ellis, *Tudor Ireland: Crown, Community and the Conflict of Cultures, 1470–1603* (Harlow, 1985), pp. 11, 307–8. Essex would certainly have approved of Andrewes' sermon, however, and was a firm advocate of instilling moral discipline in his troops. Three years earlier he had personally provided four chaplains to accompany the army on the Cadiz expedition: Paul E.J. Hammer, *The Polarisation of Elizabethan Politics: The Political Career of Robert Devereux, 2nd Earl of Essex, 1585–1597* (Cambridge, 1999), p. 230.

[47] Andrew Hadfield, *Shakespeare, Spenser and the Matter of Britain* (Basingstoke, 2004), pp. 77–89.

[48] Andrewes, *Sermons*, sig. R2r.

[49] Andrewes, *Sermons*, sig. R2v.

sinne, it would (certeinly) do the journey good.'[50] Andrewes is drawing on one
of the principal themes of late Elizabethan writing: the fear that the English,
especially those in the capital, had lapsed into behaviour so abhorrent that
God would soon have no choice other than to punish them, a fear that grew
towards the end of Elizabeth's reign with the uncertainty of her successor, and
the fear that a religious civil war might engulf the nation.[51] Andrewes argues
that '*war* is not so secular a matter', and so it is important to combine military
and religious strategy as there will be two inter-related benefits: 'Of warr, in
Divinitie: That our going forth might procure the giving over sinne. Of Divinitie, in warr: that our giving over sinne might procure good speed to our going
forth; even an honorable and happy returne.'[52] War can only be won by the
sinless, but, if properly pursued, it will have the benefit of removing the sins of
the righteous army pursuing just war: 'If they which goe to warr must keepe
themselves from sinne, then is warr no sinne, but lawfull; and, without sinne,
to be undertaken.'[53]

Andrewes' logic is circular: if Essex's army triumphs it is because it is sinless,
but if it fails then it will have failed because the soldiers were too entrapped
in sin. War should be fought against sin not with it, because 'the very nature
of Warre […] is an act of Justice, and of Justice corrective, whose office is
to punish sinne.'[54] Only when sin has been eradicated should war be waged
because war is a just instrument invented by God to punish the transgression
of men:

> For, sure it is, that for the transgression of a people, GOD suffereth these divi-
> sions of Reuben within; GOD stirreth up the spirit of Princes abroad, to take
> peace from the earth: thereby to chasten men, by paring the growth of their
> wealth, with this His hired razor; by wasting their strong men (the hand of the
> enemies eating them up;) by making widdowes and fatherlesse children; by
> other like consequents of Warre.[55]

Reuben was the eldest son of Jacob and Leah who played an instrumental role
in the plot against Joseph which led to the divisions between the brothers and
caused their suffering in Egypt.

Andrewes outlines what will happen in war. Behind these words, of course,
lurks an anxiety that the Irish might prove too stubborn and slippery to

---

[50] Andrewes, *Sermons*, sig. R2v.
[51] See, for example, Thomas Nashe, *Christs Teares Over Jerusalem*, *Works*, ed. R.B. McKer-
     row, rev. F.P. Wilson. 5 vols. (Oxford, 1966), 2: 1–175; Robert Greene and Thomas Lodge,
     A Looking Glass for London and England (London, 1594).
[52] Andrewes, *Sermons*, sigs. R2v–R3r.
[53] Andrewes, *Sermons*, sig. R2v.
[54] Andrewes, *Sermons*, sig. R4v.
[55] Andrewes, *Sermons*, sig. S1r.

succumb quickly and easily; that English military tactics might not prevail in Irish conditions; and that conditions in Ireland, in particular the notorious Irish bogs which spread 'the country disease, the flux' (dysentery), would seriously undermine the war effort.[56] All of which, of course, proved only too true – as Essex fled the country having achieved little – until the campaign was run by a far more effective general, Charles Blount, eighth baron Mountjoy (1563–1606), who realised that strategically placed garrisons would hem in the elusive Irish.[57] Accordingly, the wrath of God was visited upon both English and Irish for failing to obey his laws. The Irish because they were recalcitrant Catholics, who refused to convert to Protestantism even though they had been exposed to the true word of God; the English because they were not good enough Protestants and could not escape the consequences of their failings. In waging war without expunging sin they were bound to suffer alongside their opponents.

Sermons were surely just as important on campaign in Ireland. Unfortunately, as Raymond Gillespie has noted, scant evidence survives of the pastoral activity of Hanmer and fellow 'new colonial preachers'. All that remains are a few manuscript notes taken by listeners, and other notes taken by the preachers themselves as memory aids.[58] A number of papers found in Hanmer's collection of historical notes seem to belong to the latter group. Although there is some doubt concerning hand and authorship, these notes indeed preserve a sample of the sermons that may have been heard in Dublin cathedrals or in the field by the garrison during the war campaigns.[59] The scriptural sources he favours are the Acts of the Apostles, the Psalms, and epistles to the Philippians, the Ephesians and Corinthians.

The notes indicate that the sermons would have shared similar structural characteristics: all begin with a quotation from a scriptural passage followed by an explanation of its meaning and its place in the Scriptures. There follows the exposition, and in one instance what appears to have been the full *divisio* of the theme has been preserved. This appears in the notes for a sermon on the

---

[56]   John McGurk, *The Elizabethan Conquest of Ireland: The Burdens of the 1590s Crisis* (Manchester, 1997), p. 241.

[57]   John J. Silke, *Kinsale: The Spanish Intervention in Ireland at the End of the Elizabethan Wars* (Liverpool, 1970).

[58]   Raymond Gillespie, 'Preaching the Reformation in Early Modern Ireland', *Oxford Handbook of the Early Modern Sermon*, ed. McCullough et al., p. 289.

[59]   The duct and inclination are consistent with Hanmer's hand but single letter forms are not, as compared to the main hand in the historical notes and in his identified holograph letters. This may very well be an alternative hand used by Hanmer, but could be that of someone else. Although they appear at different points of the collection bound as TNA, SP 63/214, the sermon notes are all written on the same paper in the same style: the text is written in two columns, rubricated with the scriptural reference and introduced by the relevant quotation from the Scriptures.

Acts of the Apostles 4: 32–7 (fols. 113–14), which constitute the most complete fragment. Four parts of the division are listed immediately after the explanation.[60] The passage cited from Acts 4: 32–7 beginning 'And the multytude of them that beleved were of one harte and of one sowle', is used by the author to discuss the state and condition of the primitive Church, and the meaning of the responsibility of the Apostles as witnesses to the truth.[61] The four parts of the exposition would have developed the theme of the apostolic duty to affirm the resurrection of Christ against the enemies of the truth, which, as is repeated, was a responsibility shared by all preachers, and that required that the ministry was well instructed in order to pursue continuous teaching, affirmation and testimony of true faith.[62] The draft ends abruptly after the introduction of the second part of the *divisio*, in which the preacher seemingly aimed to expound the meaning of the consent of the primitive Christian community. We can reconstruct at least the focus of the remaining two parts thanks to the list brought forth at the beginning of the sermon. Interestingly, the preacher intended to give an account of the temporal goods needed by the Church, and to explore the theme of unity in terms of the consent of the Christian community to share possessions and wealth. The fourth part, to conclude, would have discussed the example of Barnabas, a native of Cyprus and a member of the early Christian community in Jerusalem, who sold some of his land to give the proceeds to the community. The connection between the themes touched upon by the preacher in his sermon and the reality of clerical life in Ireland, as it has emerged from our chapter, appear striking: the sermon could have sent a powerful message regarding the fundamental role of the preacher, who has inherited the duty of the Apostles to witness the truth. Furthermore, it might have been a forceful reminder of the virtues of liberality, especially towards the Church and its representatives, developing the theme from Acts 4: 34–5 that 'Neither was there any among them, that lacked, for as many as were possessors of lands or houses, sold them, and brought the price of the things that were sold,/ And laid it down at the Apostles' feet, and it was distributed unto every man, according as he had need.'

The fragments of the second draft sermon are scribbled on the verso of historical notes in Hanmer's own hand, then crossed out. The theme was drawn from the Epistle of Paul and Timothy to the Philippians, again an exhortation to unity and consent, to pursue compassion and humility, and possibly, again, to share riches (fol. 166). The notes for a sermon on Psalm 89: 20 suggest that this would have included an articulate explanation of the passage used by the

---

[60] TNA, SP 63/214. All subsequent references from Hanmer's notes are cited parenthetically in the text.

[61] Biblical quotations are from the 1560 Geneva Bible.

[62] TNA, SP 63/214 fol. 114, column 1.

preacher as a testimony of the godly foundation of the realm of Kind David: 'I have found david my servant with my holy oyle have I anoynted hym &tc.' (fol. 184). The notes indicate that the preacher intended to focus on the divine foundation of earthly powers and aimed at stirring the conscience of the listeners, particularly of leaders: 'The which teacheth a good lesson to all princes and majestrates chefely but generally to all men[,] that is first that though they be preferr[ed] above the[i]re brethren, yet that sty[ll] they are the Lordes servauntes' (fol. 184). The notes on the second epistle to the Corinthians 4: 3–4 and on Ephesians 2: 9 are fragmentary. The passage from the Ephesians must have been chosen in preparation for a sermon on the theme of grace and salvation achieved through faith rather than works. An outline for a division of the matter lists the two parts of salvation, and salvation by grace through faith (fol. 270v). The notes on Corinthians indicate that the sermon would have dealt with the theme of the inaccessibility of the gospel: 'If the Gospel be then hid, it is hid to them that are lost' and with the objection that it is evident to all that even though many hear the Gospel, yet they are not necessarily lightened by it. The notes proceed then to examine the question of whether this was the fault of the preacher or of the gospel, reaching the conclusion that

> there some that are lost […] that as wel for that they are not of them selves able to understand it beyng [infi]deles as also for that there is one that doth blind them also in their mynde that the glorye thereof should not so shine unto them in such wyse as they myght therein see christ to be the Image of god. (fol. 309v)

A note of a division into three parts follows the explanation, showing to whom the gospel is hidden, and why and how to remedy this state of things, but the notes indicate that the intention of the author was to expound further the meaning of the words of the apostle concerning himself and fellow preachers, incorporating readings of the passage from Calvin and other sources.

Military sermons, as might have been expected, exploited the tradition of *Militis Christiani*, casting the army as God's soldiers valiantly struggling to establish his will. Preachers had an obvious frame of reference and series of tropes which they could exploit and their sermons repeatedly emphasise the bond between the military and the clergy, both imagined working together as complementary, mutually reinforcing components of Christian culture. Through the use of military imagery to describe the conflict between good and evil, and the re-borrowing of the metaphor of the spiritual struggle to speak to the martial vocation of soldiers, military and religious identities became so profoundly linked that they appear to coalesce into a common identity as fighters against evil and as defenders of Christianity.[63] If Christian culture played a crucial role in the shaping of military identity through sermons, so

---

[63] Hale, *Renaissance War Studies*, p. 488.

too did the preachers by adapting their profession to martial culture, as in the example of Hanmer, a preacher who followed generals and their soldiers in their campaigns.

Conclusion

This brief survey of the relationship between the clergy and the military in late Elizabethan Ireland – largely based on the career of Meredith Hanmer in Ireland and the words of Lancelot Andrewes – reveals, as we might expect, an intimate, symbiotic relationship between two of the central professions of the period. It should certainly not surprise us that scholars and writers ended up spending large parts or all of their lives in the church or the army. By the mid-sixteenth century, universities were no longer solely institutions for training young men for a church career, although this was still one of their principal functions; if graduates were not about to inherit a landed estate they had to pursue a career somewhere, which often meant an ecclesiastical or military profession.[64] Hanmer's career makes sense in a variety of ways. He appears to have been attached to his studies as well as his faith, but his sustained pursuit of personal gain also implies that the Church was a convenient career as much as a calling.

We also have further evidence of the central importance of the sermon in Elizabethan culture – and military culture – as a regular and frequent dramatic performance which served to order the nature of everyday life in both its significant and trivial moments. Andrewes' important sermon situates the invasion of Ireland in an apocalyptic context, the struggle for good and evil which many thought was reaching a crisis point in the late 1590s. Accordingly, it should be compared to literary works which share identical premises, such as *The Faerie Queene*, the author of which had fled Ireland and died in Westminster less than a month before Andrewes delivered his sermon.[65] According to Andrewes, good can – and should – triumph over evil but only if the godly understand their need to eschew sin at all costs and labour to distinguish themselves from evil sinners. The Bible is crammed with examples of lazy backsliders who failed to understand this message and initiated God's wrath. The notes we have of Hanmer's sermons, although not extensive, provide us

64   See Richard Helgerson, *The Elizabethan Prodigals* (Berkeley, 1976), pp. 22–6; D.J.B. Trim, 'The Art of War: Martial Poetics From Henry Howard to Philip Sidney', *The Oxford Handbook of Tudor Literature, 1485–1603*, ed. Mike Pincombe and Cathy Shrank (Oxford, 2009), pp. 587–605; Andrew Hadfield, 'War Poetry and Counsel in Early Modern Ireland', *Elizabeth I and Ireland*, ed. McGowan-Doyle and Kane, pp. 239–60.
65   Florence Sandler, '*The Faerie Queene*: An Elizabethan Apocalypse', *The Apocalypse in English Renaissance Thought and Literature* ed. C.A. Patrides and Joseph Wittreich (Manchester, 1984), pp. 148–74.

with enough information to establish that he shared the same premises as those closer to the crown, and that there was little real difference in the nature of sermons preached to the court and in the field. Soldiers had to believe that they were fighting for a righteous cause. Preachers had to inspire them, but also teach them to control their baser instincts so that they would work as a more effective fighting unit. They also had to make soldiers understand that if victory on the battlefield eluded them, more than bad luck was at stake, and they had failed through their own sinfulness, and needed to become more worthy of God's favour if they were to triumph in the future.

6

'Trust, Desert, Power and skill to serve': The Old English and Military Identities in Late Elizabethan Ireland

RUTH A. CANNING

From the twelfth-century introduction of Anglo-Norman rule in Ireland, the Pale and a few scattered quasi-independent English lordships had represented beacons of 'Englishness' in an uncivil Irish wilderness. Without these precious footholds, and especially that of the Pale, English rule in Ireland could not survive. Yet it was not England which provided the military might for protecting these enclaves; this heavy responsibility had been the hereditary obligation of the Old English descendants of Ireland's original Anglo-Norman conquerors. Charged with maintaining the administrative, judicial and martial legitimacy of English overlordship on a distant frontier, this community had always led a highly militarised existence. Major and minor wars erupted every year, internecine strife was routine, and at all times the Pale borders were threatened by marauding Gaelic Irish neighbours. The martial defence of all things English was therefore central to the Old English community's sense of identity and they took great pride in having 'spent their bloode and lost their lives [...] resisting the Rebells and enemyes' of the crown.[1] Over the course of the sixteenth century, however, the position of pre-eminence once enjoyed by this community was gradually eroding as Tudor monarchs took a greater interest in Ireland and dispatched increasing numbers of English-born officers to direct Irish affairs. At the very same time, these New English officers and their patrons back in England became ever more sceptical about Old English allegiances. This was partly because the Old English were competition for Irish offices, but it was largely because their Irish birth and continuing attachment to the Catholic faith made them less than perfect subjects. Determined to prove otherwise, the Old English believed that their continued support of the crown's military enterprise would be a measurable expression of their unfaltering dedication to crown interests.

---

[1]   TNA, SP 63/202(4)/60 (The greevances of the Englishe Pale, 1598).

While military service was routine, especially for the lords who lived along the Pale borders, the Nine Years War (1594–1603) marked an intensification in their military activities as well as the crown's expectations of this population more generally. The actual military contribution of the Old English community to the progress of this war has been largely overlooked, as has how Old Englishmen considered this service to be a manifestation of their continued Englishness and their historic responsibility to uphold crown authority in Ireland. Because the Pale border elite were the most active and vocal Old English servitors during this conflict, this chapter will focus on records representing their point of view. It aims to offer some insight into how military traditions conditioned their responses during the war and how they drew on this to reinforce their declarations of loyalty. To do so, a brief assessment of security issues and military traditions within the Pale will establish that this community occupied a unique status and identity as 'Englishmen' living on a distant Tudor frontier, and that a constant state of military preparedness helped shape individual and collective mentalities. It will then focus on the war-time career and petitions of Patrick Plunkett, seventh baron of Dunsany (1565–1601), to explore how members of the Old English community drew on military traditions and personal service to articulate political and cultural identity. This identity will be considered in the context of Old English displacement from the crown's military ranks alongside their pleas to be recognised as 'the old experienced learned with bloody hands'.[2]

The key to Old English identity was a combination of geography and history. The Pale – roughly comprising counties Dublin, Louth, Meath, Westmeath and Kildare – along with a few other isolated English enclaves had represented the English crown's hold on Ireland for four centuries. These pockets of Englishness, and especially the administrative and economic hub of the Pale, had to be maintained or else England's claim to Ireland would be nothing more than an ambitious yet hollow title, like that of France. Although Ireland had long been regarded as a necessary western flank protecting the island of England from foreign invasion, English monarchs had always been reluctant to provide the men, equipment and finance for this holding operation. In fact, only three English monarchs had visited Ireland since the original Anglo-Norman invasion and, prior to 1534, sporadic interventions by English deputies and commissioners were brief, expensive and generally ineffective.[3] English monarchs tended to be distracted by what seemed like more pressing, or perhaps more prestigious, concerns at home and on the continent; Ireland did, however, present severe logistical problems which also served as a deterrent.

---

[2] Valerie McGowan-Doyle, *The Book of Howth: Elizabethan Conquest and the Old English* (Cork, 2011), pp. 101–2.

[3] The last English monarch to visit Ireland was Richard II in 1399.

Simply put, it took a great deal of time and money to raise soldiers who might desert on ships that might sink.[4] Shipments of victuals, supplies and pay for those soldiers were not only expensive, but consignments were perpetually late, rarely arrived in sufficient quantities, and foodstuffs were prone to spoiling. What awaited English soldiers in Ireland was an elusive enemy, a shortage of shelter, and an abundance of disease. To make matters worse, the captains and victuallers charged with meeting the needs of these troops were disposed to defrauding them in order to line their own pockets.[5] Consequently, exasperated English rulers were inclined to rely on the cheaper and more convenient option of delegation to the aristocracy whereby the defence of their Irish territories was left in the hands of Ireland's Old English population.

In order to fulfil this role, the Old English nobility and gentry had been permitted an enormous amount of independence and authority, and certainly far more than their counterparts living in southern England. They constituted a ruling elite, but one whose mandate was firmly grounded in their ability to fend off foreign and domestic threats through military might. Since the original Anglo-Norman settlement, the march surrounding the Pale had been described as a physical and psychological socio-political barrier separating a carved-out land of civility from the dark savagery and tyranny of the Gaelic beyond. As Robin Frame has succinctly noted, 'from the beginning to the end the Irish lordship was a land of marches [and] [c]oncern with fortifying and inhabiting the borderlands was a constant theme in the colony's history'.[6] War was common, and even in the sixteenth century, contemporary sources sometimes recorded two or three unrelated conflicts within the space of a single year. Although most of these struggles were small in scale, violence was nonetheless endemic. Sudden raids by neighbouring Gaelic septs were frequent and some clans, like the O'Tooles, made their livings by these spoils.[7] In addition to external threats, dynastic and territorial disputes were common within the Old English community.[8] Thus, in order to protect themselves and

---

4   John McGurk has provided an excellent study of the logistical issues which crippled the crown's military machine during the Nine Years War: *The Elizabethan Conquest of Ireland: The 1590s Crisis* (Manchester, 1997); see also Cyril Falls, *Elizabeth's Irish Wars* (London, 1950).
5   Ciaran Brady, 'The Captains' Games: Army and Society in Elizabethan Ireland', *A Military History of Ireland*, ed. T. Bartlett and K. Jeffery (Cambridge, 1996), pp. 149–51.
6   Robin Frame, 'Power and Society in the Lordship of Ireland 1272–1377', *P&P* 76 (1977), 7.
7   Steven G. Ellis, 'The Tudors and the Origins of the Modern Irish States: A Standing Army', *A Military History of Ireland*, p. 119. For a more detailed study of these Gaelic septs: Christopher Maginn, *'Civilizing' Gaelic Leinster: The Extension of Tudor Rule in the O'Byrne and O'Toole Lordships* (Dublin, 2005).
8   Seán Ó Domhnaill, 'Warfare in Sixteenth-Century Ireland', *IHS* 5.17 (1946), 31; David Edwards, 'The Escalation of Violence in Sixteenth-Century Ireland', *Age of Atrocity: Violence and Political Conflict in Early Modern Ireland*, ed. Edwards, P. Lenihan and C. Tait (Dublin, 2007), p. 66.

their livelihoods from these regular interruptions, the inhabitants of the Pale, and especially those residing along the borders, had to be ready to engage an enemy at a moment's notice.[9] Although they did not constitute a standing army – trained, armed and paid by the state – they did form a defensive buffer zone, or 'military frontier'.[10] Indeed, unlike the comfortable country houses being erected in England during the late Tudor period, the houses of the Pale nobility and gentry were still built and organised for defence.[11] Private armies were maintained to defend and expand the lordships of leading magnates, and these were put at the disposal of the crown when need arose. These same lords were also responsible for raising and leading local forces to respond to localised threats or campaign further abroad. The unstable nature of life in Ireland necessitated that all tenants of English blood were answerable for unpaid military service, and hostings – military expeditions assembled through mustering local inhabitants – had been a frequent occurrence since the arrival of the Anglo-Normans. Local participation was mandatory and, as in England, military tenure was established by regulation; all able-bodied men between the ages of 16 and 60 were required to maintain weapons appropriate to their status and perform up to forty days of military service each year.[12] Undoubtedly, there were years during which the Palesmen were required to exceed their traditional terms of service but, for the most part, conflicts were short-lived and these provisions sufficed.[13]

In the 1590s, however, with the outbreak of war on a scale never before witnessed, martial demands on the Old English community far exceeded what had been traditionally expected of them. Hostings became more frequent, longer, and more demanding.[14] The government also made additional and frequent appeals to the Palesmen to prepare and arm themselves for self-defence.[15] Like hostings, these defensive services were expected and generally considered an

---

[9]   Brady, 'Captains' Games', p. 146; David Edwards, *The Ormond Lordship in County Kilkenny, 1515–1642* (Dublin, 2003); Edwards, 'The Butler Revolt of 1569', *IHS* 28.111 (1993), 228–55; *Age of Atrocity*, ed. Edwards et al., *passim*.

[10] Rhys Morgan and Gerald Power, 'Enduring Borderlands: The Marches of Ireland and Wales in the Early Modern Period', *Frontiers, Regions and Identities in Europe*, ed. Steven G. Ellis et al. (Pisa, 2009), p. 120.

[11] For example, a comparison of Hardwick Hall in Derbyshire and Delvin Castle in Delvin, Westmeath, reveals houses built and maintained for very different purposes.

[12] For a detailed discussion of certain tenurial requirements: William Gerrard, 'Lord Chancellor Gerrard's Notes of his Report on Ireland', *Analecta Hibernica* 2 (1931), 93–291; Ellis, 'Tudors', p. 120.

[13] Edwards, 'Escalation', pp. 34–78.

[14] See Ruth A. Canning, *The Old English in Early Modern Ireland: The Palesmen and the Nine Years War in Ireland, 1594–1603* (Woodbridge, 2019), ch. 4.

[15] For example, TNA, SP 63/186/51 (Irish Council to Privy Council, 9 Feb. 1596); TNA, SP 63/191/15(I) (J. Norreys and Fenton to Irish Council, 27 Jun. 1596); London, Lambeth Palace, MS 612, fols. 4r–5v, 10 (Russell's Journal, Aug. and Nov. 1594); CUL, MS Kk. I. 15,

extension of their natural duty to their sovereign and state. But, in addition to carrying out these customary obligations, many Old Englishmen volunteered to serve the crown as members of fully functioning companies wholly composed of native troops.[16] Some of these were companies of kerne – as Irish foot soldiers were known – which continued to be led by their traditional territorial captains while enjoying the queen's pay.[17] Other companies were composed of loyalist volunteers or adherents of Irish magnates and landowners, like the barons of Dunsany, Delvin and Howth.[18] The service tenure of these companies varied; some were only temporary bands raised during periods of emergency, while others, including Dunsany's, formed a more permanent part of the military establishment. Many of these volunteers served at their own expense or at the expense of their local lords, but there were a significant number of Old English soldiers employed directly by the crown.[19] Due to the inadequate quality and number of soldiers dispatched from England during these war years, the administration was constrained to rely heavily on native recruits – Old English and Gaelic Irish alike – to augment the strength of the crown's English companies.[20] Initially, there had been an allowance of twenty soldiers of Irish birth in each company of one hundred,[21] but by February 1598 the Irish Council reckoned that Irishmen made up at least 'three partes of 4'.[22] This partly reflected necessity, but it was also a product of official greed. Because Irish troops received half the pay of their English counterparts, many army captains saw the financial benefit of employing native soldiers, especially for

---

fols. 387r–89v (Some errors to be reformed in the government of Ireland, Aug. and Nov. 1594).

[16] For example, TNA, SP 63/178/31 (R. Lane to Burghley, 2 Feb. 1595).

[17] K.W. Nicholls, *Gaelic and Gaelicised Ireland in the Middle Ages* (Dublin, 2003), p. 98; M. Ó Báille, 'The Buannadha: Irish Professional Soldiery of the Sixteenth Century', *Journal of the Galway Archaeological and Historical Society* 22.1–2 (1946), 49–94; Fergus Cannan, '"Hags of Hell": Late Medieval Irish Kern', *History Ireland* 19.1 (2011), 14–17.

[18] TNA, SP 63/175/5(XXVII) (Note of the new erected companies, 1594); TNA, SP 63/175/10(I) (Disposition of the forces in Leinster and Ulster, 10 Jun. 1594); HMC, *Salisbury MSS*, 6: 543–4 (Her Majesty's Forces in Ireland, Dec. 1596); Fynes Moryson, 'The Rebellion of Hugh Earle of Tyrone', *An Itinerary*, Part II (London, 1617), p. 43.

[19] For example, Theobald Dillon of Westmeath commanded 25 horsemen paid by the queen; he also commanded a group of kerne and, although it is unclear who paid these troops, it is very likely that he personally employed the men. TNA, SP 63/197/29 (J. Dillon to Cecil, 15 Jan. 1597).

[20] TNA, SP 63/175/52 (Russell to Cecil, 16 Aug. 1594); TNA SP 63/178/101 (Lord Deputy to Privy Council, 20 Mar. 1595); TNA, SP 63/179/5 (Russell to Burghley, 3 Apr. 1595); TNA, SP 63/202(3)/1 (Irish Council to Privy Council, 2 Aug. 1598); TNA, SP 63/202(3)/91 (Irish Council to Privy Council, 2 Oct. 1598); TNA, SP 63/202(2)/96 (Ormond to Cecil, 5 Jul. 1598); Falls, *Elizabeth's Irish Wars*, p. 185.

[21] TNA, SP 63/181/66 (Fenton to Buckhurst, 30 Jul. 1595).

[22] TNA, SP 63/202(1)/56 (Irish Council to Privy Council, 27 Feb. 1598).

muster checks to fill places left vacant by sickness and desertion.[23] Administrators regularly lamented the proliferation of Irishmen in the crown forces but, with few Englishmen of quality and little money to pay them, it had become a necessary evil.

In addition to active military service, Old Englishmen also assisted the crown with intelligence, advice, victuals, manual labour and financial aid. They were killed in combat, died of famine and disease, their lands were spoiled and left waste, their goods stolen, their homes abandoned, and money borrowed from them never repaid. All of this helped the crown towards its eventual victory over the Irish Catholic Confederacy and yet many administrators were determined to block Old Englishmen from positions of trust and authority. Crown administrators had grave concerns about the loyalties of the Old English population and suspected that they might find more in common with their rebellious co-religionist Gaelic countrymen than with the English Protestant crown. These fears were justified. The rebellions of Kildare, Desmond and Baltinglass earlier that century had demonstrated that the Old English were not only capable of challenging crown authority, but that they were also willing to forge alliances with their Gaelic neighbours. Thus, in a vehement attack on the nature of Irish loyalties, the author of *The Supplication of the Blood of the English* averred that no man of Irish birth could be trusted: 'Althoughe assuredly there are some, whose faith if it were thoroughly knowne doth well deserve trust. Yet that some are soe fewe as that it is better for you to trust none, then to hazard the lightinge on them that are disloyall.'[24] He further argued that protestations of loyalty and oaths of fealty were meaningless: 'Have they not often sworne and forsworne themselves? by what god can they sweare, but theyr God will dispence with it? absolve them? and make you goe seeke newe subjects?'[25] He therefore insisted that until the inhabitants of Ireland provided concrete tokens of their obedience, via personal sacrifice or hostages, they could never be trusted.

Much has been said about Old English alienation in the decades preceding the Nine Years War, and while their exclusion from administrative offices continued apace during these war years, their deteriorating position was most noticeably felt in the military establishment. Since the middle of the sixteenth century, efforts had been made to demilitarise the country and, where appropriate, replace the private retinues of local magnates with forces loyal to the English crown and government. These forces, sent from England, formed the basis of a growing standing army in which commands were given to New

[23] TNA, SP 63/178/31 (Lane to Burghley, 2 Feb. 1595).
[24] Willy Maley, ed., 'The Supplication of the Blood of the English Most Lamentably Murdered in Ireland, Cryeng out of the Yearth for Revenge (1598)', *Analecta Hibernica* 36 (1995), 36–7.
[25] Maley, ed., 'Supplication', 53.

English appointees rather than servitors of Irish birth and experience. In 1584 the baron of Delvin challenged this tendency by insisting that local forces should be maintained in order to protect the Pale and that 'the noblemen on the borders wheras they dwell shuld have the leadinge of the people as they wear accustomed to have uppon all occasions of service'.[26] For Delvin and other Pale lords, their principal function was a military one and this played a fundamental role in the formation of Old English identities during the early modern period. But appeals like this were to no avail and, over time, English commentators recommended even stricter exclusion of Irish-born individuals from the army's officer ranks. With the outbreak of war in the 1590s, officials remained reluctant to reverse this trend. As Captain John Dowdall declared in 1594: 'I wold not have anie of the countrey Birthe to be a comaunder over the rest but every one that you please to hold protested as a subject shall governe his owne familie and knowen folloers, and no further'.[27] This sentiment was shared by members of the Irish Council who expressed great reservations about entrusting any military commands to native servitors. For instance, in 1598 when the English captain of Doncannon fort left a Wexford gentleman in charge of his post while he ventured to England, the Irish Council appealed to its English counterpart for the captain's immediate return because it was 'not so saffe for a place of that chardge' to be left in the hands of a local.[28]

The Old English responded to such criticisms by directing petitions to the queen and Privy Council, vigorously rejecting denigrations of their dependability while extolling their virtues. These communications are useful interpretative tools because they expose the concerns and aspirations of Old English supplicants and reveal a clear sense of their socio-political identity. Petitions were carefully crafted verbalisations of loyalty and duty, but they were also particularly cogent articulations of the martial value and skills of Old English servitors. Military service had always featured prominently in communications with monarchs and their representatives, but the extreme escalation of military activity during the Nine Years War served to confirm the martial purpose of the Palesmen's frontier existence and heighten their appreciation of their unique expertise. Supplicants commonly asserted that since the twelfth-century Anglo-Norman conquest they and their ancestors had spilled their blood in a continual struggle to preserve both their 'Englishness' and the authority of the English crown from the perceived tyranny of Gaelic Irish lordship. Similarly, countering allegations that they had somehow degenerated through contact with the Irish, the Old English drew on a long established tradition of disdain for Gaelic culture within the towns and cities

[26] TNA, SP 63/108/58 (Delvin's plot, 26 May 1584).
[27] TNA, SP 63/174/37(IX) (J. Dowdall to Irish Council, 2 May 1594).
[28] TNA, SP 63/202(1)/56 (Irish Council to Privy Council, 27 Feb. 1598).

which rendered any notion of a pan-Irish alliance inconceivable. As Nicholas Canny has argued, the Old English 'were acutely conscious of being culturally superior to their Gaelic neighbours and they belaboured the fact that they and their forebears had, over the centuries, upheld the authority of the crown in Ireland against the persistent onslaught of their Gaelic neighbours'.[29]

Prominent among Old English servitor–supplicants was Patrick Plunkett, baron of Dunsany. The Plunkett family took great pride in their 'Englishness', and the seventh baron of Dunsany was no exception. It was this pride to which his brother-in-law Richard Stanihurst appealed in the dedicatory epistle of *De Rebus in Hibernia Gestis*, a work in which Stanihurst endeavoured 'to write the history of our race'.[30] Dunsany shared Stanihurst's opinion on the nature of Old English identity; for these men, the Old English were defined by their English ancestry and culture and in no way was this marred by the accident of their geographical location. Like many of his colleagues, Dunsany believed that preserving his 'Englishness' meant defending all that was English, both physically and ideologically. Although the sixteenth century had witnessed its share of crown–community conflicts, Dunsany stood out as a man remarkably supportive of the crown and its policies. He adamantly believed that subjects should obey their prince at all times, regardless of perceived wrongs committed against them. His position on this matter was demonstrated by his behaviour during the 1580s controversy concerning the cess, an arbitrary tax imposed by the prerogative of viceroys in order to provision their households, private retinues, and later, crown garrisons.[31] While the majority of leading Palesmen, including some of the Plunketts, were vociferous in their opposition to the cess, Dunsany remained aloof and compliant with the wills of English administrators.[32] There was, however, one arena in which Dunsany did not conform to the demands of English government. He was a Catholic. Like many other leading Palesmen, Dunsany patronised Catholic religious institutions and he sent his son and heir to the Irish College at Douai where he would be immersed in the Counter-Reformation movement rather than

[29] Nicholas Canny, 'Identity Formation in Ireland: The Emergence of the Anglo-Irish', *Colonial Identity in the Atlantic World*, ed. Nicholas Canny and Anthony Pagden (Princeton, NJ, 1989), pp. 160–1.

[30] Colm Lennon, *Richard Stanihurst the Dubliner* (Blackrock, 1981), pp. 134–5.

[31] Ciaran Brady, *The Chief Governors: The Rise and Fall of Reform Government in Tudor Ireland, 1536–1588* (Cambridge, 1994), pp. 218–22.

[32] TNA, SP 63/166/57(II) (Note of the articles concerning the composition, 13 Sep. 1592). Hiram Morgan, 'Plunketts', *Oxford Companion to Irish History*, ed. S.J. Connolly (Oxford, 2007), p. 470; Valerie McGowan-Doyle, 'The Book of Howth: The Old English and the Elizabethan Conquest of Ireland', unpublished Ph.D. thesis, (University College Cork, 2005), ch. 1; Victor Treadwell, 'Sir John Perrot and the Irish Parliament of 1585-6', *Proceedings of the Royal Irish Academy* 85 (1985), 280.

the Protestantism of English universities.[33] Dunsany also had strong connections with many redoubtable Catholics, some of whom openly supported Hugh O'Neill's Confederates during the Nine Years War.[34] But, in spite of his own Catholicism and the Counter-Reformation militancy of some of his relatives, Dunsany never saw Catholicism as a barrier to his political allegiance to the English Protestant monarch. This was something he made clear in 1600 when he insisted that the Catholic clergy of the Pale condemned the actions of O'Neill and the Confederates, and thus intimated that the souls and consciences of the Palesmen were not in any real danger.[35]

Like most Pale border lords, Dunsany was a capable military man. In 1583 he gained recognition for serving against some of his Pale colleagues during the Baltinglass and Nugent revolts, for which he was rewarded with a command of twenty horse in crown pay.[36] Following the outbreak of war a decade later, Dunsany's name appeared frequently among the lists of forces actively hunting rebels. In 1594 and 1595 he was in command of twenty horsemen assigned by the queen and another 'thirtie which he held allwaies as marshall'.[37] In 1595 Dunsany and his forces were campaigning in the north under the command of Sir John Norreys.[38] Norreys, however, expressed doubts about the value and dedication of Palesmen serving so far from their homes and suggested that Pale companies serving in Ulster would be better employed if relocated to the borders where they could provide a defensive barrier against rebel stealths.[39] In accordance with Norreys's advice, Dunsany and twelve of his horsemen were relocated to Dundalk in September 1595.[40] The following July, he and his horse company were appointed to assist the Lord Deputy and Provost Marshal on the borders with the execution of martial law against any unpardoned rebels who

[33] Colm Lennon has written a detailed study of late-medieval Catholic religious institutions in Meath, many of which were founded and patronised by branches of the Plunkett family, including Dunsany: 'The Parish Fraternities of County Meath', *Riocht na Midhe* 19 (2008), 85–101; *Sixteenth-Century Ireland* (Dublin, 2005), p. 124. See also TNA, SP 12/275/135 (Unknown to Cecil, 9 Dec. 1600).
[34] The famous Jesuit Christopher Holywood was Dunsany's cousin; see James Corboy, 'Father Christopher Holywood, S.J., 1559–1626', *Studies* 33 (1944), 543–9; Hiram Morgan, 'Faith and Fatherland of Queen and Country? An Unpublished Exchange Between O'Neill and the State at the Height of the Nine Years War', *Dúiche Néill* 9 (1994), 10, 23–40.
[35] TNA, SP 63/207(I)/2 (Dunsany to Cecil, 2 Jan. 1600).
[36] TNA, SP 63/103/48 (Queen to Lords Justices, 30 Jul. 1583).
[37] Ibid.; TNA, SP 63/177/21 (Dunsany to Cecil, 18 Nov. 1594); TNA, SP 63/177/21(I) (Dunsany to Privy Council, 18 Nov. 1594); TNA, SP 63/178/64 (Docket of Irish suitors, Feb. 1595).
[38] TNA, SP 63/183/12 (Norreys to Burghley, 8 Sep. 1595); Lambeth Palace, MS 612 (Russell's Journal).
[39] TNA, SP 63/183/12 (Norreys to Burghley, 8 Sep. 1595).
[40] Lambeth Palace, MS 612 (Russell's Journal, 21, Sep. 1595).

entered the Pale.[41] Dunsany continued to serve along the Pale frontier in 1597 where Lord Deputy Burgh reported the baron and his forces were stationed along the borders of Westmeath and Longford.[42] By September 1599 Dunsany was a colonel of foot, in command of 50 horse and 150 foot at Kells and Navan and was listed again in 1600 as commanding the same number of troops in Leinster.[43] Dunsany's charge of 150 soldiers was one of the largest among Old English servitors at this time, commensurate with the earls of Kildare and Clanricard and the baron of Delvin; only the earl of Ormond and Christopher St Lawrence held superior commands.[44] Significantly, of the 350 horse and 3,200 foot registered by Moryson as available to Lord Deputy Mountjoy to take into the field against O'Neill in March 1600, Dunsany was listed with his full complement of 50 horse and 150 foot, thus making him a large contributor to Mountjoy's campaign.[45] Then in October of that year, Mountjoy noted the extreme importance of fortifying passes between the Pale and the north, and so he authorised Dunsany to 'comaund the risings owt of the county of Meath in the E. of Ormonds absence'.[46] Following the arrival of the Spanish at Kinsale in autumn 1601, Dunsany served along the borders again, and was given a special charge 'to coste and followe the Rebells and empeach them in there Journay as mutch as [he] may'.[47] Although defending the Pale was as vital a service as campaigning further afield, it effectively precluded Dunsany from participating in major military engagements where honour and accolades were typically won. Nevertheless, he did effect some very important acts of service, including in 1600 when he captured Turlough McShane O'Reilly, a notorious rebel leader, and killed up to 30 of O'Reilly's horsemen.[48] His efforts did not escape notice, and Secretary Fenton praised Dunsany, noting that 'the gentleman hath ever contynued firme, and loyall to the State, and from tyme to tyme in his owne person, hath faithfully endeavired both to annoy and bridle the rebell, and to defend his neighbors'.[49]

---

[41] TNA, SP 63/191/46(I) (Certain notes by Norreys, enclosed with document dated 27 Jul. 1596).

[42] BL, Add. MS 4819, fol. 147.

[43] Moryson, *Itinerary*, Part II, pp. 43, 61.

[44] Ibid., pp. 59–61.

[45] Ibid., p. 61.

[46] TNA, SP 63/207(5)/92(I) (Mountjoy and Councillors to rest of Dublin Council, 6 Oct. 1600).

[47] TNA, SP 63/209(2)/199 (Carey to Cecil, 23 Nov. 1601); TNA, SP 63/209(2)/168A (Mountjoy and Councillors to Loftus and Dublin Council, 25 Oct. 1601); TNA, SP 63/210/8 (Irish Council to Privy Council, 12 Jan. 1602).

[48] HMC, *Salisbury MSS*, 10: 252 (E. Herbert to Cecil, 30 Jul. 1600); TNA, SP 63/207(4)/15 (Mountjoy to Cecil, 16 Jul. 1600); TNA, SP 63/207(6)/45 (Nov. 1600. Statement by Henry Dillon, Nov. 1600).

[49] TNA, SP 63/199/124 (Fenton to Cecil, 30 Jun. 1597).

The martial contributions of Old English servitors like Dunsany were instrumental in securing a crown victory, yet their efforts were never enough to convince English observers of their loyalty. The allegiances of even the most prominent Old English servitors came under scrutiny during this conflict as questions were raised about the earls of Kildare and Ormond as well as the barons of Howth, Louth and Delvin on multiple occasions.[50] Striving to prove their worth and ability, these Old English supplicants went to great lengths to detail their many services, even so far as counting the number of rebel heads they had delivered.[51] Their petitions also functioned as declarations of personal and familial sacrifice by drawing attention to the financial and human costs of war in terms of military support proffered and the destruction of livings by rebels and marauding crown soldiers. All this, they insisted, was borne for the sake of the crown, and what they sought in return was recognition, reward and fair treatment. Unlike most of his peers, there is no evidence to suggest that Dunsany's personal loyalty ever came into question, yet he was one of the most prolific, persistent and eloquent of Old English supplicants during these war years.[52] His petitions therefore indicate that he felt the need to defend his allegiances, and this was probably because he had ample experience of the crown's discriminatory tendencies. [53] Central to Dunsany's petitions was an ancestral commitment to furthering crown interests in Ireland through military traditions and he was determined to defend his inherited role as a military man on an English frontier.

In 1583 Elizabeth granted Dunsany 20 horsemen and £1,000 in arrearages as reward for his services during the Baltinglass and Nugent uprisings.[54] These horsemen had previously been under the command of Sir Nicholas Bagenal,

---

[50]   TNA, SP 63/196/39 (Memorandum on the state of Ireland, Dec. 1596); TNA, SP 63/202(3)/14 (Cecil to Fenton, 8 Aug. 1598); TNA, SP 63/202(3)/35 (Ormond to Cecil, 24 Aug. 1598); TNA, SP 63/178/24 (R. Brown to Lord Deputy, 28 Jan. 1595); TNA, SP 12/275/5 (J. Chamberlain to D. Carleton, 13 Jun. 1600); TNA, SP 63/207(4)/2 (A. Savage to Cecil, 3 Jul. 1600); TNA, SP 63/208(1)/23 (P. Barnewall to Cecil, 29 Jan. 1601); TNA, SP 63/212/2(c) (Articles against Delvin, no date).

[51]   For example, see the suits submitted by the baron of Delvin: TNA, SP 63/198/61 (Brief of Delvin's suit, Mar. 1597); TNA, SP 63/207/88(I) (Services done by Delvin, 1600); TNA, SP 63/207(6)/45 (Statement by Dillon, Nov. 1600). Patricia Palmer has discussed how head counts like Delvin's were used to advertise political worth and angle for promotion: *The Severed Head and Grafted Tongue* (Cambridge, 2013).

[52]   It is impossible to determine whether he wrote more frequently than his colleagues or whether more of his petitions survived.

[53]   Dunsany's son, however, was suspected of fraternising with the enemy and one of his servants was apprehended on suspicion of financing seminarians. TNA, SP 63/188/8 (J. Blakney to Dunsany, 3 Apr. 1596); TNA, SP 63/189/54 (Dunsany to Cecil, 29 May 1596); HMC, *Salisbury MSS*, 7: 58 (Dunsany to Cecil, 8 Feb. 1597).

[54]   TNA, SP 63/93/48 (Queen to Lords Justices, 30 Jul. 1583).

for which the New English Marshall had received sterling pay.[55] In 1587 Dunsany sued for like payment, but it was in vain since he was still lobbying for equal pay and expenses in November 1594.[56] This was not an accidental error in accounting and the unequal distribution of pay amongst servitors of English and Irish birth is corroborated by Fynes Moryson's registers. In 1600, horse companies under Lord Deputy Mountjoy, Munster President George Carew, Henry Danvers, and Henry Docwra received 18 pence per diem, while companies under the earls of Ormond, Kildare, and Clanricard, the barons of Dunsany and Dunkellin, and Sir Christopher St Lawrence received only 12 pence.[57] And this was only a partial subsidy, and one which they rarely received.[58] Like Dunsany, most native servitors put their personal retinues at the crown's disposal but were expected to finance at least a portion of these themselves.[59]

Arrears and reduced pay were a constant irritation, but Dunsany and other Old English servitors also found that their martial authority was undermined on the rare occasions when they enjoyed promotion. In 1599 Lord Lieutenant Essex awarded Dunsany the government of Kells and the surrounding borders. Essex, however, soon fled Ireland in disgrace and Dunsany's position was downgraded by those on the Irish Council who wished to limit the authority of native-born servitors. In January 1600 he implored Cecil to intervene because the Irish Council refused to recognise his new command, arguing that they were not sure how far his authority was actually meant to extend.[60] And, notwithstanding Dunsany's appeals, the Irish Council still ruled that they would only reconsider the matter when the Lord Lieutenant returned, which, of course, he never did.[61] This was not an isolated incident and Dunsany felt the precariousness of Old English promotions again in 1600. Although he was

---

[55]   TNA, SP 63/177/21(I) (Dunsany to Privy Council, 18 Nov. 1594).
[56]   TNA, SP 63/128/30 (Dunsany to Burghley, 30 Feb. 1587); TNA, SP 63/128/86 (Dunsany to Privy Council, 9 Mar. 1587); TNA, SP 63/177/21(I) (Dunsany to Privy Council, 18 Nov. 1594). See also TNA, SP 63/201/144 (Humble suit of the baron of Dunsany, 1597); HMC, *Salisbury MSS*, 7: 476 (Dunsany to Cecil, 9 Nov. 1597); CUL, MS Kk. I. 15, fol. 21v.
[57]   Moryson, *Itinerary*, Part II, p. 59.
[58]   For example, TNA, SP 63/173/31 (Dunsany to Burghley, 15 Feb. 1594); TNA, SP 63/173/63 (Dunsany to Burghley, 27 Feb. 1594); HMC, *Salisbury MSS*, 8: 6 (Dunsany to Cecil, 7 Jan. 1598); HMC, *Salisbury MSS*, 9: 183 (Dunsany to Cecil, 27 May 1599).
[59]   TNA, SP 63/125/2 (Dunsany to Burghley, 1 Jul. 1586); TNA, SP 63/128/86 (Dunsany petition to Privy Council, 9 Mar. 1587); TNA, SP 63/133/65 (Dunsany to Burghley, 18 Feb. 1588); TNA, SP 63/142/55 (Dunsany to Burghley, 28 Mar. 1589); TNA, PC 2/17(2)/63 (Privy Council meeting, 13 May 1590); TNA, SP 63/173/31 (Dunsany to Burghley, 15 Feb. 1594); TNA, SP 63/173/63 (Dunsany to Burghley, 27 Feb. 1594); HMC, *Salisbury MSS*, 8: 6 (Dunsany to Cecil, 7 Jan. 1598); HMC, *Salisbury MSS*, 9: 183 (Dunsany to Cecil, 27 May 1599).
[60]   TNA, SP 63/207(I)/2 (Dunsany to Cecil, 2 Jan. 1600).
[61]   TNA, SP 63/207(I)/2 (Dunsany to Cecil, 2 Jan. 1600); TNA, SP 63/209(2)/155 (Bishop of Meath to Cecil, 20 Oct. 1601).

recognised as a colonel in a series of instructions directed to Mountjoy, it was noted that this was an extraordinary measure and some of Dunsany's compatriots who had been given similar commands were to be demoted.[62]

The Palesmen's reaction to this trend was well summarised by one anonymous discourse: 'th'extract of the English nation there, ought not to be excepted unto, but rather imployed against the Irishe. As they have ever ben since the conqueste, in that they are daylie seene to fight against them, for their honor, lyves, patrimonye and sepulchers of their Ancestors'.[63] This was a cause taken up in London by Dunsany's Old English lawyer, Richard Hadsor. Acting on behalf of another Mr Plunkett whose foot company had been cashiered, Hadsor implored Cecil to restore the company because 'it were fitter in my opinion to imploy him and a number of other sufficient gentlmen of English race in the Pale who received great losse in these warres and are knowen to the State there to be good subjects and faithfull to her Majestie'.[64] Another Palesman, John Lye of Kildare, likewise advised Cecil that 'the service here will be muche the better performed' if 'some of the contrie gent. dwellinge on the bordors maye be imployed therin'.[65] As Lye explained, the Palesmen had a vested interest in establishing peace in Ireland and 'will adventure much where as others haveinge noe liveinge [...] and not able to byde the like sorowe, will not care to prolonge the same'.[66]

To underscore this point, personal and familial sacrifices were presented as the inevitable consequence of living on England's embattled Irish frontier. Particularly poignant in many of Dunsany's petitions is his adulation of the services and sacrifices performed by his kinsmen for the advancement of crown interests. He detailed his own services as well as those of his family – past and present – in order to evoke a sense of unfaltering allegiance, martial prowess, and English identity from one generation to the next. Military identity was at the core of these Old English traditions and the purpose of such historical anecdotes was to convey his awareness of an ancestral obligation towards dutifulness, service and perseverance. Dunsany's petitions touted the loyalty and accomplishments of the whole Plunkett family and specifically stressed his belief that it was a noble pursuit to sacrifice one's life for the sake of the English crown and civility. What is more, according to Dunsany, his unblemished record of ancestral loyalty and service meant that he deserved the same

---

[62]   TNA, SP 63/207(5)/116 (Heads of things, 27 Oct. 1600).
[63]   TNA, SP 63/202(4)/75 ('A discourse to show "that planting of colonies [...] will give best entrance to the reformation of Ulster"', 1598).
[64]   TNA, SP 63/209(2)/153 (R. Hadsor to Cecil, 17 Oct. 1601).
[65]   TNA, SP 63/207(6)/59 (J. Lye to Cecil, 5 Dec. 1600).
[66]   Ibid.

consideration and respect as any subject born in England.[67] As he reasoned in 1595, 'the merytte of my Auncestors whose bloode and deathe have given assured testemonye of their sufficyenties in that charge [...] and the danger of this border whereon my patrymonye is beinge sp[ec]iall consideracions of their preferment thereunto'.[68]

Dunsany purposefully drew attention to the link between service, sacrifice and location of lordship. As Steven Ellis has explained, life on the Tudor peripheries differed considerably from that in stable and comparatively peaceful late Elizabethan England.[69] Dwelling in Ireland necessitated a constant state of military preparedness, especially along the Pale frontier where the lands and livings of border lords were regularly targeted by the crown's enemies. This was particularly true during the Nine Years War because, as the desperate baron of Delvin lamented, 'my distruction is required as a thing thought verie necesarie by them for the easier accomplishing of their traitorous designments'.[70] In neighbouring Meath, where 'the State hath weekely advertisements of great incursions', Dunsany and his relatives were feeling the same pressure.[71] In one attack, nine of Dunsany's relatives were killed, including his own brother, along with thirty of his retainers.[72] According to Dunsany, not only had he been deprived of manpower through the loss of kinsmen and followers, but 'all his landes and his kynsmens upon that border [were] utterlie spoiled by the emimy which was the livinge [...] for the certaine maynteynance of the said Twentie horse'.[73] Even under normal circumstances, it cost a great deal of money and manpower to secure the Pale frontier. As Dunsany explained in 1595, 'my dwellinge is where I can not keepe my owne without keepinge men, and that the more strengthe I have, the more gayne I make of my lande'.[74] But over the course of the war, rebel assaults, the cost of victualling and housing crown soldiers, and unusually bad weather were detrimental to the economic viability of servitors' estates and their ability to sustain their forces.[75] In fact, by 1597 Dunsany was already protesting that his current 'dishabilytie' in income

---

[67]   TNA, SP 63/178/65 (Dunsany to Burghley, Feb. 1595); HMC, *Salisbury MSS*, 7: 323 (Dunsany to Cecil, Jul. 1597); TNA, SP 63/201/144 (Suit of Dunsany, 1597).

[68]   TNA, SP 63/178/65 (Dunsany to Burghley, Feb. 1595).

[69]   Steven G. Ellis, *The Pale and the Far North: Government and Society in Two Early Tudor Borderlands* (Galway, 1986), p. 1.

[70]   TNA, SP 63/192/7(VII) (Delvin to Irish Council, 7 Aug. 1596).

[71]   TNA, SP 63/194/41 (Fenton to Burghley, 22 Oct. 1596).

[72]   TNA, SP 63/201/144 (Humble suit of Dunsany, 1597).

[73]   Ibid.

[74]   TNA, SP 63/178/65 (Dunsany to Burghley, Feb. 1595).

[75]   TNA, SP 63/201/146 (Petition of the inhabitants of Co. Meath, 1597); TNA, SP 63/199/58 (Burgh to Burghley, 25 May 1597); Canning, *The Old English in Early Modern Ireland*, ch. 5.

and men meant that 'I am in hazard to be a stayne to the title of honor that I am borne to and a sclaunder to her majesties service that I have lyved in'.[76]

Hoping to remedy his situation, Dunsany solicited the queen and Privy Council for assistance. His petitions all contained appeals for men, money and commands, which, he contended, were necessary for the advancement of the queen's military enterprise against Hugh O'Neill and the Confederates.[77] These were typical requests, and although petitioners sought personal advancement by these means, they frequently presented their demands as stemming from a selfless desire to better serve their queen. There was some sincerity in this claim because many Old Englishmen believed that their fate and fortunes depended on the continuation of English rule in Ireland since the Irish Confederate alternative would probably see them dispossessed, if not expulsed, if O'Neill stuck to his Utopian agenda.[78] They therefore insisted that the more the crown supported them with men and resources the better they could maintain, and even advance, crown jurisdiction in Ireland since 'her majesties profitt shall marche arme in arme with my credit in this accion'.[79]

In addition to enhancing the capabilities of servitors, Dunsany and his colleagues repeatedly reminded the queen's councillors that rewarding Old English servitors with money, soldiers and captaincies would do much to reassure their commitment to the crown and acknowledge their military worth.[80] Promotion and reward were key for securing Old English loyalty and, according to their supplications, the advancement of even a few would hearten the rest as a sign of their own possible promotion in the future.[81] Although there was fierce competition for advancement in Ireland, Old Englishmen generally advocated the promotion of one of their own before New English *arrivistes* because they were confident that their compatriots had a better understanding of the Irish situation. Thus, in 1594 the baron of Slane endorsed Ormond's elevation to the military leadership; in 1595 John Talbot recommended Sir Patrick Barnewall for promotion; and in 1600 Dunsany recommended the suits of Justice Thomas Dillon, James Dillon, Patrick Barnewall and the baron of Howth.[82]

---

76   TNA, SP 63/178/65 (Dunsany to Burghley, Feb. 1595).
77   Ibid.
78   BL, Add. MS 33743, fols. 81–3 (Thomas Lee, 'The Discovery and Recovery of Ireland with the Author's Apology'). See also TNA, SP 63/202(4)/75 ('A discourse to show "that planting of colonies … will give best entrance to the reformation of Ulster"', 1598); BL, Cotton Titus MS B XII, fols. 112–17.
79   TNA, SP 63/178/65 (Dunsany to Burghley, Feb. 1595).
80   TNA, SP 63/207(3)/108 (Dunsany to Cecil, 15 Jun. 1600); TNA, SP 63/207(5)/34 (Dunsany to Cecil, 18 Sep. 1600). For another example of this opinion: TNA, SP 63/178/20 (W. Smythe to Burghley, 25 Jan. 1595).
81   TNA, SP 63/207(3)/149 (Petition of the inhabitants of the Pale, Jun. 1600).
82   TNA, SP 63/174/48(VII) (Slane to R. Gardener, W. Weston, A. Sentleger and G. Fenton, 12 May 1594); TNA, SP 63/181/35 (J. Talbot to Cecil, 17 Jul. 1595); TNA, SP 63/207(3)/108

In return, Dunsany was the recipient of like commendations. For instance, in November 1600 Henry Dillon presented a statement on Dunsany's many services in order to support the baron's suit for the command of Knockfergus, Cavan or the forts of Leix and Offaly.[83] And, according to Dunsany, after 'wayinge my longe and chargeable abode here', his peers would 'with more reason dispise my goinge without it, then despite [sic] my havinge of it'.[84] Although Dunsany may have exaggerated enthusiasm for his own personal advancement, Old English camaraderie was fostered by their belief that they were both better experienced and equipped to deal with Irish warfare than those sent over from England. The reality was that defending Ireland's English frontier had defined generations of Old Englishmen whose main, if not only, role had been just that. But military service was not merely an inherited necessity; it was an essential part of their identity and their social relationships. Feudal ties continued to bind the community with the result that the loyalty of a lord could secure the outward conformity of his followers.[85] This was highlighted by Captain Thomas Lee when he defended the loyalty of his friend James Fitzpiers Fitzgerald. Lee argued that Fitzpiers's constancy served to deter his less sturdy neighbours from rebellion because they 'dare not whilest he stands in, ffor [...] they feare him muche, for he is a tall man, and a good executioner'.[86] These bonds formed the basis of each lords' military strength; as Frame has argued, a strong lineage culture was the product 'of constant insecurity within the lordship, which made the protection afforded by strong leadership and kin solidarity of first importance'.[87] This certainly applied to the Plunkett family, and Dunsany declared that '[y]f power of horsmen to sarue I dare affirme that I am behynde none'.[88] As the head of his family and a leading member of his community, Dunsany was sure he could marshal the forces of the extended Plunkett family as well as the men in his locale:

> for of my surname there be three Barons Kylleen, Dunsaney, and Lowthe, Knightes and gentlemen of possessions above three score all serviceable with many followers, who beinge all borderers [...] beinge all unyted (as they desyre to be) in her majesties service [...] Besydes the Reputacion of auncyent valure, the emulacion of neighborhode wilbe such entysemente as joyned to their

---

(Dunsany to Cecil, 15 Jun. 1600); TNA, SP 63/207(5)/34 (Dunsany to Cecil, 18 Sep. 1600).
[83] TNA, SP 63/207(6)/45 (Statement by Dillon, Nov. 1600).
[84] TNA, SP 63/178/65 (Dunsany to Burghley, Feb. 1595).
[85] Ellis, *Pale*, p. 17.
[86] TNA, SP 63/202(3)/171(IV) (Substance of speeches between T. Lee and R. Hoper, 24 Nov. 1598).
[87] Frame, 'Power and Society', 20.
[88] TNA, SP 63/178/65 (Dunsany to Burghley, Feb. 1595).

comunion of kynred, yt wilbe ympossible to breake or devyde them, but by the sheadinge of that blood whereby they are so knytt together.[89]

Old English supplicants believed that they deserved rewards, but they were also of the firm opinion that they were the best qualified for positions of martial importance. The reality was that a great many of the officers and soldiers sent from England were ill-prepared for the Irish war, and this, combined with the arrogant assumption that the Irish would not meet them in the field, led to disasters like Clontibret, the Ford of Biscuits, Yellow Ford and the Pass of Plumes. As Dunsany lamented to Cecil in 1597: 'I have alwayes bene of oppinyon, that this age is too full of hott bloud, for our younge men that are w[i]thout experience, alwaies give forth hott wordes promisinge the like deedes, which many tymes they put in execucion to the losse of their lyves and suche as they lead.'[90] As if predicting Essex's disastrous campaign and Bagenal's foolhardy defeat at Yellow Ford, Dunsany warned against the employment of 'younge Cap:ens whoe without either witt or knowledge have depraved their temperance and Judgments advancinge theise rashe fightes under the coulor of the vertues resolucion.'[91] Poor judgement and reckless actions were a plague amongst New English military men in Ireland, but Old Englishmen like Dunsany were confident that they could do much better. He pointedly objected to the crown's unjust tendency to discriminate against individuals born in Ireland in favour of those whose first encounter with the island coincided with their appointment to Irish office. As Dunsany argued, these 'warrs [are] contrary unto all heate of humors [and] are not overcome with rashe fight, but by the grave and mature Judgment of olde and experienced Captaines.'[92]

Dunsany was one of these 'olde and experienced Captaines', but conscious that some in England might find fault with Old English servitors' lack of foreign military experience, he carefully noted that they 'doth measure our affaires by a wronge square, and doe bringe many tymes for lack of conciderate distinccion thinges unto confusion.'[93] While officers like Essex and Norreys cut their teeth on the continent, Ireland presented entirely different challenges for which experience of continental warfare was of little consequence – as both Essex and Norreys tragically discovered. However, by virtue of their long abode in Ireland, the Old English had a special understanding of Irish society, politics and warfare, 'haveing good experience howe to prosecutte the rebles.'[94] As such, they believed they were best equipped to judge how to proceed and

---

[89]   Ibid.
[90]   Hatfield House, Cecil MS CP 54/23 (Dunsany to Cecil, 11 Aug. 1597).
[91]   Ibid.
[92]   Ibid.
[93]   TNA, SP 63/178/65 (Dunsany to Burghley, Feb. 1595).
[94]   TNA, SP 63/207(6)/59 (Lye to Cecil, 5 Dec. 1600).

what tactics should be used. Dunsany made this point in his petitions by detailing his many skills and qualities. For instance, in his 1600 bid for one of three vacant military commands – Knockfergus, Cavan and the forts in Leix and Offaly – Dunsany placed particular emphasis on the distinctive knowledge and skills acquired by men who lived on the Irish frontier, making it clear that these were qualifications which no English contender could rival. In fact, he specifically noted that Captain Street, the former New English commander of Cavan, had 'quitt the place, as not being hable to defende yt'.[95] Dunsany then insisted that whomever was entrusted with these commands would need 'to be well understode' of the Ulstermen's 'factions and fewdes ther allyances and aptness to be emploied'.[96] Dunsany was, of course, fully acquainted with these matters, and he offered a full report on the principal men of the north, their locations, relations and rivalries. This knowledge had been acquired through long-established relationships with his Gaelic neighbours and Dunsany could use this information to play one faction off another. Similarly, his familiarity with these parties could be extremely advantageous during times of negotiation and the exchanging of hostages. Therefore, with respect to the position in Cavan, Dunsany noted his personal relations with the ruling O'Reillys, both through marriage and neighbourhood, 'wherby I have good meanes to drawe in Oreylie and all that county from the Traytor'. His similar knowledge of the O'Moores, O'Connors and O'Dempseys in Leix and Offaly likewise endowed him with advantageous connections for more successful negotiations.[97] Dunsany was acutely aware that neighbourhood, friendship and even kinship ties fostered greater trust and discourse between Old English agents and Gaelic Irish insurgents than could be achieved by any New English outsider.

Equally significant though was that these associations between individuals on both sides of the socio-cultural divide greatly facilitated intelligence-gathering, and a number of Palesmen were known to operate their own spy networks. Another unique skill that Palesmen like Dunsany possessed was 'the language very well for advantage'.[98] Fluency in Irish permitted better communication and understanding between parties, but it also enabled Old Englishmen to translate intercepted enemy communications or overhear private conversations.[99] Administrators must have been conscious of this since Dunsany had

---

[95] TNA, SP 63/207(6)/46 (Dunsany to Cecil, Nov. 1600).

[96] Ibid.

[97] Ibid.

[98] Ibid.

[99] Delvin was particularly active in this regard: TNA, SP 63/186/86(XVII) (Delvin to Russell, 24 Feb. 1596); TNA, SP 63/186/86(XVIII) (P. O'Reilly to Delvin, 20 Feb. 1596); TNA, SP 63/190/11(V) (Bishop of Meath to Russell, 4 Jun. 1596); TNA, SP 63/190/44(IX) (Bishop of Meath, Delvin, and Killeen to Russell, Jun. 1596); TNA, SP 63/190/30(I) (Bishop of Meath to Russell, 18 Jun. 1596).

been specially selected in 1591 to translate a communication which disclosed an international conspiracy to put Arabella Stuart on the throne.[100]

As Dunsany's petitions demonstrate, Old English gentlemen placed great emphasis on their martial role, expertise and heritage. They lived by the sword and, in Dunsany's case, died by it.[101] Their location and ancestry demanded this, and it defined who they were and how they described themselves to their monarch and her councillors. Political independence, combined with a militaristic mission and frontier position, formed the foundation upon which their identity had been built.[102] It endowed them with cultural skills and martial experiences which could not be rivalled by New English *arrivistes*. For these reasons, they thought they were indispensable to the crown and the advancement of English interests in Ireland. They had been arguing this for some time, but the need to defend and define their role as experienced military men protecting a vital Tudor frontier became more and more pressing during the Nine Years War. Contrary to the condemnations of many English commentators, records detailing the war-time services of Old Englishmen reveal that they provided many proofs of their loyalty and they sacrificed a great deal by doing so. Nevertheless, Old English servitors felt compelled to counter allegations that their religion and birthplace made them unreliable subjects by offering comprehensive accounts of their activities, accomplishments and sacrifices. They had, in effect, inherited a military vocation from their ancestors and they found it troubling that their services, experience and special skills were overlooked in favour of hot-blooded young Englishmen who advanced 'rashe fightes'.[103] What the crown really needed, at least according to Dunsany and his peers, were men who had 'Trust, Desert, Power and skill to serve'.[104] Perhaps the course of this war would have been different if the crown had enlisted the advice and leadership of 'olde and experienced Captaines' like Dunsany.[105] We will never know. What we can say with relative certainty is that the administration had underestimated the quality of crown loyalty and martial expertise amongst the Old English Pale community while, at the very same time, this community naively and vainly strove to prove their worth through military action. But, for them, this was the embodiment of their loyalty because being military men was as essential to the Old English sense of identity as their

[100] TNA, SP 12/239/164 (J. Ricroft to Cecil, Aug. 1591).

[101] The details of Dunsany's death are not clear, but Captain Laurence Esmond said he was present at 'that deasaster which happened to the deseased lord donsany': TNA, SP 63/211/3 (L. Esmond to earl of Shrewsbury, 8 Apr. 1602).

[102] For examples, see Steven G. Ellis, *Tudor Frontiers and Noble Power: The Making of the British State* (Oxford, 1995).

[103] Hatfield House, Cecil MS CP 54/23 (Dunsany to Cecil, 11 Aug. 1597).

[104] TNA, SP 63/178/65 (Dunsany to Burghley, Feb. 1595).

[105] Hatfield House, Cecil MS CP 54/23 (Dunsany to Cecil, 11 Aug. 1597).

Englishness. Although they kept saying this, it was to no avail. In spite of having upheld the authority of the English crown for centuries, following the English victory in 1603 there was shrinking space for Irish-born Catholics in the crown's Irish administration. This was, without a doubt, appalling to men whose very existence and identity had been defined by spending their blood and losing their lives in the service of the English crown.[106]

---

[106] TNA, SP 63/202(4)/60 (The greevances of the Englishe Pale, 1598).

7

Artifice in *Ormonius:*
Why a Renaissance Latin Epic
Falsified the Military History of a
Tudor Irish General

DAVID EDWARDS

Seated in the white plaster-worked gallery of Carrick Castle in Tipperary, his favourite house, surrounded by some of the paintings he had collected over a lifetime but could no longer see, the blind old earl of Ormond listened attentively to his Gaelic poet, Dermot O'Meara. A physician by training, O'Meara was reciting in perfect Latin the lines of a major new composition. It was summer 1614. The room was hushed as O'Meara spoke. Partly this was because Ormond, grown increasingly cantankerous in his old age, disliked noise and disruption, and ordinarily demanded quiet from his household servants.[1] But it was also because the poem was important for the earl. He was its central subject. What it said about him, and how it said it, would affect his honour and reputation. It was his strong hope that O'Meara's Latin verses would help to secure his and his family's fame and renown in perpetuity. Called *Ormonius*, the poem would place the Butlers' military identity within an ancient classical tradition of martial celebration. It contained a history of the recently completed Tudor conquest of Ireland, but one that was written from the earl's 'Old English' (or Anglo-Irish) point of view. Line after flowing line it recounted scenes from the battlefield, recalling the younger, vigorous Ormond who for almost fifty years prior to 1603 had repeatedly summoned his Butler troops to serve under the royal banners. As much a political testament as a literary entertainment, it asserted the rights of the Old English Butler family to continued crown favour by placing the earl and his followers at the heart of the conquest storyline.[2]

---

[1]   David Edwards, *The Ormond Lordship in County Kilkenny, 1515–1642: The Rise and Fall of Butler Feudal Power* (Dublin, 2003), pp. 107–8.
[2]   David Edwards and Keith Sidwell, ed. and trans., *Dermot O'Meara's Ormonius (1615): The Tipperary Hero* (Turnhout, 2011). Hereafter cited as *Ormonius*.

Like other poems of its type, *Ormonius* was immodest in its praise – hag-iographical, sycophantic. It implied Ireland had been subdued for the crown not only by English-born officers and soldiers, but by a hero-earl of unequalled military prowess and his brave and steadfast kindred, who, like him, were Irish-born subjects of English descent. Successively military commissioner of Munster and Thomond (1570–1), Lord General of Munster (1579–81, 1582–4), General of the queen's army in Leinster (1594, 1596–7), and Lord Lieuten-ant-General of all the royal forces in the country (1597–1601), Earl Thomas had embodied all that was most distinguished about his kind.[3] Of Irish birth but ancient English stock, no-one had done more than him to restore his homeland to proper order (as he would have seen it) under English royal rule. The poem he commissioned – written, appropriately, by a loyal Gaelic Irishman – would boldly proclaim this. It would also assert his right, and that of the Butlers, to be recognized as 'the kingdom's column' ('*regnique columnam*') by the English, having become, by unparalleled feats of arms, '*Hybernorum decus*': 'the glory of the Irish'.[4]

There was another reason, however, why in Carrick gallery a hushed silence greeted the poet's reading. Ormond was tetchy. At his behest O'Meara had begun writing the poem in the latter part of 1609.[5] More than four years had since passed, yet still O'Meara was not finished. Indeed, to judge by the drop in quality between the last section of the poem (Book V) and the markedly more accomplished earlier sections, it is likely that by 1614 O'Meara had com-pleted just four books of verse for his noble patron, possibly fewer. And given that *Ormonius* was very likely being written to a six-book plan, in (scaled down) emulation of Virgil's *Aeneid* or Silius Italicus' *Punica*, much remained to be done.[6]

It was not simply that Ormond was concerned that the poem would still be unfinished when he died; rather, he feared that the whole point of having commissioned its writing in the first place was now in danger of negation by a growing deterioration in the political climate. In just a few years the ground that Ormond had so long commanded had shifted beneath him. Ireland had been both conquered and subjected to a new royal ruler, a Scottish sovereign with little knowledge of the country, James VI and I. The predominantly Protestant 'New English' army officers, with whom Ormond had served in numerous campaigns down the years, were in the process of seizing complete

---

[3] Edmund Curtis, ed., *Calendar of Ormond Deeds*, 6 vols. (Dublin, 1937–43), 5: nos. 115 (2), 359; 6: nos. 97, 122, 1267, 129, 133, 136; *Irish Fiants of the Tudor Sovereigns*, ed. K.W. Nicholls, 4 vols. (Dublin, 1994), 4: Eliz. I, nos. 6020, 6116, 6166, 6291; NAI, Lodge MSS, Articles with Irish chiefs, p. 101.

[4] *Ormonius*, pp. 154, 158, 268, 464, 471.

[5] Ibid., p. 20.

[6] Ibid., pp. 30–2.

control of the kingdom, confident that James would accept this in the interests of broader Anglo-Scottish co-operation and a British Protestant triple monarchy. Intent on re-modelling Ireland in their own image and on controlling its exploitation, the New English interest sought to exclude Old English lineages like the Butlers from power and influence on religious grounds.[7] Though Ormond himself had long conformed to the Protestant church, his family and followers mostly had not. Mounting New English disregard for the earl and the Butlers had become more than ever marked since 1607, when the security crisis sparked by the Flight of the Ulster Earls exposed Catholic lineages everywhere to intensified scrutiny and suspicion. The Butler territories in Kilkenny and Tipperary were experiencing extensive interference when O'Meara first picked up his pen.[8]

   If *Ormonius* was to serve its purpose and prevent the Butlers' long record of military service from slipping into oblivion, disregarded by the English state that it served, O'Meara needed to hurry up, particularly as the 'history' the poem purported to tell was hardly a model of factual accuracy. In *Ormonius,* poet and patron appear to have connived in the creation of a counter-narrative designed to serve current political necessities rather than strict historical truth. This chapter will explore some of the liberties that O'Meara took with the historical facts of the mid-Tudor and Elizabethan Irish wars of 1554–1603. In doing so it will try to reveal the dilemma faced by his aged patron at a time of rapid political, social and religious change in Ireland – change that was confronting the Butlers of Ormond and their centuries-old military identity with the threat of obsolescence. Earl Thomas listened intently to O'Meara's every word because the poem was an important exercise in identity politics; every word counted.

   In attempting to reclaim the Tudor conquest of Ireland as a Butler/ Old English achievement as much as a New English one, *Ormonius* shows how heavily invested the earl and his family were in their military identity early in the seventeenth century, and reveals their pressing need to invoke it as a basis for negotiation with the new governing regime. As a major military lineage, with generations of 'heroic' leaders stretching back into the High Middle Ages, the poem implies that Ormond and the Butlers specially merited a prominent place in the new Jacobean state and its hierarchy. Yet, because the poem also had to take liberties with the Butlers' more recent service record, close reading shows that their military identity had already begun to lose some of

---

[7]   Aidan Clarke, 'Pacification, Plantation and the Catholic Question, 1603–23', *New History of Ireland 3: Early Modern Ireland, 1534–1691,* ed. T.W. Moody, F.X. Martin and F.J. Byrne (Oxford, 1976), pp. 187–214; John McCavitt, *Sir Arthur Chichester, Lord Deputy of Ireland, 1605–16* (Belfast, 1998), chs. 6–7; Victor Treadwell, *Buckingham and Ireland, 1616–1628: A Study in Anglo-Irish Politics* (Dublin, 1998), pp. 33–43.
[8]   Edwards, *Ormond Lordship,* pp. 263–74.

its accustomed political currency. The poem's extraordinary immersion in the martial values of antiquity was at once a seemingly confident declaration of the Butlers' abiding historical status as great soldiers, and a worried ruse to alter their dynastic history and identity, and make it fit the present. Recent research has recognized that the genre of military memoir-writing that boomed during the later fifteenth, sixteenth and seventeenth centuries from Paris to Vienna – and indeed to Mexico – owed more to the pursuit and recognition of honour and 'nobility' than to the production of factual truth.[9] Close study of *Ormonius* suggests that a similar conclusion might apply to the rather less well-studied area of Neo-Latin epic poetry. Written as events were actually unfolding, *Ormonius*'s manipulations of the truth capture a sense of the response of its author and subject to current and ongoing developments.

In the artifice of *Ormonius* it is possible to appreciate how difficult it had suddenly become in the early seventeenth century for a major Old English lineage to celebrate its military identity as a new order took hold, displacing them. Even a soldier as great as Ormond felt compelled to lie about his achievements. By exploring the extent to which he and his poet manipulated his military record, this chapter reveals for the first time how one of the principal figures of Elizabethan Ireland tried to construct a different identity the better to accommodate his family to Jacobean realities. Five examples of misleading history in the poem will be highlighted: (1) its extended and exaggerated account of Ormond's service in England against the Wyatt rebels in 1554; (2) its omission of any treatment of the earl's political identity, to suppress the awkward truth of his frequent clashes with New English officers in Ireland; (3) its exclusive concentration on the earl during the wars of the Tudor conquest, to avoid acknowledging many of the senior New English commanders who also had helped shape events; (4) its attempts to suppress evidence of the earl's Butler kinsmen who had rebelled against English rule; and (5) its remarkable reorientation of the earl and his family as tamers of the wild Gaelic north, to enhance the Butlers' appeal to James as his government was proceeding with the Ulster Plantation and reduction of the Scottish Western Isles. But first it is necessary to explore why Ormond chose a Latin poem as the medium to project this substantial remodelling of his and the Butlers' military history and identity.

I

In one sense at least, it is not surprising that the earl chose to be commemorated in Latin verse. 'Black' Thomas Butler, tenth earl of Ormond was among the best educated noblemen in England and Ireland, having as a teenager

9   See Yuval Noah Harari, *Renaissance Military Memoirs: War, History and Identity, 1450–1600* (Woodbridge, 2004), pp. 27–42.

attended the special academy created for Prince Edward and Princess Elizabeth at the Tudor royal court.[10] As an adult, besides maintaining several poets
and chroniclers in Ireland, who wrote chiefly in English and Gaelic,[11] he had
displayed a strong interest in Latin and Greek literature, and had even had a
translation of Horace's *Ars Poetica* dedicated to him in 1567.[12] This had served
Ormond well through the long reign of Elizabeth I, enabling him to both bur-
nish his power in England and Ireland, and also, crucially, to strengthen his
standing with the queen, who took genuine pleasure in classical allusion and
word-play. Ormond's ability to engage with her interests and play along with
her games and diversions had made him good company, and was one of the
reasons he rated among her favourites – a unique position for an Irishman in
England, and something which, at home, had made him virtually unassailable
by members of the government while Elizabeth lived.

After the queen's death in 1603, however, Ormond's great challenge was how
to impress her successor. Because of his age and blindness and the onset of
other infirmities, Ormond had been physically unable to travel to England to
visit King James in the years following his succession.[13] Consequently, he had
not had the opportunity to take the measure of the new monarch, who he had
never met. Initially he had relied upon three of James's principal English privy
councillors, Robert Cecil, earl of Salisbury, Charles Howard, earl of Nottingham, and Gilbert Talbot, earl of Shrewsbury, to lend him support at the heart of
James's government.[14] Yet as each of these was an ally from the previous reign,
it gradually became apparent that continued membership of the Elizabethan
old boys' network would not be sufficient to guarantee Ormond and his family
a secure place in the emerging Jacobean political order. More personal links
to the king were needed. To this end, after 1610 the old earl decided to offer
employment to the Scottish adventurer Sir James Craig, son of the famed jurist
Sir Thomas Craig of Riccarton in Ayrshire, who was a 'personal friend of the

[10]   *Letters and Papers, Henry VIII*, 19, part 1, no. 473; W.K. Jordan, ed., *The Chronicle and Political Papers of Edward VI* (London, 1966), p. 3; Stephen Alford, *Kingship and Politics in
the Reign of Edward VI* (Cambridge, 2002), pp. 44–6; Jennifer Loach, *Edward VI* (New
Haven, 2002), pp. 11–14.
[11]   Gearóidín de Buitléir, 'Na Buitléaraigh agus Cultúr na Gaeilge', unpublished Ph.D. thesis
(University College Cork, 2007); Maryclaire Moroney, 'Mirrors for (Irish) Magistrates:
Elizabethan Counsel and the Tenth Earl of Ormond', RSA Washington, DC conference
paper, March 2012.
[12]   Thomas Drant, *Horace, His Arte of Poetrie, Pistles and Satyrs Englished, and to the Earle
of Ormounte* [...] *addressed* (London, 1567). I owe this reference to the intrepid Tom
Herron.
[13]   *CSPI, 1603–6*, p. 215; Rothe's Register, 1616 (TCD, MS 842, fol. 161r).
[14]   HMC, *Salisbury MSS*, 10: 127; 12: 301–2, 358–9, 410, 506–7; 15: 72; HMC, *Shrewsbury and
Talbot Papers*, 1: 109; 2: 264; Edmund Curtis, ed., *Calendar of Ormond Deeds*, 6 vols.
(Dublin, 1937–43), 6: 161–5; *CSPD, 1603–10*, p. 452; Bodleian, Carte MS 30, fol. 43r (Walsh
and Everard to Nottingham, Shrewsbury and Cecil, 26 March 1603).

king'.[15] By making Craig one of his officers in the liberty of Tipperary, Ormond brought a Scotsman with ready access to the monarch right into the centre of his private affairs.[16]

That he hired Craig just as O'Meara began writing *Ormonius* was probably not a coincidence. Almost certainly O'Meara's Latin epic was the earl's other main overture to James. This can be deduced from a number of pointers. First, producing a major Latin poem seemed a promising way to get the king's attention, as James himself had long cultivated a reputation for classical and humanist learning; he also wrote poetry to quite a high level of proficiency.[17] Second, by summer 1614, if not earlier, arrangements had been made for *Ormonius* to be published in London by Thomas Snodham, a printer with strong ties to James's court who had previously produced works by the comptroller of the royal household and by Ben Jonson.[18] Third, *Ormonius* contains a dedicatory epistle addressed to an unnamed 'Illustrious Reader' who in all probability was the king; it openly supports James's own views on monarchy, and does so using language strikingly reminiscent of his 1598 treatise *The Trew Law of Free Monarchies*:

> *The Trew Law*: 'Kings are called Gods […] because they sit upon GOD his Throne in the earth, and have the count of their administration to give unto him'.
> *Ormonius*: 'Reges Deos esse terrenos, quibus ex divino pracepto omnis obedientia debetur'.
> *Translation*: 'Kings are gods on earth, to whom all obedience is owed by command of God'.[19]

And fourth, as a contribution to Renaissance ideas of honour and heroism grounded in a classical past, *Ormonius* makes a sustained effort to appeal directly to the monarch's known intellectual preferences. James was an active critic of late sixteenth-century literary and cultural trends, particularly neostoicism, which he believed inculcated an unhealthy cynicism in the young.[20]

---

[15] Pauline Croft, *King James* (Basingstoke, 2003), p. 2; Jenny Wormald, 'James VI and I, *Basilikon Doron*, and *The Trew Law of Free Monarchies*: The Scottish Context and the English Translation', *The Mental World of the Jacobean Court*, ed. Linda Levy Peck (Cambridge, 1991), pp. 53–4.

[16] NLI, MS 11,044 (Tipperary liberty papers), no. 23. Craig visited James's court in 1613: HMC, *Hastings MSS*, 4 vols. (London, 1928–47), 4: 164.

[17] J. Craigie, ed., *The Poems of James VI of Scotland*, 2 vols. (Edinburgh, 1955–8); Roderick J. Lyall, 'James VI and the Sixteenth-Century Cultural Crisis', *The Reign of James VI*, ed. Julian Goodare and Michael Lynch (East Linton, 2000), pp. 55–70.

[18] *Ormonius*, p. 395.

[19] Ibid., pp. 27, 88; C.H. McIlwain, ed., *The Political Works of James I* (Cambridge, MA, 1918), pp. 54–5.

[20] J.H.M. Salmon, 'Seneca and Tacitus in Jacobean England', *The Mental World of the Jacobean Court*, ed. Levy Peck, pp. 185–8.

Here was an opening for Ormond and the Butlers. A celebration of their military identity was the very antithesis of neostoicism. In the dedicatory epistle O'Meara assures the 'Illustrious Reader' that concerns over wayward youth underpinned the writing of *Ormonius*, and that one of the main reasons for the poem's prolonged praising of Ormond's many martial exploits was 'to arouse the spirits of our youth to perform deeds with vigour and bravery for King and Country'.[21]

The epistle concerned rather more than simple flattery of the king. Addressing its principal reader it also attempted to draw a veil over the poem's central flaw, namely that the truth O'Meara purported to tell about the heroic soldiering of Ormond and the Butlers was *not* in fact entirely historical: 'Illustrious Reader, insofar as History is a witness to Truth, and in it nothing fictitious [...] you will perchance wonder what has impelled me to insert some poetical embellishment into this history of mine'. Claiming that 'nothing deceitful' had motivated him, O'Meara admitted to having altered (or 'embellished') Ormond's story because in his heart of hearts he was a poet, and could not help himself. In a sense this was utterly conventional. Many poets of the Renaissance admitted struggling to achieve a satisfactory form of truth when commemorating recent historical events in verse imitating classical epic.[22] More conventional still, O'Meara quoted Horace's *Ars Poetica* to justify his decision to manipulate his hero's story, for 'Poets wish both to please and to do good'. But the really clever move was to link his conventional poetic embellishments to the desire of his powerful royal reader to nurture obedience to the monarchy among the youth of the realm and to combine this with a celebration of military service. The historical content of *Ormonius*, O'Meara claimed, would earn Ormond everlasting fame in posterity; the embellishments, however, would serve a more immediate purpose, coaxing young men away from modern vice and corruption towards the age-old pursuit of glory through service and action. And so it was that O'Meara sought royal acceptance of a significantly misleading historical military epic.

II

Of course, O'Meara's deceptions were well masked. At first glance *Ormonius* seems like a comprehensive chronicle-in-verse of the old earl's former glories.

---

[21] 'Alter juuentutis animos ad res strenue et fortiter pro Patria et Principe gerendus excitare' (*Ormonius*, pp. 88–9). Hereafter, to save space, I will quote only from Keith Sidwell's translation.

[22] William Nelson, *Fact or Fiction: The Dilemma of the Renaissance Storyteller* (Cambridge, MA, 1973); Andrew Fichter, *Poets Historical: Dynastic Epic in the Renaissance* (New Haven, 1992); Michael Murrin, *History and Warfare in Renaissance Epic* (Chicago, 1994).

Arranged into five books of poetry, it presents a richly detailed treatment of Ormond's exploits as a senior commander of pro-government forces confronting and vanquishing rebels in the field.[23] Book I accordingly extols the bravery and decisive leadership Ormond exhibited even as a young man when, in England in 1554, he had helped defeat the Kentish rebels led by Sir Thomas Wyatt outside the walls of London. Although O'Meara inflates the earl's role – incredibly, he makes Ormond the equal of the duke of Norfolk, under whom he had served only as a lieutenant of horse – it was a matter of public record that Ormond *had* assisted in the routing of Wyatt's followers, and earned Mary I's praise for his actions. By embellishing the events in Kent and London at such length, O'Meara was able to emphasize what he and his master must have decided was one of Ormond's unique selling points, and a key element of the identity he needed to project: that he was an Irish nobleman and military leader of such exceptional loyalty that he had defended the English crown in England as well as in Ireland.[24] And the fact that he had fought those Englishmen who opposed Mary's 'legitimate' succession and her right to marry a foreign prince was well worth embellishing all these years later, in the wake of James's own 'legitimate' succession, as a foreigner, to the English and Irish thrones.[25] Ormond was someone who, by 'heavenly impulse', would support the monarchy through thick and thin; he always had.

Book I advances this view with considerable skill, deftly weaving history and classical mythology to present Ormond as the embodiment of his family's seemingly immortal tradition of exceptional loyalty and service. In one of its best passages, the god Jupiter, appalled by Wyatt's rebellion, ordered his son Mercury to visit the earl in London, to stir him to action and make him an agent of divine retribution. 'It is the gods, not men, who give the sceptre', the poem announces, echoing, of course, the well-known views of King James, the theorist of 'divine monarchy'.[26] It then contends that of all the English lords available to the crown in 1554, 'the Hibernian general' Ormond seemed the one best suited to the role of divine avenger, partly because of his personal military ability, but also because of his ancestry.[27] Speaking to the earl in a dream, Mercury reminded Ormond that all his forebears were great defenders of monarchy, for which they had been justly rewarded with a place of honour in the 'palace of highest heaven', literally as stars sparkling in the night sky. It

---

[23]   For the structure and organisation of the poem: *Ormonius*, 'Introduction', pp. 21–34.

[24]   This, too, was misleading. The eleventh earl of Kildare and the Gaelic lord Barnaby Fitzpatrick had also served against Wyatt, as may other Irishmen at the court at this time.

[25]   David Edwards, 'Securing the Jacobean Succession: The Secret Career of James Fullerton of Trinity College, Dublin', *The World of the Galloglass*, ed. Seán Duffy (Dublin, 2007), pp. 191–3.

[26]   *Ormonius*, p. 126; Wormald, 'James VI and I'.

[27]   *Ormonius*, p. 148.

was Ormond's destiny, he promised, to join them in the firmament when he died, for the military traditions that he embodied were divinely approved. At which point

> The earl in mind look[ed] to the heav'n
> And [saw] in long, fine order at its height
> All of his forebears 'midst the shining stars
> And as he watch[ed could] not sate his gaze.[28]

Having in Book I re-affirmed the military identity of Ormond and the Butlers as steadfast defenders of a divine English monarchy, and placed them on a par with the Howards, one of the greatest English noble families, Books II to V press home another of the earl's distinctions, of being the crown's most senior, most experienced, and, ultimately, most successful commander in Ireland: 'Hail Earl invincible, never to yield'.[29] Following his return to Ireland in the autumn of 1554, he had played a leading role in most of the main government campaigns, accompanied to all four corners of the country by his ubiquitous Butler forces. From his first major expedition in 1556 until he went blind and had to retire in 1601, he and his men had suppressed rebellions in Connacht in the west (Book II), in Ulster in the north (Books II–III and V), in Munster in the south (Books IV–V), and in Leinster in the east (Book V). The poem shows that in the process Ormond had fought against most of the major rebels in later sixteenth-century Ireland – Shane O'Neill, James FitzMaurice Fitzgerald, Sorley Boy MacDonnell, Garret Fitzgerald, earl of Desmond, and Hugh O'Neill, earl of Tyrone – and inflicted defeats or setbacks on each in turn.

No less striking, by paying only fleeting attention to the various New English commanders who had also served in the Irish wars, *Ormonius* asserts Earl Thomas's right to be remembered as the crown commander most responsible for securing English dominion in Ireland before the death of Elizabeth I ('The greatest glory in the whole emprise/ Goes to the Butler satrap').[30] Without Ormond's many years of soldiering, James might not have had a fully intact Irish kingdom to inherit from Elizabeth; instead, rebels and foreign enemies might have controlled it (or large parts of it).

This was quite a claim. In the opening years of the seventeenth century the New English interest in Dublin Castle had assumed ownership of the conquest storyline. Propagandistic pamphlets, 'letters' and celebratory verses had appeared in print in the wake of the victory at Kinsale extolling the leadership of the English viceroy Lord Mountjoy and the sacrifices of English officers

---

28 Ibid., p. 128.
29 Ibid., p. 266.
30 Ibid., p. 350.

and troops.[31] In one of the most trenchant publications, Rafe Birkenshaw's *A Discourse Occasioned Upon the Defeat Given to the Arch-Rebels Tyrone and ODonnell*, all of the victories over Irish rebels since the 1550s were presented as the product of outstanding English soldiering overseen by English governors:

> Sussex was one worthie of such a charge,
> Sidney another held of good account,
> Fitzwilliam had the like authoritie,
> Lord Grey did also rule by like command.[32]

Of the important role played by loyalist native lords and soldiers such publications had little to say; of the Butlers they said nothing at all. Post-Kinsale it was as if there was no room for them in the government's victory narrative. The blatant partisanship of *Ormonius* was a predictable response.

III

Superficially, what makes *Ormonius* seem like a convincing historical epic is the extent to which it adheres to actual events. Ormond may not have been a 'general' when he confronted Wyatt's followers, but he *had* confronted them. Likewise, once in Ireland, he had confronted the great rebels listed above. No other crown officer still living in the 1600s could claim the same. And Ormond had indeed fought in all four provinces. If he had not always been as victorious as O'Meara claimed, it was nonetheless true that he had never suffered a serious defeat as a commander, a remarkable achievement in such a lengthy career. His military accomplishments were real.

And yet, for those of its readers who possessed more than a passing familiarity with the old nobleman's life, what really stood out about *Ormonius* was how on the one hand it bypassed large parts of the earl's career, omitting some of his successes, and how on the other it manipulated and misrepresented several of the things that it showed he had done. O'Meara and his patron had not simply 'embellished' the earl's story; they had deemed some parts of his career suitable for inclusion, and other parts not. Though the poem was all about the cut and thrust of Ormond's martial valour, it had managed to remove some of its rougher edges. It had edited his life and finessed his identity, censoring much of its context.

This is at its most obvious in the poem's treatment of Ormond's political career. Ormond was as much a major political figure as a military one. For decades before his enforced retirement, he had been at or near the centre of

---

[31]   See Hiram Morgan, ed., *The Battle of Kinsale* (Bray, 2004), pp. 351–2, 379–414.
[32]   Ibid., p. 402. Sussex was chief governor 1556–65, Sidney 1565–71 and 1575–8, Fitzwilliam 1571–5 and 1588–94, Grey 1580–2.

major public events in England as well as Ireland. Indeed, the English side of his career was extensive, and given that *Ormonius* was designed to celebrate his contribution to the preservation of English monarchical power it is surprising that the poem makes little of his role as a significant personage at Elizabeth's court. The closest the poem comes to acknowledging the earl's status in England is when the goddess Anglia is shown pressing Ormond's case for higher honours, persuading the queen to install him as a Knight of the Order of the Garter in 1588.[33] However, instead of dwelling on the uniqueness of his subsequent investiture – Ormond was the first Irish Garter knight since Henry VII's reign – or grasping the chance to portray him as rising in importance just as the Spanish Armada headed for English shores, the poem cuts straight back to Ireland, and the stirring of fresh troubles there. Possibly it was just that by this stage in the poem (Book V), O'Meara had to rush his lines, to get it all finished before the earl died. But considering that Elizabeth and her court barely appeared in the earlier, more polished books, it seems safer to deduce that Ormond's prominent place in England was never intended to feature strongly in the work. As an element of his new Jacobean identity his success at the Elizabethan court required only passing acknowledgement.

Ormond's political achievements in Ireland were likewise sidelined. His appointment to senior political office, as 'Chief Treasurer of the Kingdom of Ireland' and 'Lord Privy Councillor', is mentioned on the title page, but the role this gave him in the deliberation and implementation of crown policy in his homeland is never mentioned. Nor is anything made of the political leadership he offered to his fellow Irishmen. During the 1570s and 1580s the earl had (selectively) challenged the policies and personnel employed by a succession of New English viceroys in the country, and become a figurehead of a growing native loyalist opposition. Elizabeth replaced several of her viceroys partly because of Ormond's hostility.[34] After 1584 the earl had also emerged as probably the most effective obstacle to 'New English' colonization plans in Munster. He had not only secured for himself all the forfeited rebel lands in Tipperary, but championed the rights of various dispossessed Irish landholders in Counties Cork, Kerry and Limerick.[35] Such interventions were considered important at the time. They augmented his honour and status among the native population, and extended his political sway over parts of the country

---

[33] *Ormonius*, pp. 332–4.
[34] Ormond's disputes with Elizabeth's viceroys are approached from different perspectives in Ciaran Brady, *The Chief Governors: The Rise and Fall of Reform Government in Tudor Ireland, 1536–1588* (Cambridge, 1994), pp. 171–93, 235–6; and Edwards, *Ormond Lordship*, pp. 201–3, 205–7, 215–28, 230–4, 237–45.
[35] Anthony J. Sheehan, 'Official Reaction to Native Land Claims in the Plantation of Munster', *IHS* 23.92 (1983), 307–8; Nicholas Canny, *Making Ireland British, 1580–1650* (Oxford, 2001), pp. 84, 140.

in which he and his family had previously lacked influence. Even so, these developments too are omitted from the pages of *Ormonius*. The poem was not pitched at a native audience. Presenting Ormond and his kin as heroic defenders of English rule in Ireland, it had little to gain by dwelling on his struggles against aspects of English policy that he had disliked, or his besting of New English servitors whom he had despised, irrespective of how much of his time and energy he had actually expended on such matters.

It was precisely to rise above the rancorous world of politics in which Ormond had so often laboured, and to gloss over his sometimes irreconcilable differences with the New English government officers, that *Ormonius* took the form that it did. The greatly altered political situation that obtained in Jacobean Ireland necessitated this. Where formerly the earl could with impunity obstruct English-born officials attempting to advance policies he had deemed detrimental to his interests as a loyal Old English magnate, it was now the English that held the whip hand. His former objections to them, as dangerous upstarts bent on overthrowing the *status quo* the better to take possession of the country for themselves, were best forgotten. Instead, by framing the poem as an exclusively military epic, O'Meara sought to fulfil Ormond's urgent requirement to position him and his family's collective public identity more securely in the new order. What better way to convince the royal government of the Butlers' value to the state than to elaborate upon the earl's many feats of arms? With his Butler troops ever ready at his side, had he not repeatedly performed the task of his ancestors, of English blood and descent, to uphold English power in Ireland, to defend it, if need be, to the last man? Though Irish-born, had not he and his men risked all for England, its empire, and its 'true Augustan line'?[36]

IV

The Butlers were not, however, always the paragons of loyalty that the poem implied. Nor had their identity been exclusively English. By concentrating so heavily on Ormond as the soldier–hero, O'Meara was in fact attempting to draw a veil over the rest of the earl's extensive kindred. Apart from Earl Thomas's father, grandfather, and his medieval ancestors, *Ormonius* rarely mentions by name other Butler family members. Extraordinarily, of the earl's six brothers not one is named in the text of the poem.

There was a reason for this. From early in his career Ormond had experienced great difficulty controlling the behaviour of his siblings. Though his brothers John Butler of Kilcash, Walter Butler of Nodstown and James Butler

---

[36]   *Ormonius*, p. 106. The poem contains several assertions of English sovereignty in Ireland: ibid., pp. 114, 158, 170, 212, 224.

of Duiske usually seem to have done his bidding, Ormond's problems with Sir Edmund Butler of Cloghgrenan, Piers Butler of Grantstown and Edward Butler of Ballinahinch had been acute. Resenting his efforts to curb their traditional Irish military practices and to impose English-style administration over their armed retainers in Kilkenny, Carlow and Tipperary, in 1569 the latter three had all joined in a major inter-provincial rebellion directed against growing New English government interference in local affairs and the earl's role in facilitating it.[37] Ormond had soon crushed them, but the episode was both embarrassing to him, and profoundly damaging.

In Book IV, O'Meara's 'historical' poem passes over the Butler revolt in silence, instead attributing Ormond's expeditions in the south and southeast to the need to suppress the 'Geraldine squadrons' of James FitzMaurice Fitzgerald and the host of other lineages that had joined him – while of course excluding FitzMaurice's chief ally, the earl's dissident brothers.[38]

> Besides MacCarthys and O'Donoghues,
> The Sheehys and the O'Sullivans Beare and Mór,
> Th' O'Driscolls, O'Ciosáns, O'Donovans,
> And the MacFinians and countless clans more,
> West Munster sen[t] her nurslings, and the South
> Of Leinster thy O'Connors with the O'Mores.[39]

Far from mentioning Ormond's brethren as belonging to FitzMaurice's 'evil webs', O'Meara's poem actually portrays the Butlers collectively as having remained entirely steadfast to the crown, undivided, and even as having played the leading role in the suppression of the 1569 rebellion:

> Ormond midst this storm of woe
> As general forced the Butler youth to arm;
> And blazing with desire to meet the foe
> And battle join on equal field, he flies
> With energy onto the enemy's lands.[40]

And so it proceeds, claiming over a thousand 'rebel souls' are put to death by 'Butler arms'. Surviving documents contradict this: far fewer rebels killed; and a significant proportion were actually the followers of Sir Edmund, Piers and Edward Butler.[41]

---

[37] David Edwards, 'The Butler Revolt of 1569', *IHS* 28.111 (1993), 227–55; Edwards, *Ormond Lordship*, pp. 180–200.
[38] *Ormonius*, pp. 284–90.
[39] Ibid., p. 286.
[40] Ibid., pp. 288–90.
[41] Edwards, *Ormond Lordship*, pp. 204–7, 219, 228–9.

There were comparable difficulties a generation later with the FitzEdmunds, his nephews: in 1596 the two eldest sons of Sir Edmund Butler joined up with Feagh McHugh O'Byrne, the chief enemy of English rule in Leinster. Their breaking out added considerably to the growing crisis of English rule in the country, until Ormond hunted them down and had them both beheaded.[42] The memory of this latter rebellion was particularly noxious to Ormond at the time O'Meara composed *Ormonius*. Because his only legitimate son, James Butler, Viscount Thurles, had died in London in 1590, by the custom of primogeniture the earl's rebel nephews had been next in line to the earldom of Ormond and its vast patrimony. Under the treason laws their rebellion invalidated their right to succeed; the future course of the earldom had been placed in jeopardy.

While the earl managed in the years that followed to have the succession settled on Theobald Butler, the most junior of the FitzEdmunds, who had been too young to rebel in 1596, it had proven an unhappy arrangement. To consolidate Theobald's claim, Ormond had arranged for the boy to be married to his own daughter and heiress, Elizabeth Butler, and in so doing forfeited the chance to wed her to a senior English noble.[43] Though King James had been persuaded to acquiesce, raising Theobald to the peerage as Viscount Tully in August 1603, the marriage had quickly deteriorated.[44] The young couple had squabbled, with Theobald reportedly ill-treating his bride; estranged, they had not produced any children. As O'Meara began writing, the succession remained uncertain.

Small wonder, then, that O'Meara struggled to fit the FitzEdmunds' rebellion into his poem's heroic narrative. Their treason had to be admitted, for its chief consequence – the doubtful succession to the earldom – was common knowledge when he wrote. He decided to describe it as fleetingly as he could. Depicting it as an example of the dark forces that assailed Ormond's territories in the 1590s when Tyrone's national conspiracy crept south out of Ulster, he endeavoured to transform the FitzEdmund revolt into one of the most positive proofs of Earl Thomas's total dedication to the state:

> Pursuing his nephews, his own brother's two sons
> Who had, by unnatural taint polluted, roused
> Dire revolution 'gainst their native land
> And 'gainst th'Augustan scepter […]

---

[42] Ibid., pp. 248–52. For the extent of the English crisis, see James O'Neill, *The Nine Years War, 1593–1603* (Dublin, 2017).

[43] Edwards, *Ormond Lordship*, pp. 103–6.

[44] J.C. Erck, ed., *A Repertory of the Inrolments of the Patent Rolls of Chancery in Ireland, James I* (Dublin, 1846), pp. 6, 9; Bodleian, Carte MS 30, fol. 60r (James I to Ormond, 10 Sept. 1603).

With a payment worthy of their toils,
He punished both by cruel death and sent
Them down beneath the shades.[45]

However, in this instance O'Meara's efforts were uncharacteristically clumsy. Rather than dwell on the awful dilemma that the rebellion had presented to Ormond as the Butler patriarch, O'Meara struggled in vain to obscure its continuing toxic effects. Whereas hitherto he had quite compellingly compared Ormond the general with a variety of classical heroes such as Hercules, Scipio and Aeneas, here he strained to make the earl's fratricides heroic, and this although they were a military necessity. His intention was to portray Ormond as the rightful punisher of traitorous offspring, but by dubbing him 'a second Cassius', the suggestion buckled under its sheer preposterousness. According to Livy – O'Meara's most likely source for the attempted allusion – Cassius the Roman consul was neither supremely victorious nor, ultimately, a real hero; as his ambition soared he had had to be killed by his outraged family to prevent him becoming a tyrant.[46] Very likely the allusion was an ill-considered last-minute insertion. It must have left readers well-versed in the classics scratching their heads in confusion.

V

The last of the poem's 'embellishments' to be addressed here is in many ways its most remarkable. Early in its composition O'Meara and the earl had identified a theme which they felt would greatly improve James's perception of the Butlers and encourage him to embrace their military identity as an adornment of his Irish realm. The theme is first announced in Book II, which describes Ormond's earliest participation in the crown's Irish wars and follows the earl and his forces westwards into Thomond (County Clare) to defeat the rebel O'Briens, and then north into central and eastern Ulster, to confront Shane O'Neill and the Hiberno-Scottish MacDonnells. In strict chronological terms the outline of events constitutes very dubious history. From other sources Ormond is known to have accompanied the royal army into Ulster twice (August 1556, August–September 1557), *before* he ventured into Thomond (June 1558).[47] Additionally, in 1556 Shane O'Neill was actually on good terms with the crown, and was cooling towards the MacDonnells.[48] But no matter:

---

[45]   *Ormonius*, pp. 352, 596–7.
[46]   Ibid., pp. 437, 448–9, 542, 557, 569.
[47]   HMC, *Haliday MSS*, p. 18; *Cal. Carew MSS*, 1: 275; David Edwards, ed., *Campaign Journals of the Elizabethan Irish Wars* (Dublin, 2014), pp. 3–11.
[48]   J. Michael Hill, *Fire and Sword: Sorley Boy MacDonnell and the Rise of Clan Ian Mór, 1538-90* (London, 1993), pp. 42–3.

Book II was designed to build towards an Ulster crescendo, because O'Meara and his master intended to show the Butlers at their most heroic in the north of the country, where the Irish O'Neills and 'Hebridean' MacDonnells clung stubbornly to their Gaelic independence, defying the monarchies of England and Scotland alike. *Ormonius*, in short, was advancing a case for the Butlers as subduers of Gaelic Ulster and the Scottish Western Isles. That Ormond actually performed most of his soldiering in southern Ireland was a mere detail; the poem would present him and his forces otherwise.

Book III pushes the case furthest. The entire book is taken up with a dramatic account of Ormond's journey north-east of Lough Neagh towards Glenarm and Ballycastle on the coast of Antrim, to do battle with James Mac-Donnell, the lord of Dunyveg and the Glins, and his brothers Sorley Boy and Alexander MacDonnell. The reader is treated to some of the best passages in the poem, as the earl and his followers dared to confront the MacDonnells where others – New English troops mostly – would not: in 'a fearful place of woods and shadows', 'dreadful dark', where 'the Hebridean lines' awaited them, hiding in the forest, 'fierce in the blood of war'.[49] Having defeated a company of MacDonnells after being surrounded by them, and taken a huge herd of their cattle as plunder, the Butler troops then followed their leader onto a ship to pursue their foes to Rathlin Island. They made the crossing in a stormy sea, 'Irish prows sweep[ing] o'er the Scottish blue'. On arrival, at Ormond's command, his troops laid waste to everything in sight, challenging Sorley Boy to come and stop them, before departing, 'proud with enemy spoil', back to the mainland of Ireland.[50] Again, the dating of the action is askew, with the events described actually occurring in 1557, not 1560, as O'Meara claimed. Equally misleading, Ormond and his men did not act alone, as O'Meara insinuated, but almost always were accompanied by other crown forces, often New English and Welsh in large numbers.[51]

What chiefly mattered to the poet and his patron was the impression achieved by such manipulation: that the Butlers appeared to have put manners on the most defiant clan in the Scottish Gaelic world, the MacDonnells, lords of the Isles. At the very time that *Ormonius* was conceived, in 1609, James, as king of Scots, was renewing his efforts to impose greater royal authority over the Western Isles and the Scottish Gaeltacht generally.[52] Simultaneously, the king authorised the commencement of the Ulster Plantation, and required

[49] *Ormonius*, p. 228.
[50] Ibid., pp. 262, 264.
[51] Edwards, ed., *Campaign Journals*, pp. 4–11.
[52] Martin MacGregor, 'The Statutes of Iona: Text and Context', *Innes Review* 57.2 (2006), 111–81; Alison Cathcart, 'The View from Scotland: The Scottish Context to the Flight of the Earls', *The Flight of the Earls*, ed. David Finnegan, Éamonn Ó Ciardha and Marie-Claire Peters (Derry, 2010), pp. 132–9.

the governments of his three kingdoms, in Whitehall, Dublin and Edinburgh, to cooperate in a combined drive to fully subjugate both Gaelic Ireland and Gaelic Scotland.[53]

This clearly had not gone unnoticed in Tipperary. Seated in the gallery of Carrick Castle, Ormond and his Gaelic-born poet considered how best to attach the Butlers to the gathering anti-Gaeltacht bandwagon. The skewing of his military record in the north was the agreed outcome, accompanied with suitably chosen anti-Gaelic commentary. Thus, early in Book II Ormond's intervention in the O'Brien succession crisis in the 1550s afforded O'Meara the opportunity to present the earl as an agent of a higher civilization. Through his determination to uphold English law and order Ormond had managed to bring this major Gaelic lordship back from the brink of chaos after its lords had dispensed with English rule and fallen back into their ancient, and divisive, native customs.[54] The extended description of this episode contained a positive message for *Ormonius'* intended readership: that, properly handled, some Gaelic lords were capable of 'reform', willing to adopt supposedly superior English ways and become obedient subjects of the crown. Maybe, then, all Gaels could eventually be redeemed, provided the right people were chosen to intercede with them: people like Ormond and his family, with centuries of experience of dealing with Gaelic neighbours.

Yet the poem also accepted that reforming northern Gaeldom presented a bigger challenge for the crown than Thomond and the southern territories. The native lords of Ulster and the Scottish Hebrides were Gaels of a different degree. The O'Neills of Tyrone, 'a race most fierce in hateful war', were 'still barbarian'.[55] The MacDonnells were little better. Stirred by the Fury Alecto, they fought like savages in dense woodland and mountain passes, and nurtured an undying hatred for outside authority.[56] Luckily, the poem asserted, Ormond and the Butlers had proven more than a match for them. Even when New English troops looked to retreat, frightened by the enemy, Ormond and his band of volunteers had insisted on fighting on.[57] They had shamed the New English into following them into battle, so that subsequently even the most recidivistic of Gaelic foes were compelled to fear the power of the crown as the Butlers embodied it.

[53]   Jane Ohlmeyer, '"Civilizinge of those rude partes": Colonization within Britain and Ireland, 1580s–1640s', *The Origins of Empire*, ed. Nicholas Canny (Oxford, 1998), pp. 124–47; David Edwards, 'Political Change and Social Transformation, 1603–41', *The Cambridge History of Ireland, Vol. 2: Early Modern Ireland, 1550–1730*, ed. Jane Ohlmeyer (Cambridge, 2018), pp. 48–71.

[54]   *Ormonius*, pp. 160–4.

[55]   Ibid., p. 170.

[56]   Ibid., pp. 220, 222.

[57]   Ibid., pp. 230, 232.

Lest this message be forgotten, the opening lines of Book V returned to the theme when recounting the final rebellion of Sorley Boy MacDonnell, in 1584. Having dared to light 'dire torches' 'to rouse all Ulster' again, it had (allegedly) been Ormond and the Butlers who, returning north, had defeated Sorley's forces and forced all the MacDonnells to put down their arms and, belatedly, to take up 'the plough-share and the shepherd's crook'.[58] Of course, as with Ormond's earlier northern adventures, this too was only partly true. The earl had indeed taken a leading role in the suppression of Sorley Boy, particularly at the siege of Dunluce Castle, which he oversaw at the request of viceroy Sir John Perrot.[59] But he was in no way responsible for Sorley's final capitulation, which took far longer to achieve than the poem suggests. That occurred only in 1586, in fact, while Ormond was out of the country, visiting the Elizabethan court, and it required concessions to the old MacDonnell leader that were entirely out of keeping with the poem's tale of a swift and resounding military victory.[60] Naturally, *Ormonius* was never going to acknowledge the sometimes complex political realities behind such developments. To have done so would have meant admitting that the Butlers were expendable after all, their military identity obsolete.[61]

VI

There are many other manipulations of history lurking in the pages of *Ormonius*, but the examples discussed above go furthest to reveal the complex politics of identity afflicting the head of one of the greatest Old English military dynasties in Ireland early in the seventeenth century. Ormond was irate that the history of the Elizabethan Irish wars was being manipulated by a recently dominant New English interest in the country hostile to him and his family. To reassert the Butlers' long-established position as a leading military lineage under the crown, the earl sought to win the attention and approval of the new monarch, through a Latin epic written by his Gaelic servant O'Meara. Situating him and his kinsmen within a classical tradition of military heroism, the old earl assumed the poem would appeal to the monarch's taste for classical learning and 'improving' literature. But instead of simply recounting the many historical exploits of Ormond and his men during fifty years of active campaigning 1554–1603, the poem significantly altered the Butlers' fighting record

---

[58] Ibid., pp. 326–30.
[59] For Perrot's reports from the battlefield: Edwards, ed., *Campaign Journals*, pp. 165–73.
[60] Hill, *Fire and Sword*, ch. 10.
[61] Ciaran Brady, 'East Ulster, the MacDonalds, and the Provincial Strategies of Hugh O'Neill, Earl of Tyrone, 1585–1603', *Scotland and the Ulster Plantations*, ed. W.P. Kelly and J.R. Young (Dublin, 2009), pp. 41–61.

in order to present them as instrumental in defeating rebellion in northern as well as southern Ireland, and to deflect attention from developments and occurrences in which the earl and his family had been involved that were deemed best forgotten.

Looked at in retrospect, the falsified history of *Ormonius* seems to reek of anxiety and desperation. After all, as O'Meara hurried to complete the poem in 1614, the political situation confronting the Butlers continued to deteriorate, and became a full-blown crisis after Ormond's death at the end of the year.[62] Yet the very fact that O'Meara did hurry to complete the poem, and succeeded in having it published by a court-approved printer in London in 1615, should warn against perceiving it as somehow an inevitably doomed project. In addition to desperation there was hope. The polished Latin lines of *Ormonius* testify to the Butlers' abiding sense of the continued importance of military service in political life; their martial prowess was something timeless, immortal. Though they and their followers were seriously challenged by the political and religious policies of the new government, the poem's appearance in print demonstrated that they expected the situation to improve.

True, it was misplaced optimism, but that in itself is another of the reasons why the poem is an important source for identity politics in early modern Ireland. Collectively, all the leading Old English families in Ireland, not just the Butlers, maintained an underlying (if anxious) sense of optimism throughout James's reign and into that of his son, Charles I. Many of them felt it was only a matter of time before their extensive commitment to Catholicism was no longer an obstacle to influence and advancement. All that was needed was a good war. Then the monarchy would appreciate their military traditions once more, and their role in governing the state would be restored.

They were not entirely wrong in this assessment. When the monarchy was drawn into conflict with France and Spain in the 1620s, the Old English successfully negotiated for an improvement in political conditions.[63] And had the Anglo-French war escalated after 1629, and not petered out, King Charles would have needed to honour more of the concessions that he had promised to them than in the event he delivered. Indeed, their belief that their willingness to serve the crown in war would ultimately prevail was destined to be rekindled in 1639–40, with the outbreak of the Anglo-Scottish war, and again in October 1641, following news of the Ulster rebellion.[64] But the more time passed the stronger the grip of the New English became on the reins of power in Ireland. Optimism mutated into resistance.

---

[62] Edwards, *Ormond Lordship*, pp. 108–25, 274–82.
[63] Aidan Clarke, *The Graces, 1625–41* (Dublin, 1968).
[64] Aidan Clarke, *The Old English in Ireland, 1625–1642* (London, 1966); Michael Perceval-Maxwell, *The Outbreak of the Irish Rebellion of 1641* (Montreal, 1994).

8

Irish Savage and English Butcher: Military Identities and Tyrone's Rebellion, 1593–1603

JAMES O'NEILL

The Nine Years War, also known as Tyrone's Rebellion, raged across Ireland for ten years from 1593–1603, as a confederation of Irish lords led by Hugh O'Neill, second earl of Tyrone, almost succeeded in extinguishing English power in Ireland. It retains a popular image of being a guerrilla war by Irish lords to throw off English rule that was ultimately doomed to failure, since primitive Ireland could never hope to match the economic and military strength of Gloriana's England. The conflict has often been portrayed as a no-holds-barred conflict in which brutality was the norm. The orgy of bloodshed and cataclysmic famine in Ulster which brought the war to its close helped cement this image. The war in Ireland generated a reputation in Europe as one of uncommon savagery, with subsequent English publications attributing the bulk of that aggression and cruelty to the Irish. This appears very neat and uncontentious. However, the narrative is riven with fabrications which began during the war and have proliferated in modern historiography.

Many assumptions about the nature and course of the war are not borne out by the evidence, yet they continue to permeate the historiography of the conflict. Two of the most pervasive strands of this myth are of particular concern: the primitivism of the Irish, and the savagery of the English campaign to suppress the Gaelic lords. In truth, the Irish were anything but primitive, and in many ways were more advanced and adaptive than their English adversaries. Nevertheless, both English and Irish writers sought to portray the Irish as crude and unsophisticated. The modern critical vogue for equating the closing stages of the war with genocide is equally founded upon questionable sources. A reassessment of the contemporary accounts suggests the horrors in Ulster were overstated at the time, and later interpretations have emphasised aspects of the devastation caused by war to apportion blame to one side of the conflict, in this case the English. Whilst English officers and soldiers did not view themselves as bloodthirsty or acting contrary to accepted norms, the popular and academic interpretation of the conflict has often been one of untrammelled cruelty by crown forces.

This chapter will show how narratives of Irish barbarism and English cruelty have been fabricated – by contemporary writers and in the subsequent historiography – to craft politically useful but distorted military identities of both belligerents. Where the two narratives of military identity differ is that the cruelty of the English invader has been cultivated to counter the contemporary belief (by the English) that the influence of the crown in Ireland was ultimately a civilising one. In contrast, the figure of the primitive Gael/ noble uncouth warrior icon has been preserved, encouraged and propagated by both unionist and nationalist sides of the Irish political spectrum, regardless of its historical veracity.

Imagining the Irish primitive

The Nine Years War represented both the apex of Gaelic military ability and the final destruction of native military and political power. There remains a common perception, however, that the war was a contest between the relatively backwards, and militarily weak Irish and the modern and comparatively sophisticated armies of Elizabeth I.[1] This was far from the reality of war in Ireland at the end of the sixteenth century. The conflict bore many hallmarks of the sort of warfare that was raging in contemporary France and the Low Countries. The stereotypical native hosts of armoured gallowglass, kerne and Scottish mercenaries had little part to play in a war where military pragmatism and innovation dominated and replicated many aspects of the military revolution in Europe, where firepower came to dominate the battlefield.[2] Nevertheless, many contemporary sources incorporated descriptions of Irish military identity founded on notions of indigenous Gaelic primitivism.

Denigration of Irish culture and people by English writers was nothing new. The writings of Giraldus Cambrensis in the twelfth century form the foundations of the claims of Gaelic incivility.[3] In the sixteenth century, this tone continued as the English crown's programme for reform of the Irish kingdom faced resistance from the Gaelic Irish. In his 1571 *Historie of Ireland* Edmund Campion wrote that the Irish were 'Clear men [...] of skin and hue, but of themselves careless and bestial [...] why do they not behold the blemishes,

---

[1]   James M. Hill, *Celtic Warfare 1593–1763*, 2nd edn (Edinburgh, 2003), pp. 3–4; Wayne E. Lee, 'Indigenes as "Counterinsurgents" in the British Atlantic, 1500–1800', *Defence Studies* 10.1–2 (2010), 88.

[2]   James O'Neill, *The Nine Years War, 1593–1603: O'Neill, Mountjoy and the Military Revolution* (Dublin, 2017), pp. 195–223.

[3]   Thomas Wright, ed., *The Historical Works of Giraldus Cambrensis* (London, 1905), pp. 135–6.

nay the heinous enormities and villainies that reign among them? Their car-
rows, their kerne, their thieves, their murders, their swearing, their lying, their
drunkenness, their whoredome and bloody minds'.[4] John Derricke's *Image of
Irelande* continued to perpetuate this image. Published in 1581 and designed to
promote the achievements of Lord Deputy Sir Henry Sidney, it also contrasted
the struggle of Protestant England to reform the barbarism, intransigence
and papistry of the native Irish.[5] The Irish from the north were represented as
pernicious vipers, whose woodkern displayed 'monstrous malice, ireful hearts
and bloody hands'.[6] Derricke's text was illustrated with woodcuts depicting
the Irish as mobs of cattle thieves armed with primitive weapons, in contrast
to the serried ranks of crown troops with their armour, pikes and firearms.
The illustrations also showed the Irish cavalry, traditionally composed of the
nobility, in mid-rout. Not only were the Irish primitive but they were cowardly
in battle. Ultimately, Derricke's woodcuts – like his text – celebrated English
military supremacy.[7]

In 1596 Edmund Spenser elaborated on Gaelic primitivism, by comparing
the Irish to Scythians in *A View of the Present State of Ireland*. The Scythians loom large in Greek literature as the prototype barbarian and epitome of
all that appears alien and primitive, and were used thus by Herodotus as a
contrast to the civilised Greeks. Claims that the Irish were descended from
the Scythians ultimately served to confirm the Irish as a savage people.[8] As
if barbarism was not sufficient for Spenser, lycanthropy was also evoked: 'the
Scythians said, that they were once every year turned into wolves, and so it is
written of the Irish'.[9] By the time we get to the polemical *Supplication of the
blood of the English*, the anonymous author notes that 'such was the fury of that
man-devouring beast as death could not satisfy his malice. None that lighted
into their hands escaped their beastly lust'.[10] In other words, the Irish were
brutal, barbarous, licentious cannibals, open to wanton murder and sexual
assault. Spenser noted the essentially primitive military identity of the Irish
at war: how the Irish kerne ran into battle with a terrible yell and hubbub
armed with sword, bow and shields but were unarmoured and 'trusting only

4   James Ware, *Two Histories of Ireland: The One by Edmund Campion, the Other by Mere-
     dith Hanmer* (Dublin, 1633), p. 117.
5   Hiram Morgan, 'The Messenger in John Derricke's "Image of Irelande" (1581)', *History
     Ireland* 15.1 (2007), 6.
6   John Derricke, *The Image of Irelande* (London, 1581), sigs. B1r, D1v.
7   Fintan Cullen, *Visual Politics: The Representation of Ireland, 1750–1930* (Cork, 1997), p. 7.
8   Andrew Hadfield, 'Briton and Scythian: Tudor Representations of Irish Origins', *IHS*
     28.112 (1993), 401.
9   Andrew Hadfield and Willy Maley, eds., *Edmund Spenser: A View of the State of Ireland*
     (Oxford, 1997), p. 64.
10   Willy Maley, 'The Supplication of the Blood of the English most Lamentably Murdered
     in Ireland, Crying out of the Yearth for Revenge (1598)', *Analecta Hibernica* 36 (1995), 13.

to the thickness of their glibbes, the which they say will sometimes bear of a good stroke'. Spenser's description of the apparently disordered Irish armies complements Derricke's: 'their confused kind of march in heaps, without any order or array, their clashing of swords together, their fierce running upon their enemies, and their manner of fight, resembleth altogether that which is read in all histories to have bene used of the Scythians'.[11]

English writers were not alone in emphasizing the savagery of the Gaels. The primitive identity of the Irish was also promoted as a positive trait by native Irish chroniclers. Some sixteenth-century Irish writers such as Philip O'Sullivan Beare and Peter Lombard did discard the traditional native martial identities for a more modern, progressive image of the early modern Gael; the iconic, if contrived representation of the axe-wielding heroic archetype was absent from their accounts.[12] Contemporary Irish chroniclers persisted, nevertheless, in actively propagating the image of the archaic but noble Gael. Their works harked back to a golden age of Irish warrior myth and deliberately archaised the representation of native warfare.[13] This is evident in the account of the English and Irish preparations before the Battle of Yellow Ford (1598), as documented in *The Life of Red Hugh O' Donnell* by Lughaidh Ó Clérigh. Before the battle began the English troops 'proceeded to clothe themselves with strange tunics of iron, and high-crested, shining helmets, and foreign shields of well-tempered, refined iron. They seized their broad shouldered, firmly riveted spears, their wide-edged axes, smooth and bright, their straight two-edged swords, and their long single-edged blades, and their loud-voiced shot firing guns.'[14] In stark contrast to the arms and armour of the crown's army, which were described as 'outlandish and strange', the Irish were quite different from their English adversaries:

> [They] did not wear armour like them, except a few, and they were unarmed in comparison with the English, but they had sufficient wide-bladed spears and broad grey lances with strong handles of good ash. They had straight two-edged swords and slender flashing axes for hewing down champions [...] The implements for shooting which they had were darts of carved wood and powerful bows, with sharp pointed arrows, and the English generally had quick-firing guns.[15]

[11]   Hadfield and Maley, eds., *Edmund Spenser*, p. 62.
[12]   Philip O'Sullivan Beare, *Ireland under Elizabeth: Chapters towards a History of Ireland under Elizabeth*, trans. M.J. Byrne (Dublin, 1903); Peter Lombard, *The Irish War of Defence 1598–1600: Extracts from the De Hibernia Insula Commentaries*, ed. and trans. M.J. Byrne (Cork, 1930).
[13]   Katherine Simms, 'Images of Warfare in Bardic Poetry', *Celtica* 21 (1990), 612.
[14]   Lughaidh Ó Clérigh, *The Life of Aodh Ruadh O' Domhnaill*, ed. and trans. Paul Walsh (Dublin, 1948), pp. 175–7.
[15]   Ibid., p. 177.

Ó Clérigh laboured to distinguish the English armed and equipped with modern arms and the Irish who carried the weapons of their mythic ancestors. The Irish chroniclers framed their description of military identity in terms that reflected the Irish martial ideal: noble Irish warriors, unsullied by the foreign influences brought by the Anglo-Norman invasion of the twelfth century. This was clearly how their powerful patrons, such as the O'Donnells, wished to be represented, but the representation of the Irish primitive persevered to become the prevalent image of Irish resistance to the English conquest.

The persistence of this primitivist narrative in both English and Irish sources may have made it more likely for it to endure in modern historiography concerning the Nine Years War. Irish nationalist movements idealised the warrior of pre-conquest Ireland. Nineteenth-century Celticism created a cultural history that imagined a romanticised identity, and the Irish Literary Revival drew heavily on the mythic past. The movement engaged in cultural nationalism to create a utopian image of a pre-modern past to shape the present. In reconnecting the Irish public to the myth and legends of the past, and the iconic muscular warriors dramatised within them, it hoped to create a core of native Irish historical culture. This image was portrayed as authentically Irish and free from interference from the influence of English or British rule. Ireland would return to this golden age once the invading English were removed.[16] However, many of these allusions to historical authenticity were fictions of the past with a basis more in aspirations for the future.[17] To the present day, murals across Northern Ireland deploy this imagery to promote modern political and social agendas. The image of the primitive Irish suited both nationalist and unionist interpretations of history. For one it fitted into the pure Celtic ideal; for the other, it confirmed the backwardness of Ireland and the need for outside intervention to the ultimate benefit of the natives. The idea of a modernising Gaelic Ireland would not suit either narrative and may have fallen between the cracks of nationalist and unionist conceptions of late sixteenth-century Ireland. The enduring image of Irish warfare during the Nine Years War therefore had less to do with the realities of the conflict reported (sometimes at great length) during the war than it did with modern political agendas. Clearly the primitivist military identity had a greater utility than the reality of early modern Gaelic warfare.

---

[16]   Anthony D. Smith, *National Identity* (London, 1991), p. 67.

[17]   Declan Kiberd, 'The War Against the Past', *The Uses of the Past: Essays on Irish Culture*, ed. Audrey Stockin Eyler and Robert F. Garratt (Newark, 1988), p. 37.

Hugh O'Neill's reforms

Notwithstanding contemporary English writers' assertions of the 'bestial' Gaels, it was the leadership of Hugh O'Neill which transformed the traditional Irish hosts into modernised formations of pike and shot. For most of the sixteenth century, Irish infantry forces were traditionally composed of heavy armoured gallowglass and lightly armed kerne. The gallowglass were the shock arm of Irish armies and wore heavy mail and carried distinctive long-handled axes or great swords. The kerne wore no armour and were armed with a range of weapons, such as bows, javelins (known as darts), large knives called *scian* and spears.[18] Much of the experience of warfare throughout sixteenth-century Ireland supported the view that traditional methods of Irish warfare predominated among native lords. There was a brief period after the destruction of the Spanish Armada along the north and west Irish coast during 1588, when local Irish lords equipped their men with pike and shot salvaged from the ill-fated Spanish ships.[19] Spanish officers drilled the soldiers of several Irish lords in Connacht (the O'Rourkes and O'Flahertys), though a prompt response by local crown forces crushed their nascent revolt during March 1589.[20]

Four years later it was the unlikely figure of Tyrone who challenged crown authority in Ulster. He had been brought up in the Pale as a ward of the state after ending up on the losing side of a dynastic dispute with Shane O'Neill. His father, Matthew O'Neill, first baron of Dungannon, was assassinated in 1558 and his older brother, Brian O'Neill, murdered in 1562. In 1567 the crown established O'Neill as baron of Dungannon, where it was hoped he would counterbalance the power of the incumbent O'Neill, Turlough Luineach. Hugely ambitious, Hugh's political and military power continued to grow, and he was made the second earl of Tyrone in 1587. The crown underpinned Tyrone's military strength by permitting him to retain a large force of cavalry and infantry, paid for by the state and drilled by English officers. The so-called 'butter captains' trained 50 horse and 100 infantry, but by cycling recruits, Tyrone raised far more soldiers than he was allowed, whereby the earl 'trained under that colour without any suspicion, all the lusty bodied men in all the province of Ulster, in a soldier like manner of service'.[21] Consequently, by 1593 Tyrone's potential military power was far greater than the 50 horse and 100 foot allowed to him suggested.

---

[18] John Dymmock, *A Treatise of Ireland*, ed. Richard Butler (Dublin, 1842), p. 7.
[19] TNA, SP 63/151, fol. 228.
[20] See O'Neill, *Nine Years War*, pp. 199–200; *CSPI, 1588–92*: 146–7.
[21] Nicholas Dawtry, 'A Booke of Questions and Answars Concerning the Wars or Rebellions of the Kingdome of Irelande', ed. Hiram Morgan, *Analecta Hibernica* 36 (1995), 92–3.

Tyrone had served the crown faithfully in Ulster and operated with Lord
Grey in Munster in 1580. His order to execute hundreds of Spanish survivors
during the Armada emergency in 1588 helped reinforce the earl's apparent
fidelity. Yet by 1593, the threats to his lordship from ambitious English lords
like Sir Henry Bagenal (who had a personal grudge against Tyrone following
the latter's elopement with Bagenal's sister Mabel), the encroachment of crown
power, and offers of Spanish assistance should he wish to resist the English,
induced Tyrone to break with the crown.

Tyrone fought a proxy war against the English from 1593–4, using Hugh
Maguire, lord of Fermanagh and Hugh Roe O'Donnell, lord of Tirconnell to
divert English military power in Fermanagh and northern Connacht, while
he supressed, intimidated and assassinated the crown's Irish allies in Ulster.[22]
Only after the capture of the strategic English garrison at the Blackwater Fort
at the start of February 1595, did the earl openly defy the crown. The forces
he led were nothing like anything the crown's officers had faced in the past.
The earl's household troops were seen in action against the English relief force
defeated at the Battle of the Ford of the Biscuits in August 1594, marked out by
their distinctive red livery.[23] However, it was at the Battle of Clontibret on 27
May 1595 that the full extent of Tyrone's reforms was seen. Bagenal led an army
of 1,500 foot and 250 horse to resupply the beleaguered garrison at Monaghan.
Tyrone engaged the English column in a firefight at Crossdall on the march to
Monaghan, convincing Bagenal to take a more southerly route via the church
at Clontibret, but it was here that the full force of Tyrone's army was brought
to bear. After Bagenal's men passed the church, Tyrone attacked the column
on all sides. Irish shot supported by pike and horse assailed the flanks, rear
and head of the army with close-range gunfire.[24] The advance stalled and for
eight hours the survival of Bagenal's force hung in the balance as ammunition
ran critically low.[25] A near-suicidal charge by English horsemen gave pause to
the Irish attack, granting Bagenal the time to extricate his men. English losses
were heavy; the muster master Sir Ralph Lane considered them too many to be
'thought fit to be given forth upon the first advertisement'.[26] However, beyond
the immediate predicament of the army, which was trapped in Newry, the
authorities in Dublin were grievously concerned about the troops deployed
by Tyrone.

[22] James O'Neill, 'Maguire's Revolt but Tyrone's War: Proxy War in Fermanagh, 1593–4',
Seanchas Ard Mhacha: Journal of the Armagh Diocesan Historical Society 26.1 (2016),
43–68.
[23] Tyrone's troops were reported at the battle by Joan Kelly who recognised the red livery
as the earl's; see TNA, SP 63/176, fol. 171.
[24] Lorcan Ó Mearáin, 'The Battle of Clontibret', *Clogher Record* 1.4 (1956), 19–20.
[25] *Cal. Carew MSS*, 3: 109–10.
[26] TNA, SP 63/180, fol. 179.

At the start of June, Lord Deputy William Russell reported his misgivings to the Privy Council regarding Tyrone's forces. He noted

> their arms and weapons, their skill and practise therein far exceeding their wonted usage, having not only great force of pikes and muskets, but also many trained and experienced leaders as appeared by their manner of coming to the fight, and their orderly carriage therein […] these traitors are increased to a great strength in numbers, and wonderfully alter from their Irish manner of arms and weapons, and the use thereof, besides their order and discipline governing their men.[27]

Sir John Norreys had similar concerns after the engagement at Mullaghbrack four months later.[28] Norreys was a renowned English soldier with experience fighting in Ireland and on the continent. After Tyrone's men had attacked his army as it retreated to Newry (during which Norreys and several of his senior officers were wounded), Norreys wrote 'All those that have formerly seen the wars in this country confess they have not accustomly been acquainted with the like fight.'[29] Tyrone had evidently fielded something different.

Tyrone's reform of Irish forces came at a time of military transformation across Europe. Called the military revolution by modern scholars, one of the key features was the ascendancy of small arms on European battlefields, and the development of infantry tactics to exploit the advantages of firepower.[30] Tyrone embraced these reforms by utilising the fundamental precepts of the military revolution, by building pike and shot-based formations that relied on firearms as the mainstay of their combat power. This made them more in keeping with continental practice than English, as the crown forces' willingness to enter the melee with pikemen was inconsistent with accepted practice in Europe, which viewed firepower as superior to the pike.[31] Tyrone's infantry were not, however, direct copies of European or English tactics, but a hybrid that retained the Irish superiority in mobility with the advantages of close-range firepower.[32] Tyrone had a significantly greater dependence on firearms, as up to 80 per cent of his infantry were armed with guns, whereas English and

---

[27]   TNA, SP 63/180, fol. 9.
[28]   C.F. McGleenon, 'The Battle of Mullabrack, 5 September 1595', *Seanchas Ard Mhacha* 13.2 (1989), 90–101.
[29]   TNA, SP 63/183, fol. 51.
[30]   Geoffrey Parker, 'The "Military Revolution" 1560–1660 – A Myth?', *Journal of Modern History* 48.2 (1976), 196–214. See also the references to the early modern military revolution in the Introduction to this volume (pp. 4–5).
[31]   Thomas F. Arnold, 'War in Sixteenth-Century Europe: Revolution and Renaissance', *European Warfare 1453–1815*, ed. Jeremy Black (New York, 1999), pp. 40–1.
[32]   O'Neill, *Nine Years War*, pp. 222–3.

continental infantry had 30–50 per cent armed with firearms.[33] The Irish pike moved in loose order to minimise the effect of broken and scrubby ground. This enabled them to keep pace with their shot but made them vulnerable to close-order pike deployed by the crown.[34] The earl modified the reforms to minimise the restrictive effects of the Irish terrain, a feat which the English were unable to match for most of the war. Indeed, only after the English adopted many of Tyrone's changes did they begin to have any level of success against the Irish.[35]

It was clear that Tyrone had dramatically improved the arms and tactics of his native Irish troops. Moreover, the sartorial difference between Irish and English soldiers became less distinct. Soldiers deployed by both sides in the war began to resemble each other to the degree that their officers found it difficult to tell them apart. This was seen early in the war, and it was Hugh Maguire who almost fell victim. During the early stages of the conflict, Maguire fought an intense riverine campaign against Captain John Dowdall's garrison based in Castle Skeagh (modern-day Castle Balfour, County Fermanagh). Attacks were made by both sides along the waterways of Lower Lough Erne during the winter of 1593. In a stroke of luck (for Dowdall at least), while spoiling along the shores of the lough the English spotted Maguire approaching in a small boat. Dowdall deployed his loose shot, but Maguire 'came on thinking it had been his own company'.[36] An ill-disciplined shot betrayed the ruse and Maguire escaped, but not before English gunfire killed two of his companions in the boat.

Matters could be made much worse in the heat of battle, as smoke and confusion made identifying friend from foe all the more difficult, even for experienced officers. At the Battle of the Yellow Ford on 14 August 1598, the crown's army was overthrown by Tyrone as it attempted to relieve the English garrison in the Blackwater Fort (County Tyrone). The army's commander Sir Henry Bagenal was killed, and the leading regiments smashed. As the surviving officers attempted to reorganise their troops for a retreat to Armagh, one regiment under Captain Roger Billings had moved closer to Armagh than was thought safe. Billings' regiment, together with that of Captain Richard Cuney, had made up the rear of the army on the march towards the Blackwater, but

---

[33] Hatfield House, Cecil Papers, 139/54; Charles G. Cruickshank, *Elizabeth's Army*, 2nd edn (Oxford, 1966), pp. 114–15.

[34] The loose order training was described by Thomas Douglas at Dungannon in 1601: TNA, SP 63/210, fol. 192.

[35] James O'Neill, 'A Kingdom Near Lost: English Military Recovery in Ireland, 1600–03', *British Journal for Military History* 3.1 (2016), 33–4.

[36] TNA, SP 63/173, fol. 57.

Cuney later reported that 'we saw Captain Billings his regiment far beyond the place he was appointed, whom we supposed to be the rebels'.[37]

Cuney's mistake can easily be forgiven given the smoke, panic and attendant carnage of an army collapsing around him. Others had similar problems even when close to Irish troops, and not under fire. Sir Arthur Savage was transporting a shipment of money and gunpowder from Dublin to Athlone during December 1599. Sir Francis Shane provided an escort as the convoy passed through Westmeath, but five miles beyond Mullingar a company of foot was noticed travelling along the same road. Shane assured Savage that they were his soldiers accompanied by Sir Tibbott Dillon's horse.[38] As the foot drew near it became apparent that these were not Shane's men but the enemy. It was not, however, the soldiers' dress, marching order nor carriage which identified them as Irish, but their numbers. Savage noted that as column got closer 'we might plainly see that their number were too great to be his [Shane's] company'.[39] The convoy's escort panicked and ran as Savage tried to secure the gunpowder in a nearby castle, and Shane was captured after his horse was shot out from under him. Of the Irish troops, Savage later wrote 'The enemy were 140 of as good foot as any were of that kind in Ireland'.[40]

Despite the experience of the queen's officers and soldiers in Ireland, the myth of the primitiveness of Irish military identity still endured in England, causing some confusion when new drafts of troops arrived in Ireland. Robert Osborne remarked on this after he arrived with the reinforcements sent with the earl of Essex in 1599. In a letter to England, Osborne reported that they would soon be setting out for the north. He reported that the army was weak but 'God be of our side we shall do well with these strong rebel', about whom Osborne added 'in England they say they be but naked rogues, but we find them to be as good men as those who are sent us, and better'.[41] This suggests that while the war was ongoing in Ireland, the stereotypical image of the uncouth savage Irish was prevalent in England, despite the recent experience of the crown in Ireland, causing some concern when the illusion was dispelled by service against Tyrone and his allies.

The image of Irish cruelty and barbarity continued to be presented during the conflict. Beyond the bloody narrative of combat, the Irish were reported as barbaric and behaving outside the prescribed norms of 'civilised' warfare in England and the continent. Captain Dowdall referred to the Irish killing prisoners when he wrote in 1600 declaring that 'this nation is proud, beggarly, and treacherous, without faith or humanity [...] the enemy spares neither friend

---

[37] Hatfield, Cecil Papers, 177/131.
[38] TNA, SP 63/207, fol. 247.
[39] Ibid., fol. 249.
[40] Ibid.
[41] Hatfield, Cecil Papers, 179/74.

nor foe'. [42] This theme was continued by Fynes Moryson, secretary to Lord Deputy Mountjoy, who described how the Irish never spared their captives and had a tendency to kill any and all who fell into their hands. Moryson wrote how the Irish 'know not than despise the rules of honour, observed by other nations […] being terrible executioners by their swiftness of foot upon flying enemies, never sparing any that yield to mercy, yea being most bloody and cruel towards their captives upon cold blood, contrary to the practice of all noble enemies'. [43] Just as before, Irish annalists appear to substantiate these allegations. An Irish account of the Battle of the Yellow Ford claimed that after the victory Tyrone's men butchered the English wounded left on the field. Ó Clérigh described how the Irish returned to the battlefield 'and proceeded to strip the people who had fallen in the battle and behead those who were severely wounded'. [44] Nevertheless, English reports suggested a different attitude to the English wounded and prisoners.

A broader look at the course of the war shows Moryson's claims to be entirely false, indeed Irish behaviour was quite the opposite to that portrayed by Moryson. From the outset of the conflict, the Irish showed a greater proclivity for taking prisoners than did crown forces. Captain Robert Constable was captured after the Battle of Aldfreck near Carrickfergus in 1597. [45] The same was true for Captain Henry Cosby who was taken prisoner at the Battle of the Yellow Ford the following year. [46] Indeed, the largest single capitulation of English troops during the war was after the defeat at the Yellow Ford. The remnants of Bagenal's army were trapped in the precincts of Armagh cathedral. Tyrone allowed the army to depart southwards on terms that the Blackwater Fort capitulates, and the English left all their arms, armour and stores behind. [47] Moreover, Tyrone agreed to have many of the English wounded cared for in Armagh. Sir James Perrot described how sixty men, who had been severely burned in a gunpowder explosion during the battle, were left in Armagh when the English army retreated to Newry. [48] This incident is revealing for several reasons. It demonstrated that Tyrone was willing to offer quarter and medical aid to wounded English troops. Furthermore, it showed that despite the accusations of barbarity and cruelty later promulgated by Moryson and others, experienced English officers, such as Sir Thomas Maria Wingfield and Captain

[42] *Cal. Carew MSS,* 3: 353–5.
[43] Fynes Moryson, *The Irish Sections of Fynes Moryson's Unpublished Itinerary*, ed. Graham Kew (Dublin, 1998), p. 70.
[44] Ó Clérigh, *Life of Aodh Ruadh*, pp. 183–5.
[45] TNA, SP 63/201, fol. 132.
[46] TNA, SP 63/202 pt 3, fol. 337.
[47] Fynes Moryson, *An Itinerary*, part two (Glasgow, 1907–8), p. 217.
[48] Sir James Perrot, *The Chronicle of Ireland 1584–1608*, ed. Herbert Wood (Dublin, 1933), pp. 155–6.

Cuney, had enough confidence in Tyrone's promises to leave so many incapacitated men in Irish custody.

Rather than killing English troops, the Irish used sophisticated and intel-
ligent methods to deplete crown garrisons. Tyrone and his allies recognised
early in the war that the crown army could be harmed more by desertions
and surrenders than battle casualties. This was facilitated by offering generous
terms of surrender and providing support and even incentives to deserters
from the royal army. Tyrone willingly accepted fugitives from the crown forces
and for much of the war encouraged government soldiers to change sides.
The Irish established a system for transporting English troops out of Ireland.
Captain Humphrey Willis reported that men were deserting due to a public
proclamation by Tyrone that they would receive safe conduct and aid in the
form of food, money and transport into Scotland.[49] Thomas Walker corroborated this when he referred to the arrival of English soldiers at Dungannon and
noted their receipt of passes from Tyrone for transportation into Scotland.[50]
It is unclear how many English were carried over to Scotland, but it was significant enough to warrant English lobbying of James VI of Scotland to take
action to stem the flow. In January 1602, James issued a proclamation banning
Scots from transporting English deserters and resettling them as tenants in
Scotland.[51]

While Tyrone granted generous concessions to captives and English deserters from 1593–1600, Irish attitudes hardened as the tide of the war went against
them. By the closing stages of the war, English prisoners were more likely to
be executed. When the crown garrison at Newtownstewart fell in 1601, the
commander Captain Roger Atkinson was taken prisoner, but his 50 soldiers
were put to the sword.[52] During the dying stages of the war in Fermanagh in
1603, the Irish showed no quarter to the small English wards on Lough Erne.[53]
There were episodes where English troops were killed out of hand, but these
instances were rarer than Moryson or Dowdall suggested.

Regardless of the hard-fought war and the decidedly modern methods and
equipment of their Irish enemies, after the final defeat and submission of the
Irish confederation in 1603, the caricature of primitive Irish military identity
began to re-emerge. William Camden's *Britannia* had little to say about the
disciplined and ordered pike and shot fielded by Tyrone. On the contrary,

---

[49]   *CSPI, 1600–1*: 158–61.
[50]   Hatfield, Cecil Papers, 88/121.
[51]   *The Register of the Privy Council of Scotland*, ed. R.K. Hannay et al. 14 vols. (Edinburgh,
       1898), 5: 339.
[52]   *CSPI, 1601–3*: 92–5.
[53]   O'Sullivan Beare, *Ireland under Elizabeth*, pp. 175–6.

Camden described the Irish as fighting solely with spears and axes.[54] Two years later Sir John Davies gave no credit to the strength or sophistications of Tyrone's confederation. In *The Discovery of the True Causes Why Ireland was Never Entirely Subdued,* Davies blamed the prolongation of the war on the defects of the army sent by the crown to reduce the recalcitrant natives.[55] He believed it was English faults rather than Irish strength which kept the island in turmoil for ten years. This caricature has stubbornly remained entrenched in popular and academic scholarship even to the present day.

English brutality and starvation tactics

The events and historiography of the Nine Years War may have produced a skewed interpretation of the activities and military identity of the Irish, but the royal cause has not escaped unscathed. While contemporary writers and later historians helped create positive and negative images of native Irish primitivism, modern interpretations of the conflict have cast the crown officers and army in the role of the historical villain. The English campaigns have been interpreted by some as unrestrained butchery, typical of the behaviour of the colonial conquests of perfidious Albion. This was not always the case, as for many years there was little effort on the part of Irish historians to engage with the suffering and horrors inflicted on the civilian population in Ireland during the war. Alfred O'Rahilly, D.B. Quinn and Nicholas Canny all touched on the excesses of English aggression towards the Irish, but Brendan Bradshaw has criticised Irish historians for failing to engage with the impact of violence and atrocity in early modern Ireland.[56] Bradshaw's words fell on fertile ground and there have been strident efforts made by David Edwards, Clodagh Tait, Pádraig Lenihan and Vincent Carey to make up the deficit,[57] their work percolating into both the modern media and broader studies of the nature of genocide in

---

[54] William Camden, *Britain, or A Chorographicall Description of the Most Flourishing King-domes, England, Scotland, and Ireland,* part 2, trans. Philemon Holland (London, 1610), p. 147.

[55] Sir John Davies, *A Discoverie of the True Causes of Why Ireland Was Never Entirely Subdued* (Dublin, 1612), p. 75.

[56] Alfred O'Rahilly, *The Massacre at Smerwick, 1580* (Cork, 1938); D.B. Quinn, *The Elizabethans and the Irish* (Ithaca, 1966); Nicholas P. Canny, 'The Ideology of English Colonialism: From Ireland to America', *William and Mary Quarterly* 30.4 (1973), 575–98; Brendan Bradshaw, 'Nationalism and Historical Scholarship in Modern Ireland', *IHS* 26.104 (1989), 329–51.

[57] David Edwards, Pádraig Lenihan and Clodagh Tait, eds., *Age of Atrocity: Violence and Political Conflict in Early Modern Ireland* (Dublin, 2007); Vincent Carey, '"What pen can paint or tears atone?": Mountjoy's Scorched Earth Campaign', *The Battle of Kinsale,* ed. Hiram Morgan (Bray, 2004), pp. 205–16.

warfare.[58] Carey's use of the politically charged term 'ethnic cleansing', in his work on Mountjoy's orchestration of famine in Ulster in 1602–3, drew direct parallels between policies of the crown in Ireland and twentieth-century war crimes.[59] Elsewhere, Carey's use of incendiary terminology such as 'genocidal fury' and 'war crimes' suggests that the pendulum may have swung too far back towards the traditional narratives of English cruelty.[60]

So why pick the Ulster famine of 1602–3 as an example of English brutality? One reason could be the significant amount of suitably lurid and highly quotable accounts by English officers, which made it much easier to paint a picture of bloodthirsty and brutal crown forces. Sir Arthur Chichester, for example, considered that the Irish were only worthy of slavery, and boasted that his troops killed 'man, woman, child, horse, beast and whatever we found'.[61] Chichester was also one of many who advocated the deliberate creation of famine amongst the Irish, where 'a million swords will not do them so much harm as one winters famine'.[62] Mountjoy agreed and engaged in a programme of systematic crop destruction. Yet citing the famine of 1602–3 as evidence of English brutality ignores the possibility that the English were not entirely responsible, nor was it the first time that famine visited Ireland during the Nine Years War. Five years earlier there was a devastating agricultural collapse in northern Connacht. It was on a smaller scale but produced descriptions that would not have been out of place in Ulster in 1602. The English muster master in Connacht, Maurice Kyffin, specifically mentioned 'so many dead hungerstarven carcasses of men and women lie spread up and down the fields and ways'.[63] In Connacht, 1597 was a period of intense spoiling by the Irish confederates, and the control of the north of the province was contested by Tyrone's allies and Sir Conyers Clifford, the English chief commissioner. This – combined with a poor harvest – was the likely cause of the shortages, though the Irish annals make no mention of famine and the historiography of the period is equally silent on the matter.

The declared intention of the crown's officers to create famine in Ulster and the accounts of civilian victimisation in the north has led most analysis of the pacification of Ulster in 1602–3 to claim that the English were responsible.[64] It

---

[58]   Ben Kiernan, *Blood and Soil: A World History of Genocide and Extermination from Sparta to Darfur* (New Haven, 2007).

[59]   Carey, 'What pen', p. 209

[60]   Vincent Carey, 'Elizabeth I and State Terror in Sixteenth-Century Ireland', *Elizabeth I and the 'Sovereign Arts': Essays in Literature, History and Culture*, ed. Donald V. Stump, Linda Shenk and Carole Levin (Temple, 2011), pp. 202, 215.

[61]   *CSPI, 1600–1*: 332–5.

[62]   *CSPI, 1600*: 192–3.

[63]   *CSPI, 1596–7*: 291.

[64]   Carey, 'What pen', pp. 205–16; John McGurk, 'The Pacification of Ulster, 1600–3', *Age of Atrocity*, ed. Edwards et al., pp. 119–29.

would be wrong to suggest that the destruction of food supplies and property did not exacerbate the hardships of the local population, but it is likewise difficult to claim that crown military operations were the sole or even primary causative factor. There was no systematic crop destruction in Connacht in 1597, but the famine still broke out. The Ulster famine visited both the Irish and English equally in the north. The English had some relief from imports from England, but as the Irish did not, they were driven to extremes of want.[65] By January 1603 the entire country was facing famine.

The onset of famine in Ulster was far faster than the crown could have anticipated. During Sir George Carew's scorched earth operations in Munster in 1601, the impact of crop destruction was not expected to manifest until the following year. [66] In Ulster it did so in a matter of months. When Mountjoy finally entered Dungannon in June 1602, he described the area as 'so eaten I think we can hardly live there'.[67] O'Neill's lands to the north of the Blackwater were already subject to a subsistence crisis before Mountjoy arrived. By September, O'Hagan detailed how 1,000 dead lay between Tullahogue and Toome, and 3,000 had died in Tyrone since the start of July.[68] Given that Mountjoy found Tyrone in a poor state when he arrived and the short time taken for horror stories to emerge, it was likely that Mountjoy's campaign coincided with an emerging disaster. He certainly made it worse but did not cause the crisis. The demands of O'Neill's war effort appear to have severely depleted Tyrone's resources. The earl moved his forces into Fermanagh in August 1602, prompting Mountjoy to observe that Tyrone's concentration of troops did as much damage to the country as the lord deputy's spoiling operations.[69]

Concurrent with the campaign in the north there was a poor harvest in the Pale, with expectations of famine to follow.[70] Inclement weather had damaged much of the crop in Munster, and shortages were aggravated by the crown's debasement of the Irish coinage. The imposition of base coins combined with rapid inflation of prices meant that merchants found it impossible to pay for imported goods and commodities.[71] Shortages continued into 1603, with famine and pestilence reported in Dublin in November, and the Irish annals recorded starvation throughout Ireland. The famine was island-wide by 1604, suggesting that while the first effects were felt in active war zones, military activity was not the immediate cause of the unfolding disaster.

---

[65] C. Litton Falkiner, 'William Farmer's Chronicles of Ireland from 1594–1613', *English Historical Review* 22.85 (1907), 129.
[66] *CSPI, 1601–3*: 517–18.
[67] TNA, SP 63/211, fol. 161.
[68] Moryson, *Itinerary*, part three, p. 208.
[69] TNA, SP 63/212, fol. 110.
[70] Moryson, *Itinerary*, part three, p. 260.
[71] Moryson, *Itinerary*, part three, p. 281; *CSPI, 1601–3*: 559–61.

Depopulation of the countryside, as described in Ulster and elsewhere, did not necessarily mean people had been killed or died from famine or disease. It is possible that many inhabitants migrated out of the conflict zones, either to less troubled regions or refuges in woods or upland areas. Due to crown depredations in the Midlands in 1600, the inhabitants fled to Ulster and did not return until the end of the year.[72] In direct response to crop devastation, many of the rural inhabitants of Tyrone and Kerry relocated to Armagh and Limerick respectively.[73] Civilians were reported to have left the country entirely to escape the ravages of the war. In 1605 Chichester referred to Irish refugees in France and Spain, stating that they had escaped Ulster, Munster and Connacht during the famine at the end of the war.[74]

Examples of the misery caused by the famine in Ulster have been regularly deployed by modern historians to highlight the extreme situation unfolding in the north. Two of the most common were reports of cannibalism in Armagh during 1602. One involved attacks by women on children near Newry. They lit fires to attract children minding cattle, and when they gathered to warm themselves, the women attacked, killing and eating the children. The other was a story of children who, according to Moryson, were 'eating and gnawing with their teeth the entrails of their dead mother, upon whose flesh they had fed twenty days past, and having eaten all from the feet upward to the bare bones, roasting it continually by a slow fire, were now come to eating her said entrails in like sort roasted, yet not divided from the body being as yet raw'.[75] These examples are frequently used in modern literature to underline the horrors of the English scorched earth campaign in Ulster, but both tales are spurious at best. Why did the women not seize the cattle for food instead of the children? Furthermore, the figure of the cannibalistic crone was a stock feature of folkloric tales in early modern Europe. Indeed, the *Compendium Maleficarum* of 1608 depicts just such a scene.[76] Moryson had spent most of the 1590s travelling around Europe and the Middle East, and it was entirely possible that he heard or read of the eponymous witch or crone during his travels. Moryson may have added this to his narrative as a dramatic flourish to what was a decidedly monotonous but brutal phase of the war, but more likely the story was intended to epitomise the barbarism of the Irish.

[72] *Annals of the Kingdom of Ireland by the Four Masters from the Earliest Period to the Year 1616*, ed. and trans. John O'Donovan, 3rd edn. 7 vols. (Dublin, 1990), 6: 2187.
[73] Thomas Stafford, *Pacata Hibernia: Ireland Appeased and Reduced; or, A History of the Late Wares of Ireland, Especially in the Province of Munster under the Command of Sir George Carew*, ed. Standish O'Grady, 2 vols. (London, 1896), 2: 291; Moryson, *Itinerary*, part three, p. 202.
[74] *CSPI, 1601–3*: 345–6.
[75] Moryson, *Itinerary*, part three, p. 282.
[76] Charles Zika, 'Cannibalism and Witchcraft in Early Modern Europe: Reading the Visual Images', *History Workshop Journal* 44 (1997), 77–8, 80.

With regards to the children eating their mother, the biological progress of putrefaction after death suggests that the horrifying tableau of the children eating their mother presented by Moryson was impossible, as *post mortem* the bacteria in the human intestines ensure that the said organs become rapidly corrupted.[77] Nevertheless, both reports are often cited as fact in modern literature on the subject.[78]

English attitudes to Irish prisoners

The treatment of Irish prisoners by English troops during the conflict has been used as further evidence for the crown's disregard for the customs of war, and is consistent with the exceptional levels of brutality used to suppress the Irish.[79] Undoubtedly, from 1593 the queen's army had a poor record for taking captives or offering quarter to Irish soldiers taken in arms. From the earliest engagements of the war, English officers spared few if any men, with survival only assured if the Irish managed to evade capture. Bagenal took none during his 1593 campaign in southern Ulster. In the same year, Captain Henry Street recorded that in one engagement the only Irish to survive were those who escaped by boat.[80] Dowdall executed most if not all of those he found in Enniskillen castle after it fell in February 1595.[81] Captain Thomas Lee later reported that the Irish had surrendered upon terms, but were later 'dishonourably put to the sword in a most miserable state'.[82] Sir Conyers Clifford was one of the few English commanders who recognised the utility of granting quarter and took many prisoners during his Connacht campaigns.[83] He hoped that demonstrating the queen's mercy would gain the loyalty of local chiefs.[84] Regardless of the efficacy of Clifford's sensible approach, he was the exception to the norm. Nevertheless, English officers had every reason to believe their actions were sanctioned by the prevailing customs of war; indeed, their actions may have underpinned their own self-belief as the upholders of accepted values of law and order. They certainly did not consider themselves to be brutal or in any way immoral in their conduct against the Irish. Moreover, most viewed the war as a continuation of the programme for civilising the barbarous Gaels.

---

[77]   Arapad A. Vass, 'Beyond the Grave: Understanding Human Decomposition', *Microbiology Today* 28 (November 2001), 190.

[78]   Carey, 'What pen', p. 214.

[79]   David Edwards, 'The Escalation of Violence in Sixteenth-Century Ireland', *Age of Atrocity*, ed. Edwards et al., pp. 56–8.

[80]   TNA, SP 63/172, fol. 160.

[81]   TNA, SP 63/173, fol. 104.

[82]   BL, Harleian MS 35, fols. 258–65.

[83]   *CSPI, 1596–7*: 280.

[84]   TNA, SP 63/199, fol. 7.

Spenser noted that through many thorny and hard ways the Irish had been eventually brought to civility, and he considered violence against the Irish as necessary to subdue natives' savage manners.[85] Mountjoy referred to the English campaigns in Ireland as a means to recover to civility the wild and uncouth people still in rebellion.[86] If the forces under Tyrone were the 'enemy to all virtue and civility; defiled with all sensualities and barbarism' then it was the task of crown forces to re-establish such order in the face of Irish resistance.[87] The very act of rebellion by the Irish necessitated a hard response from the English troops in Ireland.

Contemporary principles of lawful warfare appear to have influenced the English proclivity for executing prisoners during the war. Lawful wars could only be fought by legitimate governments or sovereigns; rebellion was tantamount to heresy.[88] Queen Elizabeth was quick to correct her senior officials in Dublin for misusing the terms 'war' and 'peace' instead of 'rebellion'.[89] Conceptualising the conflict itself in such terms had significant consequences for how its participants' military identities were activated. The use of the word 'war' instead of 'rebellion' might suggest that O'Neill and his allies were legitimate belligerents rather than recalcitrant or treasonous subjects. Lord Burgh later reacted strongly against Tyrone's use of the word 'peace' as this was made 'betwixt equals', whereas the earl should 'ask forgiveness on his knees'.[90] Rebellion placed the Irish beyond the contemporary customs of war. The surrender of the Spanish garrison at Kinsale was accepted as they were there on order from their sovereign and therefore viewed as lawful belligerents; the Irish were not.[91] Therefore, from the outset of the war, the actions of O'Neill and his allies were interpreted by the crown as falling under the proscriptions of rebellion. Given the negative predisposition of the state and its officers towards rebellion, the chances of Irish prisoners receiving mercy were limited.

English authorities may have been disinclined to accept prisoners due to their limited logistical and supply infrastructure. For most of the war, traffic of food and supplies to the crown's army in Ireland was irregular and prone to failures, which could leave garrisons on the verge of starvation. In the latter stages of the conflict the situation had improved, but the supply of food for the troops remained vulnerable as scarcity increased in war-ravaged Ireland, and

---

[85] Hadfield and Maley, eds., *Edmund Spenser*, p. 21.
[86] *CSPI, 1601–3*: 380.
[87] *CSPI, 1600–1*: 135.
[88] Quoted in Geoffrey Parker, 'Early Modern Europe', *The Laws of War: Constraint on Warfare in the Western World*, ed. Michael Howard et al. (London, 1994), pp. 43–4.
[89] TNA, SP 63/183, fol. 354.
[90] BL, Lansdowne MS 84, fol. 90.
[91] Hiram Morgan, 'Disaster at Kinsale', *The Battle of Kinsale*, ed. Morgan, pp. 136–8.

foreign commerce ceased due to the debasement of the coinage.[92] Given the precarious supply situation, there was no practical way for the English military to process Irish prisoners. English commanders were faced with only two choices if they kept them alive: restrain them or let them go. The first option was impossible as the crown had few enough resources to feed and house their troops, let alone substantial numbers of prisoners. Releasing trained soldiers meant crown forces were likely to face them again in another skirmish or battle. With limited options the only solution was brutally pragmatic. Prisoners of note or intelligence value were retained or sent to larger towns or garrisons for questioning and detention; the rest were killed out of hand.

Though many Irish soldiers were executed or refused quarter, the likelihood of Irish surrenders being accepted increased as the war came closer to its conclusion. The long lists of pardons issued by the crown during the latter stages of the war suggest that a substantial number of the Irish were receiving clemency. Many of the names appearing in a pardon issued in September 1601 were recorded as soldiers, specifically those armed with swords, pike and shot.[93] Sir Henry Docwra spared the defenders of the crannog at Islandmachugh, obliging them only to hand over their arms.[94] Bonnaghts in Munster received crown protections, as surrenders critically weakened the Irish cause.[95] Submissions were accepted from common Irish soldiers in the closing stages of the conflict, though this was more a softening of the crown's attitude rather than a reversal of policy, as executions still occurred to the end of the war. Nevertheless, it is clear that surrendering to the forces of the crown was not always tantamount to a death sentence for the Irish.

In summary, it has not been my intention to suggest that the uncouth kerne or grim gallowglass never existed, since they evidently did. Indeed, their primitive arms and equipment fed into the idealised image of the heroic Gael, an image cultivated by contemporary Irish lords and their chroniclers. Yet at the end of the sixteenth century, there was little that was primitive about the Irish forces running amok over the forces of the English crown. Instead, there was a reformed and modernised Irish military fighting in a manner consistent with the most modern methods of continental Europe. Though Irish chroniclers deliberately framed the actions of Tyrone's army in terms reminiscent of the

---

[92]   Richard Stewart, 'The "Irish Road": Military Supply and Arms for Elizabeth's Army during the O'Neill Rebellion in Ireland, 1598–1601', *War and Government in Britain, 1598–1650*, ed. Mark Fissel (Manchester and New York, 1991), pp. 30–1; *CSPI, 1601–3*: 304–5.

[93]   *Irish Fiants of the Tudor Sovereigns*, ed. K.W. Nicholls, 4 vols. (Dublin, 1994), 3: 352–634.

[94]   *CSPI, 1601–3*: 566.

[95]   Stafford, *Pacata Hibernia*, 2: 282.

mythological past, in reality the earl's troops, arms and methods were modern and highly effective. The Irish abided by customs of war and regularly accepted surrenders and took prisoners, a fact which was well known to officers serving against them, although defeat has obscured the military reality and left room for the propagation of a comfortable but deceptive myth. Moreover, the stubborn perseverance of the uncouth Irish warrior suited later political movements which preferred the myth of a primitive Irish military identity untainted by English modernity. Conversely, the English and their portrayal as engaging in a campaign of genocide against the Irish is patently untrue. Contemporary English officers viewed their campaigns as justified by their intention to replace Irish barbarism with English laws and civility. While their methods during the Nine Years War were unquestionably brutal and unconscionable by modern standards, they fall somewhat short of an attempt to eradicate the Irish in Ulster. Though the English may have intended to induce a famine, an agricultural collapse was already underway caused by ten years of war. Their treatment of Irish prisoners may appear brutal and gratuitous to modern readers though this behaviour was entirely warranted by the customs of the day.

The dominant contemporary narrative of English military identity involving the civilisation of the barbarous Irish prevailed into the twentieth century until a historiographical backlash against the brutality of the conquest of Ireland emphasised instead an identity characterised by unrestrained savagery towards the native Irish. As this chapter has shown, commonly held perceptions of both the Irish primitive and English brutality are untrue, and are no longer suitable models of military identity with which to view and discuss the nature of war in Ireland at the end of the sixteenth century. Divested of these well-worn and much-abused tropes, scholars should be better equipped to approach the subject of early modern British and Irish history of this period without the attendant need to assign blame, assuage guilt or commemorate victimhood.

9

'A print in my body of this day's service': Finding Meaning in Wounding During and After the Nine Years War

CLODAGH TAIT

In October 1600 Lord Deputy Mountjoy attempted to lead his army into Ulster via the Moyry Pass, a route strongly fortified and defended by the troops of Hugh O'Neill, earl of Tyrone. According to the *Annals of the Four Masters*, O'Neill sent forth

> fierce and energetic bands of soldiers against him, like unto swarms of bees issuing from the hollows of bee-hives. They proceeded to wound, pierce, hew, and hack them, so that they were compelled to return back [...] to the camp, after the killing of countless numbers of their gentlemen, officers, recruits, and attendants.[1]

In sixteenth-century Ireland, few soldiers and commanders who served for any length of time escaped being wounded; neither could they escape wounding others. Those snatches of combat that are recorded in the Irish annals, State Papers and other sources routinely tell of flesh-piercing, bone-crunching encounters.

Reading wounds

The late Elizabethan Irish wars generated a growing level of violence between soldiers and towards civilians. Casualty levels were increased by mindsets that characterised enemies as 'Irish rebels' or 'English churls', and that legitimised atrocity as a means of dealing with opposition cheaply and definitively.[2] Advances in tactics and weapons had a significant impact on the means of killing and wounding by the end of the sixteenth century: the large numbers

---

[1] *Annals of the Kingdom of Ireland by the Four Masters,* ed. and trans. John O'Donovan. 7 vols. (Dublin, 1856), 6: 2225.

[2] See David Edwards, Pádraig Lenihan and Clodagh Tait, eds., *Age of Atrocity: Violence and Political Conflict in Early Modern Ireland* (Dublin, 2007).

of gunshot wounds reported in the State Papers in the 1590s provides one indication of how warfare in Ireland had been affected by the spread of the 'military revolution'. James O'Neill's research on the Nine Years War demonstrates
how Tyrone had modernised his army, creating a 'hybrid force that combined
the advantages of modern firepower-oriented infantry with the flexible and
highly mobile nature of Irish warfare'.[3] Though more were in possession of
firearms, soldiers still also relied on standard weapons like pikes, swords and
the 'horseman's staff', a wooden staff that might be tipped with metal. The Irish
also fought with javelins ('darts'), bows and their long knives known as *scians*.
As protective armour was expensive, heavy and cumbersome, and required
significant maintenance, for most soldiers the main forms of personal protective equipment were small shields (or 'targets'); morions (light metal helmets);
and cuirasses or breastplates that covered the upper body, possibly with tas-
sets extending over the thighs. Many among the infantry would have been
lucky to have a padded leather or canvas corselet or jack incorporating steel
plates. With most of their lower legs, arms, necks and faces left unarmoured
for manoeuvrability, and given that even body armour might be penetrated by
gunfire, all soldiers were very vulnerable to sustaining some sort of injury on
the battlefield.[4]

    It can be difficult to estimate casualty levels in Irish military engagements
since all sides had a vested interest in minimising reported numbers on their
own side and maximising those of the enemy. It is especially difficult to work
out how many of those reported as 'hurt' subsequently survived their injuries.
Military medical care was often rudimentary and surgeons were few: the outlook for the ill and wounded could thus be bleak. Soldiers without money to
pay for treatment or friends to assist them while they were incapacitated fared
especially badly. Commanders did attempt to provide some medical aid, both
for the wounded and those suffering from the hardship of campaigning, but
this was usually limited. For example, even though the contemporary chronicler William Farmer praised the efforts of the army's Surgeon General during
the siege of Kinsale, he also noted the crown's soldiers there dying of cold, and
losing toes 'from standing and lieing on the coulde grownde'. Illnesses like
dysentery also plagued the crown forces: disease was always a greater killer

[3]   James O'Neill, *The Nine Years War, 1593–1603: O'Neill, Mountjoy and the Military Revolution* (Dublin, 2017), esp. pp. 195–233; O'Neill, 'An Introduction to Firearms in Post-Medieval Ireland, 1500–1700', *The Post-Medieval Archaeology of Ireland 1550–1850*, ed.
Audrey Horning et al. (Dublin, 2007), pp. 467–84.
[4]   Wayne E. Lee, *Barbarians and Brothers: Anglo-American Warfare, 1500–1865* (Oxford,
2011), pp. 13–62; Cyril Falls, *Elizabeth's Irish Wars* (London, 1950).

than battle. Despite all of this, as will be seen, those who could access medical care regularly survived quite serious wounds.[5]

In this context, it is unsurprising that a preoccupation with wounding is evident in contemporary Irish political discourse. Metaphors visualising the state as a body with the monarch at its head abounded in early modern culture.[6] As the Elizabethan reconquest of Ireland continued, administrators and observers, many of whom had military experience, increasingly resorted to graphic analogies of wounding and blood-letting to describe and imagine solutions to Ireland's ills. In 1572, for example, Lord Deputy William Fitzwilliam wrote of Ireland as a 'wretched and moste deformed and cursed Islande which every daye growethe more crooked and mishapen'. He bemoaned the failure of reform despite the funds already expended, which 'lyke a mediscine applyed to some greevous wounde which with the sorenes draweth to it great atche [itch] and for the tyme easeth that payne and helethe nothinge, and so the plaster gone the wounde [is] as greevous as before'.[7] In September 1595, Sir Geoffrey Fenton wrote to Lord Burghley encouraging an increase in the number of troops in Ireland to deal with Tyrone's rebellion 'which will make a short war, or else to harken after some course of pacification to stop the bleeding of the wound before it languish to extremities'.[8] The power and urgency of wounding as metaphor derived from the potentially devastating impact of physical injuries on those who suffered them.

[5]   C. Litton Falkiner, ed., 'William Farmer's Chronicles of Ireland from 1594–1613', *English Historical Review* 22 (1907), 122; John McGurk, 'The Dead, Sick and Wounded of the Nine Years War (1594–1603)', *History Ireland* 4.3 (1995), 16–22; Benjamin Hazard, 'Combat Medics and Military Medicine: Irish Experience During the Tudor and Stuart Period', paper presented at Tudor and Stuart Ireland Conference, University College Dublin, 1 Sept. 2012; Steve Murdoch, 'Medic!: An Insight into Scottish Field Surgeons, Physicians and Medical Provision During the Thirty Years' War, 1618–1648', *Northern Studies* 48 (2017), 51–65. On earlier Irish treatment of wounds, see the fourteenth-century tract 'On Wounds', ed. Winifred Wulff, http://celt.ucc.ie/published/T600012/index.html, accessed 7 May 2019. See also Larissa Tracy and Kelly DeVries, *Wounds and Wound Repair in Medieval Culture* (Leiden, 2015); Ole Peter Grell, 'War, Medicine and the Military Revolution', *The Healing Arts: Health, Disease and Society in Europe 1500–1800*, ed. Peter Elmer (Manchester, 2004), pp. 257–83; Eric Gruber von Arni, *Justice to the Maimed Soldier* (London, 2001).

[6]   Jennifer C. Vaught, ed., *Rhetorics of Bodily Disease and Health in Medieval and Early Modern England* (Farnham, 2010); Sarah Covington, *Wounds, Flesh and Metaphor in Seventeenth-Century England* (Basingstoke, 2009); Jason G. Harris, *Foreign Bodies and the Body Politic: Discourses of Social Pathology in Early Modern England* (Cambridge, 2008). For similar examples: Patricia Palmer, 'Where Does It Hurt?: How Pain Makes History in Early Modern Ireland', *The Body in Pain in Irish Literature and Culture*, ed. Fionnuala Dillane et al. (Basingstoke, 2016), p. 24.

[7]   TNA, SP 63/36, fols. 2–3.

[8]   *CSPI, 1592–6*, p. 381.

This chapter considers how wounds were written about, how men represented their own wounds and those of others, and how wounds and their representation become a means of constituting and displaying military identity during and after the Nine Years War. The aim is to uncover what wounds meant to victims, engaging with both the initial experience of the agony of wounding and – using Sir Griffin Markham and Sir Henry Danvers as case-studies – its longer-term physical and emotional effects. Wounding could play a formative role in shaping military men's reputations. In his 1597 tract, *The Mirror of Honor*, John Norden reminded his patron, the earl of Essex, that 'To be wounded in the warres is glorie, and to dye in a just cause purchaseth immortal memorie'. Wounds and death 'gotten in the field in the face of the enemie' were marks of courage and 'true magnanimitie' that 'bring immortal fame to the valiant'.[9] As Yuval Harari argues, 'in early modern European martial culture injuries and scars were badges of honour, and thus important constituents of a combatant's identity'; they were 'tangible testament to *mental* qualities'.[10] Wounds were thus marks of a fight well fought, testifying to a soldier's valour and steadfastness and his triumph over timidity and doubt.

But even for the most valiant, enduring the pain and indignity of wounding and the fear of its practical consequences was hard emotional work. Furthermore, as Rob Boddice points out, the cultural environment and social norms of particular places and times tend to shape how pain is spoken about and understood. Pain, he says, is 'historical, cultural and emotional'. As well as being a physical sensation, pain is an emotion that is felt within particular historical and cultural contexts. Like the other emotions aroused by wounding, its expression occurs as 'a dynamic process of negotiation between inward feelings and outward expectations, norms, taboos and so on'.[11] Ways of describing and acting upon emotions were above all 'inflected by gender'.[12] Dianne Hall has noted that 'In early modern Ireland the meanings of male bodies wounded and killed in war were mediated through contemporary

---

[9]   John Norden, *The Mirror of Honor* (London, 1597), pp. 48, 58.

[10] Yuval Noah Harari, *The Ultimate Experience: Battlefield Revelations and the Making of Modern War Culture, 1450–2000* (Basingstoke, 2008), pp. 108–10. See also Covington, *Wounds*, pp. 95–100.

[11] Rob Boddice, 'Introduction: Hurt Feelings?', *Pain and Emotion in Modern History*, ed. Boddice (Basingstoke, 2014), pp. 1–14. On the burgeoning history of emotions: Barbara Rosenwein, *Generations of Feeling: A History of Emotions, 600–1770* (Cambridge, 2016); Rosenwein, 'Worrying about Emotions in History', *American Historical Rreview* 107 (2002), 821–45; Rob Boddice, 'The Affective Turn: Historicizing the Emotions', *Psychology and History: Interdisciplinary Explorations*, ed. Cristian Tileagă and Jovan Byford (Cambridge, 2014), pp. 147–65.

[12] Susan Broomhall, 'Introduction', *Ordering Emotions in Europe, 1100–1800*, ed. Broomhall (Leiden, 2015), p. 11.

ideas of honour and masculinity'.[13] For military men, there were significant cultural constraints on how pain and wounding were spoken and written about. At a time when male 'capacity for governance [...] was demonstrated through control of one's own mind and body',[14] it was necessary for those who had been wounded to retain control over their emotions and to attempt to react 'manfully', even 'cheerfully', with as much patience and stoicism as possible.[15] Suffering was understood to be purposeful – a means to the recovery of health – and to have elevating and redemptive qualities.[16] However, the wounded also hoped for practical and emotional responses to their suffering. Though expected not to be too voluble about their hurts, wounded soldiers sought compassionate acknowledgement of them, as well as some reward for the service that their scars continued to make visible even after physical pain might (or might not) have subsided. But in all ages, compassion can be conditional and limited, and some sufferers may be 'excluded from the realm of sympathy' for a variety of reasons: if their suffering, or the cause for which they have suffered, seems irrelevant; if the victim is considered to be responsible for their own misfortune, or something about their morals or character seems flawed; or if the emotional or material costs of compassion to the observer seem too great.[17] What happened when compassion was lacking, responses were inadequate, or when manful patience failed? Sarah Covington argues that an 'acute kind of ambivalence attached itself to the warrior's battered flesh [and] while many veterans or writers attempted to find in wounds a kind of elevating masculine power and grace, others failed in the face of interpreting injuries that stood as reminders of the soldier's, and the country's, own deep fragilities'.[18] This chapter therefore also examines the fundamental ambivalence and shifting signification of wounds and wounding, and the impact of this in the fashioning of military identity in early modern Ireland.

---

[13] Dianne Hall, '"Most barbarously and inhumane maner butchered": Masculinity, Trauma, and Memory in Early Modern Ireland', *The Body in Pain*, ed. Dillane et al., p. 50.

[14] Susan Broomhall and Jacqueline van Gent, 'Introduction', *Governing Masculinities in the Early Modern Period: Regulating Selves and Others*, ed. Broomhall and van Gent (London, 2011), pp. 16–17.

[15] Covington, *Wounds*, p. 93.

[16] Javier Moscoco, 'Pain and Suffering', *Early Modern Emotions: An Introduction*, ed. S. Broomhall (Oxford, 2017), pp. 45–7; Michael Schoenfeldt, 'The Art of Pain Management in Early Modern England', *The Sense of Suffering: Constructions of Physical Pain in Early Modern Culture*, ed. Jan Franz van Dijkhuizen and Karl A.E. Enenkel (Leiden, 2009), pp. 19–38.

[17] Boddice, 'Introduction', p. 3; Jennifer E. Stellar and Dacher Keltner, 'Compassion', *Handbook of Positive Emotions*, ed. Michele M. Tugade et al. (London, 2014), pp. 330–1.

[18] Covington, *Wounds*, p. 84.

Discussing and describing wounding in early modern Ireland

Lists of casualties in the State Papers often give some sense of the nature of the injuries suffered by soldiers. For example, in June 1599 Captain William Constable chronicled some of the misfortunes endured by crown forces in the Midlands and south in the previous six weeks:

> In the fight with Ony MacRowry O'Moore, Captain Boswell and Lieutenant Gardiner was killed. At the siege of the castle of Cahire, Captain Brett and Captain George Cary received the wounds they died of, both shot into the body. In the Desmond's country did Sir Henry Norice receive his shot which caused his leg to be cut off. Sir Thomas Norice, in a fight (with my Lord Burck his bro[ther] that was traitor) was hurt in the head with a pike [the weapon went in under his jaw and he died two months later]; at another place Sir Henry Davers shot in the face, Captain Foliatt his arm broke with a shot, Captain Jenninges in the body [...] We have in all our fights beaten the rebels, yet those men that they have hit of ours proved of the best sort. The particularities of every accident were too tedious. Ned Bushell I omit, for that he is well again, but he received an honourable hurt with a pike in his breast, which after he had taken out, he killed one of the rebels, and the rest with him 6 more.[19]

A similar list was produced after the battle of Kinsale (1601):

> There were of the Irish Rebels 1,200 dead bodies left in the place, and, as we hear from themselves, about 800 hurt, whereof many of them died that night [...] On our side only Sir Richard Greame's cornet was killed, Sir Henry Davers hurt with a sword slightly, Sir William Godolphin a little rast [razed] on the thigh with a halberd, Captain Crofts, the scout-master, with a shot in the back, and not above five or six common soldiers hurt; many of our horses killed, and more hurt.
>
> The Earl of Clanricard had many fair escapes, being shot through his garments, and no man did bloody his sword more than his Lordship that day, and would not suffer any man to take any of the Irish prisoners, but bid them kill the rebels. After the retreat was sounded the Lord Deputy did give the order of knighthood to the Earl of Clanricard in the field in the midst of the dead bodies.

It goes without saying that the actual numbers killed in June 1599 and at Kinsale were higher than indicated. It was the injuries and deaths of officers that mostly concerned commanders. Lord Deputy William Russell assessed his losses in the Monaghan and Newry area in May 1595 at '31 or 32 slain and some 90 hurt, but none of accompt, but Sir Henry Duke, Captain Cuney, 5

---

[19] HMC, *Salisbury MSS*, 9: 213.

lieutenants, an ensign, and a serjeant'. [20] While, as Patricia Palmer points out, little sympathy was shown for dead and wounded enemies – note Clanricard's order that 'rebels', presumably including those injured, were to be killed – casualties among soldiers of no 'name', 'mark' or 'accompt' also received little official attention or compassion. [21]

High-profile commanders in Ireland tended to be proactive leaders in the field and thus were themselves well-acquainted with being wounded. The State Papers and other sources regularly note the wounding of commanders such as the earl of Thomond, hurt when the earl of Ormond, lieutenant-general of the army, was taken hostage during a parley with the O'Mores in April 1600. In a joint letter to the Privy Council, Thomond and Sir George Carew described how they and their men fought their way out of the melee:

> We had more hanging upon us than is credibly to be believed; but our horses were strong, and by that means did break through them, tumbling down on all sides those that were before and behind us; and, thanks be to God, we escaped [...] their pikes, which they freely bestowed, and the flinging of their skeynes, without any hurt, saving that I, the Earl of Thomond, received with a pike a wound in my back.

Thomond also saved Carew from capture. [22] Sir Henry Docwra received a severe wound fighting against O'Donnell's troops in July 1600:

> At the first encounter I was stricken with a horseman's staff in the forehead, in so much as I fell for dead, and was a good while deprived of my senses [...] but the captains and gentlemen that were about me enforced the enemy to give ground [...] by means whereof I recovered myself was set up on my horse and so safely brought off and conducted home [...] I kept my bed of this wound by the space of a fortnight, my chamber a week after, and then I came abroad to take view and muster of all the companies. [23]

Sir John Norreys, Lord President of Munster, was a veteran of the Tudor wars throughout Europe. During his military career he sustained at least nine wounds. He was shot in the shoulder by an arrow in Ireland in 1575 and, back in action there during the Nine Years War, received a minor wound in September 1595, subsequently suffering a fall from his horse and several bouts of illness. In early 1597 he retired to Mallow lamenting that he had spilt more of his own blood in the queen's service than anyone else, and he died there,

---

[20] David Edwards, ed., *Campaign Journals of the Elizabethan Irish Wars* (Dublin, 2014), p. 218.
[21] Palmer, 'Where Does It Hurt?', pp. 24–35; Hall, 'Masculinity, Trauma and Memory', p. 39.
[22] *Cal. Carew MSS*, 3: 380–4.
[23] William P. Kelly and John O'Donovan, eds., *Docwra's Derry: A Narration of Events in North-west Ulster, 1600–1604* (Belfast, 2003), pp. 47–8, 101.

possibly of gangrene, in July 1597. (A more colourful account, put about by his enemies, suggested that the devil had appeared in person at Mallow Castle to take his soul).[24] Pain, trauma and field surgery were thus the lot of many soldiers serving in Ireland in the Nine Years War, no matter their rank.

Military leaders faced particular challenges with regard to their own wounding. The subject needed to be handled delicately, and commanders who wanted to keep their jobs conspicuously avoided dwelling in too much detail on their own wounds and misfortunes in dispatches to Dublin and London. The earl of Thomond, for example, made sure to record his own injury in 1599, but did not elaborate upon it. On the one hand it risked looking like vainglory, especially when the injury had occurred in the context of military failure. It may also have been feared that questions would be asked of one's continued competence as a leader – hence, perhaps, Docwra's keenness on the one hand to note the consequences of his wound, which kept him from his duties for three weeks, but on the other to demonstrate that he had resumed those duties in full. He plays down the seriousness of his head injury, saying merely that it was caused by a horseman's staff, when in fact Irish observers suggested he was hit in the forehead by a dart that penetrated his helmet. Appearing to spring back from misfortune might also be a means of countering rumours spread by one's rivals and enemies. The Irish *Annals of the Four Masters* claimed that rather than Docwra being the subject of a heroic rescue, 'the English, seeing their chief, their adviser, and their mighty man, wounded, returned home in sorrow and disgrace'.[25]

It is instructive in this context to consider the earl of Tyrone's account of his wounding in 1593. In the years before he entered into outright rebellion in 1594, Tyrone occasionally opted to give some impression of loyalty to the crown, while simultaneously pursuing his own interests. Hiram Morgan describes O'Neill's reluctant participation in Sir Henry Bagenal's campaign against Maguire in the autumn of 1593, which James O'Neill believes was part of 'a sophisticated deception to divert the crown's military resources in an ineffective campaign, and to prolong Tyrone's façade of loyalty' as he built up his own military capacity.[26] After being obliged to take to the field in the battle of Erne ford, Tyrone sent a belated and strongly self-justificatory account of events to London:

---

[24] John S. Nolan, *Sir John Norreys and the Elizabethan Military World* (Exeter, 1997), pp. 29, 234, 237–9.

[25] Palmer, 'Where Does It Hurt?', p. 23; Kelly and Donovan, eds., *Docwra's Derry*, pp. 100–1.

[26] Hiram Morgan, *Tyrone's Rebellion: The Outbreak of the Nine Years War in Ireland* (London, 1999), pp. 154–6; Nicholas Canny, 'Hugh O'Neill, second earl of Tyrone', *ODNB*; O'Neill, *Nine Years War*, pp. 32, 35.

If I had been in good state of health able to have written to you of the good success which we have had against Maguire I would before this time have informed
you of the manner of that service, and how every man played his part in the
same, to the honour of Her Majesty, and to the confusion of the rebel's force, but
by reason it was my hap in that day's service to receive a dangerous wound in
my right leg, which [was] run quite through with a spear, on account of which
wound I am not yet able to go or stand but upon a crutch. Thus I could not, as
I fain would, inform your Lordships of that matter. Now that I feel in myself a
little recovery and amendment of my hurt, I thought good to signify unto you
how that service was taken in hand and performed; being glad, though my hurt
was sore, that for a testimony of my loyalty and faithfulness to serve Her Majesty
it was my chance to have a print in my body of this day's service, as I have had
many other before this time; not doubting that my blood now lost in this and
other services heretofore will satisfy the Queen's Majesty, and confirm her good
opinion of me and also your Lordships.[27]

Tyrone uses his wound to seek advantage. But his repeated insistence on soliciting empathy and commendation means that his letter conspicuously fails to
conform to the business-like modesty expected of a truly loyal military commander and seems to have been designed in its obvious double-speak to make
the readers uneasy. On the one hand he declares his willingness to spill his own
blood in the queen's cause: he claims that once various matters alleged against
him were cleared up, 'I will venture both the other leg and the whole body
in Her Majesty's service as occasion shall be offered'.[28] On the other, Tyrone
points out that the queen had not previously been satisfied by similar evidence
of his loyalty, and hints that his wounds from 'this day's service' (not *good*
service) might be something for himself to cherish or regret as he chose.

What is particularly striking in Tyrone's letter is the vivid description of his
wound as 'a print in my body'. The soldier's flesh becomes a text, and on it his
spilled blood writes tales of his personal history and his fortitude. It reminds
him of his enemies – and it demands recognition and recompense. Medical
treatises spoke of wounds as having lips that needed to be drawn together to
effect a cure, and Covington has discussed the appearance in Shakespeare and
elsewhere of the idea of wounds as 'mouths', mute yet eloquent.[29] Tyrone was
hinting that rather than providing a 'testimony' to loyalty and success, his
wounds might instead come to tell a story of regret and recrimination.

[27]   *CSPI*, *1592–6*, p. 170.
[28]   *CSPI*, *1592–6*, p. 171.
[29]   Covington, *Wounds*, p. 163.

The meaning and mobilisation of wounding

Tyrone put his hurt down to 'chance' (he uses the word twice), perhaps deliberately avoiding any suggestion of divine intervention, or any imputation against his own skill as a fighter. However, he piously placed his recovery in God's hands: 'so soon as God sends me strength again that I may be able to serve I mean to do mine endeavour still in her service'.[30] (This, of course, left it open to Tyrone to state that God's work was only slowly being accomplished.) Many other soldiers also spoke about wounding and recovery in providential terms.[31] Norden reminded his audience that whether or not a soldier died in battle was ordained by God, and therefore should not be feared and could not be avoided.[32] The writer of Mountjoy's official account of the defeat at Moyry Pass attributed his own survival to the protection of 'God, whose providence stretcheth even to the bullets that fly [...] for I was shot through the cloak, and my horse was shot underneath me and slain'.[33] The outcome of serious wounds was likewise in the hands of God. Sir Ralph Lane (former colonist at Roanoke, North Carolina), writing from Kilkenny in May 1594, described how a wound that had been healing had worsened to the extent that he feared for his life: 'Albeit my recoverie is neither in myne owne feelings nor in the opinyone of the chicurgions soe hopeless but that at the good pleasure of the allmightie the same is possible enough'.[34] He thus sought to set his affairs in order.

Where one side saw God's intervention in wounding, the other might see the devil's: Mountjoy claimed that the valour of Captain Berrey, despite his having received five wounds, was of 'so great admiration to the rebels themselves, that to use their own words, they would not believe but he was a devil'.[35] Other occasions of seemingly miraculous escapes from wounding and valiant feats of wounding and killing attracted attention and awe, as in the case of the earl of Clanricard, mentioned earlier, who avoided injury at Kinsale, despite being in the thick of the action. Quick recoveries from what looked like serious or mortal wounds might also be noted, like the fact that Ned Bushell – as described in Captain Constable's letter excerpted above – received a pike-wound to the breast, pulled the weapon out and went on to kill an opponent. Writers also regularly noted cases where men's horses were killed under them, both in order to indicate lucky escapes and to highlight the bravery of those who continued to fight on foot after they had been unhorsed. In a skirmish in

---

[30] *CSPI, 1592–6*, p. 170.
[31] Covington, *Wounds*, pp. 100–3.
[32] Norden, *Mirror*, pp. 57–9.
[33] *CSPI, 1600–1*, pp. 30–1.
[34] *CSPI, 1592–6*, p. 44.
[35] *CSPI, 1600–1*, p. 38. This may refer to the man at Moyry Pass who was wounded several times and played dead as the rebels stripped him (pp. 27–8).

June 1600 (a month before the injury noted above), Docwra's horse was 'shot twice and slain under him; who quit his horse, and made a stand, till six others came to his rescue [...] All men that saw him in that danger, and his valour in the quitting himself, do highly commend him.'[36]

Given that wounding was generally interpreted as a sign of honourable and valiant conduct, petitions for assistance from or on behalf of soldiers soliciting assistance in the aftermath of disabling wounds can be a useful source for revealing individuals' reactions to their own wounds. The petitions of soldiers after the Wars of the Three Kingdoms have been discussed by Matthew Neufeld, Mark Stoyle, Sarah Covington and others, but similar documents also regularly issued from Elizabeth's Irish wars.[37] Former soldiers petitioning potential patrons for financial and practical aid frequently pointed to their wounds as proof of their courage and devotion to the advancement of the crown's cause: 'the wounds that the veteran had suffered could be taken as bodily confirmation of the principles that his service had upheld'.[38] Sir Charles Danvers thanking the earl of Southampton in 1599 for news of his brother Henry's improvement after he had been shot in the face (as is discussed in more detail below), commented 'I hope it will turn him to some good, for that wounds in the wars, being the mark of well deservers, cannot lose their reward in grateful time.'[39]

Petitions tend to be relatively brief and to follow a formula, setting out the petitioner's service and the losses he had sustained as a result, including any episodes of wounding. For example, John Thurste petitioned the Privy Council in 1582 seeking relief after having been wounded 'with a poysoned bullett' at the siege of the castle of Ballamore. He had been under the care of surgeons for nine months, 'to his greate hynderament, and thutter undoing of hym and his poore wife forever'. He cited his twenty years of service to the queen 'beinge dyvers and sundrye tymes hurte'.[40] Wounds might be recollected and made use of long after they had been acquired. When Captain John Baxter petitioned Sir Robert Cecil for 200 marks in 1600, he cited his long service, his losses in the Irish rebellion and his financial outlay in advancing the queen's cause. He also reminded Cecil that 'in Sir Richard Bingham's time I was maimed while saving his life in the wars of the MacWilliams in 1586'.[41]

[36] *CSPI, 1600*, p. 270.
[37] On soldiers' war stories from petitions for relief and memoirs after the English Civil Wars: Matthew Neufeld, *The Civil Wars After 1660: Public Remembering in Late Stuart England* (Woodbridge, 2013), pp. 55–86; Mark Stoyle, 'Memories of the Maimed: The Testimony of King Charles' Former Soldiers, 1660–1730', *History* 88 (2003), 207–26; Covington, *Wounds*, pp. 111–15.
[38] Neufeld, *Civil Wars*, p. 64.
[39] HMC, *Salisbury MSS*, 9: 236.
[40] TNA, SP 63/90, fol. 111.
[41] HMC, *Salisbury MSS*, 10: 35.

Military commanders regularly added their voices to the petitions of honourable soldiers. Thurste claimed his petition could be verified by the earl of
Ormond, who he described as a 'ffather to all good soldiers'. Sir George Carew,
wrote in 1601 in support of 'some maintenance' for a 'maimed soldier', Thomas
Beard, who had lost lands in Queen's County and had thereafter been obliged
to enter military service where he 'received a maim in his leg wherof he has
lain long under cure'. He was now 'out of all hope to recover the use thereof'
and 'extreme needy through his long sickness and charge to the surgeons'.
Carew claimed he did not normally seek such favours: 'I write not for many,
yet I could not in honour deny him my letters, having received his hurt under
my command'. Wounding set up obligations between the wounded and the
men they had followed into battle: Carew would lose honour if he neglected
Mr Beard's pitiable state, while Thurste expected Ormond's fatherly support.[42]

The frequent use of the terms 'maim' and 'maimed' in such petitions is
instructive. Contemporaries understood that while a 'wound' or 'hurt' might
recover, even if it left a scar, a 'maim' was an injury causing 'the loss of a limb,
or of the use of it [...] a mutilating wound'.[43] Those who were 'maimed' considered these injuries to be permanently disabling. From the 1590s, an increasing amount of aid was made available in England and Wales to deal with the
problem of demobilised disabled soldiers. Previously, it was mostly left up to
local parishes to provide maimed men with stipends or accommodation in
almshouses. Acts passed by the Privy Council from 1593 'created a system of
compulsory parochial taxation to be administered on a countrywide basis'.
Entitlement to the pensions now being provided was on grounds not of poverty but 'physical disability suffered in the service of the state'. Soldiers' injuries
and service were certified by their captains and presented to the muster-master
general in London to be countersigned: successful applicants then applied for
relief in the county in which they had been pressed or born.[44] That the scheme
was already being used by the end of the 1590s is evident in the petitions of
some veterans of the Nine Years War. Examples include George Sherley's letter
to Robert Cecil in 1599, claiming he had been 'maimed in the Irish wars and
dismissed and cannot obtain relief'. He asked Cecil to write to the justices of
Middlesex 'where he was pressed'.[45] Likewise in February 1599, Docwra wrote
to Essex on behalf of a man who had served with him for two years

---

[42] HMC, *Salisbury MSS*, 11: 572.
[43] *OED*, s.v. 'maim'.
[44] Geoffrey L. Hudson, 'Disabled Veterans and the State in Early Modern England', *Disa-
      bled Veterans in History*, ed. David A. Gerber (Ann Arbor, 2000), pp. 117–44; Hudson,
      'Ex-servicemen's Own Stories in Early Modern England', *Medicine, Madness and Social
      History: Essays in Honour of Roy Porter*, ed. Roberta Bivins and John V. Pickstone (Bas-
      ingstoke, 2007), pp. 105–18.
[45] HMC, *Salisbury MSS*, 9: 436.

having been before an ensign to Captain Worlock in Ireland, under whom he was maimed in the right arm in service there, for which he received a small pension in the county of Norfolk where he was born, which being in danger to lose by his absence, he desires letters from you [...] that he may not be prejudiced by his willingness to continue in the wars'.[46]

Clearly maims were effectively used to gain relief after service in Ireland, even when continued military employment was possible. Similar locally organised pensions do not seem to have been available in Ireland, however, with veterans to a large degree continuing to be dependent on ad hoc grants or private foundations, like the almshouses in Youghal founded by the first earl of Cork 'for owld decaied Soldiers' in the 1630s.[47] A memorandum of 'Pensions' being paid by the Dublin administration, compiled c.1609, indicates continuing support to a number of wounded veterans, including: Christopher Wackley 'in consideration of loss of both eyes in service'; Martin Lindsey 'an old maimed soldier'; Henry Borrowes 'having lost his arm in service'; Nicholas Crehill and Captain Francis Gameforth, each 'in recompense of his maim in service'; James Delahide whose leg had been maimed in service; and William Hethrington, 'in respect of divers hurts and maims in service'. Several of these individuals had been collecting their pensions since the 1590s.[48]

When petitioning, it was necessary to draw attention to the fact that any abandonment of military duties was due to wounds honourably sustained, rather than cowardice or desertion. In November 1595, Norreys wrote to Cecil recommending Captain Richard Wingfield 'whose sore hurt enforceth him to go into England for his recovery'. Wingfield had been 'maimed in one of his arms, with danger' the previous September, though he later returned to active service in Ireland, becoming Marshal of the army.[49] In April 1601 Geoffrey Fenton wrote to Cecil asking that the queen show compassion towards George Greame who 'having received many dangerous hurts in Her Majesty's service [...] is now in his old years determined to show himself there [in London] as a crushed soldier' as he had become 'disabled to toil and venture in the wars'.[50] In the same month, Thomas Jones, bishop of Meath, wrote to Cecil on behalf of Sir Francis Shane, asking that he be excused from his duties in Ireland as 'his wound forces him to travel to England, to seek for help and cure', and describing him as being 'in Her Majesty's services very forward, and always ready to adventure his life'. Shane had been 'maymed in one of his leggs' in January 1599, and suffered two further wounds in December 1599 (when he was

[46] HMC, *Salisbury MSS*, 9: 56.
[47] Alexander B. Grosart, ed., *The Lismore Papers*, 10 vols. (London, 1886–8), 1, 4: 7.
[48] *CSPI, 1608–10*, pp. 336–8; *CSPI, 1603–6*, pp. 125–30.
[49] *CSPI, 1592–6*, pp. 382, 428.
[50] *CSPI, 1600–1*, p. 296.

captured) and March 1600. In Shane's case, however, his quest for a cure was largely an excuse to allow him to plead his case for a pension and recompense from the crown for his losses during the 1590s. John King wrote sceptically to Sir George Carey that 'Sir Francis Shane and Sir James Dillon are commended into England, and purposed to be suitors to her Majesty for remittal of their rents[...] Sir Francis giveth out that his going is to the baths for his hurt leg, but indeed it is chiefly about his rents.'[51]

This latter case, like Tyrone's 1593 letter quoted above, reminds us that while wounds might be manipulated to personal advantage, their interpretation might be unstable, and was not always under the control of the sufferer. An Irish spy for Spain met on the continent by an English informer in 1601 was described as tall and thin, having a red beard and hair, a wart on his upper lip, and 'a scar in the middle of his forehead, which he got last year in a skirmish with the [earl of]Tyrone against Sir Samuel Bagenall.'[52] Scars thus could remind observers of their sufferer's previous disloyalty. Some men feared their wounds would be used against them. Ralph Lane, whose providentialist view of his slow recovery was mentioned above, provides a possible example of this. Statements by his detractors that Lane had 'grown weak in his brains' after being wounded have been accepted as fact. However, Lane's letters about his role as muster-master of the army are very cogent, and very unsparing of the endemic corruption that weakened the crown forces during the Nine Years War. In May 1601 he complained to Cecil about a 'sinister endeavour' to supplant him. He reminded Cecil of his previous successes 'to use it as an armour of some sound proof against the paper bullets of reproachful slanders at random shot at me by my injurious competitors.'[53] This early use of the term 'paper bullets' is an interesting choice for a man who knew the effects of wounding, and whose former injuries may have been regularly resurrected to question his capacity for his role.[54]

---

[51] *CSPI, 1600–1*, pp. 205, 265–6, 311. See Joseph Mannion, '"As trew Englishe as any man borne in Myddlesex": Sir Francis Shane, 1540–1614', *Frontiers, States and Identity in Early Modern Ireland and Beyond*, ed. Christopher Maginn and Gerald Power (Dublin, 2016), pp. 177–81.

[52] *CSPI, 1600–1*, p. 209.

[53] *CSPI, 1596–7*, p. 309; *CSPI, 1600–1*, pp. 249–50, 362, 449.

[54] He died in 1603. Edward E. Hale, 'Life of Sir Ralph Lane', *Archaeologia Americana* 4 (1860), 339–42; S.M. Thorpe, 'Ralph Lane', *The History of Parliament: the House of Commons 1558–1603*, ed. P.W. Hasler, 3 vols. (London, 1981), 2: 435–6. David Edwards believes Lane's insistence on uncovering corruption and fraud made him unpopular (personal communication). The earliest published usage of the term 'paper bullets' is in Andrew Willet, *Synopsis Papismi* (London, 1592): many thanks to James McCracken of *OED* for kindly supplying me with this reference, and to Bríd McGrath of Trinity College, Dublin for her assistance.

Petitions and letters by wounded officers can offer useful insights into anxieties that plagued sufferers and the means by which they attempted to come to terms with their changed circumstances. Francis Rushe wrote to Edward Reynolds on 12 October 1598, describing himself as a 'poor, honest thankful man', passing on Irish news and asking that Reynolds speak well of him. Only at the end of the letter does he mention that he had been wounded five weeks ago: 'No remedy but patience. The bone a little touched and the sinews shrewdly rent.' He had also suffered from flux and other ailments 'But time and patience, I hope, will give conquest of all'. Without the goodwill of a patron, however, he claimed he would have to leave soldiering. Rushe's associations with the earls of Sussex and Essex ensured his further employment: he became Governor of Maryborough in January 1599 and was knighted by Essex the following May.[55] Also in October 1598, Sir Callisthenes Brooke wrote to Cecil anxiously requesting that his command of his company (then in England) not be taken from him: he had been detained in Ireland by 'casualty and not will', having been shot in the body 'which has cut so many sinews that go to my thigh and leg as I am not yet for pain and the shortness [of breath] able to ride or go. Besides my hurt is kept open for splinters that are coming out of one of my ribs.'[56] Brooke survived his wound and the dreadful rigours of its treatment, but although he previously had been a rising name in military circles, his career and finances were compromised. On 1 April 1599 we find Essex recommending him to the Privy Council and asking for their favour to him as he had 'both done good service and been undone in his body and [e]state'.[57] Despite his 'good service', Brooke's colourful personal life may subsequently have discouraged patrons from assisting him. He served in the army again in the Low Countries for a short period, but by 1609 Lady Anne Cobham, his mother, was petitioning for him for a pension on account of his wounds when 'serving against the rebels in the Irish wars'.[58]

[55] HMC, *Salisbury MSS*, 6: 387. Rushe had formerly served in English continental armies; see Paul Hammer, '"Base rogues" and "gentlemen of quality": The Earl of Essex's Irish Knights and Royal Displeasure in 1599', *Elizabeth I and Ireland*, ed. Valerie McGowan-Doyle and Brendan Kane (Cambridge, 2011), pp. 199–200. He went on to become a Privy Councillor, acquired lands in Meath, and died in 1623: NLI, GO MS 79, Funeral Entries Vol. 17, pp. 119–20.
[56] HMC, *Salisbury MSS*, 6: 393.
[57] *CSPI, 1599–1600*, p. 1.
[58] *CSPD, 1603–10*, p. 487. Not all Brooke's wounds were sustained in Ireland: in November 1599 he was injured in a duel in London with Lord Dunkellin (later earl of Clanrickard and St Albans), allegedly after he got Dunkellin's sister pregnant and then refused her: *Letters of Philip Gawdy of West Harling, Norfolk, and of London to Various Members of his Family 1579–1616*, ed. Isaac Herbert Jeayes (London, 1906), p. 103; Claire Carroll, *Circe's Cup: Cultural Transformations in Early Modern Ireland* (Cork, 2001), pp. 72–3; A.L. Rowse, *Sex and Society in Shakespeare's Age: Simon Foreman the Astrologer* (London, 1974), pp. 18–19. Brooke married abroad and died in The Hague in 1611: Sarah

Lady Cobham's intervention to assist her son reminds us that their social standing made the position of wounded gentleman and captains somewhat more precarious than that of men in the ranks. Some had already expended large sums during their time in Ireland. The upper levels of Elizabeth's Irish army contained many 'voluntaries' who used their own funds to raise troops in support of a patron or in the hope of recompense and reward. Paul Hammer cites the example of Sir John Harington who expended £300 'to join the action in Ireland in 1599'.[59] Career officers likewise usually had a large personal financial investment in their Irish service. If this was not repaid, and if further service to recoup it was impossible, serious repercussions awaited. Sir Francis Stafford, for example, petitioned the Privy Council in 1590 for over £500 owed to him, and claimed that he was entitled to a pension 'in consideration of his service and grievous wound', he having occupied the position of Sergeant-major of Ireland for ten years before he was disabled by his injuries.[60] Furthermore, though former officers might have personal or family means to support them in their recovery and through any lingering disability, they usually did not have a claim to standard pension funds, which in any case would have provided far too little cash to provide them with an income suited to their social rank. Instead, they had to continue to rely on leveraging personal connections and on rewards that might be granted on an ad hoc basis. While Rushe's and Brooke's letters, written soon after their injuries, are models of modest self-promotion and stoical suffering, it cannot have been easy for men facing the potential ruin of their ambitions and finances to summon the patience that Rushe calls upon so valiantly.

Two case studies

Sir Griffin (or Griffith) Markham's debilitating wounds certainly spoke to him of failure and of the neglect of those who, he believed, should have rewarded his service with patronage. Markham had been 'shot through the arm with a musket' while leading Clifford's cavalry at the Battle of Curlew Pass in July 1599.[61] His cousin, Sir John Harington, described Markham's leadership as one of the few bright points in what became a rout of the crown forces. According to Harington, though initially Markham 'bare the hurt admirable

---

Williams, ed., *Letters Written By John Chamberlain* (London, 1838), pp. 2, 122, 179; *CSPD, 1601–3*, pp. 64, 122, 293; TNA, PROB 11/119/37, will of Anne Haddon Brooke, alias Cobham.

[59] Hammer, 'Earl of Essex's Irish Knights', esp. pp. 192–5.

[60] TNA, SP 63/156 fol.135. Stafford went on to become a Privy Councillor and Governor of Ulster. He was granted a pension by letters patent and was still receiving 5s a day at the time of his death in 1609: *CSPI, 1603–6*, pp. 130, 254; *CSPI, 1608–10*, pp. 47, 84, 438.

[61] O'Neill, *Nine Years War*, pp. 90–3.

well', he subsequently became ill, for a time being 'in danger of his arm by the hurt, and of his life by an ague'. In a letter of July 1601 seeking assistance from Cecil, Markham's wound seems to support his attempt to secure a role within the council of Connacht 'in which I now begin to fear the success', and he reminded Cecil of 'my standing in the wars being now above 10 years and not slackly followed'. He especially cited his service in Connacht, where he had been 'maimed'. As well as the physical suffering from his injury, he also described his emotional suffering at his lack of reward: 'It grieveth me much to see all men employed and myself wholly neglected'. Anxiety about his future also comes through in his apologies to Cecil ('If I have been too importunate').[62]

By 1603 the Markham family was hugely in debt and the difficulties of Griffin and several of his relatives were compounded by suspicions of recusancy. Harington wrote to Cecil on Markham's behalf in May 1603, vividly encapsulating his troubles in an allusion to the Trojan hero Aeneas: 'old Markham dotes at home, and his honest sonne Sir Griffin yowr kinsman like an Eneas that would carry his father owt of the flames, is like to burn in it with him, the lubber is so heavy to ly on his maimed sonnes showlders'. Markham's grievances had festered further as he was frustrated in other attempts to gain advancement, and that July he participated in the failed Bye Plot to kidnap James I and oblige him to grant religious toleration. His disability is confirmed in the proclamation for his arrest, which described his appearance – a 'large broad face, of a blacke [bleak?] complexion, a bigge nose', a thin beard, and 'one of his hands is maimed by an hurt in his arme received by the shot of a Bullet'. He was subsequently convicted of treason, though he was spared the death sentence and went into exile in the Low Countries. Mark Nicholls is inclined to view his participation as 'an aberration born of disappointed hopes in an abnormal time': Harington certainly blamed Markham's 'discontent' about his 'decaying' estate.[63] Markham's brothers also testified to his 'despair'. He allegedly recruited them to the plot because of his 'disability for action' (another indication that he would no longer have been able to pursue a military career), as well as for the Catholic faith and 'the raising of our house'.[64]

By contrast Sir Henry Davers (or Danvers) found military service and maiming wounds to be the making of his career. Like Markham, Danvers had considerable military experience on the continent before he came to Ireland in

[62] HMC, *Salisbury MSS*, 11: 301.
[63] Mark Nicholls, 'Sir Griffin Markham', *ODNB*; Nicholls, 'Treason's Reward: The Punishment of Conspirators in the Bye Plot of 1603', *Historical Journal* 38 (1995), 821–42.
[64] HMC, *Salisbury MSS*, 15: 93, 98, 183–4, 193, 196, 212, 231, 233; John Harington, *The Letters and Epigrams of Sir John Harington*, ed. Norman E. McClure (London, 1930), pp. 101–7; 396–7; *CSPD, 1603–10*, pp. 23, 57, 246, 493, 538.

Essex's entourage.[65] We have already encountered him being wounded at Kinsale and shot in the face while in County Cork in 1599.[66] After that 'great wound in his head', Danvers was obliged to return to England for a time for treatment.[67] Also during his Irish career he was shot through the thigh at Moyry Pass on 14 October 1600, 'the bone of his leg being broken by a bullett'.[68] After Kinsale, though he continued his commands in Ireland, he was also regularly sent to London bearing letters between the English and Irish Privy Councils. Those letters refer to his injuries: Sir George Carew wrote 'His wounds prove his loyal service', while in November 1602 the Irish Council remarked 'Sir Henry Davers has served long and well here and been often wounded. Pray recommend him to the Queen.'[69] In 1603 he was described as having 'received more wounds in his body by the rebels than any other captain or commander of his rank'.[70]

The two surviving portraits of Danvers emphasise these wounds, especially a prominent scar by his eye, presumably from the 'great wound' sustained in 1599.[71] It is shown both in the portrait of him in armour in front of a campaign tent from about 1600–03, now in Woburn Abbey (see Figure 9.1), and in a full-length Anthony van Dyck painting from the 1630s, now in the State Hermitage Museum, St Petersburg.[72] The motto on the Woburn portrait is 'Omnia Praecipi' ('I have foreseen everything') from Virgil's *Aeneid*. In the referenced passage, Aeneas contemplates going into the underworld and says: 'These toils [...] have no new aspect, in them arises no surprise. I have foreseen everything and gone over it all previously in my mind.' It is a passage that alludes to Aeneas' – and, by implication, Danvers' – stoicism in the face of danger.[73] The message of soldierly stoicism also pervades the van Dyck portrait. For example, though he is splendidly dressed in the robes of the Order of the Garter, Danvers retains a full 'spade' beard, a style by then unfashionable in

[65] See John McGurk, 'Henry Danvers, earl of Danby', *ODNB*.
[66] Danvers' account of Kinsale is in Thomas Wright, *Queen Elizabeth and Her Times, A Series of Original Letters*, 2 vols. (London, 1838), 2: 490–3.
[67] Charlotte Carmichael Stopes, *The Life of Henry, Third Earl of Southampton, Shakespeare's Patron* (Cambridge, 1922), p. 156.
[68] Thomas Birch, *Memoirs of the Reign of Queen Elizabeth, from the Year 1581 Till Her Death* (London, 1754), p. 405.
[69] *CSPI, 1601–3*, pp. 244, 516.
[70] *CSPI, 1603–6*, p. 11.
[71] On facial disfigurement: Patricia Skinner, *Living With Disfigurement in Early Medieval Europe* (Basingstoke, 2017), and other work by the 'Effaced from History' group: https://effacedblog.wordpress.com.
[72] According to Victoria Poulton, assistant to the Curator at Woburn Abbey, the Danvers portrait there was probably painted by either Gheeraerts or Miereveldt. Many thanks to Ms Poulton for discussing the image with me. Interestingly, some later photographic reproductions of the van Dyck image delete the scar; see *The Works of Anthony van Dyck*, 2 vols. (New York, 1943), 2: 378.
[73] Nicholas Horsfall, *Virgil, Aeneid 6, A Commentary* (Berlin, 2013), pp. 9, 133.

Figure 9.1. Circle of Marcus Gheeraerts, Portrait of Henry Danvers, c.1599–1603.
From the Woburn Abbey Collection

court circles, but understood as the mark of a soldier.[74] He poses turned so that the startlingly black scar is in the centre of the top of the picture; the colour may be due to the substances used to cauterise the wound, or a patch covering it. He holds himself upright, but stiffly and, unusually for this type of portrait, his left leg is hidden behind his robes, possibly to simultaneously conceal and draw attention to the physical effects of the leg injury suffered in Ireland.

A man aware of the power of grand gestures – the display on his installation as Knight of the Garter was especially theatrical – it seems likely that Danvers embraced his disfiguring scars and paraded his military identity in part to make up for his colourful early history.[75] He had been imprisoned for duelling in 1593, and in 1594 he and his brother, Charles, were attainted for killing a member of the Long family against whom the Danvers family had sustained a feud. He also needed to make up for his family connections since Charles Danvers was executed for taking part in Essex's abortive rebellion in 1601. Henry was pardoned for his earlier transgressions, restored in blood, and created Baron Danvers of Dauntsey by James I in 1603. He subsequently became a favourite of the martially minded Prince Henry, and after Charles I's accession he also took advantage of the new king's admiration for military men and conviction 'that his identity as a king was, ultimately, tied up with success in war'. Danvers became earl of Danby in 1626, and was appointed a member of Charles's council of war and eventually to the Privy Council. His elevation to the Order of the Garter in 1634 was credited to the 'evident proofs of his courage and conduct in the wars of Ireland'.[76] By highlighting the wounds he had sustained in the service of the monarchy, Danvers played to Charles's attraction to the idea of what Richard Cust calls a loyal 'brotherhood in arms […] exemplifying the old fashioned, "Elizabethan", martial virtues of courage and steadfastness'.[77]

Danvers' scarred face and body influenced his other interests as well. In his later years, he took up gardening; his brother John was also a gardener, setting out his gardens in Chelsea in the Italian style.[78] The earl was especially interested in medicinal plants. In the 1620s and 30s he spent £5,000 on creating a

[74]   Mark Albert Johnston, *Beard Fetish in Early Modern England* (Farnham, 2011), p. 55.
[75]   William Knowler, ed., *The Earl of Strafforde's Letters and Dispatches*, 2 vols. (London, 1739), 1: 242.
[76]   Richard Cust, *Charles I and the Aristocracy, 1625–1642* (Cambridge, 2013), pp. 127–9.
[77]   Cust, *Charles I*, pp. 138–9.
[78]   The poet George Herbert had family connections to the Danvers family and stayed with them. It is tempting to suggest that some of the references in his work to wounds and the healing products of gardens may stem from this; see, for example, 'Sunday' and 'The Church Militant': F.E. Hutchinson, ed., *The Works of George Herbert* (London, 1945), pp. xxxiii, 76, 191, 259–62; Robert H. Ray, *A George Herbert Companion* (London, 1995), p. 62; Sean Kelsey, 'Sir John Danvers', *ODNB*; John Drury, *Music at Midnight: The Life and Poetry of George Herbert* (London, 2014), pp. 197–200.

'garden of simples' (medicinal plants) or 'physick garden' in Oxford that he gifted to the university; it still exists as the Botanic Gardens in Oxford. This was intended as a teaching resource for the medical faculty, and the fact that Danvers secured the services of the most famous naturalist and gardener of the day, John Tradescant, who had previously worked with the duke of Buckingham and the king, indicates the seriousness with which he approached the enterprise. Danvers also funded an elaborate gateway to the garden in the form of a triumphal arch (allegedly created by Nicholas Stone), on which a bust of himself, typically bearded and in armour, is flanked by classical statues depicting Charles I and Charles II, which were added in the 1690s.[79] Danvers' military identity was further emphasised on his tomb in Dauntsey church, Wiltshire, whereon he was described as a veteran of wars in the Low Countries, France and Ireland. The inscription also rehearsed his other services to the crown. 'Declining further employments in his later time, by reason of his imperfect health', he died 'full of honours, woundes, and daies' in 1644.[80]

The earl of Tyrone's description of his wounds as 'a print in my body', Ralph Lane's concern about his detractors' 'paper bullets', and Griffin Markham's grief and grievance at the lack of recognition of his service and maiming alert us both to the agony of wounding and to the meaning of wounds to those who suffered them. Wounding and stoical endurance were evidence of honourable military masculinity. They could be the making of personal reputations: decades after Henry Danvers suffered his injuries, he continued to highlight the scars he had sustained in the service of the crown. But, in the longer term, wounds also had the potential to compromise and effeminise men, making them incapable of fulfilling societal expectations of them. Lack of compassionate recognition of patient suffering and of sacrifices of health, finances and career could heap further emotional wounds on suffering shoulders, hence the power of Harington's image of Markham as a maimed Aeneas, staggering under his father's weight as he attempted to rescue him from the ruins of Troy. The wounds of former soldiers were continually present, indelibly imprinted in their flesh. If these complex emblems of military service and identity went unrecognised they risked evoking anxiety, regret and resentment rather than patience, relief and pride.

---

[79] Jennifer Potter, *Strange Blooms: The Curious Lives and Adventures of the John Tradescants* (London, 2006), ch. 20; 'The Physic Garden', *A History of the County of Oxford: Volume 3, The University of Oxford*, ed. Herbert E. Salter and Mary D. Lobel (London, 1954), pp. 49–50; Charles Daubeny, *Oxford Botanic Garden* (Oxford, 1853), pp. 3–5.

[80] Francis Nottidge MacNamara, *Memorials of the Danvers Family* (London, 1895), pp. 292–3.

PART III
Staging Military Identities

10

Othello and the Braggart Soldier in the Context of Elizabethan War Veterans

ADAM N. MCKEOWN

> It was not the reputation of a famous leader in the wars which he sought (as it was construed a great while) but only power and greatness to serve his own ends, considering he never loved virtue nor valor in another, but where he thought he should be proprietary and commander of it, as referred to himself.

Francis Bacon on the earl of Essex[1]

Critics have long noted Othello's connection to the *miles gloriosus* or 'braggart soldier' of classical comedy and Italian *commedia dell'arte*, but on what to make of this connection there is little agreement.[2] Thomas Rymer commented in the late seventeenth century that Othello's 'love and his jealousy are no part of a soldier's character, unless for comedy'.[3] But *Othello* is not a comedy or, if it is a comedy, it is not a very funny one. Rymer called the play a 'bloody farce' but 'without salt or savour', and recent critics have found the lack of salt and savour sufficient reason to question its connections to the braggart soldier tradition.[4] Kenneth Muir suggests the comic echoes are misleading. 'Far from being a braggart soldier, Othello is modest in his claims', Muir contends, and 'his frequent expressions of self-esteem would be regarded by Shakespeare's

---

[1] Francis Bacon, *A Declaration of the Practices and Treasons Attempted and Committed by Robert Late Earl of Essex and His Complices* (London, 1601), sig. B1r. Here and throughout I have modernized spellings in early texts.

[2] In addition to the works cited in the text, see also Gerald M. Pinciss, *Why Shakespeare: An Introduction to the Playwright's Art* (New York, 2006), p. 87; Adrian Kiernander, 'A Comic Vision of *Othello*', *Re-visions of Shakespeare: Essays in Honour of Robert Ornstein*, ed. Robert Ornstein and Evelyn Gajowski (Newark, 2004), pp. 150–64; Francis N. Teague, 'Introduction', *Acting Funny: Comic Theory and Practice in Shakespeare's Plays*, ed. Francis N. Teague (Madison, NJ, 1994), pp. 9–28; and Martha Tuck Rozett, '*Othello, Otello*, and the Comic Tradition', *Bulletin of Research in the Humanities* 85.4 (1982), 386–411. On the related subject of Othello's pride and honour: Jean Klene, 'Othello: "A Fixed Figure for the Time of Scorn"', *Shakespeare Quarterly* 26.2 (1975), 139–50.

[3] Thomas Rymer, *A Short View of Tragedy* (1693; rpt London, 1971), p. 93.

[4] Rymer, *A Short View of Tragedy*, p. 146. See also Barbara Everett, '"Spanish" Othello: The Making of Shakespeare's Moor', *Shakespeare and Race*, ed. Catherine M.S. Alexander and Stanley W. Wells (Cambridge, 2000), pp. 64–81.

audience, not as vanity, but as legitimate and proper pride'.[5] Other critics have
found the comic echoes to amplify *Othello's* tragic force. The shadow of the
comic braggart creates a 'strange and contradictory experience', in Teresa J.
Faherty's reading. As Othello's noble facade erodes, the features he shares with
the braggart soldier – his bullying and misogyny – become 'newly disturbing'.[6]
Stephen Rogers contends that 'Othello is not the *miles gloriosus*. But the music
of his utterance and the splendor of his nobility are reduced to the solemn and
pathetic counterparts of the comic soldier's vanities'.[7]

The comedic echoes in *Othello* are less confusing, however, when both the
play and the braggart soldier are viewed in the context of the discourses on
Elizabethan veterans.   Although the braggart soldier appeared in Nicholas
Udall's academic comedy *Ralph Roister Doister* in the mid-sixteenth century,
it developed extensively in England during Elizabeth's war years. In 1585, just
one year after Anthony Munday introduced Captain Crackstone in his adaptation of Luigi Pasqualigo's *Il Fidele* as *Fidele and Fortunio*, England entered
the Dutch Revolt and would continue its direct and indirect conflict with
Spain until 1604. During these years, the stage was characterized, as Nick de
Somogyi has suggested, by a 'proximity between wartime theatres and theatres
of war', and in this environment the braggart soldier became a repository for
discourses on soldiers and veterans.[8]

These discourses are deeply conflicted. The number of war veterans
increased during the war years and, with them, the representations of veterans
in literature. As this chapter will flesh out in greater detail, veterans came to
be identified with their physical disabilities, with their struggles to readjust to
civilian life or make a legitimate living, and with their suffering at the hands
of a neglectful and ungrateful country. Then again, they were also represented
as overstating or misrepresenting their military exploits, faking or lying about
injuries, turning to crime, and complaining incessantly about their compensation. In both sympathetic and antagonistic representations, veterans were
talkers: tellers of war stories and critics of strategy and tactics but also reciters
of military jargon, exaggerators and liars. Distinguishing expert opinion from
bluster, or truth from lies, was not easy given that information about foreign
war was unreliable and veterans themselves were often its best source. Nor, for
this reason, was it easy to distinguish veterans from those who falsely claimed
to be veterans in order to leverage benefits, status and sympathy. These anti-
pathetic discourses on veterans accumulated around the braggart solider, who
became on the early modern stage not just a windbag and/ or womanizer, as

---

Kenneth Muir, 'Introduction', *Othello*, ed. Muir (New York, 1968), p. 30.
Teresa J. Faherty, '*Othello dell'Arte*: The Presence of *Commedia* in Shakespeare's Tragedy',
     Theatre Journal 43 (1991), 180, 189.
Stephen Rogers, '*Othello*: Comedy in Reverse', *Shakespeare Quarterly* 24.2 (1973), 220.
Nick de Somogyi, *Shakespeare's Theatre of War* (Aldershot, 1998), p. 169.

he was in classical and Italian comedy, but also a know-it-all, a purveyor of news and fashions from abroad, and a grumbler who burdened the state with his disaffections, his misbehaviour and his complaints. As De Somogyi sums up the matter, '[The] comic conventions of the *miles gloriosus* mingle-mangle with the topicalities of counterfeit veterans, unverifiable news-reports from the front, and the martial paradigm of the Soldier-Scholar.'[9]

The comic shadow that falls on *Othello* is a function of the play's engagement with the conflicting discourses on veterans that accumulate around the braggart soldier. The braggart soldier borrows from and also shapes the discourse on veterans, and the two are not, in terms of how they are represented, all that different, especially with regard to their supposed tendency to self-promote through war stories. A veteran and accomplished soldier such as Othello cannot leverage his military expertise or ask for considerations based on his service without resembling the braggart soldier. The tragedy of *Othello* depends, as this chapter will discuss, on the inability of the veteran to assert himself as a veteran without invoking this resemblance. The words Othello speaks in order to establish his identity as a noble, valiant and, above all, deserving soldier are not so much reduced, as Rogers suggests, to their 'solemn and pathetic counterparts' as they are confused in the first place with 'the comic soldier's vanities'.[10]

'Epithites of War'

De Somogyi briefly addresses the problematic nature of martial self-fashioning in *Othello* in passing when he locates the lies Iago tells to precipitate the tragedy within the larger problem of the unreliable words of soldiers – not their fabrications exclusively, but the sum of the inaccessible and affected language De Somogyi calls the 'new Esperanto of war'.[11] This esoteric language includes unverifiable first-hand reports replete with exotic place names and foreign phrases, the specialized terminology of tactics and strategies, the nomenclature of weapons systems, recycled descriptions of combat and phrases borrowed from military handbooks.

The reliance on this language is characteristic of Shakespeare's most memorable braggart soldiers: Armado in *Love's Labours Lost*, Parolles in *All's Well That Ends Well,* and Falstaff in *1 and 2 Henry IV*. As De Somogyi notes, however, this unreliable language is also characteristic of Shakespearean soldiers who are not braggarts (Iago in *Othello*, Pistol in *2 Henry IV* and Jamy in *Henry V*) and soldiers who are demonstrably valiant (Hotspur in *1 Henry IV* and the

---

[9]   De Somogyi, *Shakespeare's Theatre of War*, p. 154.

[10] Rogers, '*Othello*: Comedy in Reverse', 220.

[11] De Somogyi, *Shakespeare's Theatre of War*, p. 161.

young gallants who expose Parolles in *All's Well*). The noble soldier and the braggart soldier both adopt this new occupational register, and speak about actions that cannot be verified. Iago exploits this conflation of the language of war and the braggart soldier's vanities when he introduces Othello as being 'Horribly stuff'd with epithites of war' (1.1.14).[12] This description of Othello complements his description of Michael Cassio as full of 'bookish theoric' (1.1.26) and serves to discredit Othello's promotion of the latter, even though the military experiences backing up Othello's epithets are not in question. Othello's 'bumbast' (1.1.13) itself suffices to cast doubt on his judgment in military matters and to connect him to the pedantic imposters strutting about the early modern stage.

The similarity between the language of the braggart soldier and that of the noble soldier becomes especially apparent with regard to the rewards of military service, which are central to *Othello*. When a soldier, however valiant, overvalues his service or leverages his record of service to make demands on the state, the epithets and the bombast function almost exactly as they do for the braggart soldier insofar as they are used to gain status, rewards or sympathy. The example of Hotspur, one of Shakespeare's most valiant soldiers, provides invaluable context. When Hotspur is introduced to the audience in *1 Henry IV* he speaks in the 'epithites of war' to justify his decision to defy his king's orders and retain the rewards of battle for himself. His justification stands on the difference between himself as a battle-tested soldier and the king's envoy as a pretender. Hotspur describes a 'certain lord, neat, and trimly dress'd', a 'popinjay' who mouths a litter of military clichés many in the audience would have recognized from contemporary books. The lord's advice that 'the sovereignest thing on earth was parmeceti for an inward bruise' is a borrowing from Barnabe Rich's 1581 *Farewell to Military Profession*, and his lament on 'vile guns' could be right out of Ariosto.[13] The lord's military clichés mark him, in Hotspur's estimation, as a counterfeit soldier with no right to make demands on a tested soldier who is, at that moment, 'Breathless and faint, leaning upon [his] sword' (1.3.32). But the purpose of the contrast Hotspur draws is to make demands (on his sovereign) that he himself has no right to make. In this respect the 'epithites of war' of the two soldier types are conflated. The vapid

---

[12]   All citations of Shakespeare's plays are from *The Riverside Shakespeare*.

[13]   'But the Doctor took Sparmaceti, and such like things that be good for a bruise', from Barnabe Rich, *Riche His Farewell to Military Profession* (London, 1581), sig. T1r. See also G.C. Moore Smith, 'Riche's Story "Of Phylotus and Emilia"', *Modern Language Review* 5.3 (1910), 344. Ariosto laments the way impersonal military technologies like artillery impact upon military identity, obviating a 'manly heart' and discouraging 'soldiers brave, and valiant men of war' from taking the field: Lodovico Ariosto, *Orlando Furioso in English Heroicial Verse*, trans. John Harington (London, 1591), canto 11, stanzas 23–4. On Ariosto and the hostility to guns: Michael Murrin, *History and Warfare in Renaissance Epic* (Chicago, 1994), pp. 123–37.

recitations of the court popinjay and the proud vaunts of the valiant soldier blur in the familiar rhetoric of the vain and self-interested soldier.

At stake in the formulation of Hotspur's character is what Muir calls, apropos of Othello, a 'legitimate and proper pride'. Legitimate Hotspur's pride may be in that his military exploits support his epithets, but proper it is not in that it implicitly holds valour in higher estimation than loyalty. It may be debated whether or not Shakespeare's audiences would have viewed Othello's pride as legitimate and proper, but unquestionably Shakespeare's audiences would have recognized the tension between the rights of valour and the bonds of loyalty as part of contemporary discourse on soldiers.

Due estimation and valorous desert

'It is held / That valour is the chiefest virtue', Cominus remarks in *Coriolanus* (2.2.81–2); this is not to say that valour is the chiefest virtue but that many think it is. Shakespeare, as Steven Marx has suggested, may not have agreed with Cominus, but regardless of whether or not Shakespeare was a pacifist, in *Coriolanus* valour is not a greater virtue than loyalty to one's country.[14] Supposing valour an absolute virtue would have been an easy mistake to make, however, given the cult of valour that developed during Elizabeth's war years. This cult of valour found its exemplars not only in the romances of Ariosto and Tasso but also in the living memory of Sir Philip Sidney.[15] It took its direction from humanist writers like Niccolò Machiavelli, who viewed the battlefield as a proving ground for 'excellent men'.[16] But more than a proving ground it was a stage on which valour could be displayed. Baldassare Castiglione recommends that a soldier 'undertake his notable and bold feats which he hath to do with as little company as he can, and in the sight of noble men [...] and especially in the presence and (if it were possible) before the very eyes of his king'.[17] A soldier who proves his valour should also be jealous of his 'due estimation'.

---

[14] Steven Marx, 'Shakespeare's Pacifism', *Renaissance Quarterly* 45.1 (1992), 51–3. On valour as a relative virtue, see Jonathan Dollimore, *Radical Tragedy*, 3rd edn (Basingstoke, 2004), pp. 218–30.

[15] On the making of the Elizabethan martial ideal: Roy Strong, *The Cult of Elizabeth* (Berkeley, 1977), esp. pp. 129–86; and Louis Montrose, 'Spenser and the Elizabethan Political Imaginary', *ELH* 69.4 (2002), 907–46. See also Rory Rapple, *Martial Power and Elizabethan Political Culture: Military Men in England and Ireland, 1558–1594* (Cambridge, 2009); Brendan Kane, *The Politics of Honour in Britain and Ireland, 1541–1641* (Cambridge, 2010); and Mervyn James, *Society, Politics and Culture: Studies in Early Modern England* (Cambridge, 1986), pp. 308–415.

[16] Niccolò Machiavelli, *The Chief Works and Others*, trans. Allan Gilbert, 3 vols. (Durham, NC, 1965), 2: 621–2. On the citizen soldier, see book 1 throughout. See also Marx's discussion of Machiavelli in 'Shakespeare's Pacifism', 51–3.

[17] Baldassare Castiglione, *The Book of the Courtier*, trans. Thomas Hoby, ed. Virginia Cox (New York, 1994), p. 109.

By 'due estimation', Castiglione refers to the good reputation that is a right of valour, which squares with his claim that praise alone 'is the true reward of virtuous enterprise'.[18] Elizabethan soldiers, however, also expected to be compensated for their valour. The earl of Essex, Sir Walter Ralegh and other ranking participants of the 1596 Cadiz expedition were, for example, no doubt angling for praise, but they were angling for rewards and advancement as well.[19] The reputation Essex earned at Cadiz directly resulted in his commission to command the 1599 invasion of Ireland, the largest Elizabeth ever deployed and – although it would ruin him – a ripe plum for the earl at the time. At the lower levels of gentleman volunteerism, there was every expectation of prof-iting from the spoils of war or from conventional forms of corruption such as 'dead-pays', the practice of keeping dead soldiers' names on the muster books to collect their wages.[20]

Fair compensation for the 'chiefest virtue' was a controversial point, how-ever, and part of the discourse on soldiers is their sense of being shortchanged. Rich protests in *The Pathway to Military Practice* (1587) that while the soldier upholds English society many English people are 'bountiful in rewarding pipers, parasites, singers and dancers and like ministers of their pleasures, and suffer poor soldiers to beg'.[21] The idea that soldiers are not paid what they are owed also surfaces in the literature surrounding the 'Spanish Fury' to which Antwerp fell victim in 1576. As such it becomes a feature of the period's alarm-ist and jingoistic literature that functioned as an appeal to increase military spending and compensation for veterans.[22]

No less a part of the discourse on veterans was their tendency to over-value their service. 'Thinking over well of himself', as George Whetstone com-plains, is a 'foul common fault, to be hated of a soldier', but so was asking too

---

[18] Castiglione, *Book of the Courtier*, p. 109.
[19] See Paul E. J. Hammer, 'Myth-Making: Politics, Propaganda and the Capture of Cadiz in 1596', *Historical Journal* 40.3 (1997), 621–42.
[20] See Charles G. Cruickshank, 'Dead-Pays in the Elizabethan Army', *English Historical Review* 53.209 (1938), 93–7.
[21] Barnabe Rich, *A Path-way to Military Practise* (London: 1587), sig. B2r. See also Thomas Churchyard's description of the soldier as a 'hackney horse cast off when turn is served' in 'The Prayes of our Soldiars', from *Churchyardes Chippes* (London, 1575), sig. N3v; George Gascoigne's criticism of 'the proud ungrateful prince' who makes soldiers beg in *The Steele Glas*, *The Complete Works of George Gascoigne*, ed. John W. Cunliffe. 2 vols. (Cambridge, 1907–10), 2: 158–9; and Sir John Harington's reflections upon returning from Ireland, in *The Letters and Epigrams of Sir John Harington*, ed. Norman E. McClure (Philadelphia, 1930), p. 24.
[22] See for example Barnabe Rich, *Alarum to England* (London, 1578); Henry Haslop, *News Out of the Coast of Spain* (London, 1587); and Anon., *Alarum for London* (London, 1602). The latter is often associated with George Gascoigne's *The Spoyle of Antwerpe* (London, 1576).

much in exchange for valiant service.[23] An epistle to the reader in William Segar's *Honor, Military and Civil* says the book will describe 'what commendations and prizes belong to valorous desert', but most of the book is dedicated to what 'penalties and punishments appertain to disloyalty, and arms abused'.[24] In one way, the epistle's concern with soldiers seeking by abuses more than valour deserves merely affirms the idea that soldiers 'should learn to leave spoiling [...] and content themselves with their own wages', as George Wither complains in his *A.B.C. for Layman*.[25] In another way, however, the epistle contends with the idea that 'valour is the chiefest virtue' and that soldiers can and should demand 'due estimation' with regard to it. Soldiers can and should expect 'valorous desert' but not beyond the limits of the state's wages, beyond which is 'abuse of arms' or even 'disloyalty'.

The expectation that veterans should obligingly return to their civilian lives at war's end was also part of the discourse on soldiers and accords with the idea that the right to 'due estimation' and 'valorous desert' was constrained by the needs of the state even while the needs of the state were not to be constrained by the limits of the rewards offered.[26] Reflecting on some draftees assembled at Kent, the Henrician propagandist Thomas Becon urged soldiers to 'neglect their domestical travails, their private businesses, [and] their dear wives and sweet children' in the interests of 'the public weal of England'.[27] When the war is over, however, soldiers are to 'quietly return home' and 'walk in a new life, every man doing his office according to his vocation and calling'.[28] Becon's emphasis on returning to civilian life is reiterated by Thomas Styward in *The Pathway to Martial Discipline*, which also stressed that soldiers are not to make a living with their weapons and training upon returning home:

> [Their captains] letting them to understand that the wars being ended; the Prince is not further to use them, exhorting every man, quietly to deport into his country from whence he was pressed, or to the place of his longest abode, not looking to make an art or exercise of arms for that is not to be used.[29]

By making 'an art or exercise of arms', Styward means the use of weapons and training for illicit purposes more than making a career as a soldier, but the overlap between the two activities is implied nonetheless. Indeed, the

---

[23] George Whetstone, *The Honorable Reputation of a Soldier* (London, 1585), sig. E3r.
[24] William Segar, *Honor, Military and Civil* (London, 1602), unpaginated prefatory epistle.
[25] George Wither, *An A.B.C. for Laymen* (London, 1585), sig. L1r.
[26] On the impact of the new Tudor sense of commonwealth on the practice and ideology of war: Ben Lowe, 'War and the Commonwealth in Mid-Tudor England', *SCJ* 26.2 (1990), 171–92.
[27] Thomas Becon, *The New Pollecye of Warre* (London, 1542), sigs. B2r–B3v.
[28] Becon, *New Pollecye*, sig. K3r.
[29] Thomas Styward, *The Pathwaie to Martiall Discipline* (London, 1581), sigs. X4v–Y1r.

professionalization of soldiers in the sixteenth century is one of the features of what modern historians have called the 'military revolution', although professional soldiers were nevertheless overwhelmingly disparaged in the discourses of the period.[30] Thomas Smith wrote in the mid-sixteenth century that 'the word *soldier* now seemeth rather to come of *sold* and *payment*, and more to betoken a waged or hired man to fight, than otherwise'.[31] Speaking specifically of mercenaries but making the same point nevertheless, Barnabe Barnes says that theirs are 'hollow valors' who 'fight only for a little wages'. Better that soldiers fight for honour, he adds, because 'excellent valor proceedeth' from soldiers 'hope of a glorious conquest wherein the largest portion of just reputation happeneth to themselves'.[32]

The anxieties surrounding professional soldiers also accumulate around the braggart soldier, who is typically in early modern England represented as one who makes (or pretends to make) 'an art or exercise of arms'. Ben Jonson's braggart soldiers are often figured as shiftless, sketchy, or otherwise impoverished *capitanos*.[33] So are Shakespeare's Parolles and Falstaff, the latter of which is represented as making money from the exercise of arms in every possible way. He is a professional soldier who lives on highway robbery when there is no war to fight and robs churches while fighting. As a captain he will 'prick' (i.e. enlist) the dregs of society and even joke about filling up his muster roll with 'shadows', soldiers who are there in name only in order to swell the company payroll (*2 Henry IV*, 3.2.133–5). And ironically (or not), it is Falstaff in his capacity as a braggart soldier who correctly identifies the discretionary power soldiers have with regard to the problem of fair compensation for valiant service. As he says in the final act of *1 Henry IV*, 'The better part of valor is discretion, in which the better part I have sav'd my life' (5.4.119–21). The idea that it

---

[30]   On the early modern military revolution, see the Introduction to this volume.

[31]   Thomas Smith, *The Commonwealth of England and the Maner of its Government* (London, 1589), sig. D4v. Italics added.

[32]   Barnabe Barnes, *Four Books of Offices Enabling Private Persons for the Special Service of all Good Princes and Policies* (London, 1606), sig. Z2r. Matthew Woodcock notes a similar point made by Churchyard: *Thomas Churchyard: Pen, Sword, and Ego* (Oxford, 2016), pp. 207–8.

[33]   Ben Jonson, as both a rigorous classicist and a cynical war veteran, seems particularly interested in the possibilities of this character type. Sir Politic Would-be in *Volpone* and Sir Glorious Tiptoe in *The New Inn* are very close to Armado and the braggarts of Terence and Plautus. In his *Epigrams* included in the *Works* of 1616, Jonson creates such memorable soldiers as 'Cashiered Captain Surly' (p. 82), 'Captain Hazard the Cheater' (p. 87), 'Captain Hungry' (p. 107), and 'Lieutenant Shift' (p. 12), the last of whom also appears in *Every Man Out of His Humour* as a 'thread-bare Shark' who the clown Carlo Buffoni describes as 'the most strange piece of military profession that ever was discover'd' (3.5.31–2). Parenthetic references in this note are to *Ben Jonson*, ed. C. H. Herford, Percy Simpson and Evelyn Simpson, 11 vols. (Oxford, 1925–52). *Epigrams* are in vol. 8; *Every Man Out* in vol. 3.

is better to keep one's life than hazard it in the name of valour aligns with the comment he later makes in 2 *Henry IV* that 'I never knew yet but rebuke and check was the reward of valor' (4.3.31–2). In sum, a soldier is never going to be paid more for his valour than his life is worth to himself, so it is better to keep one's life than to risk it in exchange for an inadequate reward. Then again, by adopting this cynical and lamentable position one becomes a braggart soldier.

But it would seem a soldier could scarcely avoid becoming a braggart soldier when matters of compensation arose. As this review of early modern English discourses on soldiers and compensation for military service suggests, there was a very small window in which veterans could maintain and perhaps even profit from their military experiences without becoming something like the braggart soldier. A soldier could not practise arms unless fighting a war and, then, only if fighting for reputation and not for money – and then only with the understanding that reputation as a soldier is only as valuable as the state needs it to be. The soldier is to go back to his peacetime profession when the war is over and not to question how he was compensated for fighting or claim 'due estimation' or 'valorous desert' beyond what is readily given. Any soldier who fails to act within these narrow confines risks becoming the buffoon, no matter how valiant or noble or deserving he might be. *Othello* is about one soldier's tragic discovery of these hard truths.

Valiant Othello, we must straight employ you

Othello's connections to the classical braggart soldier are unmistakable and far more than superficial. For example, in telling his Othello what he wants to hear in order to keep himself employed until he can 'serve [his] turn upon him' (1.1.42), Iago assumes the role of the parasite who typically drives the plot in the earlier braggart soldier plays. Iago also describes Othello as a man who '[loves] his own pride and purposes' (1.1.12). From these early exchanges the audience might expect a play about a clever and resourceful parasite whom they are invited to trust (even while he deceives the captain he serves). They might expect to find one who ranges freely across the different strata of the fictional world of the play, who forms and destabilizes relationships between the other characters (and especially those between the braggart soldier and women), and who ultimately creates circumstances that expose the braggart for the fraud he is. This is almost exactly what happens in *Othello*, but the soldier who is undone by the clever parasite is not a buffoon but the 'Valiant Othello' (1.3.48).

The previous sections of this chapter established how the braggart soldier becomes a repository for discourses on soldiers at a time when the number of war veterans was increasing in England. When compensation – 'due estimation' and 'valorous desert' – are in question the braggart soldier tends to subsume other military identities. This is the case in *Othello*, in which the shadowy presence of the braggart soldier haunts a valiant soldier who nevertheless speaks in the 'epithites of war' to maintain his social position and, later, to justify the demands he makes on the Venetian state. The play amplifies this discursive connection to the braggart soldier by importing the structure of earlier braggart soldier plays in a manner that has confused critics for generations. This confusion rests on Othello's indisputable valour, but as the example of Hotspur demonstrates, valour is not sufficient to wrest military identity from the connection to the braggart soldier, especially when it is staked against compensations offered by the state and loyalty to the state.

The Venetian state looms over *Othello*. References to 'state', 'state-matters' and service to the state are everywhere repeated. Many of the supporting characters in the play are presented as 'brothers of the state' (1.2.96), as Brabantio calls them. 'State' holds pride of place in the play's final couplet, voiced by Lodovico.[34] And it is to the 'state' that Othello famously appeals prior to his suicide: 'I have done the state some service, and they know't' (5.2.339). Very often in the play, it is Othello himself who invokes the 'state' – or its 'signiors' and 'senators' – often to make demands on the state or to define what kinds of treatment he deserves in exchange for his service. In his first speech in the play, he dismisses the ramifications of Brabantio's outrage with 'Let him do his spite;/ My services which I have done the signiory/ Shall out-tongue his complaints' (1.2.17–19). He later makes good on this boast in what is the longest and most braggart-soldierly speech in the play, one that includes, among its self-aggrandizing references, tall tales of 'Cannibals' and 'men whose heads/ Do grow beneath their shoulders' (1.3. 43–4).

Othello's rhetorical performance in the ducal palace in the first act must have struck, on some level, a very sour and all-too familiar chord in 1604. Here is a soldier boasting about his accomplishments like a comic *capitano*, but here also is a soldier who, consistent with contemporary discourses on presumptive soldiers, rehearses the legend of his own service in order to advance his personal interests. That Othello *is* the soldier he pretends to be makes this problem more acute. The audience must recognize that a man who, with a cool word, defeats the 'bright swords' (1.3.59) drawn against him is not the *miles gloriosus* they were led to anticipate, but this separation collapses when, almost immediately, Othello starts making excessive demands on the state in the name of valour.

Those demands become increasingly bold. As the first act progresses Othello moves from invoking his past service to shield himself from Brabantio's

<hr>

[34] 'Myself will straight aboard, and to the state/ This heavy act with heavy heart relate' (5.2.371–2).

wrath to posturing that service to make requests of the Duke. Before embarking to Cyprus, Othello presumes to have the Duke himself see to the 'place and exhibition' (1.3.237) of Desdemona while he is fighting Venice's wars. Othello's gesture of obedience – his 'bending to [the] state' – is coterminous with a carefully phrased demand on the state. Othello's presumption would not seem to be lost on the Duke, who does not make Desdemona's 'disposition' his personal problem. 'If you please/ Be't at her father's', is his reply (1.3.239–40), but in the First Folio he is far less deferential, saying only, 'Why, at her father's' (1.588).

Not surprisingly, the fourth-act catastrophe is set up when Lodovico delivers an order to Othello from the Venetian state that he refuses to obey. As with Hotspur's snubbing of his king, rewards and the obligation of the soldier to obey the state as a condition of rewards are at issue. Faced with the loss of the greatest reward that his valour earned, Desdemona, Othello becomes blind to any obligation other than his own interests. As if to emphasize the flaw in Othello's civic reasoning at this moment, the play depicts Othello as railing against what he takes as feigned obedience in Desdemona at the same time that he is himself feigning obedience to the state:

> And she's obedient, as you say, obedient;
> Very obedient. – Proceed you in your tears. –
> Concerning this, sir – O well-painted passion! –
> I am commanded home. – Get you away;
> I'll send for you anon. –Sir, I obey the mandate,
> And will return to Venice. (4.1.255–60)

He literally plays the obedient, deferential soldier in order to buy time to see to his personal agenda in spite of direct orders to remove to Venice, which he dismisses as a mere 'instrument' of the state's 'pleasures' (4.1.218). More than hypocrisy or rage, Othello's act of punishing and perpetrating disobedience in the same breath exposes a relationship between himself and the state hinted at all along but not revealed until this moment. Beneath Othello's show of obedience is a *quid pro quo* relationship in which he reserves the right to set the rate of exchange for his military service or to cancel the relationship at his discretion. As Falstaff might have told him, Othello's option is to decide how valiant he will be in exchange for the state's wages, not what the state is obliged to pay for his valour or how loyal he is obliged to be if the payment is inadequate.

The extent of Othello's presumption can be measured by comparing two instances of self-representation, both liberally employing 'epithites of war'. At the moment of his greatness in Venice, when he is called upon in the middle of the night to defend both the city and his marriage to Desdemona, Othello says of himself,

Rude am I in my speech
And little bless'd with the soft phrase of peace;
[...]
And therefore little shall I grace my cause
In speaking for myself. (1.3.81–9)

Later, convinced that his relationship with Desdemona no longer confirms his greatness but authors his humiliation, he employs a similar contrast between himself as a rough-cut man of action and the 'chamberers' of Venice with their 'soft parts of conversation' to claim, 'Yet, 'tis the plague of great ones,/ Prerogativ'd are they less than the base;/ 'Tis destiny unshunnable, like death' (3.3.264–75). As Hotspur does in contrasting himself with the court 'popinjay', Othello plays his soldierly toughness against a pampered society that speaks in 'soft' words in order to invalidate its demands on him. In the first instance, Othello quite reasonably postures his valour before a *de facto* jury of state officials as part of a defence against some serious accusations by a well-connected citizen. But in the second instance this posturing transcends public performance. Discomfited and demoted as both a man and an officer of the state, Othello fashions himself into a valiant soldier abused by a world unworthy of him, and his conclusion that to be abused is 'the plague of great ones' is more or less the same as Coriolanus' complaint to the Roman people (also uttered in the name of valour) that 'Who deserves greatness/ Deserves your hate' (1.1.176–7). But Coriolanus at least has an audience; in the third act Othello is speaking these words and reinforcing this conviction to himself alone.

When his sense of entitlement has run its bloody course, even Othello must recognize that the performance of one who has 'done the state some service' cannot offset the crime of murdering Desdemona. And yet in a remarkable reconfiguration of the *corpus delicti*, Othello acknowledges the blameworthiness of his action at the same time as he transfers the agency of that action to an imaginary 'Turk', assigning to himself instead the heroic task of killing a 'circumcised dog' who 'traduc'd the state':

And say besides, that in Aleppo once,
Where a malignant and a turban'd Turk
Beat a Venetian and traduc'd the state,
I took by th' throat the circumcised dog,
And smote him, thus. (5.2.352–6)

On the level of the plot there is not much left for Othello to do having been caught red-handed but kill himself. In the context of this discussion, however, what is important is Othello's readiness to employ 'epithites of war' to posture himself as a valiant soldier, even to the last breath, whenever the state's rewards or punishments are at stake – whenever he wants something from the state or when the state wants something from him.

Conclusion

Through the 'epithites of war' uttered before his suicide Othello inflates himself into the only soldier valiant enough to destroy an enemy as dangerous as himself. The words he speaks over Desdemona's corpse, however, indicate that he is not a braggart soldier (i.e. a self-conscious pretender) but resembles the braggart soldier insofar as his personal investment in 'due estimation' and 'valorous desert' comes across as a vanity. Looking skyward for 'a huge eclipse/ Of sun and moon' (5.2.99–100), Othello cannot see that he is just a soldier who thinks, to quote Whetstone again, 'over well of himself'. The action he thinks has 'affrighted [the] globe' (5.2.100) is just a soldier's action, the kind Shakespeare's audience would have read about in the alarmist war stories that flooded England during the violent last decades of Elizabeth's reign. He kills a virtuous maiden, the daughter of a respected citizen, in her own bed. That is what soldiers do when the state asks them to and for which they are paid whatever they are paid. No eclipses and no great alterations. If there is redemption for Othello at play's end, it comes not because he should necessarily be taken at his word that he 'lov'd not wisely but too well' (5.2.344) but that he exposes the tension in the social and political forces through which military identities were established.

Robin Headlam Wells observes that 'Shakespeare's martial heroes' tend to be 'a liability to the state', an observation that echoes one made by Paul Jorgensen a decade after the Second World War that Shakespeare will often stage the rocky translation of the soldier 'from the battlefield into a milieu of peace'.[35] If in Shakespeare's plays soldiers tend not to go gently into a milieu of peace and if his military heroes are liabilities, one reason is that real-life Elizabethan veterans had trouble existing as veterans.

The Elizabethan state notoriously shirked its responsibilities towards its large veteran population, but it also created conditions in which even a 'legitimate and proper pride', to borrow Muir's words again, or circumspect concerns over fair compensation for military service could scarcely avoid taking the discursive shape of the braggart soldier's vanities. As *Othello* makes clear, the valiant soldier was shadowed in popular discourses by the braggart soldier, and the potential for these two soldiers to collapse into one served the interests of a Tudor state for whom soldiers were to perform their duties, accept their

---

[35]   Robin Headlam Wells, '"Manhood and Chevalrie": *Coriolanus*, Prince Henry, and the Chivalric Revival', *RES* 51.203 (2000), 395; Paul Jorgensen, *Shakespeare's Military World* (Berkeley, 1956), p. 208.

wages, and return to their domestic occupations when told. It was a convenient arrangement that allowed the state to employ soldiers however it wished, discouraged them from posturing their valour or trading upon it, and tainted any concerns they might voice with charges of vanity and seditious pride.

While *Othello* also makes clear that there is no action on the state's part for which treason or the murder of the innocent is a reasonable reaction, what Falstaff – that great braggart soldier – says at the end of *1 Henry IV* resonates nevertheless: 'let them that should reward valor/ bear the sin upon their own heads' (5.4.144–5). In the final analysis, the state requires valour from its soldiers, and while the precise form valour takes may shift with ideological pressures, what soldiers do or fail to do in the name of valour is on some level a product of the way they are rewarded for it. Othello's expectations are, as Essex's perhaps were, a reflection of the way his valour had been rewarded. If in his fall he becomes a threat to the state and a vainglorious self-promoter he is also the state's most pitiable victim, a useful icon of a certain kind of martial identity that works best when, as in the case of Sidney, it does not survive the battlefield. The play would seem to understand this problem on the human level, and it gives Othello a chance at fashioning a suitably admirable identity by taking on the noble mission of ridding the state of himself.

11

'Lay by thine Armes and take the Citie then': Soldiery and City in the Drama of Thomas Middleton

ANDREW HISCOCK

My Lorde,

Touchynge our matters here, and what hathe fallen oute sithence you departed, maye perchance not be unpleasente to you to heare. Manie have beene the made caps rejoicinge to oure new kynges cominge, and who in good trothe darede not have set forthe their good affection to him a month or two agoe; but, alas! what availeth truthe, when profite is in queste? You were true and liege bondsman to her late Highnesse, and felte her sweete bounties in full force and good savour. Nor dide I my poor self unexperience her love and kyndness on manie occasions; but I cannot forbeare remembringe my dread at her frownes in the Iryshe affair, when I followede my General, (And what shoude a Captaine do better?) to Englande a little before his tyme: If Essex had met his appoynted time, as Davide saithe, to die, it had fared better, than to meet his follie and his fate too. But enoughe of olde tales; a new kynge will have new soldiers, and God knowethe what men they will be.[1]

It is in this way that Sir John Harington, godson to Elizabeth I, addressed a letter to Lord Thomas Howard in the accession year of 1603. At this critical moment of political parturition, uppermost in the correspondent's mind was the radical re-configuration of political and military allegiances in the aftermath of the earl of Essex's vain attempt at a *coup d'état* in the armed revolt of 1601 and the death of the last Tudor sovereign in 1603, the year this letter was written. Harington had been knighted during the 1599 Irish campaign under Essex's command but, faced on his return with his godmother's implacable ire, he had soon come to wish that he 'had never received my Lorde of Essex's honor of knighthood'.[2]

---

[1] Sir John Harington, *Nugae Antiquae*, 2 vols. (London, 1769), 1: 101, 'Letter to Lorde Thomas Howarde, from Sir I.H. 1603'.
[2] Harington, *Nugae Antiquae*, 1: 46.

Decades earlier, in *A Generall Rehearsall of Warres* (1579), Thomas Church-yard recalled a time when

> all Chevalrie was cherished, Soldiours made of, and manhoode so muche esteemed, that he was thought happie and moste valiaunt, that sought cred-ite by the exercises of Armes, and dissipline of warre [and] he was counted nobodie, that had not been knowen to bee at some valiaunte enterprice [for the] advaunsement of his Countrey.[3]

Now, however, as one century gave way to the next, there was even less reason to associate such social advancement with military distinction. As will become apparent in the course of this discussion, Thomas Middleton's drama repeat-edly invested in problematizing military identities for his Jacobean audiences. Across his career, he continued to interrogate the changeful cultural status of the war veteran, the war wounded, the soldier-beggar, the *miles gloriosus*, the soldier-as-public-servant, the trained expert in military violence and so on in order to revisit prevailing social theories of power for audiences in early seventeenth-century London. Nonetheless, if Harington observed that mad-caps might be found rejoicing at the advent of a new reign, there were those who also found themselves agreeably with newly 'made caps' in these times of dynastic transition. The son of Norfolk gentry, Philip Gawdy, wrote from London to his brother in the final week of May 1603

> I doubt not but that you have heard of the multitude of Knightes made in many places [...] I knowe one knighte in Suffolke that followed the courte so long for a knighthood, as whether it wer for want of good lodging, or shifte of rayment, he and his men were so lousye as it was most wonderfull, and yet in the end (paying well for it) he was made a lowsy K[night].[4]

To crown this growing mood of frantic preferment, in Middleton's *The Puritan Widow* (1606) playhouse audiences had the opportunity to make acquaintance with one Sir John Pennydub.

Amongst the growing throng, Harington's contemporary, Francis Bacon, was also knighted by the Scottish king in this first regnal year; and in his work dating from this period, the *Temporis Partus Masculus* (1603–4), the rising jurist also acknowledged that the age was one of political rupture, but med-itated that 'it is important to understand how the present is like a seer with two faces, one looking towards the future, the other towards the past'.[5] The

3   Thomas Churchyard, *A Generall Rehearsall of Warres Called Churchyardes Choise* (Lon-don, 1579), sig. A1r.
4   Philip Gawdy, *Letters of Philip Gawdy of West Harling, Norfolk, and of London to Various Members of his Family 1579–1616*, ed. Isaac Herbert Jeayes (London, 1906), pp. 130, 136.
5   See translated text of the *Temporis Partus Masculus* (1603–4), in Benjamin Farrington, *The Philosophy of Francis Bacon* (Liverpool, 1964), p. 68.

importance of assuming such an attitude for an aspiring servant of the state had been demonstrated in his earlier support of the crown against his former patron Essex; and indeed, in *A Briefe Discourse, Touching the Happie Vnion of the Kingdomes of England, and Scotland* (1603), Bacon resolved upon commending in fulsome terms 'this happye union of your Majesties two Kingdomes of England and Scotland'.[6]

More generally, the momentous arrival of James VI of Scotland in the southern kingdom was inevitably being widely signalled in all manner of writings and entertainments from the period. As we have seen, squarely in Harington's mind was the radical re-configuration of political and military allegiances under the new political dispensation, yet his conviction that the 'new kynge will have new soldiers' was, in the event, to be put severely to the test by the Stuart *rex pacificus*. However, in the opening years of the reign, even with the drawing to a close of hostilities with Spain, there seemed little reason to believe that the need for men-at-arms in the newly unified British nations would diminish in that bellicose age. Strikingly, if many acknowledged the potential in the body politic for conflict and contestation at this precarious moment of political transition, public ceremonial and performance might often be sought out with the express hope of exorcising, or at least quelling, such anxieties.

The present chapter considers how the work of one dramatist, Thomas Middleton (1580–1627), and his collaborators engaged with the ongoing cultural debate surrounding militarism and the militarising of civil society in the early decades of the seventeenth century. Their productions were not only exercized by questions of the deployment of military violence as an organizing principle for political discourse and governance, but also frequently disclosed how desperate bids to secure identities and knowledge associated with the battlefield might shape the construction of everyday selves during the reign of a royal peace-maker.

Entertainments for a new age of peace

For many Jacobeans, if the name of Thomas Middleton was associated at all with the business of performance, it is all too possible that this association would be with civic pageantry rather than fare for the public playhouses.[7] His involvement in such productions over the broad length of his career varied widely. Thus, an examination of his *modus operandi* with reference to the world

---

[6] Francis Bacon, *A Briefe Discourse, Touching the Happie Vnion of the Kingdomes of England, and Scotland* (1603), sigs. C2r, C5r.

[7] For further discussion here, see Heather Easterling, *Parsing the City: Jonson, Middleton, Dekker, and City Comedy's London as Language* (London, 2007), pp. 43ff.

of armed hostilities cannot be exhaustive, but in this section three examples are considered for the ways in which such pageantry could engage with questions of military import for Jacobean audiences. The first finds Middleton as a very minor contributor, for it was, as is typical of the form, highly collaborative in nature: *The Whole Royal Magnificent Entertainment of King James through the City of London, 15 March 1604* involved the pens of Thomas Dekker, Ben Jonson, Stephen Harrison and, to a very much lesser degree, Middleton.[8] Intentionally striking a chord with a king who took as his motto *beati pacifici*, the audience to the *Entertainment*'s first pageant was duly informed that the nation had refused to give way to the

> sorrow and amazement that like an earthquake began to shake the distempered body of this island, by reason of our late sovereign's departure, being wisely and miraculously prevented, and the feared wounds of a civil sword [...] being stopped from bursting forth by the sound of trumpets that proclaimed King James, all men's eyes were presently turned to the north (Pageant 1: 212–20)

Thus, forsaking the Iron Age of conflict, the capital might greet its 'Augusto Novo' who was resolved upon the forging, and the mythologizing, of an 'Empyre': 'foure Kingdomes by your entrance blest/ By Brute divided, but by you alone,/ All are againe united and made One' (Pageant 7: 2518, Pageant 6: 2159–61). Middleton's contribution to the whole performance has been isolated to the speech of the choric figure Zeal in the sixth pageant. Here, the thematic emphasis of the opening is reiterated as the symbolic figure laments 'our English isle/ Seemed to move backward at the funeral pile/ Of her dead female majesty', but 'Our globe is drawn in a right line again./ [...] See at the peaceful presence of the king/ How quietly [the elements] move' (Pageant 6: 2122–4, 2136–7). The dynamics of collaborative authorship inevitably varied enormously across the early modern period and, in this instance, the printed text grudgingly acknowledges, 'If there *be* any glory to be won by writing these lines, I do freely bestow it (as his due) on Thomas Middleton, in whose brain they were begotten' (Pageant 6: 2182–4).

However, the subsequent pageant (in which Middleton had no hand) unfolding at Temple Bar, marking the limits of the cities of Westminster and London, unveiled appropriately a Temple of Janus to signify this watershed in the life of the nation. Here, as so often in the later Jacobean period, audiences were being asked not only to identify the withdrawal from armed hostilities as

---

[8]   Middleton's contribution has been isolated to the speech for Zeal at the sixth arch. See R. Malcolm Smuts, '*The Whole Royal and Magnificent Entertainment*', in Thomas Middleton, *The Collected Works*, ed. Gary Taylor et al. (Oxford, 2007), pp. 219–23. All references to texts by Middleton (single-authored or collaborative) and translations from Latin texts are taken from this edition for this discussion. Citations from the *Entertainment* are to pageant and line numbers.

a divinely ordained motion of state, but also as a return to a state of existence confirmed by nature which gravitated inexorably towards union and cooperation – 'pax optima rerum' (Pageant 7: 2316). Moreover, in this seventh pageant, in a temple newly erected within the City's limits for the Scottish king, Irene 'or Peace' is envisaged as 'the first and principal person in the Temple', and Jonson has 'ENYALIUS, or Mars' discovered 'grovelling, his armour scattered upon him in several pieces, and sundry sorts of weapons broken about him'. Irene reminds the assembled company that '*UNA TRIUMPHIS IN NUMERIS POTIOR./ pax optima rerum/ Quas homini novisse datum est.*' ['One more powerful in numerous triumphs. Peace is the best thing that man may know.'] (Pageant 7: 2299, 2298, 2311–17). In this staged, recursive motion drawing deeply upon the legitimizing authority of myth and antiquity, an altar inscription is discovered: 'D. I. O. M. BRITANNIARUM. IMP. PACIS. VINDICI. MARTE. MAJORI. P. P. F. S. AUGUSTO. NOVO.' ['To Lord James the Best and Greatest, Emperor of the Britons, guarantor of peace, greater than Mars, father of his country, saviour of the faith, new Augustus.'] (Pageant 7: 2515–18).

If, in the event, James was never to resolve his very different kingdoms into one cohesive political community, the state and civic pageantry dedicated to him at the opening of his reign was determined to invest in this eirenic vision for an imperially minded sovereign. For, as Tracey Hill has demonstrated in her magisterial study of Jacobean civic pageantry, if such performances were often characterized by lavish expenditure, collaborative authorship and management, they catered to very large audiences (not infrequently from home *and* abroad) and remained attentive in acknowledging the undertakings of their patrons and/or dedicatees.[9] Moreover, equally importantly, Hill underlines (in a consideration here of Lord Mayor's Shows, but with wider import for this discussion) that civic productions sought to impress upon their audiences the need to flex their collective memories in order to realize the full extent of the nation's political inheritance:

> The rhetoric of the Shows, with its recurrent invocation of notable historical and mythical moments and figures, would have gained most of its effect from the audience's ability to relate what they were seeing and hearing to a collective narrative of the past. [...] Indeed, in important ways the Shows can be said to fashion or even create that sense of the past through what they include, what they highlight and what they omit (at times there is as much a collective forgetting as a collective remembering).[10]

---

[9]   Tracey Hill, *Pageantry and Power: A Cultural History of the Early Modern Lord Mayor's Show, 1585–1639* (Manchester, 2010), p. 119.
[10]   Hill, *Pageantry and Power*, p. 9; see also in this context, pp. 1, 8, 89.

In the instance of the *Magnificent Entertainment*, the authors repeatedly sought to lay claim once again to the mythical, originary narratives of a British imperialism and this collective political life of an expanding empire might be clearly emblematized for the crowd of onlookers in their very own community of the city. Nonetheless, this new-born Augustan age remains selective in its commitments: the grandiloquent claims to universal peace are strategically allowed here to eclipse any concerns with conquest and expansion which might conventionally be associated with a *pax romana*.

Some two decades later, the *Honourable Entertainments* (1620) might be taken as a clear example of Middleton engaging more broadly with an ambitious range of issues having currency in contemporaneous debate. The collection of *Entertainments* ranges in focus from masque-like performances on the occasions of Christmas and Easter to more familiar examples of the genre in civic pageantry, recital and performative debate. Moreover, in direct comparison with works Middleton composed in this later period of his career, these *Entertainments* may often be seen to take cognizance at regular intervals of the divisions and conflicts unfolding on the European continent at that time in the shape of the Thirty Years War. The fourth *Entertainment*, for example, addresses specifically the question of the poor state of military preparedness (notably in the nation's capital) in such profoundly uncertain times and, thus, the man-at-arms as a figure of social neglect. If funding were finally being made available in the City for military equipment and training for its militia, the in-fighting between civic bodies concerning matters of precedence and access to the city's spaces inevitably impeded any substantive progress. In addition, numbers within the city's militia companies continued to diminish alarmingly.[11] Thus, the text of this civic address targets anxieties 'Upon discontinuance, and to excite them to practise. A Speech intended for the generall Training, being appointed for the Tuesday next [...] but uppon some occasion, the Day deferred' (4: Prol.). Significantly, the *Entertainment* was never performed because the occasion of the city's muster was cancelled by the City's Aldermen in 1620, but the reader of its printed version is reminded that 'Pallas on Horsebacke [...] thus should have greeted the L. Generall the L. Mayor Sir William Cokaine, at his entrance into the Field, the worthy Colonels, the right Generous Mr: Alderman Hamersley, President of the Noble Councell of Warre':

> [...] Lieutenants, ensigners, sergeants of Bands,
> Of worthy citizens the army stands,
> Each in his place deserving faire respect;
> I can complaine of nothing but neglect,

11 See Anthony Parr, '*Honourable Entertainments* and *An Invention*', in Middleton, *Collected Works*, p. 1433.

That such a noble city's armed defence
Should be so seldom seen. I could dispense
With great occasions, but alas, whole years
To put off exercise gives cause of fears.
[…]
Let every year at least once in his round
See you like sons of honour tread this ground;
And heaven that both gives and secures just wealth,
The city bless with safety, you with health. (4: Prol., 27–34, 65–8)

If this particular appeal to arms (or, at least, to have familiarity with arms) failed to enjoy a public hearing, earlier in the collection, the second *Entertainment* addressed a question which had already figured prominently in late Elizabethan pamphleteering: the status and function of the modern archer in the nation's military forces. Sir John Smythe's *Certain Discourses* [...] *Concerning the Formes and Effects of Divers Sorts of Weapons, and Other Verie Important Matters Militarie* (1590), for example, had been a notable intervention in the period, hailing the victories throughout English history which might be attributed to the skills of the bowman: 'the great daunger that uppon divers accidents may hereafter happen to the Crowne and Realme of England and English Nation, hath been, and is to seeke to abolish and extinguish the notable exercise and use of our Long-bowes and Archerie'.[12] Forming part of an ongoing and vigorous series of exchanges concerning the relative merits of military technology, Smythe went on to argue that those who advocated discarding the longbow had only learned their craft 'in the disordered and tumultuarie warres of the Lowe Countries under the States, or (peraduenture) some litle divers yeres past, in the intestine and licentious warres of *France*'.[13]

In the event, this publication would continue to generate a number of contrary responses in print. Indeed, two years later, Humfrey Barwick in his *Breefe Discourse, Concerning the Force and Effect of all Manuall Weapons of Fire and the Disability of the Long Bowe or Archery* (1592) engaged sceptically and in some detail with the arguments of Smythe's publication, retorting, 'what, shall we refuse the Cannon and fall to the Ram againe[?]'.[14] Middleton himself had

---

[12] John Smythe, *Certain Discourses* [...] *Concerning the Formes and Effects of Divers Sorts of Weapons, and Other Verie Important Matters Militarie* (London, 1590), sig. A2r.

[13] Smythe, *Certain Discourses*, sig. *3v. Interestingly, in this context, Parr, '*Honourable Entertainments*', p. 1433, notes that 'In 2.13–16 Middleton borrows from Roger Ascham's *Toxophilus* (1545) to underline the idea of archery as a distillation of English skill and nobility, and uses this to develop an elaborate analogy with wise government'. See also Jim Ellis, 'Archery and Social Memory in Sixteenth-Century London', *HLQ* 79.2 (2016), 21–40.

[14] Humfrey Barwick, *A Breefe Discourse, Concerning the Force and Effect of all Manuall Weapons of Fire and the Disability of the Long Bowe or Archery* (1592), sig. A4r.

acknowledged the cut-and-thrust of this debate in *The Penniless Parliament of Threadbare Poets* (1601), for example. Here, the unruly gathering recognizes the timeliness of

> a necessary statute that there shall great contentions fall between soldiers and archers, and, if the fray be not decided at a pot of ale and a black pudding, great bloodshed is like to ensue.
>
> [...]
>
> Amongst these controversies we will send forth our commission to god Cupid, being an archer, who shall decide the doubt and prove that archer is heavenly, for in meditation thereof he hath lost his eyes. (lines 229–40)

If developments in firearms would ultimately foreclose participation in this debate concerning the bowman-as-combatant as the century wore on, it was clear even before the end of Elizabeth's reign that participation in archery contests could be patchy at best. Thus, in 1620, on the notable annual occasion of 'the Shooting day' at Bunhill near Moorfields in London, Middleton's second *Entertainment* proposed that one 'habited like an Archer' address 'the L. Mayor and Aldermen after they were placed in their Tent':

> Why, this is nobly done, to come to grace
> A sport so well becomes the time and place.
> Old time made much on't, and it thought no praise
> Too dear for't, nor no honour in those days.
> Not only kings ordained laws to defend it
> But shined the first examples to commend it;
> In their own persons honored it so far
> A land of peace showed like a field of war.
> But chiefly Henry, memory's fame, the Eighth,
> And the sixth Edward, gave it worth and weight [...] (2: Prol., 1–10)

If the figure of the bowman is unsurprisingly celebrated on the occasion of an archery contest, it remains worthy of note that Middleton's civic pageant draws once again upon the authority of time-honoured practice and the power of cultural intervention in the gift of kings as key sites for promoting conflict resolution in the nation, most especially with reference to the changing political fortunes of the soldier.

In collaboration with William Rowley, Middleton did, however, conceive of ceremonial performance in a qualitatively different manner for a masque commissioned (probably also in 1620) by the future Charles I. The entertainment was designed for presentation before the king and the court at the Prince's newly acquired residence of Denmark House in the capital. In a number of ways, *The World Tossed at Tennis* seeks to challenge in a sustained manner the policies of the *rex pacificus* for an elite audience at a time when Europe was being torn apart by the remorseless bloodletting of the Thirty Years War. If, in the event, there is no evidence that Middleton and Rowley's text was performed at Denmark House (also personified in the text) for the exalted company that Prince Charles wished to assemble, we do know that it was performed at the Swan Theatre in the same year.[15] Here, in an initial scene attributed to Rowley characterized by verbal fencing between 'the Scholar' and 'the Soldier', the latter of these symbolic figures is discovered giving voice to an already familiar refrain in this discussion, that of the veteran lamenting his bitter plight as social pariah with only fairweather support from those around him in civilian society:

> We are like winter garments, in the height
> And hot blood of summer, put off, thrown by
> For moth's meat, never so much as thought on
> Till the drum strikes up storms again; and then,
> 'Come, my well-lined soldier' (with valour,
> Not velure) 'keep me warme; Oh, I love thee!' (44–9)

As the entertainment progresses, we are asked to compare and contrast the relative merits of the vocations of both figures. However, rather than formulating an interrogation, familiar from well-established humanist discourse, of the relative merits of the *vita activa* and the *vita contemplativa*, the emphasis of the proceedings falls regularly upon a redemptive narrative (supported by interventions from pagan deities and antique heroes) in which all parties may find newly minted roles, being integrated fully into the larger body of society as premier public servants for the greater prosperity and well-being of the realm as a whole:

> Pallas   […] What seeks the soldier?
> Soldier   My maintenance.
> Pallas   Lay by thine arms and take the city then.
>   There's the full cup and can of maintenance. (174–6)

In due course, the audience is encouraged to join with the Soldier and Scholar in enjoying the pageantry and concord of 'Musique' and song as the nine Worthies and the nine Muses 'are discovered on the upper stage'. Attentive to the Prince's concern that his father's kingdom engage more vigorously in support of Protestant forces in the continental wars, we learn in this entertainment that Pallas's realm is inhabited by those who may command 'fiery coursers' and devote their 'great weight in conquest' (284, 291).

---

[15] See C.E. McGee, *The World Tossed at Tennis*, in Middleton, *Collected Works*, p. 1406. Citations are to line numbers.

In the second half of *The World Tossed at Tennis*, a 'Land-Captain' is introduced in the company of 'Deceit as a soldier' (552). Here, once again, we return to an analysis of the hardships to be endured by the labourless fighter: 'The stings of thirst and hunger [...] Afflictions sharper than the enemy's swords' (558–9). After the recital of a *cahier de doléances* from the Land-Captain, the stage king resigns his power, symbolized by an orb, to this key member of his military. Now that respect and goodwill have been restored on both sides of this crucial political relationship of service and patronage in the nation, the moral mettle of the Land-Captain is acknowledged ('Though now an absolute master, yet to thee/ Ever a faithful servant' 590–1) and he duly drives Deceit from his company: 'Now 'tis the soldier's time, great Jupiter' (615).

Characteristically drawing upon psychomachic dramaturgy of medieval play-making for such pageantry, the staged account of the Land-Captain is now juxtaposed by Middleton with those in the next scene where we witness the encounter of a Sea-Captain and 'Deceit as a purser'. Here again, after some more verbal fencing with the Land-Captain over questions of precedence, the dramatic thrust is towards a more general submission to royal authority: 'I will join with thee/ Both to defend and enrich majesty' (671–2). In due course, the Flamen (or priest figure) is drawn onstage to query the larger status and function of these military figures, 'What is't to be the lord of many battles [...] Abroad to conquer, and be slaves at home?' (699, 701). Leaving the audience to ponder the verities imparted by this sanctified presence, shadowing the steps of his land-bound counterpart, the Sea-Captain relinquishes the orb to his master; the sovereign receives it declaring 'Let this be called the sphere of harmony,/ In which, being met, let's all move mutually' (811–12). Subsequently, Deceit and the Devil depart from this morally cleansed realm, but the Soldier responds nevertheless rather anxiously at the close of the proceedings: 'The World's in a good hand now, if it hold' (876). More generally, the 'courtly masque' is resolved with a symbolic re-allocation of the age's spoils as the Soldier determines 'I'll over, yonder to the most glorious wars/ That e'er famed Christian Kingdom', leaving the Scholar to settle 'in a land of a most glorious peace' (878–80). Thus, in a host of different ways in these selected entertainments across the length of the Jacobean period, Middleton and his collaborators offer their audiences opportunities not only to celebrate the communal life of the nation (and the capital) steeped in ancient myths and traditions of law-making through pageantry and civic address, but to engage with pressing questions of social and political ethics, most particularly in these instances with regard to those who have served in the field of action.[16]

---

[16]   On Middleton's ethical undertaking in his pageants and civic entertainments: Hill, *Pageantry and Power*, p. 312.

Civil society and the recourse to the theatre of war

By the time of the Stuart accession, the anonymous publication *England's Wedding Garment* (1603) had 'The Scholer and the Souldier sing', and Francis Trigge's *Humble petition of two sisters the Church and Common-wealth* (1604) asserted that the 'strength of England [...] consistes on the poore Husbandman, Cottager, and common Souldier'.[17] Some five years later, Middleton's sometime collaborator Thomas Dekker could be found arguing that 'The life of a Begger is the life of a Souldier: he suffers hunger and colde in winter, and heate and thirst in summer [...] hee's not regarded, hee's not rewarded.'[18] Such diverse cross-currents of cultural opinion formed a continuum with well-established debates which had already been unfolding in the public domain for a good number of years.[19] As we have seen, during the final decades of Elizabeth's reign, pamphlet print culture had witnessed an enormous resurgence of interest in, and interrogation of, the long-standing cultural investment in the soldier – and Middleton could not remain impervious to this thriving debate. Indeed, in these very opening years of James's reign, in *Father Hubburd's Tales, or The Nightingale and the Ant* (1604) Middleton's reader was made to keep company with the Ant, cast as an ex-soldier for part of the tale. Adopting the persona of the reluctant conscript, the latter recounts that, after some wavering, he 'entered into the entrails of black-livered policy' of fully fledged soldiery. Subsequently, a brief appearance as the *miles gloriosus* segues into a more robust account of the desperate nature of his plight:

> [the bullets] used me very courteously and gentleman-like awhile [...] they played with me [...] they lurched me of two of my best limbs, viz. my right arm and right leg, that so, of a man of war, I became in show a monster of war, yet comforted in this because I knew war begot many such monsters as myself in less than a twelvemonth [...] When I was on shore, the people gathered, which word 'gathering' put me in hope of good comfort that afterward I failed of. For I thought, at first, they had gathered something for me, but I found, at last, they did only but gather about me, some wondering at me as if I had been some sea monster cast ashore, some jesting at my deformity, whilst others laughed at the jests. (lines 913, 917, 919–23, 949–55)

Here, at a relatively early stage in his career, Middleton was already drawing attention to the multiple identities which the soldier might assume for

[17] See respectively: Anon., *Englands Wedding Garment. Or A Preparation to King James his Royall Coronation* (London, 1603), sig. A4r; Francis Trigge, *To the Kings Most Excellent Majestie* (London, 1604), sig. F1v.

[18] Thomas Dekker, *The Belman of London* (1608), sig. C3v.

[19] See, for example: Churchyard, *A Generall Rehearsall*, sigs. M2r; Barnabe Rich, *Allarme to England* (London, 1578), sig. G4v.

his contemporaries: faint-hearted combatant; intrepid man of action; *raconteur*; braggart; invalid; beggar; miscreant; theatrical spectacle; pariah. In this instance, the Ant finds himself enduring the fate which Trinculo and Stephano had hoped to reserve for Caliban on their first encounter with the islander; and both Shakespeare's and Middleton's creations are duly marketed by the onlookers as monstrous.

Indeed, just a few years earlier, Dekker's *The Shoemaker's Holiday* (1599) had also made time in its romantic celebration of the *civitas* to shine a cold light on the bitter plight of the war veteran, crippled and excluded from social exchanges in the capital's mercantile and erotic trading. Rafe returns from the wars an invalid and believes himself displaced in the energetic games of speculation and asset-stripping circulating furiously in the citizen world of London. In reality, the presence of large groups of unemployed and masterless soldiers returning from conflict zones to the home country remained an abiding concern for the authorities as one century yielded to the next. Moreover, it seems that there was the potential that the sympathy generated by the return of these battle-scarred soldiers might be exploited by the wider community of the non-combative poor. In February 1592, for example, the authorities reiterated their alarm that most illegitimate theatrics and forms of imposture were taking place in the realm:

> [there were] persons as wander abroad in the habit of soldiers [...] pretending to have served in the late wars and service [...] and some amongst these have neither been maimed nor hurt nor yet served at all in the war, but take the cloak and color to be the more pitied, and do live about the city by begging and in disorderly manner.[20]

Nonetheless, in direct comparison with the complaint of Middleton's Ant, it became a constant refrain that such homecomings by veterans might find cold comfort at the hands of their former neighbours and fellow citizens. In *A Pleasant Song, Made by a Souldier* (1614), for example, the returning combatant is (according to the title) 'now beaten with his owne rod' and stages his own 'repentance' in song:

> When I came home, I made a proofe
> What friends would do if need should be,
> My neerest kinsfolkes look'd aloofe,
> As though they had forgotten me.
> And as the Owle by chattring charmes,
> Is wondred at of other Birds,

---

20 'Ordering Examination of Vagrant Soldiers – Whitehall, 28 February 1592'; see *Tudor Royal Proclamations*, ed. Paul Hughes and James F. Larkin (New Haven, 1969), p. 105.

> So came they wondring at my harmes,
> And yeeld me no releefe but words.[21]

In this particular instance, the plangent air is in fact a swansong as the ostra-cized Soldier seeks his own end, offering a final warning to his auditor: 'Yet marke the words that I have said,/ Trust not to friends when thou art old'.[22] Nor, as we have seen in the case of *The Shoemaker's Holiday*, did this cultural debate surrounding the figure of the soldier and his place in civil society remain outside the bounds of the playhouse. In the next decade, the dramatic emphasis of Middleton's *Wit at Several Weapons* (1613) falls not so much upon the disquieting marginality of the military figure, but upon the scepticism with which any bid for social privilege based upon service at arms might now be greeted in the Jacobean age. Such, it seems, was the easy currency of claims to distinction based on military heroism by the ubiquitous figure of the *miles gloriosus* that each petitioner warranted most particular and vigorous interro-gation. In Middleton's play, Sir Ruinous undergoes this manner of cross-ques-tioning. However, the rather facile minds of his auditors, Wittypate and the Old Knight, mean that they do not prove especially resisting readers of his record of achievement:

Wittypate	In what services have you been, sir?
Sir Ruinous	The first that fleshed me a soldier, sir, was
	that great battle of Alcazar in Barbary, where the noble
	English Stukeley fell, and where that royal Portugal,
	Sebastian, ended his untimely days.
Wittypate	Are you sure Sebastian died there?
Sir Ruinous	Faith, sir, there was some other rumour
	hopped amongst us that he, wounded, escaped, and
	touched on his native shore again, where, finding his
	country at home more distressed by the invasion of the
	Spaniard than his loss abroad, forsook it, still supporting
	a miserable and unfortunate life, which where he ended
	is yet uncertain.
Wittypate	By my faith, sir, he speaks the nearest fame of
	truth in this.
Sir Ruinous	Since, sir, I served in France, the Low Countries,
	lastly at that memorable skirmish at Nieuport;
	where the forward and bold Scot there spent his life

---

[21] Anon., *A Pleasant Song, Made by a Souldier Whose Bringing up Had Bin Dainty, and Partly Fed by Those Affections of his Unbridled Youth, Is Now Beaten with his Owne Rod, and Therefore Tearmeth this his Repentance, The Fall of his Folly: To the Tune of Calino* (London, 1614), n.p.

[22] Ibid.

	so freely, that from every single heart that there fell came home from his resolution a double honour to his country.	
Wittypate	This should be no counterfeit, sir.	
Old Knight	I do not think he is, sir.	(1.2.163–85)

Like the Roman citizens of Shakespeare's city-state in *Coriolanus*, Wittypate subsequently asks for evidence of the wounds incurred in the heat of action. However, unlike the victor at Corioli, Sir Ruinous is held squarely within a comic frame of raillery and riposte. If both men demur coyly when greeted with such requests, Shakespeare's hero eventually submits to scenes of public inspection, whereas Middleton's character lights upon a more teasing rejoinder: 'I have wounds, and many; but in those parts where nature and humanity bids me shame to publish' (1.2.189–91).[23]

If, in his review of the polity in the *Sermon of the Stewards* (1602), Sir John Hayward affirmed that 'many great and precious things are committed' to the Magistrate, the Minister, the Scholar, 'the politique Captaine, the valiant souldier, the skilfull artificer, the father of the familie', the audiences of Middleton's dramatic intrigues are mostly offered precious little evidence of the cohesive society of the nation in which the soldier is allowed to join the venerated elders of his community.[24] Indeed, we are frequently introduced to the stark inversion of such a social vision. In *The Witch* (1616), Sebastian finds his cultural capital sorely depleted owing to his sustained absence from his society's power games ('My three years spent in war has now undone/ My peace forever' (1.1.1–2)), and the mores of the battlefield have now been allowed to enter the court. We discover the coarse military commander of the Duke presiding over this elite company, insisting that his Duchess toast the marriage of eminent subjects from a military trophy, a 'soldier's cup', proffered to her personally by her spouse. The cup proves to be the skull of her own father: 'a trophy/ We'll keep till death, in memory of that conquest./ He was the greatest foe our steel e'er struck at,/ And he was bravely slain' (1.1.117–20). Unsurprisingly, the Duchess remains rather less responsive to the triumphal celebrations of the moment: 'Did ever cruel, barbarous act match this?' (1.1.137).

In such sombre dramatic worlds, Middleton frequently draws attention to the ways in which the pressures of the combatant's expectations of preferment and commonplace violence continue to fashion the lives of civilians. In *Women Beware Women* (1621? pub. 1657) the eloper-turned-cuckold Leantio may earn audience attention provisionally as the wronged husband, but he

---

[23] See also the essays by Trim and Tait in this volume (Chapters 1 and 9) that discuss combat wounds and their function as blazons of military service and identity.
[24] Sir John Hayward, *A Sermon of the Stewards Danger Preached at Paules Crosse the 15. of August by John Hayward* (London, 1602), sig. A8r.

does not linger unduly on the margins of Florentine society. With a fine sense of irony, the Duke expresses his appreciation of the merchant's 'good parts, sir, which we honour/ With our embrace and love' (3.2.38–9), and dignifies his new ducal rights of ownership with public acts of patronage to Leantio: the supplanted husband may 'Rise now the captain of our fort at Ruinse' (3.2.44). Thus, the expert trader now has his state dignified with the ruins and remnants of military status that others grant him. As the tragedy unfolds, he does indeed become a counterfeit commander and fully complicit in the play world's exchanges, paying obeisance to its defective concepts of individual dedication and communal protection: 'The service of whole life give your grace thanks' (3.2.45). Elsewhere, in *More Dissemblers Besides Women* (1614? pub. 1657), the courtly world of the Italian city-state is arrested by a 'sudden shout' beyond its walls and is reassured by the Lord Cardinal that the 'victorious man' is

> Signor Andrugio, general of the field;
> Successful in his fortunes, is arrived,
> And met by all the gallant hopes of Milan,
> Welcomed with laurel wreaths, and hymns of praises. (1.3.59–63)

Nonetheless, we subsequently discover in this sordid world, riven by dilemmas of death-or-else-dishonour, that 'war's a soaker; she's no friend to us;/ Turns a man home sometimes to his mistress/ Some forty ounces poorer then he went' (2.3.99–101).

In a rather more sustained fashion, in the bitterly divided world of *The Changeling* (1622, written collaboratively with William Rowley) we find a dramatic world much more clearly historicized as belonging to the first decade of the seventeenth century, when Spaniards continued as adversaries of the 'rebellious Hollanders' (1.1.186). In such a climate, Vermandero underlines to the new arrival Alsemero that 'we use not to give survey/ Of our chief strengths to strangers. Our citadels/ Are placed conspicuous to outward view/ On promonts' tops, but within are secrets' (1.1.166–9). Strikingly, Beatrice-Joanna's father is swiftly reassured on learning that Alsemero is the son of an old friend and former fellow-at-arms fallen at the 1607 battle of Gibraltar: 'Well, he's gone;/ A good soldier went with him' (1.1.180–1). He would have avenged Alsemero's father's death, Vermandero adds, 'Or followed him in fate, had not the late league/ Prevented me' (1.1.188–9), referring to the twelve-year peace initiated by the 1609 Treaty of the Hague.

This investment in cultural allusion is widely in evidence in Middleton's *oeuvre* across a host of different genres, and it undergirds the audience experience of a whole series of dramatic worlds whose characters are given to understanding the vicissitudes of their lives in terms of the theatres of war being played out more broadly around them. Indeed, Middleton remains at pains to indicate that it is not only the *practices* of experienced combatants that may find passage into the exchanges of civilian society. Even in his frenetic city comedies we encounter his creations regularly exploiting knowledge of armed conflicts in order to render their own lives more legible. In the early play *The Phoenix* (1603–4), for example, the Jeweller's Wife reminds her auditors that a visit in the capital to a Barber's shop may be 'as dangerous as a piece of Ireland' (scene 5, line 7). Mining a similar vein elsewhere in the comedies, in *The Honest Whore* (1604) the audience discovers that 'the constancy of a woman' is 'harder to come by then ever was Ostend' (10.31–2) and that 'A harlot is like *Dunkirk*, true to none,/ Swallows both English, Spanish, fulsome Dutch,/ Back-doord Italian, last of all the French' (scene 6, lines 405–7). And in *Michaelmas Term* (1604–6), offering generalized reference to the Dutch siege upon the Spanish military encampment at Middleburgh in Zeeland in evidence some thirty years earlier, Falselight informs Shortyard of the latest news: 'The passage to Middleburgh is stopped, and therefore neither Master Stillyard-down nor Master Beggarland, nor any other merchant, will deliver present money upon't' (2.3.400–3).

Middleton's dramatized societies are frequently defined critically by their propensities for inexhaustible competition, insatiable ambition and reluctant fellowship. Moreover, it is in the nature of his dramaturgy that these abiding concerns with the collapse in the economies of human intercourse into a violence familiar from the battlefield are played out in a resolutely urban environment. The city communities which dominate his intrigues, rather than being evidence of the fulfilment of civic aspiration, remain dynamic but hopelessly subject to moral incontinence and a terrifying dearth of self-knowledge. Since 'the cessure of the wars' in *The Puritan Widow* (1606), for example, the soldier or 'old lad of war' Peter Skirmish has found himself, like so many Middletonian veterans, 'put to silence like a sectary[.] War sits now like a justice/ of peace and does nothing. Where be your muskets,/ calivers and hotshots?' (1.2.1–6). In direct comparison with Jonson's *The Alchemist* (1610), also composed for the stage in these opening years of the new reign, Middleton's comic dramas repeatedly underline the similarities of military and criminal professions. As we have seen, King James had sought to usher in a world in 1603 (with his newly unified kingdoms) in which *beati pacifici* – Blessed are the Peacemakers. However, again and again on Middleton's stages, such policies remain little source of comfort for the inhabitants. Skirmish protests, 'in my conscience, I think some kind of peace has more hidden oppressions and violent heady sins (though looking of a gentle nature) then a professed war' (1.2.20–6) and meets with a keen rejoinder from his auditor, a decayed gentleman-scholar, George Pieboard, who is equally disaffected with this new order:

for my part [I] wish a turbulency in the world, for I have nothing to lose but
my wits

[...]

an honest war is better then a bawdy peace

[...]

The multiplicity of scholars, hatched and nourished in the idle calms of peace
makes 'em like fishes, one devour another. (1.2.49–55)

If the political commitment to eirenicism is thus put severely to the test in
such dramatic intrigues, *The Puritan Widow* also strikes another chord in
evidence elsewhere in Middleton's writing. Like Jonson's 'venture tripartite' in
The Alchemist, Middleton's comic dramas also occlude the hitherto reassuring
distinctions between survival in urban and military environments. The tactics of battle operations have now been adopted by the criminal subculture of
most unruly citizens in the capital. Here, Piebald later convinces his auditor
the Captain that whereas he has been but a 'poor soldier', if he chose to dabble
in the art of conjuring he would be new-born as 'a commander of rich fools,
which is truly the best purchase peace can allow you, safer then highways,
heath, or cony groves, and yet a far better booty. For your greatest thieves are
never hanged' (3.5.50–4).

The biting social critique to be found in *The Puritan Widow* finds its ana-
logue elsewhere in Middleton's works with the invariably disturbing appearance of the soldier-as-duellist in civilian society.[25] Such was the level of concern
about the phenomenon that the authorities outlawed the broadcasting of news
concerning duels in 1613 and prohibited the challenges which triggered such
contests in the following year. Middleton's pamphlet *The Peacemaker; or, Great
Britain's Blessing* (1618) sought to promote 'England, Insula pacis. The Land of
Peace, under the King of Peace', recognizing the need for such an argument
was warranted in a nation where 'Detraction snarles':

What blood shall the Revenger dare to shed? Or what Fame shall the
schoolmaster of duels achieve, with all his vainglorious and punctual orders of
firsts and seconds, lengths of weapons, distances of place, heights of grounds,
equalities of wind and Sunne? (702–6)

Equally importantly, such concerns are widely responded to in Middleton's
dramas for the playhouse. Indeed, in *A Fair Quarrel* (1616) such contentions
are placed centre-stage as the Colonel and Captain Ager negotiate their new

---

[25] See V.G. Kiernan, *The Duel in European History* (Oxford, 1988).

roles away from the battlefield through the heated question of military *degree* and gendered prowess:

Colonel	[...] In terms of manhood
	What can you dispute more questionable?
	You are a captain, sir, I give you all your due.
Captain Ager	And you are a colonel, a title
	Which may include within it many captains.
	Yet, sir, but throwing by those titular shadows,
	Which add no substance to the men themselves,
	And take them uncompounded, man and man,
	They may be so with fair equality.
Colonel	Y'are a boy, sir. (1.1.75–84)

In the subsequent action, Ager's 'Second Friend' contends that 'War has his court of justice, that's the field,/ Where all cases of manhood are determined,/ And your case is no mean one' (3.1.6–8). Similarly, in *The Nice Valour* (1622?), audiences are once again urged to attend to the ways in which the customs of the lawless battlefield are imported into the passionate chaos of civilian society. Here, the 'Soldier' finds himself displaced in the courtship of his mistress by the mocking 'Passionate Lord' who accuses his rival of most poorly executed practices and apes how he might 'woo you in a skirmish' (2.1.87). In this, the intrigue's subplot, the Soldier, driven to address his 'wrong's expiation', enters the palace chambers, stabs the Passionate Lord, and subsequently 'throws down and tramples Lepet and the clown Galoshio, and exits' (5.1.88–91). Meanwhile, the hero of the piece, his brother Chamont, is chastened by his ruler with a motion of a switch:

Chamont	I cannot love you, never, nor desire to serve you more.
	If your drum call me, I am vowed to valour,
	But peace shall never know me yours again,
	Because I've lost mine own. (2.1.289–92)

Thus, once again at a key moment in a Middleton dramatic intrigue, audiences are compelled to witness a spectacular moment of humiliation and displacement for the combatant and, as a consequence, we become increasingly sensitive to the potential unravelling of this society as all bonds of allegiance and service are now placed in question.

Conclusions

This chapter began with a consideration of the ways in which the arrival of a Stuart on the English throne – a Stuart committed to withdrawal from European theatres of war – excited yet further cultural debate on the status and function of the soldier in seventeenth-century political culture. At this key moment in the life of the nation, the lawyer John Manningham wrote that, 'The people is full of expectacion, and great with hope of his [James's] worthines, of our nations future greatnes; every one promises himselfe a share in some famous action to be hereafter performed.'[26] As we have seen, the 'share' to be apportioned to those in the military continued to be a source of much debate in the years which followed as the potential identities of public servant, social dependant, pariah, seditious agent, criminal, braggart, *raconteur* and so on were greeted often with attitudes of mistrust or disbelief. Indeed, it became increasingly problematic during James's reign to promote the political deployment of the soldier on the battlefield in any context as an unqualified good.

For decade upon decade across Europe during the sixteenth century, humanist voices had been heard scorning warfare as an ethical, or even effective, instrument of political policy. The English translation of Henry Cornelius Agrippa's *Of the Vanitie and Uncertaintie of Artes and Sciences* (1569), for example, had denigrated soldiers as 'the barbarouse dregges of wicked men, whom a naughtie will, and naughtie minde, stirreth to all mischiefe.'[27] Twenty years later, Francisco de Valdés argued in his *Espeio y deceplina militar* (1589) that 'The day a man picks up his pike to become a soldier is the day he ceases to be a Christian.'[28] Moreover, as J.R. Hale underlined, the early modern state might easily exacerbate the situation and become complicit in actively encouraging morally and politically suspect recruits to join the ranks of its military forces: 'To reinforce the troops besieged at Le Havre, Elizabeth I licensed the export of men from Newgate [in 1562]; in 1596 criminals were released from the royal prison in Seville on condition that they helped beat back the English raid on Cadiz.'[29]

If this chapter has focused upon the changing political and social investments which characterized the treatment of the soldier during the Jacobean period on Middleton's stages, one additional, and again collaborative, work also affords this question sustained attention. The place of *Timon of Athens*

---

[26] John Manningham, *Diary*, ed. Robert Parker Sorlien (Hanover, NH, 1976), p. 209.

[27] Henry Cornelius Agrippa, *Of the Vanitie and Uncertaintie of Artes and Sciences* (London, 1569), sig. 126v.

[28] Quoted in John A. Lynn II, *Women, Armies, and Warfare in Early Modern Europe* (Cambridge, 2008), p. 41.

[29] J.R. Hale, *War and Society in Renaissance Europe 1450–1620* (Leicester, 1985), p. 86. See also Jonathan Davies, *The Tudor Art of War 1485–1603* (Bristol, 2001), p. 11ff.

has often been problematized on account of its singular nature in the Shake-spearean canon.[30] Nonetheless, in more recent decades, a growing number of critical studies have identified in persuasive detail the hand of Middleton in this disquieting play, leading latterly to its integration into the Oxford *Collected Works* of Middleton as a text in which both Shakespeare and his younger contemporary collaborated.[31] The initially bountiful but always vociferous protagonist recognizes the Athenian general Alcibiades as 'a soldier, therefore seldom rich./ [...] for all thy living/ Is 'mongst the dead, and all the lands thou hast/ Lie in a pitched field' (2.224–7).[32] Ultimately, it is in the nature of this flawed and bitterly survivalist dramatic world that both general and patron must endure a remorseless regime of ingratitude. When the General ('worse than mad') petitions in vain for clemency for a fellow soldier before obdurate senators, he rails at the patriciate that having 'kept back their foes,/ While they have told their money [...] Is this the balsam that the usuring senate/ Pours into captains' wounds?' (10.104–5, 108–9). Like *Coriolanus*, examined above, the disaffected premier warrior summons up an apocalyptic fate for a society which refuses to recognize the worth of its armed forces: 'It is a cause worthy my spleen and fury,/ That I may strike at Athens. I'll cheer up/ My discontented troops' (10.111–13). As has already been seen, Pallas in *The World Tossed at Tennis* invites her military auditor to 'Lay by thine arms and take the city then', and in the final movement of *Timon of Athens*, Alcibiades is minded to adopt a similar attitude, resolving, 'Bring me into your city,/ And I will use the olive with my sword,/ Make war breed peace, make peace stint war' (19.82–4). In both instances, if peace is to be dispensed throughout the commonwealth, it must be in the gift of the seasoned commander, fully conversant with the theatre of war.

By way of conclusion and a final insight into Middleton's dramaturgical practice as it relates to military identity, it is appropriate that this discussion returns to the opening years of James's reign where it began. *The Meeting of Gallants at an Ordinary; or, The Walks in Paul's* (1604) is a broadly conceived dramatized narrative, but it is initiated with a metatheatrical framing device of a competitive 'Dialogue between War, Famine, and the Pestilence, blazing their several Evils' where, again, we find Middleton tapping the resources of

30   For further discussion: Andrew Hiscock, '"Cut my heart in sums": Community-Making and Breaking in the Prodigal Drama of Thomas Middleton', *Community-Making in Early Stuart Theatres*, ed. Roger D. Sell et al. (London, 2017), pp. 311–37.
31   See Jonathan Hope, *The Authorship of Shakespeare's Plays* (Cambridge, 1994); John Jowett, 'The Pattern of Collaboration in *Timon of Athens*', *Words that Count: Early Modern Authorship*, ed. Brian Boyd (Cranbury, NJ, 2004), pp. 181– 208; Brian Vickers, *Shakespeare, Co-Author* (Oxford, 2004); James P. Bednarz, 'Collaboration: The Shadow of Shakespeare', *Thomas Middleton in Context*, ed. Suzanne Gossett (Cambridge, 2011), pp. 211–18.
32   Quotations from *Timon* are also from the Oxford *Collected Works* of Middleton.

allegorical play-making familiar from medieval and early Tudor dramatic conventions to establish the thematic thrust of his textual undertaking. The 'Genius of War' unveils at the outset of the debate the spectres of 'Famine and Pestilence, cowards of hell,/ That strike in peace, when the whole world's unarmed' (1–2), contending that these ills are more than a match for the possible gifts proffered by 'the ghost of crimson passing War' (8). In the event, the focus of attention remains upon a piquant, if resolutely cynical dissection of a deeply flawed and fractious London society by fashionable wits in which it is 'as commmendable to go ragged after a plague as to have an ensign full of holes and tatters after a battle' (148–50). Such conclusions are emblematic of a *modus operandi* that remained in evidence throughout Middleton's career, a desire to render the workings of late Elizabethan and Jacobean society more transparent by analysing them at close quarters with the contemporaneous practices and expectations of the garrison and the battlefield.

The figure of the soldier re-appears with striking frequency in the drama, prose and pageants of Middleton. Moreover, as has been explored, his writing demonstrates a sustained determination to problematize military identities and soldierly roles in order to unmask a troubled, degenerate, corruptible or effeminate society. His audiences were constantly invited to reflect upon the public service that the combatant might offer society as a whole, and to question the value systems conventionally associated with the man-at-arms. Ultimately, however, Middleton's abiding anxieties concerning the consequences of military violence percolating through into every recess of civilian society would soon be realized for the next generation across the British nations as the seventeenth century yielded to the blood-letting of the Civil Wars.

12

'Sometimes a figure, sometimes a cipher': Dramatic Assertions of Martial Identity, 1580–1642

VIMALA C. PASUPATHI AND BENJAMIN J. ARMINTOR

In his examination of 'Occupational Identity in Early Modern England', Mark Hailwood argues that broadside ballads not only 'provide a valuable entry point for learning how occupational identities were constructed' but also 'played an important role in the process of identity formation itself'.[1] The present study began with a similar contention regarding the more specific identity of the pre- or proto-professional soldier, though its 'point of entry' is not the ballad, but rather, the play. With characters who identify explicitly as soldiers featuring in hundreds of works performed and printed over multiple decades, drama must have helped to shape contemporary perceptions of soldiers in the Tudor and Stuart periods.

Although we are not alone in addressing dramatic works in this volume, this chapter departs from the others within it in both its particular archive and the methodology we rely on to examine it: the claims we make in this chapter are based on what we have learned from mining an electronic corpus containing 1,244 dramatic works for specific linguistic patterns. We will contextualize some specific instances in plays by taking recourse to more traditional primary and secondary sources of military history, but much of what we discuss here hinges on structures of speech that can be detected at a relatively large scale by simple machine processes. Specifically, we compile and examine over 300 assertions about soldiers' identities that make use of any form of the stative verb 'to be'. As Wilfrid Sellars contends, constructions of this sort are ontological, establishing both the existence of a category of being and its associated qualities.[2] We will demonstrate here that these types of utterances regarding soldierly identity are more common in early modern dramatic texts than in other contemporary works that circulated in print.

---

[1] Mark Hailwood, 'Broadside Ballads and Occupational Identity in Early Modern England', *HLQ* 79.1 (2016), 188.

[2] Wilfrid Sellars, 'Grammar and Existence: A Preface to Ontology', *Mind* 69 (1960), 499–533.

Of course, scholars were mining English drama for insights about early modern identity long before the advent of widespread digitization, and there is a well-established body of scholarship going back half a century devoted to examining 'the self' and person-hood as primary concerns of the stage. As A.J. Piesse's survey of such scholarship makes clear, much of this work has approached identity in relation to the concepts of subjectivity and self-con-sciousness.[3] That is to say, in most cases, the most significant facet of characters' identity is the extent to which these figures make clear in speeches that they have *thought* about that identity. Drama scholars may disagree on whether the soliloquy or dialogue is the most appropriate form of discourse from which to draw insights, but their critical formulations of early modern identity con-sistently privilege the notion of interiority and evidence of a character's deep contemplation.[4]

This emphasis on the psychological processes of self-reckoning may account for the relative lack of attention to occupation in studies of identity of the early modern period, a lack that coincides with the centrality of Shakespeare in many of these critical works.[5] It seems indisputable that, as James P. Driscoll noted in a 1983 study, Shakespeare 'found the question of identity persistently fascinating', and, as a great many studies of warfare and drama demonstrate, scholars have felt similarly about the martial plots and protagonists that fea-ture prominently in his works.[6] It is not hard to see why: Othello, Henry V and

---

[3] A.J. Piesse, 'Identity', *A Companion to English Renaissance Literature and Culture*, ed. Michael Hattaway (Oxford, 2003), pp. 634–43.

[4] Sylvia Adamson has noted the narrowness of this focus on the 'self-contained, self-ex-pressive self'; see 'Questions of Identity in Renaissance Drama: New Historicism Meets Old Philology', *Shakespeare Quarterly* 61 (2010), 56–77. As Adamson suggests, work from the past two decades in the field of linguistics presents an interesting contrast to the emphasis on interiority in literary scholarship that Piesse describes; for other exam-ples: Beatrix Busse, *Vocative Constructions in the Language of Shakespeare* (Philadelphia, 2006); Jonathan Culpepper, *Language and Characterisation: People in Plays and other Texts* (New York, 2001).

[5] On the lack of attention to occupation, see Hailwood, 'Broadside Ballads', 187, who con-tends 'Historians of identity of this period have rarely taken occupations as their start-ing point. The roles of religion, office-holding, marital status, wealth, education, degree of financial independence, a sense of belonging to civic or parish institutions: all have been explored as important foundations of individual and collective identities to an extent that occupation, as yet, has not.' On the issue of Shakespeare's representative-ness in the age of digital corpora: Heather Froehlich, 'Thus to make poor females mad: Finding the "Mad Woman" in Early Modern Drama', *The Pragmatics and Stylistics of Identity Construction and Characterisation*, ed. Minna Nevala et al., Studies in Variation, Contacts and Change in English 17 (2006). E- publication series http://www.helsinki.fi/ varieng/series/volumes/17/froehlich/

[6] James P. Driscoll, *Identity in Shakespearean Drama* (Lewisburg, 1983), p. 9. Scholarship on drama and military affairs includes studies such as Paul Jorgensen's *Shakespeare's Military World* (Berkeley, 1956), and recent work such as Susan Harlan, *Memories of War in Early Modern England* (New York, 2016). For a useful survey of this work up to 2011:

Macbeth all identify as soldiers and offer multiple speeches about themselves *as* selves and soldiers. But it is also the case that these elite and exceptional men understand their respective identities very differently from a great many other figures who also claim to occupy the same identity in other plays.

We intend for this chapter to complement, rather than challenge, the basic assessments of soldiers offered in seminal and more recent works of scholarship that focus primarily (if not exclusively) on Shakespeare. Our contribution to this larger body of work is to consider the implications of simple identity assertions rather than contemplative speeches, and to examine these structures in all available dramatic texts rather than a handful of works by familiar playwrights. What can we learn when we set aside the exceptional *cogito* and privilege the pervasive *sum*?

In the first section of the chapter, we provide a detailed description of the corpora we have mined as well as the steps we took to prepare and search them. These efforts ensure our process is transparent (and replicable) and provide necessary context for the primary claims we can make about our results. We also outline this chapter's first and fundamental claim: that the number and frequency of identity assertions we have found in drama is statistically significant when compared to the much larger body of printed texts from the period. From this finding, we can move into a variety of additional comparisons between the body of texts containing our desired patterns and the drama corpus at large. We explain how our matches map onto genre (the concentration of identity assertions in comedy, tragedy and so-forth); presumed authorship (the concentration of these assertions in raw counts of matches and number of works by specific playwrights); and date (the number of matches in plays printed or performed by decade relative to the general and generic concentration of plays by decade in the larger corpus).

In section two of the chapter, we continue to narrow our focus, turning from comparisons of our matches to broader corpora to examine them in subsets featuring particular syntactic forms. Augmenting the practices associated with distant reading with the labour of close reading, we discuss variations of matches with respect to grammatical person (the number of first-, second-, and third-person constructions) and number (the distribution of singular and plural forms), and again consider how these formal elements of identity assertions are distributed in plays with respect to genre. We build on these findings in the third section, which looks in more detail at how specific grammatical forms of identity assertions also embed value. Here, we survey the attributes and actions that these utterances associate with 'being' a soldier, attending to

---

Andrew Hiscock, '"More Warlike than Politique": Shakespeare and the Theatre of War. A Critical Survey', *Shakespeare* 7 (2011), 221–47.

assertions that take the form of vows and oaths, expletives or similarly abstract constructions.

Our discussion concludes with an analysis of two additional significant groups of matches: declarations that invoke the soldier's identity in relation to other identity categories and contested assertions in which characters deny or are denied the identity. Attending to the negating claims as well as the various entities to which 'soldier' is verbally appended in our matches, we ask the following: how is being a soldier like or unlike being someone or something else? To what extent did military identities preclude the inhabitation or occupation of other commonly articulated types of person-hood? In the fictional and real worlds in which 'counterfeiters' and actors might claim the role – and, in a realm whose governing elites relied on local militias instead of standing armies – could any subject convincingly play a soldier?

We ponder these and other questions using quantitative and qualitative data. We support our claims with examples from plays in the form of brief quotations. Our approach to citing these examples will appear unconventional and requires some contextualization. First, in most cases, we opt not to identify these works by author and title; this choice is in keeping with our larger focus on drama as a type of work rather than on particular playwrights or plays. Second, we do not provide identifying bibliographical information for these texts in the instance of their quotation. While our matches derive from actual literary texts in print, the words we quote (as we will explain at the outset of the first section) come from resampled electronic files of those works. These files constitute a semi-modernized version of a play, but that version is unique to our resampling and therefore is effectively not the same as the specific edition of that play in print from which our text file originated. For readers who would like to track down specific quotations, we have made our full list of matches with accompanying bibliographical metadata available online through CORE, Humanities Commons' Open Access Repository.[7] Beyond what we have normalized automatically, we do not emend errors of punctuation or spelling in quotations from matches unless such errors impede their basic sense.

Corpora, search patterns and basic findings

Our examination of martial identity is enabled by the transcribed texts in Early English Books Online (EEBO), produced by the Text Creation Partnership (TCP) and rendered as plain text by the Visualizing English Print (VEP) Project. Under the auspices of a Mellon grant, VEP built on the TCP by establishing techniques for extracting from it a normalized, plain text corpus that

[7]   See the dataset titled 'Stative Identity Assertions of Soldiers in Early Modern Drama TCP transcriptions', http://dx.doi.org/10.17613/M6WV4B (accessed 8 May 2019).

could be interrogated with tools for computational analysis.[8] Most notable for the present study, VEP produced several corpora, including three devoted to drama; accompanying catalogues of bibliographic metadata; and a number of exemplary tools for visualizing analyses of these corpora. These products were published online (within the licensing constraints of TCP Phase II) and presented at a December 2016 seminar at the Folger Shakespeare Library.[9] We attended this seminar, and our collaboration owes its existence in large part to the data and processing standards provided to us by members of VEP.

This chapter is concerned with one VEP corpus in particular, the 'Expanded Drama to 1700' corpus (ED1700), comprised of 1,244 plays. This collection allows us to define drama in broad terms since it includes masques, civic pageants and closet dramas in addition to plays composed for performance at court, the universities, Dublin's Werburgh Street, and the commercial playhouses of London's 'liberties'. We have also used VEP's 'Early Modern 1080' corpus (EM1080), which consists of a random sample of 40 TCP texts per decade from 1530 to 1799, a total of 1,080 dramatic and non-dramatic works.[10] EM1080 provided a model for the production and subsequent processing of a larger sample of TCP texts that we used to compare features of the dramatic works in the ED1700 to all texts that circulated in print during the same period. This sample, which we refer to as TCP-R (i.e. Text Creation Partnership Resampled), consists of 5,272 texts, a size that allows us to estimate the matches across EEBO-TCP with an appropriate level of confidence and margin of error.

In attempting to re-purpose the tools and processes developed under VEP, we found some additional work was necessary to prepare corpora that would be suitable for the kinds of queries we wanted to perform. For instance, VEP could not distribute the plain text renderings of the entire EM1700 corpus under the licensing constraints of TCP Phase II, which restricts access to some plays to users at TCP partner institutions. Additionally, a number of these restricted plays were transcriptions of works that had been printed together

---

[8]   See 'About', The Visualizing English Print Project, http://graphics.cs.wisc.edu/WP/vep/about/ (accessed 8 May 2019).

[9]   Texts identified as TCP phase II will not be publicly available until 2020; see 'EEBO-TCP: Early English Books Online' Text Creation Partnership, http://www.textcreationpartnership.org/tcp-eebo/ (accessed 8 May 2019).

[10]   Michael Witmore describes the process of creating EM1080 as follows: 'We assembled the corpus by drawing 40 texts at random from 27 decades within the corpus, beginning with the decade 1530–9 and ending with 1790-9. Texts under 500 words in length were excluded from selection. We knew that this selection could not be truly random, since the TCP project selected texts for transcription that it felt would be of interest to scholars. [...] We did want to frustrate the natural urge to pick texts we knew and liked: that would limit the kind of lexical and generic variation we want to study'; see 'Visualizing English Print, 1530 –1800: The Corpus, Tag Sets, and Topics', Wine Dark Sea: https://web.archive.org/web/20150327202652/http://winedarksea.org/?p=1770 (accessed 8 May 2019).

Table 12.1. Corpora used and referred to in this chapter

Expanded Early Modern Drama to 1700 (includes Early Modern Drama to 1642)	Produced by VEP, re-normalized by the authors. Contains all dramatic texts in print up to 1700	ED1700: 1,244 plays ED1642: 680 plays
Early Modern 1080	Produced by VEP, re-normalized by the authors. Contains 40 TCP Texts per decade from 1530–1799	EM1080: 1,080 texts, diverse genres
Text Creation Partnership Resampled	Produced by the authors from TCP. Random sample of TCP texts, resampled and re-normalized	TCP-R: 5,272 texts, diverse genres

in folios. In electronic form, they were large files containing multiple plays rather than smaller files consisting of single works, a state that reflected these texts' original mode of circulation, but is not consistent with VEP's handling of non-restricted folio plays. To ensure these plays could be included as individual works in our searches, we have followed VEP's practice of making them into single files. Doing so required reproducing, to the best of our ability, the VEP algorithm for extracting individual works from collections, and then applying it to transcriptions of the printed volumes available to TCP partner institutions at the University of Michigan's EEBO-TCP interface.[11] The preparation of our corpora was complete after one final step: although the VEP text processing algorithms standardize spelling in their simple text files, we found after an examination of the normalization dictionaries that the pattern-matching we desired would require some additional normalizations to capture a wider range of variant spellings of 'soldier' and the diverse syntax of 'to be' forms in early modern English.[12]

We conducted our searches for characters claiming to be (or claiming others to be) soldiers using regular expressions, a method for describing text patterns to a text processing engine. This process entailed the generation of a list of abstract syntactic forms that our assertions could take. We opted to look exclusively at forms of identity expression that emphasize the simple state of being as opposed to forms with adjectival emphasis. Accordingly, our patterns include 'I am a soldier' and variations of it with respect to tense, mood,

---

[11]   The interface is available at https://quod.lib.umich.edu/e/eebogroup/.
[12]   For a fuller account of our process and emendations, see 'Stative Identity Assertions', http://dx.doi.org/10.17613/M6WV4B (accessed 8 May 2019).

number and gender, but not constructions that indicate a *kind* or degree of soldier. We are not concerned with instances in which a character claims (or is claimed) to be a 'good' soldier (nor, an 'old', 'fresh' or 'common' one, for that matter). Such patterns are informative in their own right, but because their function is as much evaluation as identification, they are also more likely to tell us something about a specific character than what it means to be a soldier generally. We have also ruled out constructions that begin with the phrase 'A soldier is' or 'Soldiers are' on similar grounds: phrases that take 'soldier' or 'soldiers' as the subject rather than the *subject complement* are too often followed by adjectives to be useful for the queries we intend.

In initial tests of these expressions, we were able to observe an apparent correlation of claims to being a soldier with being a 'gentleman' in many iterations. This discovery led us to set up additional scripts to search for constructions linking 'soldier' with a variety of other categories of person-hood, including courtiers, scholars and lawyers, and various types of trades. With two primary sets of search patterns in place, we compiled the outputs from both the ED1700 corpus and the TCP-R sample along with relevant metadata from VEP, such as author, title, decade of writing and printing, and – for drama – date of first performance.

Our first task in analyzing our results was to compare the number and frequency of matches in ED1700 with printed texts in EEBO-TCP generally in order to establish the range of occurrences that may result from sampling error. We estimated the rate at which assertions match across EEBO via the TCP-R sample and applied this rate to the ED1700 by decade to generate an expected number of works containing the identity assertions. As Figures 12.1 and 12.2 demonstrate, we observed in ED1700 a significantly higher number of works with these identity assertions and aggregate assertions per decade than would be predicted by the estimated rates for EEBO-TCP overall.[13]

The minimum departure from expected number of works is in the decade from 1580–9, during which the number of matching works predicted by the overall EEBO-TCP rates was approximately 2, but, in fact, ED1700 contains 6 works featuring a match. The peak departure from expectation is in the decade from 1610–19, in which we would predict 11 matching works but instead observe 35; this number constitutes 31 per cent of the 113 dramatic works in ED1700 that were printed in that decade. A similar pattern can be seen in the overall number of identity assertions in ED1700 for each decade (Figure 12.2), and, in every decade from 1580–1699, ED1700 significantly exceeds the

---

[13] In our comparisons between corpora, we use VEP's 'decade' metadata, based on proposed dates of writing, for all works in ED1700; this date, we think, is preferable to date of publication and performance, since plays were published sometimes much later than they were composed, and performance dates are unknown or non-applicable for some plays. Decades for TCP-R are determined from the date of printing listed in EEBO-TCP.

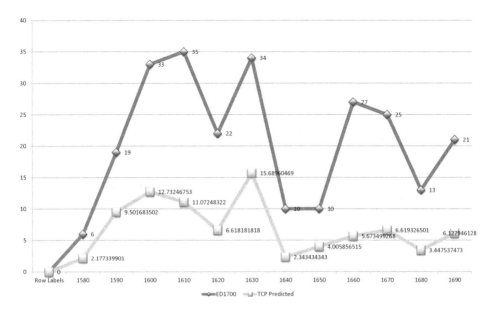

Figure 12.1. Observed vs predicted works asserting soldier identity by decade of composition

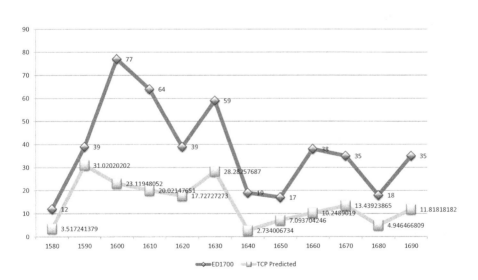

Figure 12.2. Observed vs predicted identity assertions by decade of composition

expected number of assertions and works containing them. In short, phrases such as 'I am a soldier' and 'he is a soldier' are significantly more frequent in plays than in other texts, and this distinction is borne out in every decade between 1580 and 1699.

To be sure, the presence of matches in the TCP-R demonstrates that our expression patterns are not exclusive to drama; the TCP-R sample's densest works for identity assertions represent a range of genres. Still, the titles in the top percentile in numbers of matches are telling: they include Richard Hakluyt's *The Principal Navigations, Traffics, and Voyages* (1599), which contains 26 matches, and Shakespeare's 1623 folio, which contains 25. Also included in this percentile are Ben Jonson's 1616 folio and Samuel Purchas's *Purchas His Pilgrimes* (1625), each with 13 matches, and the latter very closely related to Hakluyt's *Navigations*. Titles in the next percentile each had 9 matches, including Robert Barret's *The Theorike and Practike of Moderne Warres* (1598) and Urian Oakes's sermon *The Unconquerable, All-Conquering, and More-Then-Conquering Souldier* (1692), but also Thomas Dekker's *The Second Part of the Honest Whore* (1605/ 1630).[14] The number of matches in TCP-R, a representative sample of the texts circulating in print broadly during the period, never gets close to the number of matches of the texts we see in the corpus of plays; moreover, as we see in TCP-R's highest counts, many of the texts with matches in the general print corpus are themselves plays.

The printed texts that survive from this period cannot tell us everything we might want to know about how these assertions worked in performance, and we have no specific evidence that explains *why* they appear in drama more frequently than in other genres. On one hand, it should not surprise us to find that, at a time prior to the emergence of the novel, identity assertions appear most often in works built almost exclusively around dialogue; such assertions required, after all, a speaker who can make the utterance and another person, whether that person's presence is diegetic or in an audience, to witness the claim.[15] On the other hand, the frequency with which they appear in dramatic texts compared to printed works overall indicates that plays were more than merely adequate platforms for soldiers to identify themselves or be identified by others. The simple fact of this frequency and the data supporting it is reason enough to eschew further speculation about the merits of drama for these forms and instead focus on the concrete features of the matches we compiled.

---

[14] While our main concern is highlighting the extent to which these assertions constitute a dramatic phenomenon, we would also like to point out the imperialist nature of the non-dramatic works that contain them. Even Oakes's camp sermon mentioned here, touted on the title page as delivered in New England, is engaged in colonial enterprise.

[15] It is perhaps worth noting that the non-dramatic military treatise (by Barret) featuring the most matches is also a dialogue.

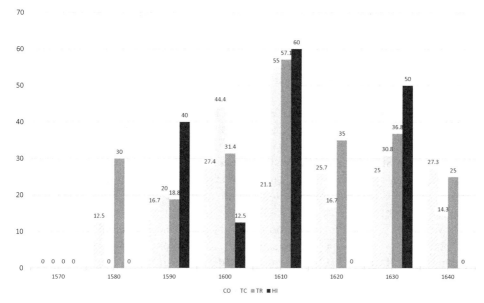

Figure 12.3. Percentage with assertions by genre and decade
(Key: comedy; tragicomedy; tragedy; history)

Through metadata provided by VEP, we can describe these matches in terms of the generic status of the plays in which they appear, the ascribed authors of those plays, as well as the decades within which the plays were composed.[16] We are also able to use this metadata to remove texts with probable dates of composition after 1642 from our match list. This smaller subset of plays and matches, which we will refer to as ED1642, is the basis for the remainder of our claims and comparisons. It contains 680 works out of the total 1,244 in ED1700. Our searches of these 680 works produced 329 unique iterations of stative identity assertions in a total of 174 distinct works from ED1642. Approximately one quarter of the total plays in the corpus feature expressions of martial identity in forms matching our queries.

Looking only at the data on genre in aggregate, one might be tempted to regard the identity assertions we are studying as a comic phenomenon; most of the assertions are in comedies. However, a more careful read of the metadata points towards the opposite conclusion: the prevalence of comedy in our matches is a function of the greater number of surviving comedies, and the phenomenon of interest adheres more strongly to other genres (Figure 12.3).

[16] See 'Metadata', The Visualizing English Print Project. http://graphics.cs.wisc.edu/WP/vep/metadata/ (accessed 8 May 2019); and Beth Ralston and Jonathan Hope, 'Expanded Drama to 1700'. http://vep.cs.wisc.edu/VEPCorporaRelease/Readmes/READMEforExpandedDrama1700corpus.pdf (accessed 8 May 2019).

While 66 of the 265 comedies in ED1642 (24.9 per cent) contain one or more of these assertions, the proportions of histories (14 of 43, 32.6 per cent), tragicomedies (29 of 80, 36.3 per cent), and tragedies (52 of 142, 36.6 per cent) are noticeably greater than of comedies.[17] Cross-tabulating the genre of matching texts against their dates of composition reveals even greater disparity in certain decades.

Some of this disparity may be explained by known trends in genre production – for instance, we might account for the preponderance of matches in history plays in the 1590s this way (not to mention the number of matches in works by Shakespeare). Even so, the percentage of histories containing matches in the 1590s, and the percentages of tragicomedies and tragedies from 1600–39, are sufficiently high as to warrant further consideration in other parts of this chapter.

With respect to authorship, among the 175 plays that contained matches, a total of 10 works containing 15 assertions are of anonymous or unknown authorship. Of works that have been assigned authors in VEP metadata, John Fletcher is at the top with the most matches and the most works with matches in plays for which he is credited as the sole-author or a collaborator.[18] These figures and those for the additional 9 dramatists with the highest number of matches are featured in Figure 12.4, which also includes data on the total number of works that are included in ED1642 for each playwright.

We find a few things noteworthy here: first, our list of matches includes a total of five works by Ben Jonson, the only playwright here to identify as a soldier himself on occasion; in works containing these matches, he has a higher ratio of matches (3.2) per work than all the other dramatists in the top ten, including Fletcher (3.05). The works containing matches by Jonson are, however, only a small percentage of the total works by him in the corpus (5 out of 48, or 10.4 per cent). Fletcher, by contrast, has matches in 40 per cent of his works (20 out of 50). We assume readers will register the absence of a third canonical playwright who wrote enough about soldiers to warrant a

---

[17] Although our searches included masques, interludes, entertainments and dialogues, we have excluded them from our charts in order to focus on the major genres in which our matches appear; masques and related forms account for only 13 of the total works in our sample.

[18] On Fletcher's interest in soldiers: Eugene M. Waith, 'Mad Lovers, Vainglorious Soldiers', *Research Opportunities in Renaissance Drama* 27 (1984), 13–19; and Vimala C. Pasupathi, 'Furious Soldiers and Mad Lovers: Fletcherian Plots and *The History of Cardenio*', *The Creation and Re-creation of Cardenio: Performing Shakespeare, Transforming Cervantes*, ed. Gary Taylor and Terri Bourus (New York, 2013), pp. 83–94, 'Shakespeare, Fletcher, and the "The Gain O' the Martialist"', *Shakespeare* 7.5 (2011), 296–308, 'The King's Privates: Sex and the Soldier's Place in John Fletcher's *The Humorous Lieutenant* (ca. 1618)', *Research Opportunities in Medieval and Renaissance Drama* 47 (2008), 25–50.

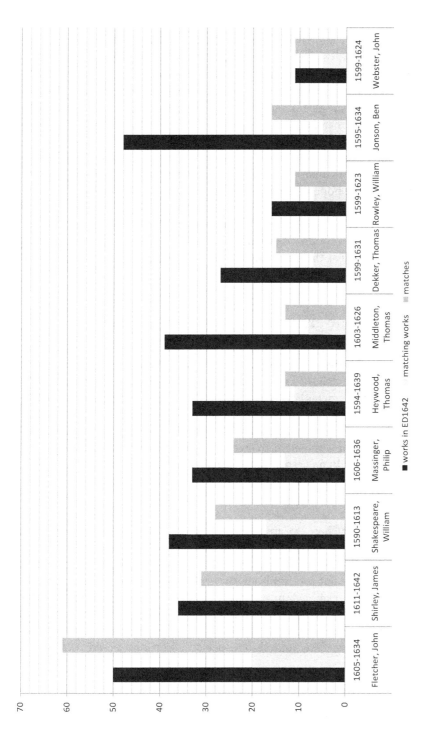

Figure 12.4. Top 10 ED1642 authors by identity assertion

monograph devoted to them.[19] Relative to other playwrights, Christopher Marlowe used very few constructions that follow our specified pattern, though the number of raw matches for the playwright of *Tamburlaine* (3 in 2 works) must be further contextualized with his foreshortened career and the resulting small number of total plays (7) in ED1642 associated with him. His data provide an interesting contrast with the prolific and enduring James Shirley, identified with 31 matches dispersed over 18 plays, exactly half of the works by him in the full drama corpus.

We could certainly spend additional time and space contemplating the relationship between matches and particular playwrights' investment in soldiers' identities, and we hope that others will find the above information generative of new queries. For our purposes, it is necessary to leave such matters to future work and we will turn instead to the grammar and mechanics of our matches. In the next section we discuss elements such as grammatical person, number and mood, as well as the implications of these features' concentrations within specific genres.

The grammar of a soldier's identity

The great majority of those identifying (or being identified) as soldiers are male characters. The complementary subjects of these assertions are female characters in 8 matches, though the status of this identity is, in most cases, rooted in a joke, a metaphorical comparison, or an allusion to deception. Perhaps unsurprisingly, women and soldiers are held up in opposition in some of our matches ('Why man, art thou a soldier and do talk/ Of womanish pity and compassion?'; 'For women are no soldiers; be not nice', 'Behold me in my Sex, I am no Soldier'). In one especially telling instance, female characters who are disguised as Amazons make the case that they 'Are Soldiers too' more convincing by chastising their male audience for 'turn[ing their] Camp into/ A soft Receipt of Ladies'.

Of the 329 matches, 122 are uttered in the firstperson (I/ we); 117 are in the third-person (he/she/they), and 90 in the second person (you/ thou/ you all). From these numbers, we can think in broad terms about the discursive contexts in which our assertions appear based on what these forms generally imply about the relationship between the soldier invoked and the speaker. We would expect third-person assertions to establish the martial identity of a person or persons who are not immediate participants in a given conversation. Conversely, first- and second-person assertions would establish or

[19]   Alan Shepard, *Marlowe's Soldiers: Rhetorics of Masculinity in the Age of the Armada* (Aldershot, 2002). See also Nina Taunton, *1590s Drama and Militarism: Portrayals of War in Marlowe, Chapman and Shakespeare's Henry V* (Farnham, 2001).

highlight relationships between the subject of the utterance and other characters through direct exchange. We can see from the sum of instances of first and
second person that the latter type of interaction is at work in more than half
(64 per cent) of our matches.

Breaking down the counts of grammatical person further by way of the
four most-represented genres in our match list, we learn the following: in history plays, identity claims more often take the form of first- and third-person
claims than second-person claims; there are twice the number of third-person
claims than first-person claims, with 16 and 8 matches, respectively. In comedies, first- and third-person constructions were roughly equal, constituting 55
and 56 utterances, respectively, and 30 in the second-person. In tragedies, the
matches in first and second person were about even, with 28 and 29 utterances
respectively, and there were more instances of claims in the third person (35). In
tragicomedy, the number of first- and second-person assertions were close to
equal, at 25 and 23, respectively, and only 6 instances were in the third person.
Overall, 35.9 per cent of our total matches are third-person utterances and
27.4 per cent are second-person; compared to matches in other genres, then,
tragicomedies feature a relatively high number of second-person utterances
and a particularly low number of third-person assertions.[20] Much more often
than not, soldiers' identities in tragicomedy are constructed in social contexts
in which the soldier or soldiers in question are typically present and take an
active role in defining their relationship to that form of personhood. Tragedies
and histories, by contrast, feature more instances in which these assertions
were made *about* a character in the third person than were made *by* characters
in the first and secondperson. From the latter observation, we can infer these
genres' proclivity for scenarios in which a soldier's identity is something to be
taken up by other characters for evaluation or gossip.

Only 62 out of the 329 matches use plural pronouns and nouns. Though
a few instances with singular forms imply that the identity is shared with
others in a conversation – for instance, 'I am no stranger, but (like you) a
Soldier' – in the great majority of these cases, the utterance confers on the
soldier a state of relative distinction from others. Twenty-seven (43.5 per cent)
of these plural forms appear in tragic plays; tragedy has the most first- and
second-person plural assertions and is tied with comedy (which outnumbers
tragedy in our match list and in the ED1642 corpus as a whole) for the most
third-person plural assertions. Tragedies contain 28 per cent of the assertions
and are 31.7 per cent of the matching works; however, 43.5 per cent of the plural

---

[20]   One of the few third-person instances actually does the work of a second-person construction, since it is part of a larger declaration in which a character addresses another in
second person before referring to him immediately thereafter in the third: 'O Melintus,
you must not wish it; Melintus can bravely suffer, he is a Soldier'.

subjects are in tragic works, and constitute half (48.6 per cent) the plural first- and second-person subjects in total. These findings are compelling in part because much of the scholarship on soldiers (and tragic soldiers in particular) has drawn attention to their isolation from others and from 'civilian' society. Our data suggest that scenarios in which soldiers are described or describe themselves as part of a collective occur more often in tragedy than in other genres, though without additional enquiries into whether or not the speaker in question is the protagonist in each tragedy, it is difficult to know the full significance of this result. Regardless, these plural forms of identity assertions, and their relative paucity, raise questions about the degree to which soldiers experience and express the sense of 'corporateness' that D.J.B Trim describes as a feature of professional (military) identity. To what extent do our 62 plural iterations convey 'a feeling among group members that they constitute a sub-culture distinct from the rest of society'?[21] How many of these matches entail self-proclaimed soldiers acknowledging shared ties with other soldiers, and how many feature speakers who are *not* soldiers projecting a collective identity and sense of solidarity onto groups of soldiers?

On their own, stative expressions are insufficient data for determining whether soldiers in drama see themselves in the terms of fraternal camaraderie that Shakespeare's Henry V projects onto his men on St Crispin's Day. Still, our dataset allows us to make some observations about our plural matches and their implications. Roughly half of the instances in the third person (26) are statements that define soldiers' identities in the abstract; as such, they attribute qualities to the category of soldier without attributing qualities to concrete relationships among or between soldiers. Even in the iterations that refer to specific people, the appeals we see do not project a sense of martial community so much as promote qualities or entitlements that individual soldiers are assumed to have ('In them I trust: for they are Soldiers'; 'give their Graves the rites that do belong To Soldiers/ They were Soldiers both'). The same appears to be true of the 8 instances of second-person plural iterations ('you are Soldiers and Men of Honour'), and also in most of the 28 first-person assertions ('We are soldiers, and not used to complement'). Only in a few cases do these utterances invoke shared experiences in military enterprise in order to link two or more characters' fates and future actions together: 'Fabricio, we two have been soldiers'; 'remember we are Soldiers/ As well as Courtiers, lets cast off this dissembling'; and 'We shall rule the world, we that are soldiers'. In claims such as these, we can detect at least some degree of collective thinking, though they do not rise to the level of Trim's description of a 'mythology and

---

[21]   D.J.B. Trim, 'Introduction', *The Chivalric Ethos and the Development of Military Professionalism*, ed. D.J.B Trim (Leiden, 2003), p. 7.

culture of a particular social body' that conditions 'how its members view their activities characteristic to their profession'.[22]

In addition to 'corporateness', our matches can offer clues into contemporary perceptions of the permanence (or lack thereof) of a soldier's status, another basic criterion Trim cites as constitutive of military professionalism. Along these lines, it is interesting to note that 246 of the iterations in our results are simple present-tense formulations. The present tense is also linked to, or implied, in several additional forms: 16 instances are in present perfect, 10 in present progressive, and 12 take infinitive forms. In aggregate, these present forms entail over 86 per cent of the assertions and demonstrate that most plays with matches are concerned with characters who 'are' soldiers at the precise moment in which the utterance occurs. This moment, it should be noted, takes place in a variety of settings. 'Being' a soldier does not require that one 'is' engaged in warfare or battle-field acts. It seems clear that, more often than not, the subject of the assertion is *not* in the field, where a discussion of that identity would be, in most cases, unnecessary.

While the 32 instances relayed in the past tense suggest that there might be limitations upon the period in which a person can claim to be a soldier, the 15 iterations relayed in the present progressive convey the sense that being a soldier in the past has lasting effects on the present ('I have been/ A soldier, and perhaps am apt to anger', and 'We have bin Soldiers, and we cannot weep'). Forms of the past tense (simple past and past perfect) occur in a relatively narrow band of matches in tragedies and comedies, but are especially rare (3) in tragicomedies.[23] As with the frequency of first- and second-person utterances, the infrequency of past tense forms hints at the exceptional immediacy that characterizes soldiers' identity claims in tragicomedy.

Finally, only 13 matches are phrased in future tense, and of these, nearly half (6) are metaphorical, 3 are invoked about women, and 2 are negations in which characters declare they will *not* be a soldier. These constructions, and more so the lack of future constructions that genuinely convey a person who will be a soldier, suggest that a person's assumption of the identity was something that could not be predicted or planned. It is also the case, however, that subjunctive forms did, in some matches, suggest future-oriented thinking, and we were able to find 35 additional statements about prospective identity in unrefined searches that looked for other verbs. Preliminary searches for 'to make', 'to

---

[22]   Trim, 'Introduction', p. 10.

[23]   Assertions in tenses other than the present appear in the following percentages within generic categories: 14.2 per cent of the matches in comedy are past or future tense; 14.1 per cent in tragedies; 18.5 per cent in histories; and 9.2 per cent tragicomedies. Matches in the past tenses alone have a similar pattern: 9.9 per cent, 10.8 per cent, 14.8 per cent and 5.5 per cent respectively. Because there are so few history plays in our match list, we have not commented on them here.

become', 'to play', and 'to turn' allowed us to find 38 references indicating transitional states of the identity, and additional research that builds on our preliminary assessments may determine these verbs to grapple substantively with characters' intentions to become. In a cursory analysis of these matches, we found the future tense to be similarly rare; the tenses in a large majority are forms of the past or present ('I am turned soldier'; 'that fellow was not made a Soldier') or subjunctive forms ('Mr Secretary might have let Jacques play the soldier, He has a black patch').

The essential soldier

Thus far, we have mentioned the characteristics associated with identity claims only in passing. Having covered the most basic grammar of these iterations, however, we can now look more closely at how these constructions embed attributes associated with martial identity and consider the particular qualities that soldiers in plays are supposed to have. The aforementioned 'black patch' aside, these qualities will be unsurprising to readers of the present volume, but they are worth rehearsing, if only in brief. In the same moments that characters identify or are identified as soldiers, we learn that soldiers are people who bear arms and are experienced and valiant in battle. They are plain-speaking and plain-dealing, such that others must be careful when speaking with them ('Take heed what you say Sir, he is a Soldier'). Soldiers are also well-travelled in the identity assertions, though this worldliness is at times fabricated (as we discuss in our conclusion) or, if genuine, has made them weary or hard-hearted ('As have been Soldiers bred, whose eyes inured to slaughter'). As many of our instances demonstrate, they are also often maimed or wounded ('thou art a Soldier, and thy wound-plow'd face/ Has every furrow filled') as well as impoverished. These qualities evoke sympathy in those that witness them and lay claim to the identity in some cases ('As you are Soldiers truly valiant, I honor you, as poor, I pity'; 'Be kind to him he is a soldier'); in others, they are condemned for related (but more negative) qualities. They are aggressive and volatile ('Take heed what you say Sir, he is a Soldier./ If you cross him, he'll blow you up with Gunpowder'), and, in the *miles gloriosus* tradition, prone to bragging, swearing, drinking and whoring.[24]

In this chapter, we are less interested in the characteristics themselves than we are the ways in which a particular grammatical structure embeds them. While we are not surprised to find references to soldiers' bravery, conviction, and the moral code with which they conduct themselves in these assertions, we find it noteworthy that 33 (10 per cent) of our matches take the form of

---

[24] On the *miles gloriosus* tradition, see McKeown's chapter above.

abstractions, and several of these rely on double negative constructions. With claims such as 'He is not a Soldier that does fear any dou[b]t'; 'For you he is no soldier dares not fight' and 'there is no soldier but has a piece of [a conscience], tho it be full of holes', we see appeals not only to these attributes, but also the notion that these attributes are understood to be shared. The same is true of the 43 matches (12.7 per cent) that take the form of vows or oaths. regardless of whether characters make vows based on their own identities as soldiers ('I am not guilty, as I am a Soldier') or whether other characters appeal to soldiers on those grounds ('Will you now answer me as y'are a Soldier'; 'Then, as you are a Soldier, take it, and protect it'; 'Touch not the Princess, as you are a soldier'). With few exceptions, these constructions offer the tacit sense that a claim to be a soldier is a claim for being trustworthy. Howsoever these statements might be qualified, they convey a *de facto* equation of conduct in the field and camp with honest-dealing outside of them. Even a conscience 'full of holes' can imply a soldier's persevering (if metonymically wounded) honour, a constant in the face of constant danger and strife.

We also find 9 matches among this set in which vows are buttressed by the addition of a second identity. Constructions such as 'as he is a Soldier and a Knight Cornelius vows to be a friend to Spain' and 'he is a Gentleman and a Soldier, he will not hurt you' suggest that in some cases, a soldier's virtue is doubly reliable, a function of occupying not one, but *two* honorable states. The same function is at work in an additional 10 instances that are not vows but similarly establish persons as both soldiers and members of the nobility. Constituting 20 iterations, we can see an allusion to the affinity Trim and others note between early modern warfare and the traditional or feudal role of the aristocracy. Our data suggests that characters reinforce this connection in dramatic works, but also that playwrights treated it as suspect.

These matches with claims to dual identity are part of a broader phenomenon that we can detect when we assess stative constructions about soldiers in aggregate: we see numerous examples that suggest a great deal of variability within the conditions that allow a character to identify as a soldier and that also call into question the prospect that this identity is all-encompassing or static. Indeed, there are several iterations of stative expressions that suggest soldiers can be something 'other than' or in addition to soldiers even *while* they identify as such. Some of these other categories of personhood are not ones that we would expect to be mutually exclusive. It makes sense that a person who identified as a soldier could also be named a 'Roman', a 'father' or a 'friend'; although playwrights are often at pains to depict soldiers as misogynists and inept suitors, a sizeable number of matches (59, or about 18 per cent) invite audiences to imagine (if not admit) them as 'lovers'.

Yet even the dually occupied positions unsurprising in the single iteration are significant in aggregate: we see by them that the persons who are described or describe themselves as being soldiers – but never are they a monolith. As one character in our matches puts it, one might 'be a Soldier, a Scholar, and every thing'. Some of the categories of personhood linked to soldiers in our matches are surprising with respect to Jorgensen's pioneering scholarship as well as characters like Hotspur, supposed, with respect to 'military rules' and 'humors of blood' to be 'the mark and glass, copy and book/ That fashion'd others'.[25] In these formulations, the soldier stands in opposition to lawyers, courtiers, poets and scholars; collectively (and in somewhat unexpected ways), our matches give the lie to them.[26]

Of the 9 identity assertions making claims about courtiers and soldiers, 3 set up courtiers and soldiers as distinct in sense and sensibility; for example, in one a character says 'I am a Soldier Sir,/ Least part of Courtier', and contrasts his speech in the identity of the former with the latter's 'smooth oil' and 'present flattery'. When a character muses over the person who would be capable of making a particularly soft and comfortable bed, he posits, 'A was no soldier sure, nor no scholar,/ And yet a might be ve[r]y well a Courtier'. And of course, the courtier who approaches Hotspur earns his ire by claiming 'He would himself have been a Soldier' if it were not 'but for these vile Gunnes'. Six of the courtier assertions, however, suggest that those categories are not separate or incompatible; several (3) make clear that a person is or could be both ('you, that are a courtier as a soldier'; 'He can be Courtier and a Soldier'; 'remember, he is a Courtier, and a Soldier'). In fact, among 121 constructions listing 'soldier' along with other types of personhood in stative expressions, these alternate identity categories are *distinguished* from 'soldier' only 38 times. The identities for which the distinction is drawn more than once include merchant (4 times in 3 works), courtier, lover and orator (all contrasted in 3 works), gentleman (contrasted in 2, but linked in 20), and woman and rogue (both contrasted in 2).

Lawyers are compared in only one of our matches. In this rather amusing iteration, the playwright suggests their respective abilities to shift in a crisis, establishing loose morals and resourcefulness as mutually associated traits: a soldier tells us 'in this vacation time am forced to do like Lawyers; when suites do not make them, they make suites: because the wars will not maintain me, I maintain the wars'. We find similar bases of alignment in instances wherein soldiers are compared to scholars. When one character asks of a man 'Is he a Scholar, or a Soldier?', we are encouraged to see practitioners of what are usually understood as very different kinds of action as being distinguished from

---

[25]   William Shakespeare, *2 Henry IV*, 2.3.30–2; cited here from *The Riverside Shakespeare*.
[26]   See Jorgensen, *Shakespeare's Military World*, p. 230, for instance, who argues '[The military profession] not only found itself temperamentally opposed to courtiers, scholars and lawyers, but boasted of this fact'. On connections between soldiers and scholars, see also the chapters above by Woodcock, O'Mahony and Hiscock.

one another, but, because of their mutually associated leanness and poverty, they might not be *distinguishable* to observers. Eight other matches in this subset emphasize their shared homosociality (they both make poor lovers) and the fact that their tongues are more often known for their sharpness than their eloquence. In 3 of these matches ('as I am a scholar, as I am a soldier'; 'I am both a Soldier, and a Scholar'; 'you know I am a Scholar,/ And part a Soldier'; 'I am a scholar, as I am a soldier') characters lay claim to both identities. Further challenging general pronouncements that 'Scholars prove ill Soldiers' are matches informing us that 'Thou art no Soldier unless a Scholar,/ Nor thou a Scholar unless a Soldier' and exhorting 'Let every Scholar be a Soldiers friend'.[27] The play in which this last example features – Robert Wilson's *The Cobblers Prophecy* (1594) – even claims that the man who embodies both identities 'is a complete man'. All told, the soldier is compared to the scholar more often than any other identity excepting the gentleman.

These data demonstrate that 'soldier' and many other types of identity categories might exist in dynamic relation instead of strictly in opposition to another. It is also the case, however, that plays paint a rather complicated picture of these relationships when we look more closely at individual iterations. In one of our matches, an officer laments, 'Faith I could wish I had been any thing/ Rather then what I am, a Soldier', an expression that circumscribes the martial self as *essentially* martial – and therein fixed. In the longer passage containing the match, this captain compares his own unmoored self during peacetime to 'A Carriere, or a Cobler', enviable figures because 'their trades/ Are and shall be a constant way of life/ While men send cheeses up, or wear out buskins'. Here, he uses both present and future-oriented constructions to describe 'their trades', labour structured by membership in livery companies and kept active by supply and demand. Although he continues to describe himself as a soldier in the present tense, he admits that his own labour and service are not in demand; thus, it is not a soldier's personhood that lacks constancy so much as the external world. To use Trim's phrasing, we can see in this passage a 'distinctive self-conceptualisation' but also an understanding of the absence of a permanent and 'discrete occupational structure'.[28]

Along these lines, it seems noteworthy that only 4 identity assertion matches contain the word 'profession' or 'trade' in the context of their utterance; whereas the conditions defining the working conditions of artisans and

---

[27] In a separate search for non-stative constructions that feature soldiers and scholars together, we found multiple iterations of the sentiment that 'Scholars prove ill Soldiers' and vice versa'. On the typical dichotomy in early modern literature: Anthony Ellis, *Old Age, Masculinity, and Early Modern Drama: Comic Elders on the Italian and Shakespearean Stage* (New York, 2016), p. 157; and Jorgensen, *Shakespeare's Military World*, pp. 231–98.

[28] Trim, 'Introduction', pp. 7, 9–10.

labourers were established and regulated by statute, the pre-professional soldier's status was the subject of ad hoc proclamations and contingent upon less predictable factors. As one particularly compelling match formulates the state of contingency wrought by war and peace: 'Sometimes a figure, sometimes a cipher, as the State has occasion to cast up her accounts: I am a soldier'.

Despite the distancing from trades we see in the match with the plaintive captain, this 'sometimes' nature of soldiering means that we also see soldiers identify themselves *as*, rather than *in opposition to*, members of livery companies.[29] The soldiers in one of our matches begin as citizen merchants in the play that features their identity expressions; in a match from another work, a shoemaker tells others that his impressed journeyman is not only 'a brother of our trade' but 'a tall soldier' and 'a good workman'. Some characters who define themselves via soldiering *and* trades abandon one identity for the other once they return from the former: 'I was a Miller my self before I was a soldier'; 'after I have done being a soldier, I Will to cobling'. In one additional example not in our match list, military service emboldens one livery man to keep both identities and also lay claim to another one: 'I am plain honest Miles the Miller of Ruddington;/ a gentleman and a Soldier'.[30]

Of the 20 matches that establish characters as both a soldier and gentleman, 7 occur within the same play, Jonson's *Every Man in his Humour* (1598), a play well known for its boastful Captain Bobadilla. Master Stephen, the country gull, is so taken by the captain's swearing that he laments his own lack of swearing authority as a function of *not* being a soldier himself. When his companion reminds him that his 'name is entered in the artillery garden', he is cautiously optimistic: 'that is true,/ Cousin, may I swear, as I am a soldier, by that?' His companion's rejoinder, 'Oh yes, that you may. It is all you have for your money' affirms that he may indeed *swear* by the identity – but also calls into question its legitimacy.

These instances are not the only affirmation of an identity claim in our search results that is essentially a negation of one. If we simply take a match from Fletcher's *Tragedy of Valentinian* (c.1601–14) at face value, we might interpret 'You were a souldier, Chilax' as a simple statement. Chilax's reply, 'Yes, I musterd/ But never saw the Enemy' is at once confirmation that the identity belongs to him and commentary that implies it does not. While attendance at

---

[29] As Patricia A. Cahill, *Unto the Breach: Martial Formations, Historical Trauma, and the Early Modern Stage* (Oxford, 2008), p. 82, notes, 'the cobbler and the shoemaker' figure in 1590s drama 'as the prototypical pressed man'.

[30] William Sampson, *The Vow Breaker. Or, The Faire Maide of Clifton* (London, 1636), sig. J4. This instance was not in our match list because it did not meet the parameters we set for words in between the stative verb and the words 'soldier' and 'gentleman'. Although we suspect that its front-loading of other identity categories makes it atypical, we also allow that there may be other matches along these lines that our searches missed.

musters might entail some displays of weaponry and drilling, Chilax's claim to the identity would be suspect for early modern audiences – who would not be surprised when he proves a coward later in the play. They could also compare Chilax and Master Stephen's specious claims to military identity to assertions in plays that determine actions in the field and camp are essential before the name of soldier is earned. For instance, Tamburlaine tells his sons they must 'make the water mount', and 'dryfoot martch through lakes and pooles,/ Deep rivers, havens, creekes, and little seas', as well as 'make a Fortress in the raging waves'; only 'when this is done', he insists, 'then are ye soldiers'.

This rather high (but less suspect) bar leads us to a significant number of matches in which playwrights and their characters implicitly or explicitly contest the identity in statements about themselves or others. These matches are concentrated in plays performed between 1600 and 1639, and appear most particularly in the period between 1600 and 1609, when the assertions denying the identity appear only in second or third person. Whereas first-person nega-tions entail a character distancing themselves from soldiers to avoid associa-tions with negatively perceived actions or attributes ('I was never a Soldier in my life', 'A Soldier, no I scorn to be so poor'), second- and third- person nega-tions typically entail derision against those without experience in the field. Our searches turned up 42 stative assertions in which figures deny that they themselves or others are soldiers ('You are no soldier. Desert in these days?'), with 13 in the first decade of the seventeenth century. Many of these statements ('so many are Captains that are no Soldiers'; 'He a Soldier? a Pander, a Dog that will lick up six pence'; 'You are no Soldiers, but a pack of rogues') are directed at counterfeiters: characters who, like those described in Elizabethan procla-mations, had not 'served at all in the wars, but take that cloak and color to be the more pitied, and do live about the city by begging and in disorderly man-ner'.[31] A total of 31 of the claims to the identity in our 329 matches in ED1642 are made by or about characters who are either known to audiences from the outset as pretenders in disguise or are revealed to be mere actors subsequent to making their claims. These matches are clustered in dramas performed between 1604 and 1642 and, like contested claims, are particularly frequent in plays performed in the five-year period subsequent to James I's accession and his signing of the Treaty of London.

Less than 10 per cent (12/122) of the first-person claims are made by counter-feiters, and similar proportions are in effect for third-person (11/117) and sec-ond-person (8/90) claims. However, counterfeits comprise 17.8 per cent (10/56) of the third-person assertions in comedy, 23.3 per cent (7/30) second-person

---

[31] 'Ordering Examination of Vagrant Soldiers – 28 February 1592', *Tudor Royal Proclama-tions: Volume 3. The Late Tudors, 1558–1603*, ed. Paul Hughes and James F. Larkin (New Haven, 1969), p. 105.

assertions, and over a third, 37 per cent (10/27) of the first-person assertions. All of the false assertions occur in comedies except for 4; of these remaining 27, over half (15) are in plays performed between 1604 and 1609. The aggregation of counterfeits in comedy, and particularly in the first person, suggest the plays could both acknowledge the serious problem of vagrancy in peacetime and exploit it as an opportunity for light-hearted meta-performance.

But more germane to the question of identity is the net effect of these 31 false assertions and the additional matches with negations on audience perceptions. Across our works, playwrights exhibit little tolerance for such claims; however comic their approach, they enforce rather strict notions of who can lay legitimate claim to the identity. This general rigidity may be a way to signal sympathy for returning soldiers who were unemployed or owed arrears; it may also be an acknowledgement of the power of a good performance and the difficulty of identifying genuine service in an unknown person solely by visual cues. With respect to the latter, it seems worth noting that 25 of our matches are phrased directly or effectively as questions, with roughly half of the questions consisting of one character asking another 'Are you a soldier?' outright. In another 13 matches, characters use the word 'seem' or the phrase 'I think' to describe others' status as soldiers, indicating not only a sense of doubt but also anxiety about the indeterminacy of a soldier's authenticity. These matches alone cannot tell us the particular conditions that underpin this apparent regulatory desire on the part of dramatists, but it is tempting to see them as evidence of an underlying desire to project an absolute state onto what was obviously shifting and unfixed. Strident refusals to accept a character's stative assertions do the work of instructing audiences how to respond to persons 'that pretend to have served as soldiers', those that Elizabeth charged with enacting 'great outrages […] upon her Highness' good and loving subjects', but stop short of advocating more permanent structures that would ensure continuous employment and consistent pay.[32]

Without these structures, career soldiers with significant experience in campaigns abroad could muster complaints as effectively as other masterless men with more tenuous or false claims to the identity. Perhaps the most striking element of the period's drama is that even the claims of those who were not 'truly' soldiers had something to impress upon spectators. The match we cite earlier, from Dekker's c.1605 *The Honest Whore, Part Two*, wherein a soldier admits he is 'sometimes a figure, sometimes a cipher' until 'the state has occasion to cast up her accounts', is uttered by a character that civic authorities denounce as 'no soldier'. At the playhouse, a character could be a liar and a fraud and still tell the truth.

---

[32]   'Placing vagrant Soldiers under Martial Law' – 13 November 1589', *Tudor Royal Proclamations*, ed. Hughes and Larkin, p. 46.

Conclusion

The initial findings presented here demonstrate the relevance of drama to the study of military identities in the early modern period. By mining electronic corpora, we were able to determine the presence of stative constructions identifying soldiers in 25 per cent of dramatic works performed and printed between 1550 and 1642. With hundreds of iterations of these constructions, we could not only confirm these compact forms were a legitimate phenomenon in plays, but also make broad generalizations about their grammatical features and their concentration within specific genres and decades. Our commentary on them offers corroboration and nuance to previous scholarship on soldiers in literary studies, while also, in some important ways, confirming the limitations of purely algorithmic analysis. Indeed, the data provide compelling answers to some questions, but they cannot alone provide satisfactory explanations for verbal phenomena. Moreover, while humans may not always recognize a counterfeiter, they are still better at interpreting the social dynamics of identity assertions than a computer. Ultimately, we do not see these limitations as a problem so much as a reason to bring multiple methods to bear on electronic dramatic corpora. What we find with digital methods can refine and be refined by historicist approaches. We hope what we have laid out here will be the foundation for new research into the dynamic relationships of military identity to genre, narrative and existing professional and occupational classes.

Afterword: The Way Ahead

MATTHEW WOODCOCK

One of the aims of this collection has been to stimulate subsequent discussion and investigation of military identity and to foster further interdisciplinary studies of early modern warfare and its representation. One is aware, of course, that there are many other directions in which subsequent studies of military identity can be taken and that the geographic, temporal and thematic coverage could be expanded further. Although several of the chapters above discuss the significance of differences between English, Old English and Irish military identities, analysis could equally focus on the fighting men of Spain, France, the Low Countries, Italy, Germany, Sweden, or the Ottoman Empire, as well as expand beyond Europe to consider those in the New World or Japan.[1] Nearer to home, although Robert Monro was mentioned in the introduction above, it would be instructive to further examine the distinct military identity of Scottish soldiery and, indeed, both the Scots and Irish regiments active in continental Europe in the sixteenth and seventeenth centuries, as part of a wider British military identity.[2] The study of regimental identity obviously complements the broader explorations of collective military identity discussed in the essays above. It can also be set alongside other forms of martial communities found in this period in, say, garrisons (Calais, the Dublin Pale) or military societies (for example, the London Artillery and Military Garden companies).[3]

[1]   Geoffrey Parker's studies on the early modern military revolution endeavour to contextualise European technological and tactical developments alongside those of Africa, and the Middle and Far East; see *The Military Revolution: Military Innovation and the Rise of the West, 1500–1800* (Cambridge, 1996); 'The Limits to Revolution in Military Affairs: Maurice of Nassau, the Battle of Nieuwpoort (1600), and the Legacy', *Journal of Military History* 71.2 (2007), 331–72. Space precludes a full bibliography of extant scholarship on soldiery and martial cultures viewed on an international scale.

[2]   Andrew Mackillop and Steve Murdoch, ed., *Fighting for Identity: Scottish Military Experience, c.1550–1900* (Cambridge, 1996); Gráinne Henry, *The Irish Military Community in Spanish Flanders, 1586–1621* (Dublin, 1992).

[3]   On the military identity of garrison troops: David Grummitt, *The Calais Garrison: War and Military Service in England, 1436–1558* (Woodbridge, 2008). On martial communities based around the Artillery and Military Gardens (and their imitators): Barbara Donagan, *War in England, 1642–1649* (Oxford, 2008), pp. 55–9; David Lawrence, *The Complete Soldier: Military Books and Military Culture in Early Stuart England, 1603–1645*

It is easy to envisage subsequent studies that look beyond this collection's temporal scope and address military identity, citizen soldiery and martial professionalism during the Civil Wars of the 1640s, and beyond. In terms of specific stereotypes of military identities adopted and ascribed in this later period, it would be productive to discuss the figure of the cavalier in relation to that of the swordsman mentioned above, and to consider certain exemplars of this type, such as Prince Rupert of Bohemia or Sir William Cavendish.[4] To broaden the thematic range of future studies of our core concept, following the lead of Andreani and Hadfield's essay, attention needs to be given to non-combatants who formed part of what Lynn calls a 'campaign community', be it, say, as military surveyors or surgeons.[5] We might consider too how conceptions of military identity explored in this volume relate to naval identity, recognising that there was frequent overlap in personnel between land- and sea-based forces (as exemplified by figures such as Sir Humphrey Gilbert, Sir Walter Ralegh or Sir Arthur Chichester).[6]

Keith Thomas included a coda to his chapter on martial prowess in *The Ends of Life* addressing royal military identities, a topic which could easily be expanded upon.[7] Spanning Henry VIII through to George II, it reminds us of both James I's martial experience before he came to England and the representations of Queen Elizabeth I at Tilbury in 1588 that depicted her armoured and mounted on horseback. The latter construction of military identity has been scrutinised before,[8] but it leads us on to an area that still needs to be examined in far greater detail: the relationship of early modern women to military identity, and to perceptions of associations explored in this volume between masculinity and martial selfhood.[9] How are we to reconcile

---

(Leiden, 2009), pp. 216–23. O'Mahony's essay above (Chapter 3) discusses a seventeenth-century literary evocation of Norwich's Military Yard.

[4] See above pp. 9–10. For a relatively recent treatment of the cavalier figure: John Stubbs, *Reprobates: Cavaliers of the English Civil War* (London, 2011). See also Jerome de Groot, *Royalist Identities* (London, 2004).

[5] John A. Lynn II, *Women, Armies, and Warfare in Early Modern Europe* (Cambridge, 2008), pp. 33–6.

[6] Ian Roy, 'The Profession of Arms', *The Professions in Early Modern England*, ed. Wilfrid Prest (London, 1987), pp. 188–9.

[7] Keith Thomas, *The Ends of Life: Roads to Fulfilment in Early Modern England* (Oxford, 2009), pp. 76–7.

[8] Susan Frye, 'The Myth of Elizabeth at Tilbury', *SCJ* 23.1 (1992), 95–114.

[9] See Barton C. Hacker, 'Women and Military Institutions in Early Modern Europe: A Reconnaissance', *Signs: Journal of Women in Culture and Society* 6.4 (1981), 643–71; Katharine A. Walker, 'The Military Activities of Charlotte de la Tremouille, Countess of Derby, During the Civil War and Interregnum', *Northern History* 38.1 (2001), 47–64; Lynn, *Women*. The majority of evidence used by Lynn (and the few other scholars who have scouted this field) tends to be from continental and/ or later seventeenth-century sources.

literary traditions and archetypes of the martial heroine – which was explored and evolved during this period in the works of Ariosto, Tasso and Spenser – with the reductive, formulaic associations made by early modern martialists concerning gender and military identities?[10]

Finally, one could readily extend the evidence-base beyond the predominantly archival, textual and literary evidence used by the contributors above and examine representations of early modern military identity found in contemporary music, portraiture and statuary – including that armoured representation of William Herbert, third earl of Pembroke, with whom this book began.[11]

[10]   See, however, Gerry Milligan, *Moral Combat: Women, Gender, and War in Italian Renaissance Literature* (Toronto, 2018).

[11]   See, for example, Roy Strong, *Van Dyck: Charles I on Horseback* (New York, 1972), pp. 45–57; J.R. Hale, *Artists and Warfare in the Renaissance* (New Haven, 1990); Paul E.J. Hammer, *The Polarisation of Elizabethan Politics: The Political Career of Robert Devereux, 2nd Earl of Essex, 1585–1597* (Cambridge, 1999), pp. 206–11 (on martial depictions of Essex); Kate van Ordern, *Music, Discipline, and Arms in Early Modern France* (Chicago, 2005); Christopher R. Wilson, *Shakespeare's Musical Imagery* (London, 2011), pp. 62–80. Tait's essay above (Chapter 9) discusses wounding and military portraiture with reference to Sir Henry Danvers.

BIBLIOGRAPHY

Primary

Manuscripts

Brotherton Library, Leeds

MS Yorks 1
MS Yorks 2

Cambridge

CUL, MS Kk.I.15
CUL, MS Mm.i.43
Fitzwilliam Museum, MS CFM 13
St John's College, MS 548 (U.26)

Chatsworth House, Derbyshire

Cork MS 1/31–32

Dublin

NAI, Lodge MSS
NLI, GO MS 64
NLI, GO MS 79
NLI, MS 11,044
NLI, MS 43,144/4/92
NLI, MS 43,283/3
TCD, MS 566
TCD, MS 842

Folger Shakespeare Library, Washington, DC

MS V.b.303

Hatfield House, Hertfordshire

Cecil Papers

Koninklijke Bibliotheek, The Hague
MS 132.G.27

London
BL, Add. MS 4819
BL, Add. MS 28326
BL, Add. MS 33743
BL, Cotton Titus MS B XII
BL, Harleian MS 35
BL, Harleian MS 6390
BL, Harleian MS 6993
BL, Lansdowne MS 84
Lambeth Palace, MS 612
TNA, PC 2/17(2)/63
TNA, PROB 11/119/37
TNA, SP 12 State papers, domestic, Elizabeth I
TNA, SP 63 State papers, Ireland, Elizabeth I to George III

Oxford
Bodleian, Carte MS 30
Bodleian, MS Clarendon 34
Bodleian, MS Fairfax 30
Bodleian, MS Fairfax 40
Codrington Library, All Souls College, MS 129

Printed

Agrippa, Henry Cornelius, *Of the Vanitie and Uncertaintie of Artes and Sciences* (London, 1569).

Andrewes, Lancelot, *Sermons* (London, 1629).

Annals of the Kingdom of Ireland by the Four Masters, ed. and trans. John O'Donovan, 3rd edn. 7 vols. (Dublin, 1990).

Anon., *Alarum for London* (London, 1602).

Anon., *Englands Wedding Garment: Or A Preparation to King James his Royall Coronation* (London, 1603).

Anon., *A Pleasant Song, made by a souldier whose bringing up had bin dainty, and partly fed by those affections of his unbridled youth, is now beaten with his owne rod, and therefore tearmeth this his repentance, the fall of his folly: to the tune of Calino* (London, 1614).

Anon., *The Advice of that Worthy Commander, Sir Ed. Harwood, Collonel [...] Also a relation of his Life and Death* (London, 1642).

Anstey, Henry, ed., *Epistolae academicae Oxon.*, 2 vols. (Oxford, 1898).

Arber, Edward, ed., *A Transcript of the Registers of the Company of Stationers of London, 1554–1640*, 5 vols. (London, 1875–94).

Archives ou correspondance inédite de la maison d'Orange-Nassau, ed. G. Groen van Prinsterer, 2nd ser. (Utrecht, 1856–61).

Ariosto, Lodovico, *Orlando Furioso in English Heroical Verse*, trans. John Harington (London, 1591).

Bacon, Francis, *A Declaration of the Practices and Treasons Attempted and Committed by Robert Late Earl of Essex and His Complices* (London, 1601).

——, *A Briefe Discourse, Touching the Happie Vnion of the Kingdomes of England, and Scotland* (London, 1603).

——, 'An Advertisement Touching an Holy War', *The Works of Francis Bacon*, 10 vols. (London, 1861), 3: 467–92.

Barnes, Barnabe, *Four Books of Offices Enabling Private Persons for the Special Service of all Good Princes and Policies* (London, 1606).

Barret, Robert, *The Theorike and Practike of Moderne Warres* (London, 1598).

Barry, Gerrat, *A Discourse of Military Discipline* (Brussels, 1634).

Barwick, Humfrey, *A Breefe Discourse, Concerning the Force and Effect of all Manuall Weapons of Fire and the Disability of the Long Bowe or Archery* (1592).

Becon, Thomas, *The New Pollecye of Warre* (London, 1542).

Birch, Thomas, *Memoirs of the Reign of Queen Elizabeth, from the Year 1581 Till Her Death* (London, 1754).

Blakemore Evans, G., ed., *The Riverside Shakespeare*, 2nd edn (Boston, 1997).

Blandy, William, *The Castle, or Picture of Pollicy* (London, 1581).

Brancaccio, Giulio Cesare, *Il Brancatio, della vera disciplina, et arte militare sopra i Commentari di Giulio Cesare* (Venice, 1582).

Brinsley, John, *A Consolation for our Grammar Schooles* (London, 1622).

Caesar, *The Gallic War*, trans. H.J. Edwards (London, 1917).

——, *The Civil War*, trans. Cynthia Damon (London, 2016).

Calendar of the Carew Manuscripts, 6 vols. (London, 1867–73).

Camden, William, *Britain, or A Chorographicall Description of the Most Flourishing Kingdomes, England, Scotland, and Ireland*, part 2, trans. Philemon Holland (London, 1610).

——, *Annales, The True and Royal History of Elizabeth, Queene of England*, trans. Abraham Darcie (London, 1625).

Castiglione, Baldesar, *The Book of the Courtier*, trans. G. Bull (Harmondsworth, 1967).

——, *The Book of the Courtier*, trans. Thomas Hoby, ed. Virginia Cox (New York, 1994).

Charles, Amy, ed., *The Shorter Poems of Ralph Knevet: A Critical Edition* (Ohio, 1966).

Churchyard, Thomas, *Churchyardes Chippes* (London, 1575).

——, *A Generall Rehearsall of Warres* (London, 1579).

Cicero, *Brutus*, trans. G.L. Hendrickson (Cambridge, MA, 1971).

——, *On Obligations*, trans. P.G. Walsh (Oxford, 2000).

Coningsby, Sir Thomas, *Journal of the Siege of Rouen, 1591*, ed. John Gough Nicholls (London, 1847).

Cotton, Henry, *Fasti Ecclesiae Hibernicae*, 5 vols. (Dublin, 1848–78).

Craigie, J., ed., *The Poems of James VI of Scotland*, 2 vols. (Edinburgh, 1955–8).

Crosse, William, *A Generall Historie of the Netherlands* (London, 1627).

Cruso, John, *Militarie Instructions* (London, 1632).

Curtis, Edmund, ed., *Calendar of Ormond Deeds*, 6 vols. (Dublin, 1937–43).

Davies, Sir John, *A Discoverie of the True Causes of Why Ireland was Never Entirely Subdued* (Dublin, 1612).

Dawtry, Nicholas, 'A Booke of Questions and Answars Concerning the Wars or Rebellions of the Kingdome of Irelande', ed. Hiram Morgan, *Analecta Hibernica* 36 (1995), 79–132.

Dekker, Thomas, *The Belman of London* (1608).

Derricke, John, *The Image of Irelande* (London, 1581).

D.F.R. de M., *An Answer to the Untruthes Published in Spaine, in Glorie of their Supposed Victorie against our English Navie*, trans. J[ames] L[ea] (London, 1589).

Digges, Leonard and Thomas, *An Arithmeticall Warlike Treatise Named Stratioticos* (London, 1590).

Drant, Thomas, *Horace, His Arte of Poetrie, Pistles and Satyrs Englished, and to the Earle of Ormounte [...] Addressed* (London, 1567).

[Dudley, Robert], *Correspondence of Robert Dudley, Earl of Leycester, During his Government of the Low Countries, in the Years 1585 and 1586*, ed. John Bruce (London, 1844).

Dymmock, John, *A Treatise of Ireland*, ed. Richard Butler (Dublin, 1842).

Edmondes, Clement, *Observations upon the Five First Bookes of Caesars Commentaries* (London, 1600).

——, *Observations upon Caesars Commentaries Setting Forth the Practise of ye Art Militarie in the Time of the Romaine Empire for the Better Direction of our Moderne Warrs* (London, 1604).

——, *Observations upon Caesars Commentaries* (London, 1609).

Edwards, David, ed., *Campaign Journals of the Elizabethan Irish Wars* (Dublin, 2014).

Edwards, David, and Keith Sidwell, eds. and trans., *Dermot O'Meara's Ormonius (1615): The Tipperary Hero* (Turnhout, 2011).

Erck, J.C., ed., *A Repertory of the Inrolments of the Patent Rolls of Chancery in Ireland, James I* (Dublin, 1846).

Eusebius, *The Auncient Ecclesiasticall Histories of the First Six Hundred Yeares after Christ [...] Translated out of the Greeke Tongue by Meredith Hanmer* (London, 1577).

The Expedition of Sir John Norris and Sir Francis Drake to Spain and Portugal, 1589, ed. R.B. Wernham (Aldershot, 1988).

Falkiner, C. Litton, 'William Farmer's Chronicles of Ireland from 1594–1613', *English Historical Review* 22.85 (1907).

Fenne, Thomas, *Fennes Frutes* (London, 1590).

Galloway, David, ed., *Records of Early English Drama: Norwich: 1540–1642* (Toronto, 1984).

Gascoigne, George, *The Spoyle of Antwerpe* (London, 1576).

——, *Complete Works*, ed. John W. Cunliffe. 2 vols. (Cambridge, 1907–10).

Gates, Geoffrey, *The Defence of Militarie Profession* (London, 1579).

Gawdy, Philip, *Letters of Philip Gawdy of West Harling, Norfolk, and of London to Various Members of his Family 1579–1616*, ed. Isaac Herbert Jeayes (London, 1906).

Gerrard, William, 'Lord Chancellor Gerrard's Notes of his Report on Ireland', *Analecta Hibernica* 2 (1931), 93–291.

Golding, Arthur, *The Eyght Bookes of Caius Julius Caesar* (London, 1565).

Googe, Barnabe, *The Shippe of Safegarde (1569)*, ed. Simon McKeown and William E. Sheidley (Tempe, AZ, 2001).

Greene, Robert, and Thomas Lodge, *A Looking Glass for London and England* (London, 1594).

Grimeston, Edward, *A Generall History of the Netherlands* (London, 1608).

Grosart, Alexander B., ed., *The Lismore Papers,* 10 vols. (London, 1886–8).

Hadfield, Andrew, and Willy Maley, eds., *Edmund Spenser: A View of the State of Ireland. From the First Printed Edition (1633)* (Oxford, 1997).

Harington, Sir John, *Nugae Antiquae,* 2 vols. (London, 1769).

——, *The Letters and Epigrams of Sir John Harington,* ed. Norman E. McClure (London, 1930).

Haslop, Henry, *News Out of the Coast of Spain* (London, 1587).

Hayward, Sir John, *A Sermon of the Stewards Danger Preached at Paules Crosse the 15. of August by John Hayward* (London, 1602).

[Herbert, Edward], *The Life of Edward, First Lord Herbert of Cherbury,* ed. J.M. Shuttleworth (London, 1976).

Heylyn, Peter, *The Historie of that most Famous Saint and Souldier of Christ Jesus, St George of Cappadochia* (London, 1633).

HMC, *Calendar of the Manuscripts of the Marquis of Salisbury,* 24 vols. (London, 1883–1976).

HMC, *Calendar of the Shrewsbury and Talbot Papers,* 2 vols. (London, 1966–71).

HMC, *Haliday MSS* (London, 1897).

HMC, *Hastings MSS,* 4 vols. (London, 1928–47).

HMC, *Report on the Manuscripts of Lord De L'Isle and Dudley,* 3 vols. (London, 1925–36).

HMC, *Rutland MSS,* 4 vols. (London, 1888–1905).

Hogan, Edmund, *Words of Comfort to Persecuted Catholics* (Dublin, 1881).

Horsfall, Nicholas, *Virgil, Aeneid 6, A Commentary* (Berlin, 2013).

Hughes, Paul, and James F. Larkin, ed., *Tudor Royal Proclamations: Volume 3. The Late Tudors, 1558–1603* (New Haven, 1969).

Hutchinson, F.E., ed., *The Works of George Herbert* (London, 1945).

Irish Fiants of the Tudor Sovereigns, ed. K.W. Nicholls, 4 vols. (Dublin, 1994).

[James VI and I], *Basilikon Doron, Or His Majesties Instructions to his Dearest Sonne, Henrie the Prince* (London, 1603).

Johnson, George W., ed., *The Fairfax Correspondence: Memoirs of the Reign of Charles I,* 2 vols. (London, 1848).

Jonson, Ben, *Ben Jonson,* ed. C.H. Herford, Percy Simpson and Evelyn Simpson, 11 vols. (Oxford, 1925–52).

Jordan, W.K., ed., *The Chronicle and Political Papers of Edward VI* (London, 1966).

Kinney, Arthur, ed., *Rogues, Vagabonds, and Sturdy Beggars* (Amherst, MA, 1990).

Knevet, Ralph, *The Shorter Poems of Ralph Knevet: A Critical Edition* ed. Amy Charles (Ohio, 1966).

——, *A Supplement of the Faery Queene,* ed. Christopher Burlinson and Andrew Zurcher (Manchester, 2015).

Knowler, William, ed., *The Earl of Strafforde's Letters and Dispatches,* 2 vols. (London, 1739).

Kuin, Roger, ed., *The Correspondence of Sir Philip Sidney,* 2 vols. (Oxford, 2012).

Leech, Jeremy, *The Trayne Souldier: A Sermon Preached Before the Societie of the Captaynes and Gentle men* (London, 1619).

Letters and Papers, Henry VIII, 21 vols. in 33 (London, 1862–1910).

Lombard, Peter, *The Irish War of Defence 1598–1600: Extracts from the De Hibernia Insula Commentaries*, ed. and trans. M.J. Byrne (Cork, 1930).

Machiavelli, Niccolò, *The Art of War*, trans. Ellis Farneworth (New York, 1965).

——, *The Chief Works and Others*, trans. Allan Gilbert, 3 vols. (Durham, NC, 1965).

Major, Philip, ed., *The Writings of Thomas, Third Lord Fairfax* (Manchester, forthcoming).

Maley, Willy, ed., 'The Supplication of the Blood of the English Most Lamentably Murdered in Ireland, Cryeng Out of the Yearth for Revenge (1598)', *Analecta Hibernica* 36 (1995), 3–91.

Manningham, John, *Diary*, ed. Robert Parker Sorlien (Hanover, NH, 1976).

Markham, Francis, *Five Decades of Epistles of Warre* (London, 1622).

Markham, Francis, *The Booke of Honour. Or, Five Decads of Epistles of Honour* (London, 1625).

Markham, Gervase, *Honour in his Perfection* (London, 1624).

McIlwain, C.H., ed., *The Political Works of James I* (Cambridge, MA, 1918).

Middleton, Thomas, *The Collected Works*, ed. Gary Taylor et al. (Oxford, 2007).

Monluc, Blaise de, *The Habsburg–Valois Wars and the French Wars of Religion*, ed. Ian Roy (London, 1971).

Montaigne, Michel de, *The Complete Essays*, trans. M.A. Screech (London, 2003).

Morgan, Victor et al., eds., *The Papers of Nathaniel Bacon of Stiffkey: Volume IV, 1596–1602* (Norwich, 2000).

Moryson, Fynes, 'The Rebellion of Hugh Earle of Tyrone', *An Itinerary*, Part II (London, 1617).

——, *An Itinerary*, part two (Glasgow, 1907–8).

——, *The Irish sections of Fynes Moryson's unpublished Itinerary*, ed. Graham Kew (Dublin, 1998).

Nashe, Thomas, *Works*, ed. R.B. McKerrow, rev. F.P. Wilson. 5 vols. (Oxford, 1966).

Naunton, Sir Robert, *Fragmenta Regalia, or Observations on Queen Elizabeth, Her Times and Favorites*, ed. J.S. Cerovski (Washington, DC, 1985).

Neville, Alexander, *Norfolkes Furies*, trans. Richard Woods (London, 1615).

Norden, John, *The Mirror of Honor* (London, 1597).

Palmer, Thomas, *An Essay of the Meanes How to Make Our Travailes, into Forraine Countries, the More Profitable and Honourable* (London, 1606).

Peacham, Henry, *The Compleat Gentleman* (London, 1622).

Perrot, Sir James, *The Chronicle of Ireland 1584–1608*, ed. Herbert Wood (Dublin, 1933).

Plutarch, *Roman Lives*, trans. Robin Waterfield (Oxford, 1999).

Randall, David, ed., *English Military News Pamphlets, 1513–1637* (Tempe, AZ, 2011).

Register of the Privy Council of Scotland, ed. R.K. Hannay et al. 14 vols. (Edinburgh, 1898).

Relations politiques des Pays-Bas et de l'Angleterre sous le regne de Philippe II, ed. Kervyn de Lettenhove, 11 vols. (Brussels, 1882–1900).

Rich, Barnabe, *A Right Excelent and Pleasaunt Dialogue, betwene Mercury and an English Souldier* (London, 1574).

——, *Allarme to England* (London, 1578).

——, *Riche His Farewell to Military Profession* (London, 1581).

——, *A Path-way to Military Practise* (London, 1587).

——, *Roome for a Gentleman, or the Second Part of Faultes* (London, 1609).

——, *A Short Survey of Ireland* (London, 1609).

Rogers, Francis, *A Sermon Preached on September the 20 1632. At the Funerall of William Proud* (London, 1633).

Rymer, Thomas, *A Short View of Tragedy* (1693; rpt. London, 1971).

Sampson, William, *The Vow Breaker. Or, The faire maide of Clifton* (London, 1636).

Schofield, Bertram, ed., *The Knyvett Letters, 1620–44* (Norwich, 1949).

Scott, Thomas, *Robert Earle Essex his Ghost, Sent from Elizian* (London, 1624).

Segar, William, *Honor, Military and Civil* (London, 1602).

Shakespeare, William, *Othello*, ed. Kenneth Muir (New York, 1968).

——, *The Riverside Shakespeare*, ed. G. Blakemore Evans, 2nd edn (Boston, 1997).

Sidney, Henry, *A Viceroy's Vindication? Sir Henry Sidney's Memoir of Service in Ireland, 1556–78*, ed. Ciaran Brady (Cork, 2002).

Smith, Thomas, *The Commonwealth of England and the Maner of its Government* (London, 1589).

Smythe, John, *Certain Discourses [...] Concerning the Formes and Effects of Divers Sorts of Weapons, and Other Verie Important Matters Militarie* (London, 1590).

Somers Collection of Tracts, 2nd edn, ed. Walter Scott, 13 vols. (London, 1809–15).

Spenser, Edmund, *The Faerie Queene*, ed. A.C. Hamilton (London, 2001).

Stafford, Thomas, *Pacata Hibernia: Ireland Appeased and Reduced; or, A History of the Late Wares of Ireland, Especially in the Province of Munster under the Command of Sir George Carew*, ed. Standish O'Grady, 2 vols. (London, 1896).

Styward, Thomas, *The Pathwaie to Martiall Discipline* (London, 1581).

T.D., *A Briefe Report of the Militarie Services Done in the Low Countries, by the Erle of Leicester: Written by One that Served in a Good Place There* (London, 1587).

Tourneur, Cyril, *A Funerall Poeme Upon the Death of the Most Worthie and True Souldier, Sir Francis Vere, Knight* (London, 1609).

Trigge, Francis, *To the Kings Most Excellent Majestie* (London, 1604).

Trussell, Thomas, *The Souldier Pleading his Own Cause* (London, 1619).

Vegetius, *Epitome of Military Science*, trans. N.P. Milner (Liverpool, 1993).

Vere, Sir Francis, *The Commentaries of Sir Francis Vere* (Cambridge, 1657).

Ware, James, *Two Histories of Ireland: The One by Edmund Campion, the Other by Meredith Hanmer* (Dublin, 1633).

Whetstone, George, *The Honorable Reputation of a Soldier* (London, 1585).

Willet, Andrew, *Synopsis Papismi* (London, 1592).

[William of Orange], *Correspondance de Guillaume le Taciturne, Prince d'Orange*, ed. L.P. Gachard, 6 vols. (Brussels, 1854).

Williams, Sir Roger, *Works*, ed. John X. Evans (Oxford, 1972).

Williams, Sarah, ed., *Letters Written by John Chamberlain* (London, 1838).

Wither, George, *An A.B.C. for Laymen* (London, 1585).

Wright, Thomas, *Queen Elizabeth and Her Times, A Series of Original Letters*, 2 vols. (London, 1838).

——, ed., *The Historical Works of Giraldus Cambrensis* (London, 1905).

Secondary

Printed

Adams, John Henry, 'Assembling Radigund and Artegall: Gender Identities in *The Faerie Queene*', *Early Modern Literary Studies* 18.1 (2015).

Adams, Simon, 'Spain or the Netherlands? The Dilemmas of Early Stuart Foreign Policy', *Before the English Civil War: Essays on Early Stuart Politics and Government*, ed. Howard Tomlinson (London, 1983), pp. 79–101.

Adamson, John, 'Chivalry and Political Culture in Caroline England', *Culture and Politics in Early Stuart England*, ed. Kevin Sharpe and Peter Lake (London, 1994), pp. 161–98.

Adamson, Sylvia, 'Questions of Identity in Renaissance Drama: New Historicism Meets Old Philology', *Shakespeare Quarterly* 61 (2010), 56–77.

Adcock, F.E., *Caesar as Man of Letters* (Cambridge, 1956).

Alford, Stephen, *Kingship and Politics in the Reign of Edward VI* (Cambridge, 2002).

Allmand, Christopher, *The De Re Militari of Vegetius: The Reception, Transmission and Legacy of a Roman Text in The Middle Ages* (Cambridge, 2011).

Andreani, Angela, 'Between Theological Debate and Political Subversion: Meredith Hanmer's Confutation of Edmund Campion's Letter to the Privy Council', *Aevum* 3 (2016), 557–73.

——, 'Meredith Hanmer's Career in the Church of England, c.1570–1590', *Explorations in Renaissance Culture* 44.1 (2018), 47–72.

Arnold, Thomas F., 'War in Sixteenth-Century Europe: Revolution and Renaissance', *European Warfare 1453–1815*, ed. Jeremy Black (New York, 1999), pp. 23–44.

Asmussen, Susan Dwyer, '"The part of a Christian man": The Cultural Politics of Manhood in Early Modern England', *Political Culture and Cultural Politics in Early Modern England*, ed. Asmussen and Mark A. Kishlansky (Manchester, 1995), pp. 213–33.

Atherton, Ian, *Ambition and Failure in Stuart England: The Career of John, first Viscount Scudamore* (Manchester, 1999).

Austen, Gillian, *George Gascoigne* (Cambridge, 2008).

Baldo, Jonathan, 'Wars of Memory in *Henry V*', *Shakespeare Quarterly* 47 (1996), 132–59.

Baldwin, T.W., *William Shakspere's Small Latine and Lesse Greeke*, 2 vols. (Urbana, IL, 1944).

Barker, S.K., and B.M. Hosington, ed., *Renaissance Cultural Crossroads* (Leiden, 2013).

Bednarz, James P., 'Collaboration: The Shadow of Shakespeare', *Thomas Middleton in Context*, ed. Suzanne Gossett (Cambridge, 2011), pp. 211–18.

Beer, Anna, *Sir Walter Ralegh and his Readers in the Seventeenth Century* (London, 1997).

Bell, Adrian R. et al., ed., *The Soldier Experience in the Fourteenth Century* (Woodbridge, 2011).

——, et al., ed., *The Soldier in Later Medieval England* (Oxford, 2013).

Bellis, J., "'I Was Enforced to Become an Eyed Witnes": *Documenting War in Medieval and Early Modern Literature Emotions and War*, ed. S. Downes, A. Lynch and K. O' Loughlin (Palgrave, 2015), pp. 133–51.

Billows, Richard, *Julius Caesar: The Colossus of Rome* (London, 2009).

Black, Jeremy, *A Military Revolution? Military Change and European Society* (Basingstoke, 1991).

Blomefield, Francis, *An Essay towards a Topographical Study of Norfolk: History of Norwich*, ed. Charles Parkin (London, 1860).

Boddice, Rob, 'The Affective Turn: Historicizing the Emotions', *Psychology and History: Interdisciplinary Explorations*, ed. Cristian Tileagă and Jovan Byford (Cambridge, 2014), pp. 147–65.

——, 'Introduction: Hurt Feelings?', *Pain and Emotion in Modern History*, ed. Rob Boddice (Basingstoke, 2014), pp. 1–14.

Boynton, Lindsay, *The Elizabethan Militia, 1558-1638* (London, 1967).

Boys, Jayne E.E., *London's News Press and the Thirty Years War* (Woodbridge, 2011).

Bradshaw, Brendan, 'Sword, Word and Strategy in the Reformation in Ireland', *Historical Journal* 21.3 (1978), 475–502.

——, 'Nationalism and Historical Scholarship in Modern Ireland', *Irish Historical Studies* 26.104 (1989), 329–51.

Brady, Ciaran, *The Chief Governors: The Rise and Fall of Reform Government in Tudor Ireland, 1536-1588* (Cambridge, 1994).

——, 'The Captains' Games: Army and Society in Elizabethan Ireland', *A Military History of Ireland*, ed. T. Bartlett and K. Jeffery (Cambridge, 1996), pp. 149–51.

——, 'East Ulster, the MacDonalds, and the Provincial Strategies of Hugh O'Neill, Earl of Tyrone, 1585–1603', *Scotland and the Ulster Plantations*, ed. W.P. Kelly and J.R. Young (Dublin, 2009), pp. 41–61.

Breight, Curtis, *Militarism, Surveillance and Elizabethan Drama* (London, 1997).

Britland, Karen, 'A Fairy-tale Marriage: Charles I and Henrietta Maria's Romance', *The Spanish Match: Prince Charles's Journey to Madrid, 1623*, ed. Alexander Samson (Aldershot, 2006), pp. 123–38.

Broomhall, Susan, ed., *Ordering Emotions in Europe, 1100-1800* (Leiden, 2015).

Broomhall, Susan, and Jacqueline van Gent, eds., *Governing Masculinities in The Early Modern Period: Regulating Selves and Others* (London, 2011).

Burke, Peter, 'A Survey of the Popularity of Ancient Historians, 1450-1700', *History and Theory* 5 (1966), 136–40.

Burlinson, Christopher, and Andrew Zurcher, eds., *Ralph Knevet: A Supplement of the Faery Queene* (Manchester, 2015).

Busse, Beatrix, *Vocative Constructions in the Language of Shakespeare* (Philadelphia, 2006).

Butler, Judith, *Gender Trouble: Feminism and the Subversion of Identity* (rpt New York, 2006).

Cahill, Patricia, *Unto the Breach: Martial Formations, Historical Trauma, and the Early Modern Stage* (Oxford, 2008).

Cannan, Fergus, "'Hags of Hell": Late Medieval Irish Kern', *History Ireland* 19.1 (2011), 14–17.

Canning, Ruth A., *The Old English in Early Modern Ireland: The Palesmen and the Nine Years War in Ireland: An Early Modern Community, 1594–1603* (Woodbridge, 2019).

Canny, Nicholas P., 'The Ideology of English Colonialism: from Ireland to America', *William and Mary Quarterly* 30.4 (1973), 575–98.

——, 'Identity Formation in Ireland: The Emergence of the Anglo-Irish', *Colonial Identity in the Atlantic World*, ed. Nicholas Canny and Anthony Pagden (Princeton, NJ, 1989), pp. 159–212.

——, *Making Ireland British, 1580–1650* (Oxford, 2001).

Carey, Vincent, '"What pen can paint or tears atone?": Mountjoy's Scorched Earth Campaign', *The Battle of Kinsale*, ed. Hiram Morgan (Bray, 2004), pp. 205–16.

——, 'Elizabeth I and State Terror in Sixteenth-Century Ireland', *Elizabeth I and the 'Sovereign Arts': Essays in Literature, History and Culture*, ed. Donald V. Stump, Linda Shenk and Carole Levin (Temple, 2011), pp. 201–16.

Carlton, Charles, *This Seat of Mars: War and the British Isles, 1485–1746* (New Haven, 2011).

Carroll, Claire, *Circe's Cup: Cultural Transformations in Early Modern Ireland* (Cork, 2001).

Cathcart, Alison, 'The View from Scotland: The Scottish Context to the Flight of the Earls', *The Flight of the Earls*, ed. David Finnegan, Éamonn Ó Ciardha and Marie-Claire Peters (Derry, 2010), pp. 131–9.

Chaudhuri, Sukhanta, *Renaissance Pastoral and its English Developments* (New York, 1989).

Clark, Carol, 'Some Renaissance Caesars', *Companion to Julius Caesar*, ed. Griffin, pp. 356–70.

Clarke, Aidan, *The Old English in Ireland, 1625–1642* (London, 1966).

——, *The Graces, 1625–41* (Dublin, 1968).

——, 'Pacification, Plantation and the Catholic Question, 1603–23', *New History of Ireland 3: Early Modern Ireland, 1534–1691*, ed. T.W. Moody, F.X. Martin and F.J. Byrne (Oxford, 1976), pp. 187–214.

Cliffe, J.T., *The Yorkshire Gentry: From the Reformation to the Civil War* (London, 1969).

Coast, David, *News and Rumour in Jacobean England: Information, Court Politics and Diplomacy, 1618–25* (Manchester, 2014).

Cogswell, Thomas, *The Blessed Revolution: English Politics and the Coming of War, 1621–1624* (Cambridge, 1989).

Cohn, Henry J., 'Götz von Berlichingen and the Art of Military Biography', *War, Literature, and the Arts in Sixteenth-Century Europe*, ed. J.R. Mulryne and Margaret Shewring, (London, 1989), pp. 22–40.

Connor, W.J., 'The Fairfax Archives: A Study in Dispersal', *Archives* 11 (1973–4), 76–85.

Corboy, James, 'Father Christopher Holywood, S.J., 1559–1626', *Studies* 33 (1944), 543–9.

Coss, Peter, and Christopher Tyerman, ed., *Soldiers, Nobles and Gentlemen: Essays in Honour of Maurice Keen* (Woodbridge, 2009).

Covington, Sarah, *Wounds, Flesh and Metaphor in Seventeenth-Century England* (Basingstoke, 2009).

Cressy, David, 'Gender Trouble and Cross-Dressing in Early Modern England', *JBS* 35 (1996), 438–65.

Croft, Pauline, *King James* (Basingstoke, 2003).

Cruickshank, Charles G., 'Dead-Pays in the Elizabethan Army', *English Historical Review* 53.209 (1938), 93–7.

——, *Elizabeth's Army*, 2nd edn (Oxford, 1966).

Cullen, Fintan, *Visual Politics: The Representation of Ireland, 1750–1930* (Cork, 1997).

Culpepper, Jonathan, *Language and Characterisation: People in Plays and other Texts* (New York, 2001).

Cummings, R.M., *Edmund Spenser: The Critical Heritage* (London, 1995).

Cust, Richard, 'Politics and the Electorate in the 1620s', *Conflict in Early Stuart England: Studies in Religion and Politics, 1603–1642*, ed. Richard Cust and Ann Hughes (London, 1989), pp. 134–67.

——, 'Honour and Politics in Early Stuart England: The Case of Beaumont v. Hastings', *P&P* 149 (1995), 70–89.

——, 'Charles I and the Order of the Garter', *Journal of British Studies* 52.2 (2013), 343–69.

——, *Charles I and the Aristocracy, 1625–1642* (Cambridge, 2013).

Dandelet, Thomas James, *The Renaissance of Empire in Early Modern Europe* (Cambridge, 2014).

Daubeny, Charles, *Oxford Botanic Garden* (Oxford, 1853).

Davies, Jonathan, *The Tudor Art of War 1485–1603* (Bristol, 2001).

Davis, Natalie Zemon, '"Women's History" in Transition: The European Case', *Feminist Studies* 3.3/4 (1976), 83–103.

Dawson, Graham, *Soldier Heroes: British Adventure, Empire and the Imagining of Masculinities* (London, 1994).

De Groot, Jerome, *Royalist Identities* (London, 2004).

De Landtsheer, Jeanine, 'Justus Lipsius's *De Militia Romana*: Polybius Revived, or How an Ancient Historian Was Turned Into a Manual of Early Modern Warfare', *Recreating Ancient History*, ed. Karl A.E. Enenkel et al. (Leiden, 2002), pp. 101–22.

De Ornellas, Kevin, *The Horse in Early Modern English Culture: Bridled, Curbed and Tamed* (Madison, 2013).

De Somogyi, Nick, *Shakespeare's Theatre of War* (Aldershot, 1998).

Dickinson, Janet, *Court Politics and the Earl of Essex, 1589–1601* (London, 2012).

Doelman, James, '"Not as the mourning of some private fate": John Earle's Funeral Elegy on Sir John Burroughs', *ELR* 41 (2011), 485–502.

Dollimore, Jonathan, *Radical Tragedy*, 3rd edn (Basingstoke, 2004).

Donagan, Barbara, 'Halcyon Days and the Literature of War: England's Military Education before 1642', *P&P* 147 (1995), 65–100.

——, *War in England, 1642–1649* (Oxford, 2008).

Driscoll, James P., *Identity in Shakespearean Drama* (Lewisburg, 1983).

Drury, John, *Music at Midnight: The Life and Poetry of George Herbert* (London, 2014).

Dunlop, Robert, 'The Plantation of Munster, 1584–89', *English Historical Review* 3 (1888), 250–69.

Dunthorne, Hugh, *Britain and the Dutch Revolt 1560–1700* (Cambridge, 2013).

Dutton, Richard, *Mastering the Revels: The Regulation and Censorship of English Renaissance Drama* (Basingstoke, 1991).

Eales, Jacqueline, 'Anne and Thomas Fairfax, and the Vere Connection', *England's Fortress*, ed. Andrew Hopper and Philip Major (Farnham, 2014), pp. 145–68.

Easterling, Heather, *Parsing the City: Jonson, Middleton, Dekker, and City Comedy's London as Language* (London, 2007).

Edwards, David, 'The Butler Revolt of 1569', *IHS* 28.111 (1993), 228–55.

——, *The Ormond Lordship in County Kilkenny, 1515–1642: The Rise and Fall of Butler Feudal Power* (Dublin, 2003).

——, 'The Escalation of Violence in Sixteenth-Century Ireland', *Age of Atrocity: Violence and Political Conflict in Early Modern Ireland*, ed. Edwards, P. Lenihan and C. Tait (Dublin, 2007), pp. 34–78.

——, 'Securing the Jacobean Succession: The secret career of James Fullerton of Trinity College, Dublin', *The World of the Galloglass*, ed. Seán Duffy (Dublin 2007), pp. 188–219.

——, 'Political Change and Social Transformation, 1603–41', *The Cambridge History of Ireland, Vol. 2: Early Modern Ireland, 1550–1730*, ed. Jane Ohlmeyer (Cambridge, 2018), pp. 48–71.

Edwards, Peter, *Horse and Man in Early Modern England* (London, 2007).

Ellis, Anthony, *Old Age, Masculinity, and Early Modern Drama: Comic Elders on the Italian and Shakespearean Stage* (New York, 2016).

Ellis, Jim, 'Archery and Social Memory in Sixteenth-Century London', *HLQ* 79.2 (2016), 21–40.

Ellis, Steven G., *Tudor Ireland: Crown, Community and the Conflict of Cultures, 1470–1603* (Harlow, 1985).

——, *The Pale and the Far North: Government and Society in Two Early Tudor Borderlands* (Galway, 1986).

——, 'Economic Problems of the Church: Why the Reformation Failed in Ireland', *Journal of Ecclesiastical History* 41.2 (1990), 239–65.

——, *Tudor Frontiers and Noble Power: The Making of the British State.* (Oxford, 1995).

——, 'The Tudors and the Origins of the Modern Irish States: A Standing Army', *A Military History of Ireland*, ed. T. Bartlett and K. Jeffrey (Cambridge, 1997), pp. 116–35.

Eltis, David, *The Military Revolution in Sixteenth-Century Europe* (New York, 1998).

Elton, Geoffrey, 'Tudor Government: The Points of Contact. III: The Court', *TRHS*, 5th ser., 26 (1976), 211–28.

——, 'War and the English in the Reign of Henry VIII', *War, Strategy, and International Politics*, ed. Lawrence Freedman et al. (Oxford, 1991), pp. 1–17.

Evans, Robert C., *Habits of Mind: Evidence and Effects of Ben Jonson's Reading* (Lewisburg, 1995).

Everett, Barbara, '"Spanish" Othello: The Making of Shakespeare's Moor', *Shakespeare and Race*, ed. Catherine M.S. Alexander and Stanley W. Wells (Cambridge, 2000), pp. 64–81.

Faherty, Teresa J., '*Othello dell'Arte*: The Presence of *Commedia* in Shakespeare's Tragedy', *Theatre Journal* 43 (1991), 179–94.

Faini, Mario, and Maria Elena Severini, eds., *Books for Captains and Captains in Books: Shaping the Perfect Military Commander in Early Modern Europe* (Wiesbaden, 2016).

The Fairfax Library and Archive, Sales Catalogue, Sotheby's, London, 14 December 1993 (London, 1993).

Falls, Cyril, *Elizabeth's Irish Wars* (London, 1950).

Farrington, Benjamin, *The Philosophy of Francis Bacon* (Liverpool, 1964).

Ferguson, Arthur B., *The Indian Summer of English Chivalry* (Durham, NC, 1960).

——, *The Chivalric Tradition in Renaissance England* (Washington, DC, 1986).

Fichter, Andrew, *Poets Historical: Dynastic Epic in the Renaissance* (New Haven, 1992).

Fissel, Mark, *English Warfare, 1511–1642* (London, 2001).

Fletcher, Anthony, *Reform in the Provinces: The Government of Stuart England* (New Haven, 1986).

——, 'Manhood, the Male Body, Courtship and the Household in Early Modern England', *History* 84 (1999), 419–36.

——, 'Men's Dilemma: The Future of Patriarchy in England 1560–1660', *TRHS*, 6th ser., 4 (1994), 61–81.

Ford, Alan, *The Protestant Reformation in Ireland 1590–1640* (Dublin, 1997).

——, *James Ussher: Theology, History, and Politics in Early Modern Ireland and England* (Oxford, 2007)

Foucault, Michel, *Discipline and Punish: The Birth of the Prison*, trans. Alan Sheridan (Harmondsworth, 1977).

Foyster, Elizabeth A., *Manhood in Early Modern England* (London, 1999).

Frame, Robin, 'Power and Society in the Lordship of Ireland 1272–1377', *P&P* 76 (1977), 3–33.

Francisco, Timothy, *The Impact of Militarism and Social Mobility on the Construction of Masculinity in Elizabethan and Jacobean Drama* (Lewiston, 2007).

Frearson, Michael, 'The Distribution and Readership of London Corantos in the 1620s', *Serials and Their Readers 1620–1914*, ed. Robin Myers and Michael Harris (London, 1993), pp. 1–25.

Froehlich, Heather, 'Thus to make poor females mad: Finding the "Mad Woman" in Early Modern Drama', *The Pragmatics and Stylistics of Identity Construction and Characterisation*, ed. Minna Nevala et al. (Studies in Variation, Contacts and Change in English 17 (2006). E- publication series http://www.helsinki.fi/varieng/series/volumes/17/froehlich/

Frye, Susan, 'The Myth of Elizabeth at Tilbury', *SCJ* 23.1 (1992), 95–114.

Gardiner, S.R., *A History of England under the Duke of Buckingham and Charles I*, 2 vols. (London, 1975).

Geldof, Mark, 'The Pike and the Printing Press: Military Handbooks and the Gentrification of the Early Modern Military Revolution', *International Exchange in the Early Modern Book World*, ed. Matthew McLean and Sara Barker (Leiden, 2016), pp. 147–68.

Gillespie, Raymond, 'Preaching the Reformation in Early Modern Ireland', *The Oxford Handbook of the Early Modern Sermon*, ed. P. McCullough et al. (Oxford, 2011), pp. 287–93.

——, ed., *The Chapter Act Book of Christ Church Dublin 1574–1634* (Dublin, 1997).

Goldsworthy, Adrian, '"Instinctive Genius": The Depiction of Caesar the General', *Julius Caesar as Artful Reporter*, ed. K. Welch and A. Powell (Swansea, 1998), pp. 193–219.

——, *Caesar: The Life of a Colossus* (London, 2006).

Gouws, John, 'Fact and Anecdote in Fulke Greville's Account of Sidney's Last Days', *Sir Philip Sidney: 1586 and the Creation of a Legend*, ed. Jan van Dorsten et al. (Leiden, 1986), pp. 62–82.

Greg, W.W., *Pastoral Poetry and Pastoral Drama* (Oxford, 1906).

Grell, Ole Peter, *Calvinist Exiles in Tudor and Stuart England* (Aldershot, 1996).

——, 'War, Medicine and the Military Revolution', *The Healing Arts: Health, Disease and Society in Europe 1500–1800*, ed. Peter Elmer (Manchester, 2004), pp. 257–83.

Grummitt, David, *The Calais Garrison: War and Military Service in England, 1436–1558* (Woodbridge, 2008).

Gunn, Steven, David Grummitt and Hans Cools, *War, State, and Society in England and the Netherlands 1477–1559* (Oxford, 2007).

Hacker, Barton C., 'Women and Military Institutions in Early Modern Europe: A Reconnaissance', *Signs: Journal of Women in Culture and Society* 6.4 (1981), 643–71.

Hadfield, Andrew, 'Briton and Scythian: Tudor Representations of Irish Origins', *IHS* 28.112 (1993), 390–408.

——, *Shakespeare, Spenser and the Matter of Britain* (Basingstoke, 2004).

——, *Edmund Spenser: A Life* (Oxford, 2012).

——, 'War Poetry and Counsel in Early Modern Ireland', *Elizabeth I and Ireland*, ed. Valerie McGowan-Doyle and Brendan Kane (Cambridge, 2017), pp. 239–60.

Hailwood, Mark, 'Broadside Ballads and Occupational Identity in Early Modern England', *HLQ* 79.1 (2016), 187–200.

Hale, Edward E., 'Life of Sir Ralph Lane', *Archaeologia Americana* 4 (1860), 339–42.

Hale, J.R., *Renaissance War Studies* (London, 1983).

——, *War and Society in Renaissance Europe, 1450–1620* (London, 1985).

——, *Artists and Warfare in the Renaissance* (New Haven, 1990).

Hall, Bert S., Weapons *and Warfare in Renaissance Europe: Gunpowder, Technology, and Tactics* (Baltimore, 1997).

Hall, Dianne, '"Most barbarously and inhumaine maner butchered": Masculinity, Trauma, and Memory in Early Modern Ireland', *The Body in Pain in Irish Literature and Culture*, ed. F. Dillane et al. (London, 2016), pp. 39–46.

Hall, Lindsay G.H., '*Ratio* and *Romanitas* in the *Bellum Gallicum*', *Julius Caesar as Artful Reporter*, ed. Kathryn Welch and Anton Powell (Swansea, 1998), pp. 11–44.

Hammer, Paul E.J., 'Myth-Making: Politics, Propaganda and the Capture of Cadiz in 1596', *Historical Journal* 40.3 (1997), 621–42.

——, *The Polarisation of Elizabethan Politics: The Political Career of Robert Devereux, 2nd Earl of Essex, 1585–1597* (Cambridge, 1999).

——, *Elizabeth's Wars* (Basingstoke, 2003).

——, '"Base rogues" and "gentlemen of quality": The Earl of Essex's Irish knights and Royal Displeasure in 1599', *Elizabeth I and Ireland*, ed. Valerie McGowan-Doyle and Brendan Kane (Cambridge, 2014), pp. 184–208.

——, ed., *Warfare in Early Modern Europe, 1450–1660* (London, 2007).

Harari, Yuval, *Renaissance Military Memoirs: War, History and Identity, 1450–1600* (Woodbridge, 2004).

——, *The Ultimate Experience: Battlefield Revelations and the Making of Modern War Culture, 1450–2000* (Basingstoke, 2008).

Harris, Jason G., *Foreign Bodies and the Body Politic: Discourses of Social Pathology in Early Modern England* (Cambridge, 2008).

Hattaway, Michael, 'Blood is Their Argument: Men of War and Soldiers in Shakespeare and Others', *Religion, Culture and Society in Early Modern Britain*, ed. Anthony Fletcher and Peter Roberts (Cambridge, 1994), pp. 84–101.

Headlam Wells, Robin, '"Manhood and Chevalrie": *Coriolanus*, Prince Henry, and the Chivalric Revival', *RES* 51.203 (2000), 395–422.

Helgerson, Richard, *The Elizabethan Prodigals* (Berkeley, 1976).

Henry, Gráinne, *The Irish Military Community in Spanish Flanders, 1586–1621* (Dublin, 1992).

Herrup, Cynthia, '"To pluck bright honour from the pale-faced moon": Gender and Honour in the Castlehaven Story', *TRHS*, 6th ser., 6 (1996), 137–59.

——, 'The King's Two Genders', *JBS* 45 (2006), 493–510.

Hill, J. Michael, *Fire and Sword: Sorley Boy MacDonnell and the Rise of Clan Ian Mór, 1538–90* (London, 1993).

Hill, James M., *Celtic Warfare 1593–1763*, 2nd edn (Edinburgh, 2003).

Hill, Tracey, *Pageantry and Power: A Cultural History of the Early Modern Lord Mayor's Show, 1585–1639* (Manchester, 2010).

Hillyer, Richard, *Sir Philip Sidney, Cultural Icon* (New York, 2010).

Hiscock, Andrew, '"More Warlike than Politique": Shakespeare and the Theatre of War. A Critical Survey', *Shakespeare* 7 (2011), 221–47.

——, '"Achilles alter": The Heroic Lives and Afterlives of Robert Devereux, 2nd Earl of Essex', *Essex: The Cultural Impact of an Elizabethan Courtier*, ed. Annaliese Connolly and Lisa Hopkins (Manchester, 2013), pp. 101–32.

——, '"Cut my heart in sums": Community-Making and Breaking in the Prodigal Drama of Thomas Middleton', *Community-Making in Early Stuart Theatres*, ed. Roger D. Sell et al. (London, 2017), pp. 311–37.

The History of Parliament: The House of Commons 1558–1603, ed. P.W. Hasler, 3 vols. (London, 1981).

The History of Parliament: The House of Commons 1604–1629, ed. Andrew Thrush and John P. Ferris. 6 vols. (Cambridge, 2010).

Hoftijzer, Paul, 'Henry Hexham (c.1585–1650), English Soldier, Author, Translator, Lexicographer, and Cultural Mediator in the Low Countries', *Renaissance Cultural Crossroads*, ed. S.K. Barker and B.M. Hosington (Leiden, 2013), pp. 209–25.

Hope, Jonathan, *The Authorship of Shakespeare's Plays* (Cambridge, 1994).

Hopper, Andrew, '*Black Tom': Sir Thomas Fairfax and the English Revolution* (Manchester, 2007).

Hopper, Andrew, and Philip Major, eds., '*England's Fortress': New Perspectives on Thomas, Third Lord Fairfax* (Farnham, 2014).

Hudson, Geoffrey L., 'Disabled Veterans and the State in Early Modern England', *Disabled Veterans in History*, ed. David A. Gerber (Ann Arbor, 2000), pp. 117–44.

——, 'Ex-servicemen's Own Stories in Early Modern England', *Medicine, Madness and Social History: Essays in Honour of Roy Porter*, ed. Roberta Bivins and John V. Pickstone (Basingstoke, 2007), pp. 105–18.

Hunt, Arnold, *The Art of Hearing: English Preachers and their Audiences, 1590–1640* (Oxford, 2010).

Jacob, Frank, and Gilmar Visoni-Alonzo, *The Military Revolution in Early Modern Europe: A Revision* (Houndmills, 2016).

James, Mervyn, *Society, Politics and Culture: Studies in Early Modern England* (Cambridge, 1986).

Jardine, Lisa, and Anthony Grafton, '"Studied for Action": How Gabriel Harvey Read his Livy', *P&P* 129 (1990), 30–78.

Jefferies, Henry A., 'Elizabeth's Reformation in the Irish Pale', *Journal of Ecclesiastical History* 66.3 (2015), 524–42.

Jeffrey, David L., *A Dictionary of Biblical Tradition in English Literature* (Grand Rapids, 1992).

Jensen, Freyja Cox, *Reading the Roman Republic in Early Modern England* (Leiden, 2012).

Joby, Christopher, 'Classical and Early Modern Sources of the Poetry of Jan Cruso of Norwich (1592–fl.1655)', *International Journal of the Classical Tradition* 21.2 (2014), 89–120.

Johnston, Mark Albert, *Beard Fetish in Early Modern England* (Farnham, 2011).

Jorgensen, Paul, *Shakespeare's Military World* (Berkeley, 1956).

Jowett, John, 'The Pattern of Collaboration in *Timon of Athens*', *Words that Count: Early Modern Authorship*, ed. Brian Boyd (Cranbury, NJ, 2004), pp. 181–208.

Kane, Brendan, *The Politics of Honour in Britain and Ireland, 1541–1641* (Cambridge, 2010).

Keegan, John, *The Face of Battle* (Harmondsworth, 1978).

——, and Richard Holmes, *Soldiers: A History of Men in Battle* (London, 1985).

Keen, Maurice, *Chivalry* (London, 1984).

Kelly, William P., and John O'Donovan, eds., *Docwra's Derry: A Narration of Events in North-west Ulster, 1600–1604* (Belfast, 2003).

Ketton-Cremer, R.W., *Norfolk Portraits* (London, 1944).

——, *Norfolk Assembly* (London, 1957).

Kewes, Paulina, 'Julius Caesar in Jacobean England', *The Seventeenth Century* 17 (2002), 155–86.

——, 'Henry Savile's Tacitus and the Politics of Roman History in Late Elizabethan England', *HLQ* 74 (2011), 515–51.

Kiberd, Declan, 'The War Against the Past', *The Uses of the Past: Essays on Irish Culture*, ed. Audrey Stockin Eyler and Robert F. Garratt (Newark, 1988), pp. 158–90.

Kiernan, Ben, *Blood and Soil: A World History of Genocide and Extermination from Sparta to Darfur* (New Haven, 2007).

Kiernan, V.G., *The Duel in European History* (Oxford, 1988).

Kiernander, Adrian, 'A Comic Vision of *Othello*', *Re-visions of Shakespeare: Essays in Honour of Robert Ornstein*, ed. Robert Ornstein and Evelyn Gajowski (Newark, 2004), pp. 150–64.

Kishlanksy, Mark, 'Tyranny Denied: Charles I, Attorney General Heath, and the Five Knights' Case', *Historical Journal* 42.1 (1999), 53–83.

Klene, Jean, 'Othello: "A Fixed Figure for the Time of Scorn"', *Shakespeare Quarterly* 26.2 (1975), 139–50.

Knecht, Robert J., 'Military Autobiographies in Sixteenth-Century France', *War, Literature, and the Arts in Sixteenth-Century Europe*, ed. J.R. Mulryne and Margaret Shewring (London, 1989), pp. 3–21.

Knox, M., and W. Murray, ed., *The Dynamics of Military Revolution, 1300–2050* (Cambridge, 2001).

Kraus, Christina S., '*Bellum Gallicum*': *A Companion to Julius Caesar*, ed. Miriam Griffin (Oxford, 2009), pp. 157–74.

Lake, Peter, 'Anti-Popery: the Structure of a Prejudice', *Conflict in Early Stuart England: Studies in Religion and Politics 1603–1642*, ed. Richard Cust and Ann Hughes (London and New York, 1989), pp. 72–106.

Lawrence, David R., *The Complete Soldier: Military Books and Military Culture in Early Stuart England, 1603–1645* (Leiden, 2009).

——, 'Reappraising the Elizabethan and Early Stuart Soldier: Recent Historiography on Early Modern English Military Culture', *History Compass* 9 (2011), 16–33.

Lee, Wayne E., 'Indigenes as "Counterinsurgents" in the British Atlantic, 1500–1800', *Defence Studies* 10.1–2 (2010), 88–105.

——, *Barbarians and Brothers: Anglo-American Warfare, 1500–1865* (Oxford, 2011).

Lendon, J.E., 'The Rhetoric of Combat: Greek Military Theory and Roman Culture in Julius Caesar's Battle Descriptions', *Classical Antiquity* 18 (1999), 273–329.

——, 'Julius Caesar, Thinking About Battle and Foreign Relations', *Histos* 9 (2015), 9–22.

Lenihan, Pádraig, 'Conclusion: Ireland's Military Revolution(s)', *Conquest and Resistance: War in Seventeenth-Century Ireland*, ed. Pádraig Lenihan (Leiden, 2001), pp. 245–69.

Lenman, Bruce, *England's Colonial Wars: Conflicts, Empire and National Identity* (London, 2001).

Lennon, Colm, *Richard Stanihurst the Dubliner* (Blackrock, 1981).

——, *Sixteenth-Century Ireland* (Dublin, 2005).

——, 'The Parish Fraternities of County Meath', *Ríocht na Midhe* 19 (2008), 85–101.

Leonard, Amy E., 'Introduction: Attending to Early Modern Women—and Men', *Masculinities, Childhood, Violence: Attending to Early Modern Women—and Men: Proceedings of the 2006 Symposium*, ed. Amy E. Leonard and Karen L. Nelson (Newark, 2011), pp. 3–10.

Loach, Jennifer, *Edward VI* (New Haven, 2002).

Lovascio, Domenico, 'Rewriting Julius Caesar as a National Villain in Early Modern English Drama', *ELR* 47 (2017), 218–50.

Lowe, Ben, 'War and the Commonwealth in Mid-Tudor England', *SCJ* 26.2 (1990), 171–92.

Lyall, Roderick J., 'James VI and the Sixteenth-Century Cultural Crisis', *The Reign of James VI*, ed. Julian Goodare and Michael Lynch (East Linton, 2000), pp. 55–70.

Lynn II, John A., *Women, Armies, and Warfare in Early Modern Europe* (Cambridge, 2008).

MacCaffrey, Wallace T., *Elizabeth I: War and Politics, 1588–1603* (Princeton, 1992).

Macdona, Michael King, 'Thomas, 3rd Lord Fairfax and Vegetius', *Modern Language Review* 113.2 (2018), 307–20.

MacGregor, Martin, 'The Statutes of Iona: Text and Context', *Innes Review* 57.2 (2006), 111–81.

Mackenzie, Louisa, 'Imitation Gone Wrong: The "Pestilentially Ambitious" Figure of Julius Caesar in Michel de Montaigne's Essais', *Julius Caesar in Western Culture*, ed. M. Wyke (Oxford, 2006), pp. 129–47.

Mackillop, Andrew, and Steve Murdoch, ed., *Fighting for Identity: Scottish Military Experience, c.1550–1900* (Cambridge, 1996).

MacNamara, Francis Nottidge, *Memorials of the Danvers Family* (London, 1895).

Maginn, Christopher, *'Civilizing' Gaelic Leinster: The Extension of Tudor Rule in the O'Byrne and O'Toole Lordships* (Dublin, 2005).

Manning, Roger B., *Swordsmen: The Martial Ethos in the Three Kingdoms* (Oxford, 2003).

——, *An Apprenticeship in Arms: The Origins of the British Army 1585–1702* (Oxford, 2006).

——, *War and Peace in the Western Political Imagination: From Classical Antiquity to the Age of Reason* (London, 2016).

Mannion, Joseph, '"As trew Englishe as any man borne in Myddlesex": Sir Francis Shane, 1540–1614', *Frontiers, States and Identity in Early Modern Ireland and Beyond*, ed. Christopher Maginn and Gerald Power (Dublin, 2016), pp. 177–81.

Marcus, Leah, 'Politics and Pastoral: Writing the Court on the Countryside', *Culture and Politics in Early Stuart England*, ed. Kevin Sharpe and Peter Lake (Basingstoke, 1994), pp. 139–59.

Markham, Clements R., *A Life of the Great Lord Fairfax* (London, 1870).

——, *The Fighting Veres: Lives of Sir Francis Vere and Sir Horace Vere* (Boston, 1888).

Martinez, Miguel, *Front Lines: Soldiers' Writing in the Early Modern Hispanic World* (Philadelphia, 2016).

Marx, Steven, 'Shakespeare's Pacifism', *Renaissance Quarterly* 45.1 (1992), 49–98.

McCarthy-Morrogh, Michael, *The Munster Plantation: English Migration to Southern Ireland, 1583–1641* (Oxford, 1986).

McCavitt, John, *Sir Arthur Chichester, Lord Deputy of Ireland, 1605–16* (Belfast, 1998).

McCoy, Richard C., *The Rites of Knighthood: The Literature and Politics of Elizabethan Chivalry* (Berkeley, 1989).

——, 'Old English Honour in an Evil Time: Aristocratic Principle in the 1620s', *The Stuart Court and Europe: Essays in Politics and Religious Culture*, ed. R. Malcolm Smuts (Cambridge, 1996), pp. 133–55.

McCullough, Peter, *Sermons at Court: Politics and Religion in Elizabethan and Jacobean Preaching* (Cambridge, 1998).

——, Hugh Adlington, and Emma Rhatigan, eds., *The Oxford Handbook of the Early Modern Sermon* (Oxford, 2011).

McGleenon, C.F., 'The Battle of Mullabrack, 5 September 1595', *Seanchas Ard Mhacha* 13.2 (1989), 90–101.

McGowan-Doyle, Valerie, *The Book of Howth: Elizabethan Conquest and the Old English* (Cork, 2011).

McGurk, John, 'The Dead, Sick and Wounded of the Nine Years War (1594–1603)', *History Ireland* 4.3 (1995), 16–22.

——, *The Elizabethan Conquest of Ireland: The 1590s Crisis* (Manchester, 1997).

——, 'Terrain and Conquest, 1600–1603', *Conquest and Resistance: War in Seventeenth-Century Ireland*, ed. Pádraig Lenihan (Leiden, 2001), pp. 87–114.

——, 'The Pacification of Ulster, 1600–3', *Age of Atrocity*, ed. D. Edwards et al. (Dublin, 2007), pp. 119–29.

McKeown, Adam, *English Mercuries: Soldier Poets in the Age of Shakespeare* (Nashville, 2009).

McKeown, Simon, 'The Reception of Gustavus Adolphus in English Literary Culture: The Case of George Tooke', *RS* 23.2 (2009), 200–20.

McLaughlin, Martin, 'Empire, Eloquence and Military Genius: Renaissance Italy', *Companion to Julius Caesar*, ed. M. Griffin (Chichester, 2009), pp. 335–55.

Millican, C. Bowie, 'Ralph Knevet, Author of the *Supplement* to Spenser's *Faerie Queene*', *RES* 14.53 (1938), 44–52.

Milligan, Gerry, *Moral Combat: Women, Gender, and War in Italian Renaissance Literature* (Toronto, 2018).

Moelwyn Merchant, W., 'Ralph Knevet of Norfolk, Poet of Civill Warre', *Essays and Studies* 13 (1960), 21–35.

Montrose, Louis, 'Spenser and the Elizabethan Political Imaginary', *ELH* 69.4 (2002), 907–46.

Moore Smith, G.C., 'Riche's Story "Of Phylotus and Emilia"', *Modern Language Review* 5.3 (1910), 342–4.

Morgan, Hiram, 'Faith and Fatherland of Queen and Country? An Unpublished Exchange Between O'Neill and the State at the Height of the Nine Years War', *Dúiche Néill* 9 (1994), 9–65.

——, *Tyrone's Rebellion: The Outbreak of the Nine Years War in Ireland* (London, 1999).

——, 'Plunketts', *Oxford Companion to Irish History*, ed. S.J. Connolly (Oxford, 2007).

——, 'The Messenger in John Derricke's "Image of Irelande" (1581)', *History Ireland*, 15.1 (2007), 6–7.

——, '"Tempt not God too long, O Queen": Elizabeth and the Irish Crisis of the 1590s', *Elizabeth I and Ireland*, ed. Valerie McGowan-Doyle and Brendan Kane (Cambridge, 2014), pp. 209–38.

——, ed., *The Battle of Kinsale* (Bray, 2004).

Morgan, Rhys, and Gerald Power, 'Enduring Borderlands: The Marches of Ireland and Wales in the Early Modern Period', *Frontiers, Regions and Identities in Europe*, ed. Steven G. Ellis et al. (Pisa, 2009), pp. 101–28.

Morrissey, Mary, *Politics and the Paul's Cross Sermons, 1558–1642* (Oxford, 2011).

Moscoco, Javier, 'Pain and Suffering', *Early Modern Emotions: An Introduction*, ed. S. Broomhall (Oxford, 2017), pp. 45–8.

Mulier, E.O.G. Haitsma, and G.A.C. van der Lem, *Repertorium van geschiedschrijvers in Nederland 1500–1800* (Den Haag, 1990).

Murdoch, Steve, 'The House of Stuart and the Scottish Professional Soldier 1618–1640: A Conflict of Nationality and Identities', *War: Identities in Conflict 1300–2000*, ed. B. Taithe and T. Thornton (Stroud, 1998), pp. 37–56.

——, 'Medic!: An Insight into Scottish Field Surgeons, Physicians and Medical Provision during the Thirty Years' War, 1618–1648', *Northern Studies* 48 (2017), 51–65.

Murrin, Michael, *History and Warfare in Renaissance Epic* (Chicago, 1994).

Nelson, William, *Fact or Fiction: The Dilemma of the Renaissance Storyteller* (Cambridge, MA, 1973).

Neufeld, Matthew, *The Civil Wars After 1660: Public Remembering in Late Stuart England* (Woodbridge, 2013).

Neuschel, Kristen B., *Word of Honour: Interpreting Noble Culture in Sixteenth-Century France* (Ithaca, 1989).

Nicholls, K.W., *Gaelic and Gaelicised Ireland in the Middle Ages* (Dublin, 2003).

Nicholls, Mark, 'Treason's Reward: The Punishment of Conspirators in the Bye Plot of 1603', *The Historical Journal* 38 (1995), 821–42.

Nolan, John S., *Sir John Norreys and the Elizabethan Military World* (Exeter, 1997).

Norbrook, David, *Writing the English Republic: Poetry, Rhetoric and Politics* (Cambridge, 1999).

Ó Báille, M., 'The Buannadha: Irish Professional Soldiery of the Sixteenth Century', *Journal of the Galway Archaeological and Historical Society* 22.1–2 (1946), 49–94.

O'Callaghan, Michelle, '*The Shepheards Nation*': Jacobean Spenserians and Early Stuart Political Culture, 1612–1625 (Oxford, 2000).

O'Carroll, Donal, 'Change and Continuity in Weapons and Tactics', *Conquest and Resistance*, ed. P. Lenihan (Leiden, 2001), pp. 211–55.

Ó Clérigh, Lughaidh, *The Life of Aodh Ruadh O' Domhnaill*, ed. and trans. Paul Walsh (Dublin, 1948).

Ó Domhnaill, Seán, 'Warfare in Sixteenth-Century Ireland', *IHS* 5.17 (1946), 29–54.

Ó Mearáin, Lorcan, 'The Battle of Clontibret', *Clogher Record* 1.4 (1956), 1–28.

O'Neill, James, 'An Introduction to Firearms in Post-Medieval Ireland, 1500–1700', *The Post-Medieval Archaeology of Ireland 1550–1850*, ed. Audrey Horning et al. (Dublin, 2007), pp. 467–84.

——, 'A Kingdom Near Lost: English Military Recovery in Ireland, 1600–03', *British Journal for Military History* 3.1 (2016), 26–47.

——, 'Maguire's Revolt but Tyrone's War: Proxy War in Fermanagh, 1593–4', *Seanchas Ard Mhacha: Journal of the Armagh Diocesan Historical Society* 26.1 (2016), 43–68.

——, *The Nine Years War, 1593–1603* (Dublin, 2017).

O'Rahilly, Alfred, *The Massacre at Smerwick, 1580* (Cork, 1938).

O'Sullivan Beare, Philip, *Ireland under Elizabeth: Chapters towards a History of Ireland under Elizabeth*, trans. M.J. Byrne (Dublin, 1903).

Ohlmeyer, Jane, '"Civilizinge of those rude partes": Colonization within Britain and Ireland, 1580s–1640s', *The Origins of Empire*, ed. Nicholas Canny (Oxford, 1998), pp. 124-47.

Olsthoorn, Peter, 'Courage in the Military: Physical and Moral', *Journal of Military Ethics* 6 (2007), 270–9.

Oman, Charles, *A History of the Art of War in the Sixteenth Century* (London, 1937).

Osgood, Josiah, 'The Pen and the Sword: Writing and Conquest in Caesar's Gaul', *Classical Antiquity* 28 (2009), 328–58.

Paleit, Edward, *War, Liberty, and Caesar: Responses to Lucan's 'Bellum Civile', c.1580–1650* (Oxford, 2013).

Palmer, Patricia, *The Severed Head and Grafted Tongue* (Cambridge, 2013).

——, 'Where Does It Hurt?: How Pain Makes History in Early Modern Ireland', *The Body in Pain in Irish Literature and Culture*, ed. Fionnuala Dillane et al. (Basingstoke, 2016), pp. 21–38.

Parente, James A., *Religious Drama and the Humanist Tradition: Christian Theater in Germany and in the Netherlands, 1500–1680* (Leiden, 1987).

Parker, Geoffrey, 'The "Military Revolution" 1560–1660—A Myth?', *Journal of Modern History* 48.2 (1976), 196–214.

——, 'Early Modern Europe', *The Laws of War: Constraint on Warfare in the Western World*, ed. Michael Howard et al. (London, 1994), pp. 40–58.

——, *The Military Revolution: Military Innovation and the Rise of the West, 1500–1800* (Cambridge, 1996).

——, *The Army of Flanders and the Spanish Road, 1567–1659*, 2nd edn. (Cambridge, 2004).

——, 'The Limits to Revolution in Military Affairs: Maurice of Nassau, the Battle of Nieuwpoort (1600), and the Legacy', *Journal of Military History* 71.2 (2007), 331–72.

Pasupathi, Vimala C., 'The King's Privates: Sex and the Soldier's Place in John Fletcher's *The Humorous Lieutenant* (ca. 1618)', *Research Opportunities in Medieval and Renaissance Drama* 47 (2008), 25–50.

——, 'Shakespeare, Fletcher, and the "The Gain O' the Martialist"', *Shakespeare* 7.5 (2011), 296–308.

——, 'Furious Soldiers and Mad Lovers: Fletcherian Plots and *The History of Cardenio*', *The Creation and Re-creation of Cardenio: Performing Shakespeare, Transforming Cervantes*, ed. Gary Taylor and Terri Bourus (New York, 2013), pp. 83–94.

Patterson, W.B., *King James VI and I and the Reunion of Christendom* (Cambridge, 1997).

Peacey, Jason, 'Print and Public Politics in Seventeenth-Century England', *History Compass* 5.1 (2007), 85–111.

Pelling, Christopher, 'Judging Julius Caesar', *Julius Caesar in Western Culture*, ed. Maria Wyke (Oxford, 2006), pp. 15–20.

Peltonen, Markku, *Classical Humanism and Republicanism in English Political Thought, 1570–1640* (Cambridge, 1995).

Perceval-Maxwell, Michael, *The Outbreak of the Irish Rebellion of 1641* (Montreal, 1994).

Piesse, A.J., 'Identity', *A Companion to English Renaissance Literature and Culture*, ed. Michael Hattaway (Oxford, 2003), pp. 634–43.

Pinciss, Gerald M., *Why Shakespeare: An Introduction to the Playwright's Art* (New York, 2006).

Potter, Jennifer, *Strange Blooms: The Curious Lives and Adventures of the John Tradescants* (London, 2006).

Powell, Anton, 'Julius Caesar and the Presentation of Massacre', *Julius Caesar as Artful Reporter*, ed. Welch and Powell (Swansea, 1998), pp. 111–37.

Purkiss, Diane, *Literature, Gender and Politics during the English Civil War* (Cambridge, 2005).

Quinn, D.B., *The Elizabethans and the Irish* (Ithaca, 1966).

Randall, David, *Credibility in Elizabethan and Early Stuart Military News* (London, 2008).

Rapple, Rory, *Martial Power and Elizabethan Political Culture: Military Men in England and Ireland, 1558–1594* (Cambridge, 2009).

Ray, Robert H., *A George Herbert Companion* (London, 1995).

Raymond, James, *Henry VIII's Military Revolution: The Armies of Sixteenth-Century Britain and Europe* (New York, 2007).

Redworth, Glyn, *The Prince and the Infanta: The Cultural Politics of the Spanish Match* (New Haven and London, 2003).

Riggsby, Andrew M., *Caesar in Gaul and Rome* (Austin, 2006)

Roberts, Michael, *Essays in Swedish History* (London, 1967).

Rogers, Stephen, '*Othello*: Comedy in Reverse', *Shakespeare Quarterly* 24.2 (1973), 210–20.

Rosenwein, Barbara, 'Worrying about Emotions in History', *American Historical Review* 107 (2002), 821–45.

——, *Generations of Feeling: A History of Emotions, 600–1770* (Cambridge, 2016).

Rowse, A.L., *The Elizabethan Renaissance: The Cultural Achievement* (London, 1972).

——, *Sex and Society in Shakespeare's Age: Simon Foreman the Astrologer* (London, 1974).

Roy, Ian, 'The Profession of Arms', *The Professions in Early Modern England*, ed. Wilfrid Prest (London, 1987), pp. 181–219.

Rozett, Martha Tuck, '*Othello*, *Otello*, and the Comic Tradition', *Bulletin of Research in the Humanities* 85.4 (1982), 386–411.

Salmon, J.H.M., 'Seneca and Tacitus in Jacobean England', *The Mental World of the Jacobean Court*, ed. Levy Peck (Cambridge, 1991), pp. 169–88.

Salter, Herbert E. and Mary D. Lobel, ed., *A History of the County of Oxford*: Volume 3, The University of Oxford (London, 1954).

Salzman, Paul, *Literature and Politics in the 1620s: 'Whisper'd Counsells'* (Basingstoke, 2014).

Samson, Alexander, ed., *The Spanish Match: Prince Charles' Journey to Madrid, 1623* (Aldershot, 2006).

Sandler, Florence, '*The Faerie Queene*: An Elizabethan Apocalypse', *The Apocalypse in English Renaissance Thought and Literature* ed. C.A. Patrides and Joseph Wittreich (Manchester, 1984), pp. 148–74.

Scannell, Paul, *Conflict and Soldiers' Literature in Early Modern Europe* (London, 2015).

Schoenfeldt, Michael, 'The Art of Pain Management in Early Modern England', *The Sense of Suffering: Constructions of Physical Pain in Early Modern Culture*, ed. Jan Franz van Dijkhuizen and Karl A.E. Enenkel (Leiden, 2009), pp. 19–38.

Schurink, Fred, 'War, What is it Good For? Sixteenth-Century English Translations of Ancient Texts on Warfare', *Renaissance Cultural Crossroads*, ed. Barker and Hosington (Leiden, 2013), pp. 121–38.

Sellars, Wilfrid, 'Grammar and Existence: A Preface to Ontology', *Mind* 69 (1960), 499–533.

Sheehan, Anthony J., 'Official Reaction to Native Land Claims in the Plantation of Munster', *IHS* 23.92 (1983), 297–318.

Shepard, Alan, *Marlowe's Soldiers: Rhetorics of Masculinity in the Age of the Armada* (Aldershot, 2002).

Shepard, Alexandra, *Meanings of Manhood in Early Modern England* (Oxford, 2003).

Sherlock, Peter, 'Militant Masculinity and the Monuments of Westminster Abbey', *Governing Masculinities*, ed. S. Broomhill and J. van Gent (Farnham, 2011), pp. 131–52.

Siegfried, Brandie R., 'Rivalling Caesar: The Roman Model in Sir Henry Sidney's Memoir of Ireland', *Sidney Journal* 29 (2011), 187–208.

Silke, John J., *Kinsale: The Spanish Intervention in Ireland at the End of the Elizabethan Wars* (Liverpool, 1970).

Simms, Katherine, 'Images of Warfare in Bardic Poetry', *Celtica* 21 (1990), 608–19.

Skinner, Patricia, *Living With Disfigurement in Early Medieval Europe* (Basingstoke, 2017).

Skinner, Quentin, *Visions of Politics—Volume 2: Renaissance Virtues* (Cambridge, 2002).

Smith, Anthony D., *National Identity* (London, 1991).

Smith, Homer, 'Pastoral Influence in the English Drama', *PMLA* 12.3 (1897), 355–460.

Smuts, R. Malcolm, 'Court-Centred Politics and the Uses of Roman Historians, c.1590–1630', *Culture and Politics in Early Stuart England*, ed. Kevin Sharpe and Peter Lake (Stanford, 1993), pp. 21–43.

Speight, Harry, *Upper Wharfedale [...] from Otley to Langstrothdale* (London, 1900).

Stellar, Jennifer E., and Dacher Keltner, 'Compassion', *Handbook of Positive Emotions*, ed. Michele M. Tugade et al. (London, 2014), pp. 329–41.

Stewart, Richard, 'The "Irish Road": Military Supply and Arms for Elizabeth's Army during the O'Neill Rebellion in Ireland, 1598–1601', *War and Government in Britain, 1598–1650*, ed. Mark Fissel (Manchester and New York, 1991), pp. 16–37.

Stone, Lawrence, *The Crisis of the Aristocracy, 1558–1641* (Oxford, 1965).

Stopes, Charlotte Carmichael, *The Life of Henry, Third Earl of Southampton, Shakespeare's Patron* (Cambridge, 1922).

Stoyle, Mark, 'Memories of the Maimed: The Testimony of King Charles' Former Soldiers, 1660–1730', *History* 88 (2003), 207–26.

Strickland, Matthew, *War and Chivalry: The Conduct and Perception of War in England and Normandy, 1066–1217* (Cambridge, 1996).

Strong, Roy, *Van Dyck: Charles I on Horseback* (New York, 1972).

——, *The Cult of Elizabeth* (Berkeley, 1977).

——, *Henry, Prince of Wales and England's Lost Renaissance* (London, 1986).

Stubbs, John, *Reprobates: Cavaliers of the English Civil War* (London, 2011).

Supple, James J., *Arms Versus Letters: The Military and Literary Ideals in the 'Essais' of Montaigne* (Oxford, 1984).

Taithe, Bertrand, and Tim Thornton, eds., *War: Identities in Conflict 1300-2000* (Stroud, 1998).

Tallett, Frank, *War and Society in Early Modern Europe, 1495-1715* (London, 1992).

Taunton, Nina, *1590s Drama and Militarism: Portrayals of War in Marlowe, Chapman and Shakespeare's Henry V* (Aldershot, 2001).

Teague, Francis N., 'Introduction', *Acting Funny: Comic Theory and Practice in Shakespeare's Plays*, ed. Francis N. Teague (Madison, NJ, 1994), pp. 9–28.

Thomas, Courtney Erin, *If I Lose Honour I Lose Myself: Honour Among the Early Modern English Elite* (Toronto, 2017).

Thomas, Keith, *The Ends of Life: Roads to Fulfilment in Early Modern England* (Oxford, 2009).

Tracy, Larissa, and Kelly DeVries, *Wounds and Wound Repair in Medieval Culture* (Leiden, 2015).

Treadwell, Victor, 'Sir John Perrot and the Irish Parliament of 1585–6', *Proceedings of the Royal Irish Academy* 85 (1985), 259–308.

——, *Buckingham and Ireland, 1616–1628: A Study in Anglo-Irish Politics* (Dublin, 1998).

Trim, D.J.B., 'The Art of War: Martial Poetics From Henry Howard to Philip Sidney', *The Oxford Handbook of Tudor Literature, 1485–1603*, ed. Mike Pincombe and Cathy Shrank (Oxford, 2009), pp. 587–605.

——, 'Gascoigne the Soldier: Rhetoric, Representation and Reality', *New Essays on George Gascoigne*, ed. Gillian Austen (London, forthcoming).

——, ed., *The Chivalric Ethos and the Development of Military Professionalism* (Leiden, 2003).

Tuck, Richard, *Philosophy and Government, 1572–1651* (Cambridge, 1993).

Underdown, D.E., 'The Taming of the Scold: The Enforcement of Patriarchal Authority in Early Modern England', *Order and Disorder in Early Modern England*, ed. Anthony Fletcher and John Stevenson (Cambridge, 1985), pp. 116–36.

Vale, Malcolm, *War and Chivalry* (London, 1981).

[Van Dyck, Anthony], *The Works of Anthony van Dyck*, 2 vols. (New York, 1943).

Van Ordern, Kate, *Music, Discipline, and Arms in Early Modern France* (Chicago, 2005).

Vass, Arapad A., 'Beyond the Grave: Understanding Human Decomposition', *Microbiology Today* 28 (November 2001), 190–2.

Vaught, Jennifer C., ed., *Rhetorics of Bodily Disease and Health in Medieval and Early Modern England* (Farnham, 2010).

Verhoef, C.E.H.J., *Nieuwpoort 1600: De bekendste slag uit de Tachtigjarige Oorlog* (Soesterberg, 2000).

Vickers, Brian, *Shakespeare, Co-Author* (Oxford, 2004).

Von Arni, Eric Gruber, *Justice to the Maimed Soldier* (London, 2001).

Waith, Eugene M., 'Mad Lovers, Vainglorious Soldiers', *Research Opportunities in Renaissance Drama* 27 (1984), 13–19.

Waldron, Jennifer, 'Beyond Words and Deeds: Montaigne's Soldierly Style', *Philological Quarterly* 82 (2003), 38–59.

Walker, Katharine A., 'The Military Activities of Charlotte de la Tremouille, Countess of Derby, During the Civil War and Interregnum', *Northern History* 38.1 (2001), 47–64.

Webb, Henry J., *Elizabethan Military Science: The Books and the Practice*, (Madison, 1965).

Welch, Kathryn, and Anton Powell, eds., *Julius Caesar as Artful Reporter* (Swansea, 1998).

Wheeler, James Scott, *The Making of a World Power: War and the Military Revolution in Seventeenth-Century England* (Stroud, 1999).

Williamson, J.W., *The Myth of the Conqueror: Prince Henry Stuart—A Study of Seventeenth-Century Personation* (New York, 1978).

Wilson, Christopher R., *Shakespeare's Musical Imagery* (London, 2011).

Wilson, Peter H., *Europe's Tragedy: A New History of the Thirty Years War* (London, 2009).

Wintjes, Jorit, 'From "Capitano" to "Great Commander": The Military Reception of Caesar from the Sixteenth to the Twentieth Centuries', *Julius Caesar in Western Culture*, ed. M. Wyke (Oxford, 2006), pp. 269–84.

Wiseman, T.P., 'The Publication of *De Bello Gallico*', *Julius Caesar as Artful Reporter*, ed. K. Welch and A. Powell (Swansea, 1998), pp. 1–9.

Withington, Phil, 'Introduction—Citizens and Soldiers: the Renaissance Context', *Journal of Early Modern History* 15 (2011), 3–30.

Woodcock, Matthew, 'Shooting for England: Configuring the Book and the Bow in Roger Ascham's *Toxophilus*', *SCJ* 41.4 (2010), 1017–38.

——, *Thomas Churchyard: Pen, Sword, and Ego* (Oxford, 2016).

——, 'Tudor Soldier-Authors and the Art of Military Autobiography', *Representing War and Violence in Later Medieval Europe*, ed. Joanna Bellis and Laura Slater (Woodbridge, 2016), pp. 159–77.

Wormald, Jenny, 'James VI and I, *Basilikon Doron*, and *The Trew Law of Free Monarchies*: The Scottish Context and the English Translation', *The Mental World of the Jacobean Court*, ed. Linda Levy Peck (Cambridge, 1991), pp. 36–54.

Zika, Charles, 'Cannibalism and Witchcraft in Early Modern Europe: Reading the Visual Images', *History Workshop Journal* 44 (1997), 77–105.

Unpublished

Borman, Tracy, 'Sir Francis Vere in the Netherlands, 1589–1603: A Re-evaluation of his Career as Sergeant Major General of Elizabeth I's Troops', unpublished Ph.D. thesis (University of Hull, 2007).

De Buitléir, Gearóidín, 'Na Buitléaraigh agus Cultúr na Gaeilge', unpublished Ph.D. thesis (University College Cork, 2007).

Laskowsk, Eliza Fisher, 'Performance, Politics, and Religion: Reconstructing Seventeenth-Century Masque', unpublished Ph.D. thesis (University of North Carolina, 2006).

McGowan-Doyle, Valerie, 'The Book of Howth: The Old English and the Elizabethan Conquest of Ireland', unpublished Ph.D. thesis (University College Cork, 2005).

Trim, D.J.B., 'Fighting "Jacob's Wars". The Employment of English and Welsh Mercenaries in the European Wars of Religion: France and the Netherlands, 1562–1610', unpublished Ph.D. thesis (University of London, 2002).

Index

Aelian   65, 73
Agincourt, battle of   5, 44, 81
Agrippa, Henry Cornelius   253
Alarum for London   226n22
Albert, archduke of Austria   73
Alesia, battle of   57, 60–1
Alexander the Great   46, 107
Andreani, Angela   19–20, 281
Andrewes, Lancelot   19, 121–2, 130–6
Annals of the Four Masters   197, 204
Antwerp   226
archery   71, 81–2, 179–80, 182, 198, 203,
    241–2
Ariosto, Ludovico   224–5, 282
Armintor, Benjamin J.   7, 9n30, 14n54,
    22, 27n11
artillery   30, 32, 41, 50, 53–4, 81n6, 90,
    224n11, 241, 276, 280
Arundell, Thomas   50–51
Ascham, Roger   241n13
Athlone   125, 186
autobiography   7–8, 18, 48, 57, 62–3, 65,
    76–7, 101, 105, 107, 161, 207

Bacon, Francis   70, 116, 221, 236–7
Bagenal, Nicholas   148, 154, 183, 185, 187,
    193, 204
Bagenal, Samuel   210
Baltinglass rebellion   143, 146, 148
Barckley, Richard   9–10
Barnes, Barnabe   228
Barret, Robert   1–2, 6, 8–9, 15, 66, 264
Barry, Garret   80n4, 111
Barwick, Humphrey   241
Beard, Thomas   208
Becon, Thomas   19, 227

Bergen-op-Zoom   39, 42
Bertie, Peregrine, thirteenth baron
    Willoughby d'Eresby   40–3, 54, 110
Bingham, Richard   46, 111, 207
Birkenshaw, Rafe   167
Bishops' War, First   3n5, 176
Bladwell, William   86, 89
Blandy, William   9, 31–3, 36, 44–7
blood   9, 44–5, 47, 52, 57, 105, 112, 138,
    144, 151, 154, 157, 173, 199, 203, 205,
    216, 251, 274 *see also* wounds
Blount, Charles, eighth baron Mountjoy
    65, 125, 133, 147, 149–50, 166, 187,
    190–1, 194, 197, 206
Bradshaw, Brendan   189
braggart soldiers   13, 17, 21, 221–34, 246,
    253 *see also miles gloriosus*
Brancaccio, Giulio Cesare   69
Brooke, Callisthenes   211
Bruni, Leonardo   63
Burgh, John, captain   52
Burgh, Thomas, third baron Burgh   147,
    194
Burke, Richard, fourth earl of Clanricard
    147, 149, 202–3, 206
Burroughs, John   82, 90, 103
Butler, Theobald   171
Butler, Thomas, tenth earl of
    Ormond   9, 20, 125–30, 147–9, 152,
    158–76, 203, 208
Bye plot   213

Cadiz   5, 48, 113n55, 131n46, 226, 253
Calais   280
Calvinism   19, 115, 117, 135
Cambridge   34, 77, 80, 88n19, 123n7

Camden, William   33, 48–9, 69n61, 105, 188–9
Campion, Edmund   128n34, 178–9
cannibalism   61, 192–3, 230
Canning, Ruth A.   11n42, 14, 20
Canny, Nicholas   145, 189
Carew, George   149, 191, 203, 208, 214
Carey, Vincent   189–90
'carpet knights'   9–10, 32
Casimir, Ernest, count of Nassau   48, 53
Castiglione, Baldesar   63, 225–6
casualties   21, 188, 197–203, 211 *see also* disability; wounds
cavalry   47, 50, 54, 71–2, 86, 88–9, 96–7, 111–12, 124, 146–9, 151, 165, 179, 182–3, 186, 203, 206–7
Cavendish, William, first duke of Newcastle   281
Cecil, Edward   40
Cecil, Robert   124n17, 149–50, 154, 162, 207–11, 213
Cecil, William, Lord Burghley   16–17, 123, 199
Chapman, George   92
Charles I   11, 19, 80, 84–5, 94–7, 101, 110, 176, 216–17, 242–3
Charles II   217
Charles, Amy   83–5, 88n18, 91–2
Chester, Edward   39–40
Chichester, Arthur   190, 192, 281
chivalry   3, 6, 9–11, 19, 40, 46, 80, 86, 95–8, 105–6, 108, 118
Cholières, Nicolas, sieur de   64
Churchyard, Thomas   9, 13, 16, 28, 30–33, 38–49, 54, 107n31, 226n21, 228n32, 236
Cicero   58, 66–7, 77
citizen soldiery   3n5, 14, 88, 225n16, 281 *see also* militias; musters
Civil Wars, English (Wars of the Three Kingdoms)   3n5, 7, 16, 79, 81, 88n19, 99, 105, 117, 255, 281
civilians   7, 13–16, 82, 87, 189–93, 197, 222, 227, 243, 248, 250–52, 255, 270, 281
clergy   18–19, 121–37, 146 *see also* Andrewes, Lancelot; Hanmer,

Meredith; Knevet, Ralph; Loftus, Adam
Clifford, Conyers   190, 193, 212
Clifford, Henry, Lord Clifford   103, 106
Clontibret, battle of   154, 183
Cobham, Anne   211–12
Connacht   166, 182–3, 190–3, 213
Constable, William   202, 206
Conway, Edward   102
Cork   124–7, 168, 214
courage   18, 29–31, 33, 37–8, 40–9, 51–4, 60–1, 71, 82, 86, 103, 113, 159, 164–5, 200, 206–7, 216, 224n13, 248, 272
courtiers, soldiers compared with   9–10, 13, 22, 32n35, 106, 262, 270, 274 *see also* 'carpet knights'
Covington, Sarah   201, 205, 207
Cruso, John   63, 80, 84, 87–9
Cust, Richard   216

Daniel, Samuel   71, 81
Danvers, Henry   21, 149, 200, 202, 213–17, 282n11
Davies, John   189
De Somogyi, Nick   28, 30n22, 222–3
Dekker, Thomas   238, 245–6, 264, 267, 278
Derricke, John   16, 179–80
desertion   143, 188, 209
Desmond rebellion   143, 166
Devereux, Robert, second earl of Essex   6, 10, 19, 37, 66–7, 73, 109–11, 121–2, 130–3, 149, 154, 186, 200, 208, 211, 214, 216, 221, 226, 234–5, 237, 282n11
Digges, Leonard   32–3
Digges, Thomas   9, 32–3
Dillingham, William   77–8
disability   21–2, 197–217, 222 *see also* casualties; wounds
discipline   5, 12, 15, 18–20, 39, 45, 60–1, 64, 80–2, 97, 131n46, 184, 188
disease   35, 54n129, 133, 140, 143, 192, 198, 203, 208, 211
dishonour   36, 44–5, 52, 193, 249
Docwra, Henry   149, 195, 203–4, 207–9
Doesburg, siege of   48, 53

Dowdall, John, captain   144, 185–8, 193

Drake, Francis   6, 113–14

Drayton, Michael   81

drilling   4–5, 12, 14, 73, 75–6, 182, 277

Dublin   123, 125–9, 133, 139, 166, 174, 183, 186, 191, 194, 204, 209, 260, 280 *see also* Pale, the

Dudley, Robert, earl of Leicester   10, 35, 37, 42–3, 48–50, 52–3, 102, 110

Dyrrachium, battle of   57, 59

Edmondes, Clement   18, 56, 62–3, 65–78

Edward VI   39, 162, 242

Edwards, David   9, 11n42, 20, 189, 210n54

Eighty Years War   31, 33, 35, 37–54, 67–8, 73–8, 83, 88, 100, 102, 104, 108, 111–12, 178, 211, 217, 222, 247

elegies   9, 77, 90

Elizabeth I   1–2, 3n5, 6, 10, 14, 30, 32, 41, 46, 54, 76, 100, 104, 113, 123, 126, 130, 132, 142, 144, 146, 148, 152, 159, 162, 166, 168, 178, 186, 193–4, 203, 205, 207, 209, 212, 214, 222, 225–6, 233, 235, 242, 245, 253, 278, 281

Elizabeth Stuart, queen of Bohemia   13, 94, 101, 108

Ellis, Steven   126, 151

Elton, Geoffrey   25–6

emotions   21–2, 37, 45, 100, 103, 106–7, 118, 200–1, 213, 217

England's Wedding Garment   245

epic poetry   79, 87, 97–8, 158–76 *see also* Ariosto, Ludovico; Spenser, Edmund; Tasso, Torquato; Virgil

Erasmus, Desiderius   121, 131

Eusebius   69n61, 122

Fairfax, Charles   103, 112

Fairfax, Edward   100, 106–7, 109

Fairfax, John   102–3

Fairfax, Thomas, first lord   19–20, 100–18

Fairfax, Thomas, third lord   100, 104, 106n26, 110, 115, 117

Fairfax, William   102–3, 106–7, 109

famine   11, 143, 177, 189–94, 196, 254–5,

Farmer, William   198

Farnese, Alexander, duke of Parma   42, 50

Fenn, Humphrey   127, 129

Fenne, Thomas   72

Fenton, Geoffrey   147, 199, 209

field surgery   54, 124n17, 187, 198–9, 204–8, 281 *see also* casualties; wounds

FitzGerald,   Gerald, eleventh earl of Kildare 165n24

FitzGerald, Gerald, fifteenth earl of Desmond   166

Fitzgerald, Henry, twelfth earl of Kildare   147–9

Fitzgerald, James Fitzmaurice   124, 166, 170

Fitzpatrick, Barnaby, second baron Upper Ossory   165n24

Fitzwilliam, William   167, 199

Fletcher, John   266–7, 276

Ford of Biscuits, battle of the   154, 183

Foucault, Michel   12n48

France   2, 19, 32, 37, 39, 54n129, 62, 64, 72, 78n82, 81, 102, 105, 107, 108, 112, 139, 176, 178, 192, 217, 241, 247, 250, 280

Frankenthal   43, 103, 106, 111, 118

Frederick V, elector Palatine   13, 94, 101

Froissart, Jean   108

Frontinus   59, 69n61

gallowglass   178, 182, 195

Gascoigne, George   28, 45, 107n31, 226n21

Gates, Geoffrey   9, 13, 15, 31, 33

Gawdy, Philip   236

gender studies   25–9

genocide   72, 177, 189–90, 196

George II   281

Germany   13, 16, 57, 59, 62, 72, 100–18, 280 *see also* Palatinate, counties of

Gilbert, Humphrey   281

Giraldus Cambrensis   178

Golding, Arthur   62

Googe, Barnabe   36

Grafton, Anthony   67

Graves, Robert   122–3, 125, 127, 129

Greville, Fulke   54, 114
Grey, Arthur, fourteenth baron Grey de
    Wilton   167, 183
Groningen   44
Guicciardini, Francesco   69n61, 75n74
Gustavus Adolphus   4, 19, 80–81, 89,
    96–8

Haarlem, siege of   38–9
Haddington, siege of   5, 38–9
Hadfield, Andrew   19–20, 281
Hadsor, Richard   150
Hailwood, Mark   6, 256
Hakluyt, Richard   264
Hale, John   7, 19, 129, 253
Hanmer, Meredith   19, 121–30, 133–7
Harari, Yuval   107, 200
Harington, John   212–13, 217, 226n21,
    235–7
Harlan, Susan   6
Harrison, Stephen   238
Harvey, Gabriel   67
Harwood, Edward   50
Hayward, John   248
Hector of Troy   46, 87
Heidelberg   19–20, 43, 100–18
Henri, duc de Rohan   63
Henry Stuart, prince of Wales   11, 68,
    216
Henry VII   168
Henry VIII   29–30, 242, 281
Herbert, Edward, Lord of Cherbury   52
Herbert, George   99, 216n78
Herbert, Henry, second earl of Pembroke
    1–2
Herbert, William, third earl of Pembroke
    1–2, 6, 8, 282
Herodotus   69n61, 179
Hexham, Henry   9, 77, 111
Heydon, William   82, 90
Heywood, Thomas   267
Hill, Tracey   239
Hiscock, Andrew   17, 21–2, 274n26
honour   1, 3, 9–10, 12–13, 15–16, 18, 21,
    26, 29–30, 32–54, 60, 68, 75, 82, 86,
    101, 106–7, 110, 131, 147, 158, 161, 163,

    165, 168, 176, 187, 200–2, 205, 207–9,
    217, 228, 240–2, 248–9, 270, 273
Horace   89, 162, 164
hostings   141–2
Howard, Charles, earl of Nottingham   162
Howard, Thomas   235
Huguenots   38, 45
humanism   63–4, 66, 163, 225, 243, 253
Humphrey, duke of Gloucester   63

Île de Ré   80, 82, 90
intelligence-gathering   143, 155–6, 195, 210
Ireland   *see* Dublin; military identity
    and Anglo-Irish/ 'Old English'
    identity; Nine Years War; Pale, the;
    and under names of individual
    places and persons

James VI of Scotland, and I of England
    5, 10–11, 13, 19, 32, 68–9, 96, 100–1,
    103–5, 109, 112, 116–17, 159, 161–6,
    171–3, 176, 188, 213, 216, 236–46,
    250–4, 277, 281
Jardine, Lisa   67
Jesuits   20n73, 122, 128–30, 146n34
Jonson, Ben   70, 76, 92, 163, 228, 238–9,
    250–1, 264, 266–7, 276
Jorgensen, Paul   233, 274
Josephus   59, 69n61
Julius Caesar   18, 56–78, 106–7, 110

Keegan, John   65
kerne   142, 178–9, 182, 195
Kewes, Paulina   69
Kildare   123–4, 127, 139, 150
Kildare rebellion   143
Kinsale   147, 166–7, 194, 198, 202, 206, 214
Knevet, Ralph   18–19, 79–99
Knollys, Francis   46
Kyffin, Maurice   190

La Rochelle   38–9
Lane, Ralph   183, 206, 210, 217
Languet, Hubert   67n54
Latimer, Hugh   19
lawyers   262, 274, 262

Le Havre   253
Lee, Thomas   152–3, 193
Leech, Jeremy   40–1, 47, 52
Leinster   125, 147, 159, 166, 170–1
Limerick   125, 127, 168, 192,
Lipsius, Justus   5, 64, 69
Livy   69n61, 75n74, 172
Loftus, Adam, archbishop   125, 127, 129
logistics   3, 139–40, 183, 194–5
Lombard, Peter   180
London   92, 101, 122, 127–8, 150, 163,
    165, 171, 176, 204, 208–9, 211n58, 214,
    236–55, 260, 280 *see also* Treaty of
    London
Low Countries   2, 10, 16, 19, 31–46,
    48–54, 68, 73–8, 83, 88, 100, 102–4,
    108, 110–12, 114, 178, 211, 213, 217,
    222, 247, 249–50, 280
Lye, John   150

Maastricht, siege of   150
MacDonnell, Sorley Boy   166, 172–5
Machiavelli, Niccolò   14, 18, 60n16, 64,
    225
Magdeburg   94
Maguire, Hugh   123, 183, 185, 204–5
Major, Philip   5n14, 11n42, 15, 19–20
Malta   38–9
Mannheim   43, 97
Manning, Roger B.   9–11
Manningham, John   253
Mansfeld, Ernst, count   101–2
Marckham, William   45–6
Markham, Francis   32, 34, 36, 111
Markham, Gervase   110–11
Markham, Griffin   21, 200, 212–13, 217
Marlowe, Christopher   27–8, 268, 277
Martinez, Miguel   8
Mary I   2, 165
masculinity   3, 17–18, 25–55, 60, 201,
    217, 281
masque   79, 91–3, 95, 240, 242, 244, 260,
    266n17
Massinger, Philip   267
Maurice, prince of Nassau   5, 64–5,
    73–4, 76

McBrian, Collo   123
McKeown, Adam N.   17, 21–2, 27n11,
    272n24
mercenaries   7, 13, 40, 47–8, 54, 102,
    105–6, 109–10, 142, 174, 178, 226, 228
Meteren, Emanuel van 31
Middleton, Thomas   21–2, 235–55, 267
miles gloriosus   17, 21, 221–34, 236, 245,
    247, 272 *see also* braggart soldiers
militant Protestantism   10–11, 81n5,
    89 *see also* Dudley, Robert, earl of
    Leicester; Eighty Years War; Sidney,
    Philip
military identity
    and Anglo-Irish/ 'Old English' identity
       11, 17, 20, 138–76
    definitions of   2–3, 7, 22, 270–71
    and effeminacy   14, 18, 30, 32–3, 60,
       96, 217, 255 *see also* 'carpet knights'
    and family identity   1–2, 19–20,
       100–18, 150, 158–76, 212–16
    and national identity   5, 13–14, 17,
       19–22, 61, 80–82, 90, 280 *see also*
       military identity and Anglo-Irish/
       'Old English' identity
    and noble identity   2, 8–10, 12, 18,
       25–55, 161
    and occupational identity   3, 6–7,
       12–13, 224, 256–79
    and professionalism   6, 11–12, 271, 281
    and regional identity   19, 79–99
    and religion   19–20, 121–37, 80–81,
       93–8, 100–18, 121–38, 143, 145–6,
       157–60, 179, 243, 253 *see also*
       Calvinism; Jesuits; militant
       Protestantism
military memoir   *see* autobiography
military revolution, early modern   4–5,
    12, 20, 22, 65, 178, 184–5, 198, 228
militias   14–19, 80–90, 103, 108, 240, 259
    see also musters
Monluc, Blaise de   65
Monro, Robert   9, 13, 280
Montaigne, Michel de   61n19, 63–4,
    69–71, 76, 105
Morgan, Hiram   204

Morgan, Walter 39
Moryson, Fynes 147, 149, 187–8, 192–3
Moyry Pass 197, 206, 214
Muir, Kenneth 221, 225, 233
Munday, Anthony 222
Munster 122–3, 126, 129, 149, 159, 166,
    168, 170, 183, 191–2, 195, 203
Murdoch, Stuart 13
musters 8, 14–16, 33, 59, 71n69, 80–90,
    141–3, 183, 190, 203, 208, 210, 226,
    228, 240, 276–7

Naunton, Robert 9–10
neostoicism 163–4 *see also* Lipsius,
    Justus
Neuschel, Kristin 37
New World, the 7, 100, 111–14, 206, 280
news 16, 81, 97, 108–9, 113, 117, 211, 223,
    251
Nieuwpoort 67–8, 73–4, 76–8, 102, 247
Nine Years War 17, 19–21, 119–217
nobility *see* military identity and noble
    identity
non-combatants 82, 87, 121–37, 281 *see
    also* civilians
Norden, John 200, 206
Norreys, Edward 37, 51
Norreys, Henry 47
Norreys, John 12, 31, 40, 44–7, 51, 53,
    126–7, 130, 146–7, 154, 184, 203, 209
Northern Rebellion 104
Nugent, Christopher, baron Delvin 142,
    144, 147–8, 151, 155n99
Nugent rebellion 146, 148

O'Brien, Donogh, fourth earl of
    Thomond 203–4
O'Byrne, Fiach McHugh 124, 171
Ó Clérigh, Lughaidh 180–81, 187
O'Donnell, Hugh Roe, lord of Tirconnell
    180–81, 183, 203
O'Mahony, Cian 15, 21, 18–19, 274n26,
    281n3
O'Meara, Dermot, *Ormonius* 20,
    158–76

O'Neill, Hugh, second earl of Tyrone
    20, 124, 127, 146–7, 152, 166–7, 171,
    174, 177–99, 204–6, 210, 217 *see also*
    Nine Years War
O'Neill, James 16n64, 20, 198, 204
O'Neill, Shane 166, 172, 182
O'Neill, Turlough Luineach 182
O'Reilly, Turlough Shane 147
O'Sullivan Beare, Philip 180
Oakes, Uriah 264
Oge, Brian McHugh 123
Ogle, John 77–8, 102, 109–10, 117
Onosander 59, 69n61
Ostend, siege of 5, 39, 54, 72, 102, 250
Oxford 2, 63, 122–3, 217

pageantry 84, 237–44, 255, 260
Palatinate, counties of 13, 19, 43, 94,
    100–18
Pale, the (Ireland) 125, 138–41, 144–7,
    150–51, 155–6, 182, 191, 280
Palladio, Andrea 64, 69
Palmer, Patricia 148n51, 203
Parker, Geoffrey 5
Pass of Plumes, battle of the 154
Paston, William 80, 84, 99
pastoral 79, 91–5
Pasupathi, Vimala C. 7, 9n30, 14n54,
    22, 27n11
Patrizi, Francesco 64, 69
peace 11, 13, 17, 21–2, 54, 87, 112–13, 117,
    132, 150–1, 194, 229, 232–3, 237–44,
    248–55, 275–6, 278
Peacham, Henry 78n82
Pelham, William 37, 53
pensions 53, 208–12
Perrot, John 175, 187
petitions 20, 53, 139, 144, 148–52, 155–6,
    207–9, 211–12, 254
Petrarch, Francesco 63
Pharsalus, battle of 57
Philip II, king of Spain 113, 116
Phliip III, king of Spain 116
Philip IV, king of Spain 94, 112–16
Piesse, A.J. 257
Pinkie, battle of 39

Pleasant song, made by a souldier, A
    246–7
Plunkett, Patrick, seventh baron of
    Dunsany 139, 142, 145–56
Plutarch 62–4, 69n61
Polybius 59, 64, 69n61
Pompey the Great 57, 59, 61
Portugal 51, 247
prisoners of war 43, 186–8, 193–6, 202
psalms 100, 133–4
Purchas, Samuel 264

Radcliffe, Henry, fourth earl of
    Sussex 51, 167, 211
Ralegh, Walter 6, 114, 226, 281
Ramus, Peter 63, 69n61
Rapple, Rory 10
reputation 2, 5, 10, 19–20, 22, 30, 34–45,
    48–54, 60, 82, 100, 103, 158, 163, 200,
    217, 221, 226, 228–9 *see also* honour
Rich, Barnabe 13–14, 28, 32, 224, 226
Rijmenam 45–6
Roberts, Michael 4–5, 12
Rogers, Stephen 222–3
Roman army, the 5, 14–15, 56–78 *see
    also* Julius Caesar, Vegetius
Rouen 109
Rowley, William 242–3, 249, 267
Roy, Ian 6
Rudolf II, emperor 50
Rupert, prince of Bohemia 281
Rushe, Francis 211–12
Russell, William, lord deputy 127,
    129–30, 146, 155, 184, 202

St Lawrence, Christopher, tenth baron of
    Howth 142, 147–9, 152
Savile, Henry 69, 105
Savile, John 105
Scannell, Paul 7
scholars, soldiers compared with 2, 8,
    13, 18, 22, 63–7, 87–90, 106, 108–11,
    118, 136, 223, 243–4, 262, 274–5
Scotland 37, 39, 104, 124, 159–63, 172–6,
    178, 188, 237, 247, 280
Scott, John 68

Segar, William 227
Sellars, Wilfrid 256
sermons 52, 115, 121–37, 248, 264
Shakespeare, William 2, 14, 21, 27–8,
    34, 37, 41, 44, 47, 51–2, 58n5, 205,
    221–34, 246, 248, 253–4, 257–8, 264,
    266–7, 270, 274
Shane, Francis 186, 209–10
Sheffield, Edmund, first earl of Mulgrave
    102
Sheffield, Elizabeth 128
Shelton, Henry, captain 82–4, 87
Shirley, James 267–8
Sidney, Henry 65, 123, 167
Sidney, Philip 1–2, 10, 31, 38, 42, 54, 67,
    89, 106, 111, 114, 225, 234
Sidney, Thomas 51
sieges 3–5, 11, 35, 38–9, 43, 47–8, 50, 54,
    59, 61–2, 71n69, 72, 81n6, 90, 94, 103,
    106, 109, 175, 198, 202, 207, 250, 253
Silius Italicus 159
Skinner, Quentin 66
Sluys 43, 50
Smith, Thomas 228
Smythe, John 241
Spain 5, 10–11, 19, 39–40, 42–4, 46–51,
    57, 66, 68, 73–4, 81, 94, 97, 100–3,
    107–17, 147, 176, 183, 192, 194, 210,
    222, 226, 237, 250, 273, 280
Spanish Armada 5, 52, 72, 81, 113, 115,
    168, 182–3, 281
Spanish Match 94–5, 101, 109, 115–18
Spenser, Edmund 19, 79, 86–7, 89, 91,
    95–8, 123, 179–80, 194, 282
Spinola, Ambrogio 101, 112
standing armies 6–7, 141, 143, 259
Stanihurst, Richard 145
Stanley, Edward 48–9, 51, 53
Stuart, Arabella 156
Stuart, James, duke of Lennox 104n15
Stukeley, Thomas 247
Styward, Thomas 15, 36, 227
*Supplication of the blood of the English,
    The* 143, 179

Tacitus 67, 69, 105

tactics   56, 59, 64, 72, 88–9, 111, 133, 155,
    184–5, 189–93, 197, 222–3, 251
Tait, Clodagh   9, 20–21, 30n23, 189,
    248n23, 282n11
Talbot, Gilbert, earl of Shrewsbury   162
Tasso, Torquato   100, 225, 282
Taunton, Nina   28, 32–3
Thirty Years War   16, 29, 92, 94–5,
    101–18, 240, 243
Thomas, Keith   6–7, 281
Tiptoft, John, first earl of Worcester   62
Tourneur, Cyril   77
Tradescant, John   217
training   14–15, 59, 75, 83–4, 106, 227,
    240 *see also* drilling
translation   31, 56, 62–78, 80, 88, 100,
    105–6, 121–2, 131, 155–6, 162–3, 253
Treaty of London   10, 222, 237, 277
Trigge, Francis   245
Trim, D.J.B   6, 9, 11, 18, 22, 60n16,
    248n23, 270–71, 273, 275
Trussell, Thomas   13
Tuck, Richard   66
Turks   33, 38, 50, 115–16, 118, 232, 280

Udall, Nicholas   222
Ulster   122–4, 127, 146, 155, 160–61, 166,
    171–5, 177, 182–3, 190–93, 196–7
Ulster rebellion (1641)   176
Underdown, David   26

Valdés, Francisco de   253
Van Dyck, Anthony   11, 214
Vegetius   15, 59, 65, 69n61, 73, 100, 106
Vere, Francis   12, 18–19, 39, 43, 48,
    50–51, 53, 56, 65, 68, 70, 73–8
Vere, Horace   12, 76, 97, 102, 110, 117

veterans   35, 102, 105n22, 110–13, 201,
    208–9, 221–34, 246, 250
Villiers, George, duke of Buckingham
    90, 101, 110, 113, 217
Virgil   69n61, 91, 159, 172, 213–14, 217
volunteers   *see* mercenaries

Wales   1–2, 173, 208
Walsingham, Francis   46–9
Wars of the Roses   104
Webster, John   267
Wells, Robin Headlam   233
Wentworth, Thomas, first earl of
    Strafford   117–18
Wheeler, Jonas   125, 127, 129
Whetstone, George   15, 34, 226–7, 233
William, prince of Orange   38, 40, 46
Williams, Roger   12, 43, 47–51, 65, 207
Wilson, Robert   275
Wither, George   227
Withington, Phil   7
women and soldiery   18, 71, 268, 271,
    281–2
Woodcock, Matthew   11n42, 15, 18,
    110n48, 114n57, 228n32, 274n26
wounds   9, 17, 20–21, 30, 41–2, 48, 51–4,
    90, 184, 187, 197–217, 236, 247–8, 254,
    272 *see also* casualties; disability
Wyatt, Thomas, rebellion of   161, 165, 167

Xenophon   69n61, 106

Yellow Ford, battle of   154, 180, 185, 187
Yorke, Edward   112
Yorke, Rowland   46

Zutphen   42–3, 48, 53–4